# Essentials of
# SPC in the
# Process Industries

An Independent Learning Module
from the
Instrument Society of America

# ESSENTIALS OF SPC IN THE PROCESS INDUSTRIES

By
James M. Pruett
Louisiana State University
and
Helmut Schneider
Louisiana State University

 **INSTRUMENT SOCIETY OF AMERICA**

INSTRUMENT SOCIETY OF AMERICA
67 Alexander Drive
P.O. Box 12277
Research Triangle Park
North Carolina 27709


**Library of Congress Cataloging-in-Publication Data**

Pruett, James M.
    Essentials of SPC in the process industries/by James M. Pruett
and Helmut Schneider.
        p.    cm.—(An Independent learning module from the Instrument
Society of America)
    Includes bibliographical references (p.    ) and index.
    ISBN 1-55617-391-1
    1. Process control—Statistical methods—Programmed instruction.
I. Schneider, Helmut.  II. Title.  III. Series.
TS156.8.P798  1992                                            92-29678
    658.5′62′015195—dc20                                        CIP


*Editorial development and book design by Monarch International, Inc., under
the editorial direction of Paul W. Murrill, Ph.D.*

# TABLE OF CONTENTS

# PREFACE

## ISA's Independent Learning Modules

This book is an Indepedent Learning Module (ILM) as developed and published by the Instrument Society of America (ISA). The ILMs are the principal components of a major educational system designed primarily for independent self-study. This comprehensive learning system has been custom designed and created for ISA to more fully educate people in the basic theories and technologies associated with applied instrumentation and control.

The ILM System is divided into several distinct sets of Modules on closely related topics; such a set of individually related Modules is called a Series. The ILM System is composed of:

- the ISA Series of Modules on Control Principles and Techniques;
- the ISA Series of Modules on Fundamental Instrumentation;
- the ISA Series of Modules on Unit Process and Unit Operation Control;
- the ISA Series of Modules for Professional Development;
- the ISA Series of Modules for Specific Industries; and
- the ISA Series of Modules on Software-Assisted Topics.

The principal components of the Series are the individual ILMs (or Modules) such as this one. They are especially designed for independent self-study; no other text or references are required. The unique format, style, and teaching techniques employed in the ILMs make them a powerful addition to any library.

The published ILMs are as follows:

> *Fundamentals of Process Control Theory*—Paul W. Murrill—1981
>
> *Controlling Multivariable Processes*—F. G. Shinskey—1981
>
> *Microprocessors in Industrial Control*—Robert J. Bibbero—1982
>
> *Measurement and Control of Liquid Level*—Chun H. Cho—1982

*Control Valve Selection and Sizing*—Les Driskell—1983

*Fundamentals of Flow Measurement*—Joseph P. DeCarlo—1984

*Intrinsic Safety*—E. C. Magison—1984

*Digital Control*—Theodore J. Williams—1984

*pH Control*—Gregory K. McMillan—1985

*Fundamentals of Programming with FORTRAN 77*—James M. Pruett—1987

*Introduction to Telemetry*—O. J. Strock—1987

*Application Concepts in Process Control*—Paul W. Murrill—1988

*Controlling Centrifugal Compressors*—Ralph L. Moore—1989

*CIM in the Process Industries*—John W. Bernard—1989

*Continuous Control Techniques for Distributive Control Systems*—Gregory K. McMillan—1989

*Temperature Measurement in Industry*—E. C. Magison—1990

*Simulating Process Control Loops Using BASIC*—F. G. Shinskey—1990

*Tuning of Industrial Control Systems*—Armando B. Corripio—1990

*Computer Control Strategies*—Albert A. Gunkler and John W. Bernard—1990

*Fundamentals of Process Control Theory, 2nd Edition*—Paul W. Murrill—1991

*Environmental Control Systems*—Randy D. Down—1992

*Conceptual Design Analysis Applied to Offshore Control Systems*—Bill G. Tompkins—1992

*Measurement Uncertainty*—Ronald H. Dieck—1992

*Justification and Auditing of Control Systems*—N. E. (Bill) Battikha—1992

*Essentials of SPC in the Process Industries*—James M. Pruett and Helmut Schneider—1992

Most of the original ILMs were envisioned to be the more traditional or fundamental subjects in instrumentation and process control. With the publications planned over the next few years, the ILM Series will become much more involved in emerging technologies.

Recently, ISA has increased its commitment to the ILM Series and has set for itself a goal of publishing four ILMs each year. Obviously, this growing Series is part of a foundation for any professional library in instrumentation and control. The individual practitioner will find them of value, of course, and they are a necessity in any institutional or corporate library.

There is obvious value in maintaining continuity within your personal set of ILMs; place a standing purchase order with ISA.

Paul W. Murrill
Consulting Editor, ILM Series
June, 1992

## Comments about This Volume

*The Essentials of SPC in the Process Industries* presents the principles of statistical process control in a readable format with special emphasis on the process industries. Its focus on SPC in the process industries makes it unique among SPC books, and its logical, readable presentation style makes it an easy-to-learn-from text.

## Acknowledgments

Many people have contributed significantly to the completion of this book. The staff in LSU's Department of Quantitative Business Analysis (particularly Tracy Adams, Ramona Forbes, and Mike Bui) worked hundreds of hours in typing drafts and revisions. Dr. Paul Murrill provided guidance and inordinate patience.

Earlier drafts have been used in teaching an undergraduate course in LSU's Quantitative Business Analysis Department and in numerous seminars, both through the LSU College of Business Administration's Executive Education program and at several industrial plants. The people at Paxon Polymer in Baton Rouge deserve special mention. While they have been relentless in their pursuit of continuous quality improvement in their processes, they have also been gracious in allowing us to use many examples based on practical experience gained through the successful application of these tools at Paxon. Mr. Douglas Connor and Mr. Henry Tsuei, both of Paxon, have been particularly supportive. Numerous other people throughout the process industries provided criticism, insight, suggestions, and support for our work. Mr. Larry Daigre of John H. Carter Co., Inc., served as our unofficial industry conscience, reading, commenting on, and rereading the book's various drafts. His interest, keen insight, attention to detail, and positive outlook helped us through many a rough spot.

Finally, our families (particularly, our wives, Faye and Mary, and our children, Jon, Allyson, and Jed, and Caroline and Mark) have been both understanding and supportive throughout the years this project has taken. To all these people, we say a heartfelt thank you and well done.

James M. Pruett & Helmut Schneider

# Unit 1:
# Introduction and Overview

# UNIT 1

# Introduction and Overview

Welcome to ISA's Independent Learning Module *Essentials of SPC in the Process Industries*. The first unit of the self-study program provides the information needed to proceed through the course.

**Learning Objectives** — **When you have completed this unit, you should:**

      **A. Understand the general organization of the course.**

      **B. Know the course objectives.**

      **C. Know how to proceed through the course.**

## 1-1. Course Coverage

This is an ILM on the essentials of statistical process control for the process industries. This course covers:

      A. The basic theoretical concepts of statistical process control.

      B. How these basic theoretical concepts are applied in the process industries.

The principles on which statistical process control (SPC) is based are not industry dependent. However, there is considerable variation in the application of these principles in various industries. SPC was first applied in component part manufacturing and has only in the last few years been considered for use in the process industries. The material presented in this book is generally oriented toward the modern practitioner in processing industries such as petroleum, petrochemical, chemical, food processing, and pulp and paper.

The book focuses on the set of principles and tools generally considered the essentials of statistical process control in the process industries setting. No attempt is made to provide exhaustive coverage. Rather, each of the methods is described and presented in context through examples and exercises.

## 1-2.  Purpose

The purpose of this ILM is to present in easily understood terms the basic principles of statistical process control and to illustrate and teach the usage of these principles in modern industrial applications. This is neither solely a theoretical book nor solely a practical book—it is both! The purpose is to show the theoretical concepts and principles in day-to-day industrial situations and, in doing so, to show that this theory is quite practical.

## 1-3.  Audience and Prerequisites

This ILM is designed for those who want to work on their own and who want to gain a basic understanding of statistical process control. The material will be useful to engineers, first-line supervisors, managers, technicians, and operators who are concerned with the application of statistical process control. The book will also be helpful to students in technical schools, colleges, or universities who wish to gain insight into the practical concepts of statistical process control.

No elaborate prerequisites are required to take this course, though an appreciation for industrial concerns and philosophies will be helpful. In addition, it is inevitable that some mathematics will be involved in particular parts of the presentation. It is not necessary for the student to be intimately familiar with such mathematics to appreciate the concepts that are presented and applied. Quite often, mathematics becomes one of the barriers that prevents many persons from understanding and actually using statistical process control; it is hoped that in this ILM such barriers will be minimized.

## 1-4.  Study Material

This textbook is the only study material required in this course; it is one of ISA's ILM System. It is an independent, stand-alone textbook that is uniquely and specifically designed for self-study.

There is contained in Appendix A a list of suggested readings to provide additional reference and study materials for the student. In addition, the student will find it most helpful to study the other ILMs that are available from ISA.

## 1-5. Organization and Sequence

This ILM is divided into 15 separate units and an epilogue. The next five units (Units 2–6) are designed to teach the fundamental graphical techniques and statistical principles used throughout SPC. Following these, five units (Units 7–11) introduce the student to the hallmark SPC concept, the control chart. The next unit (Unit 12) discusses process capability, a concept concerned with how well a process is able to meet customer specifications. The next three units (Units 13–15) describe more advanced—and frequently more applicable—control charting techniques. The Epilogue briefly summarizes the key SPC concepts and provides general guidelines for their application.

The method of instruction used in this ILM is self-study. Basically, you will work on your own in taking this course; you select the pace at which you learn best.

Each unit is designed in a consistent format with a set of specific learning objectives stated in the very beginning of the unit. Note these learning objectives carefully; the material that follows the learning objectives will teach to these objectives. The individual units contain example problems to illustrate specific concepts, and at the end of each unit you will find exercises to test your understanding of the material. All exercises have solutions contained in Appendix C, against which you should check your solutions.

This ILM belongs to you; it is yours to keep. We encourage you to make notes in the textbook and to take advantage of the ample white space that is provided on every page for this specific purpose.

## 1-6. Course Objectives

When you have completed this entire ILM, you should:

A.  Understand the basic graphical techniques and statistical principles on which SPC is based.

B.  Understand the concept of control charting, including the risks inherent in the process.

C. Understand the advantages and disadvantages of a variety of control charts and know when each one is most applicable.

D. Understand the concept of process capability and be able to apply it.

E. Have an appreciation of the difficulties and potential benefits of applying SPC in the process industries.

In addition to these overall course objectives, each unit in this ILM contains a specific set of learning objectives for that particular unit. These objectives are intended to help direct your study of that individual unit.

## 1-7. Course Length

The basic premise of the ISA System of ILMs is that students learn best if they proceed at their own personal pace. As a result, there will be significant variation in the amount of time taken by individual students to complete this ILM. Previous experience and personal capabilities will do much to vary the time, but most students will complete this course in 60 to 80 hours.

You are now ready to begin your detailed study of the essential concepts of statistical process control. Please proceed to Unit 2.

# Unit 2:
# Introduction to SPC

# UNIT 2

# Introduction to SPC

The idea of statistical process control (SPC) is straightforward: use statistics to help determine what the process is capable of producing and then work to continuously improve it. This unit introduces the idea of statistical process control and describes where SPC fits into the overall total quality management process.

**Learning Objectives** — When you have completed this unit, you should:

A. Know the purpose of statistical process control.

B. Know the role of statistical process control in the total quality management/process improvement process.

C. Be aware of several definitions of quality.

D. Know the relationship between quality and cost.

E. Know some of the key differences between statistical process control and automatic process control in the process industries.

## 2-1. What Is Statistical Process Control?

Until early in the 1980s, the focus of quality concerns regarding production was primarily on the final product. Statistical techniques dealing with quality of the final product were called statistical quality control (SQC) methods. Products received from suppliers were customarily sampled, with the outcome of the sampling experiment determining the product's disposition. Batches failing inspection were shipped back to the supplier or screened (i.e., the good ones kept, the bad ones returned). Production batches were also sampled, with bad products either discarded or reworked. Of course, since large numbers of products often weren't inspected at all, the customer frequently had the "privilege" of discovering them. It was standard operating procedure. The flowchart in Fig. 2-1 presents the product control idea.

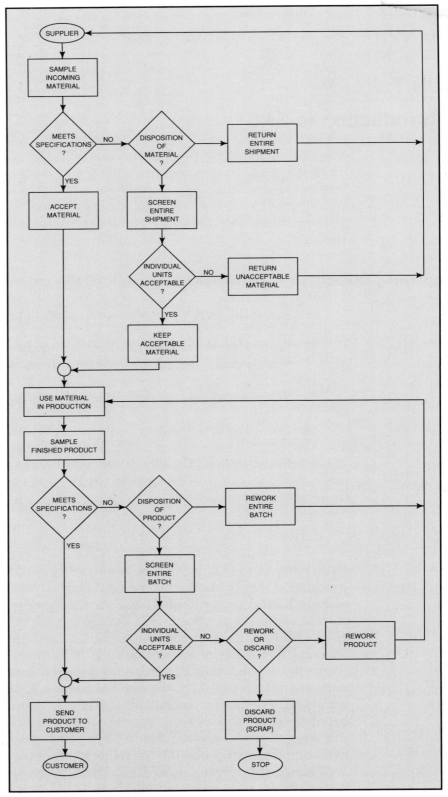

**Fig. 2-1. Product Control Flowchart**

Changes in views regarding quality originated from economic pressure, mainly in the form of international competition. As organizations began to realize that product quality was the natural result of process quality, the focus slowly changed from the product to the process. The idea is that if the process is well controlled, consistent products will follow. Since on the surface the change in perspective appears to be minor, many companies have been slow to recognize its transforming benefits. (Note: This discussion does not imply that no attention be given to finished products. Rather it implies that focusing on the process has the potential of a transforming effect on the finished product, thereby reducing the need for undue attention on the finished product.)

Fig. 2-2 shows a simplified flowchart description of the process control perspective. The chart indicates that the health of a process is centered around two questions: (1) Is the process well behaved (i.e., in control)? (2) Is the process capable of meeting specifications? While successful statistical process control may not completely eliminate the need for finished product inspection, it does reduce the need significantly.

This ILM describes techniques that are helpful in collecting and presenting data and helpful in monitoring and analyzing processes. The goal is to answer the two questions presented above affirmatively. These are the two most important questions in statistical process control.

## 2-2. A Broader View

Statistical process control does not provide all the answers. As one manager put it, "Producing quality is a lot more than SPC." While this is obviously true, SPC has a critical place in the fact-based management process necessary for higher quality products, continual improvement, and greater customer satisfaction. Appropriate and accurate data means improved information; improved information means greater understanding; greater understanding means better decisions and potentially improved processes; improved processes means higher quality products and greater customer satisfaction. Dr. W. Edwards Deming's Chain of Quality (Fig. 2-3) shows a similar view—start by improving process quality and later reap the rewards.

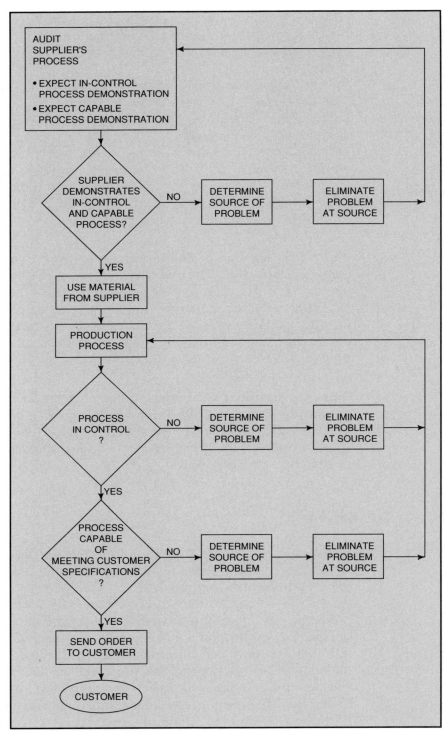

**Fig. 2-2. Process Control Flowchart**

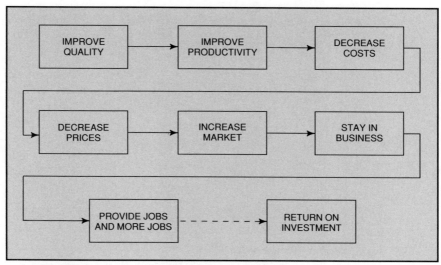

**Fig. 2-3. Dr. Deming's Chain of Quality**

Another view of the importance of statistical process control
can be seen beginning with Dr. Deming's Systems View (Fig.
2-4). His concept is that all components of the production (or
service) process must be viewed as being part of a system, from
suppliers through customers, with customer satisfaction the key
element of the system. Further, there should be continuous,
quantitative, and qualitative feedback from all parts of the
system. This is important because there is variation present in

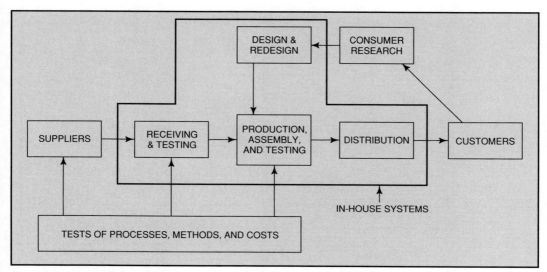

**Fig. 2-4. Dr. Deming's Systems View**

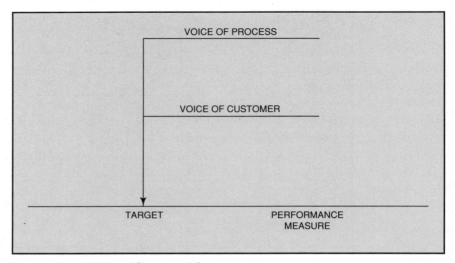

Fig. 2-5.  Aligned Voices of Process and Customer

each part of the system and one goal of the continuous improvement process is to reduce that variation.

William Scherkenbach extends Dr. Deming's views by describing the system's "voices." If each process step is viewed as having a customer, then each step has two voices—the voice of the process and the voice of the customer. Ideally, the voice of the process and the voice of the customer are perfectly aligned—the process is producing exactly what the

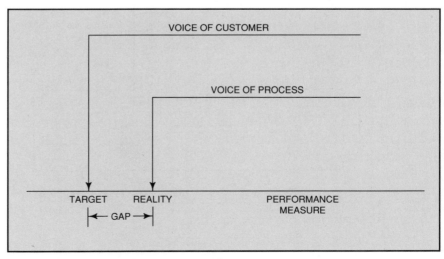

Fig. 2-6.  Gap between Voices of Process and Customer

customer requires (Fig. 2-5). In reality, however, there is usually a gap between the two voices—the process is not exactly meeting the customer's requirements (Fig. 2-6). In addition, there is variation in both the voice of the process (because process outputs are not identical) and the voice of the customer (because there are many different customers and because customer requirements change) (Fig. 2-7). Reducing the gap between the two voices (Fig. 2-8) requires information, which requires data.

Fact-based quality management involves the extensive use of SPC tools. This ILM describes the essential SPC tools. Many of

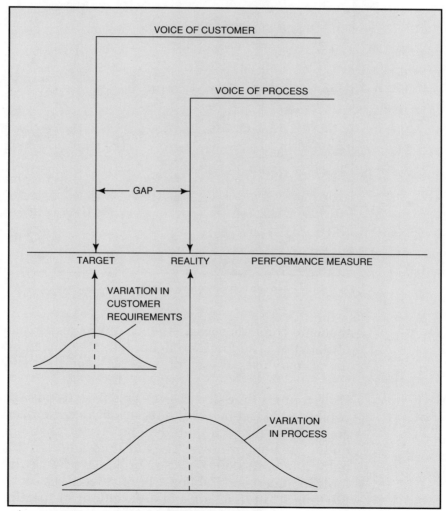

**Fig. 2-7. Variation in Voices of Process and Customer**

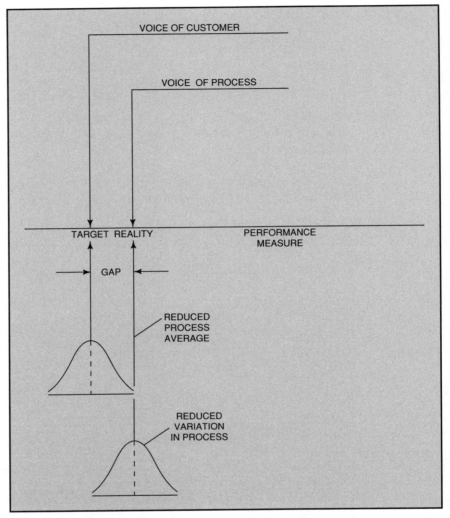

**Fig. 2-8. Reduced Gap between Voices of Process and Customer**

them are common sense; others require greater understanding of statistics. The first step in applying them is to understand the primary uses of each of the tools—and their shortcomings.

Dr. Deming's four-step PDSA Cycle (Fig. 2-9) is extremely useful in the fact-based quality management process. The steps are (1) Plan, (2) Do, (3) Study, and (4) Act, then repeat the steps on the next opportunity. The tools presented in this book are helpful in each step. Fig. 2-10 provides a framework of the tools included and Table 2-1 briefly describes each tool's function. Unit numbers and descriptions of specific tools

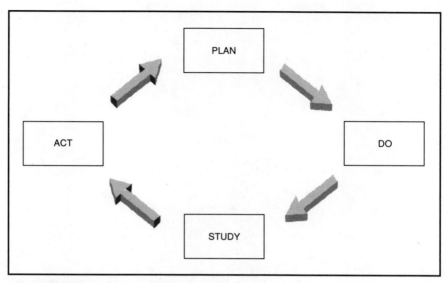

**Fig. 2-9. PDSA (Plan-Do-Study-Act) Cycle**

presented in each unit are also shown in Fig. 2-10 and Table 2-1.

In general, this ILM does not repeatedly describe the entire process improvement process. Instead, it presents a series of tools that are important to the continual improvement process, describes what makes each tool unique, and shows how each one may be applied.

## 2-3. What Is Quality?

While there are many definitions of quality, there is no single, widely accepted one. *Webster's New Universal Unabridged Dictionary* includes the following among its variations: [Quality is] ''that which belongs to something and makes or helps to make it what it is; any character or characteristic which may make an object good or bad, commendable or reprehensible; the degree of excellence which a thing possesses.''

Several other perspectives on quality are listed below:

A. Quality is conformance to requirements, not goodness.

B. Quality means fitness for use.

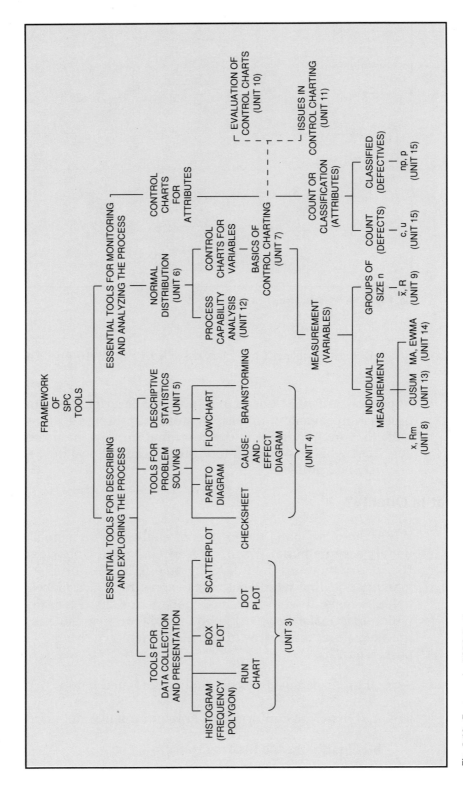

**Fig. 2-10. Framework of SPC Tools**

18

| General Category | Tool | Description |
|---|---|---|
| Tools for Describing and Exploring the Process | Checksheet (Unit 3) | Used to tally and present data; many innovative forms; sometimes called tallysheet. |
| | Pareto Diagram (Unit 3) | Helps focus attention on top-priority items; data categorized and shown in descending order. |
| | Cause & Effect Diagram (Unit 3) | Used to show relationships between problems and possible causes; also, fishbone diagram. |
| | Flowchart (Unit 3) | Graphical method of describing and sequencing an operation's activities and processes; used to develop complete and correct understanding of a process. |
| | Histogram (Unit 4) | Data grouped by frequency of occurrence and shown as bars; provides snapshot of process at fixed point in time; also useful for first-cut process capability analysis. |
| | Box Plot (Unit 4) | Used to compare multiple sets of data. |
| | Dot Plot (Unit 4) | Histogram-like plot using dots instead of bars; useful when only a few values are available. |
| | Run Chart (Unit 4) | Shows same data as histogram, but values plotted sequentially over time; used to spot trends, sudden shifts, runs, and cycles. |
| | Descriptive Statistics (Unit 5) | Variety of numeric measures including mean, median, mode, variance, standard deviation, range, coefficient of variation, signal-to-noise ratio, correlation, and autocorrelation. |
| | Normal Distribution (Unit 6) | Most important probability distribution in SPC; probability calculations; normal probability plot; central limit theorem. |
| Tools for Monitoring and Analyzing the Process (Control Charts) | Individual Measurements (Unit 8) | x and $R_m$ charts; charts for individual measurements; used when multiple measurements are impractical or homogeneous. |
| | Grouped Measurements (Unit 9) | $\bar{x}$ and R charts; charts for groups of measured values; used when multiple measurements at each sampling point are independent indicators. |
| | Process Capability (Unit 12) | Provides a numeric measure of the process' ability to produce within customer specifications. |
| | Cumulative Sum Charts (Unit 13) | CUSUM chart; especially useful in detecting small process shifts. |
| | Moving Average Charts (Unit 14) | Moving average or exponentially weighted moving average charts; used in place of x chart to more quickly identify gradual shifts in process mean. |
| | Attribute Charts (Unit 15) | c, u, p, and np charts; charts for counts (e.g., number of blemishes) and classified data (e.g., proportion of late shipments). |

TABLE 2-1. Brief Descriptions of SPC Tools

C. Quality is determined by the customer (not by engineering or marketing or management). It is the result of a customer's experience with a product or service. It is measured against the customer's requirements, which are continuously changing.

D. Customers define quality. The product or service must meet customer needs and expectations at a cost that represents value.

E. Quality is something for which you get excellent value for the money you put into it.

F. Quality is not just what you see on the surface, but also what is underneath the surface.

G. Quality is not definable, but you know what it is.

While no one definition captures every aspect of quality, the definitions touch upon several important characteristics: (1) Quality is closely related to the customer; (2) both requirements and fitness for use are important components of quality; (3) since things change, the customer's view of quality will also change; (4) there is a relationship between quality and cost.

## 2-4. Costs Related to Quality

The idea that costs are related to quality is an important one. For years the relationship between quality and cost was viewed as conflicting (i.e., the view that achieving higher quality meant accruing higher costs). In fact, the opposite is true, at least to a large extent; higher quality processes result in less rework, which leads to greater productivity and lower costs. (In most processes, however, there is a point after which quality improvement efforts are no longer cost effective. Efforts past this point are sometimes called ''gold plating.'')

Total quality-related cost is generally described as the sum of the costs in four major categories (a perspective provided by Dr. Joseph Juran): (1) prevention costs, (2) appraisal costs, (3) internal failure costs, and (4) external failure costs. (Note: While these costs can also be applied to a service, the descriptions presented here are given in terms of a product.)

Prevention costs are incurred in order to reduce failure costs and appraisal costs. The costs required to train employees (in their jobs and regarding SPC), to perform field trials, to audit and rate suppliers, and to design products with both the process and the customer in mind are examples of prevention costs.

Appraisal costs are incurred to determine the degree of conformance to quality requirements both inside and outside the plant. The costs related to the inspection of incoming products, performing process control, maintaining control charts, performing periodic audits on products and services, and maintaining measurement equipment are examples of appraisal costs.

Internal failure costs are incurred when materials or products fail to meet quality requirements before leaving the facility. The costs related to rework, scrap, and repair, troubleshooting a process, corrective actions taken by suppliers on nonconforming incoming materials (and the costs related to delays and lost production time), and material replacement costs are examples of internal failure costs.

External failure costs are incurred when products fail to meet quality requirements after delivery of the product to the customer. The costs related to returned products, warranty work, dealing with dissatisfied customers, product recalls, liability costs, penalty costs, loss of customer trust, and lost sales are examples of external failure costs.

Prevention and appraisal costs may be viewed as input costs, costs that are incurred in trying to prevent and identify problems, while internal and external costs represent output costs, the costs that are incurred when problems occur. The process of reducing total quality cost is indirectly the focus of this entire book.

The cost of quality may also be viewed as costs that are related to conformance and nonconformance. Costs related to nonconformance are all those expenses involved in doing things wrong. It has been estimated that more than one-third of the costs associated with labor, supplies, materials, and energy are nonconformance costs. Costs related to conformance are all those expenses incurred in making things come out right. All prevention costs are costs that are related to conformance.

## 2-5. Statistical Process Control versus Automatic Process Control

Statistical process control techniques were first used in the hard goods product industries. In more recent times, while statistical process control techniques were being applied to discrete production processes, automatic process control techniques were being developed and improved in continuous production industries. Of course, SPC is now being applied in the process industries. Still, the number of noteworthy differences between the hard goods and process industries and between the perspectives of statistical process control and automatic process control sometimes complicates the use of SPC.

Discrete production processes result in individual products, such as batteries, automobiles, and pencils, while continuous production processes feature product runs that result in batches of products, such as chemicals, petrochemicals, sugar, paper, plastic, and rubber. Discrete processes feature counts, discrete production steps, and linear production lines, while continuous processes feature linked operations and process flows. In discrete manufacturing, the goal is to improve processes by eliminating the causes of defects (and minimizing scrap and rework). In continuous process industries, the goal is to produce a product mix that matches market demand with a minimum energy expenditure (and minimum reblending).

There are also physical differences between the two approaches and between the methods of applying them. Process control is centered around the process engineer and a computer-driven feedback controller. The engineer-programmed controller is connected directly to sensors and final control elements (such as valves) and reacts automatically to signals to control the process. Statistical process control depends on data that is often collected and plotted by operators on charts that are later analyzed. In other words, while process control counts on the engineer-controlled computer or other device to react, statistical process control typically counts on the reaction of the operator.

There are important differences in perspectives regarding what is meant by being "in control." From the automatic process control perspective, a process is in control when adjustments are made such that the sensors, which measure the material and energy balance, track their target within some acceptable engineering tolerance. From the statistical process control perspective, a process is said to be in control (more properly, in statistical control) when only random variation is present in the process. The concept of statistical control is discussed extensively throughout this ILM.

There are also differences in focus. The fundamental concern of automatic process control is the immediate regulation of the process against frequent and sometimes large disturbances. Automatic process control reacts quickly to disturbances in the system in an attempt to bring the process back on course. The fundamental concern of statistical process control is finding out what is causing the disturbances (i.e., root causes). In fact, traditional SPC techniques emphasize the fact that variation is normal, that it is present in all processes, and that reacting to random variation actually increases the process variation. In summary, automatic process control takes a short-term view, while statistical process control takes a long-term view.

Process engineers take the perspective that relationships among process variables are known without error, that is, a view that if all equations that describe the system are included and all the parameter estimates are correct, the system output can be predicted exactly. They view the process as a cause-and-effect system that is both known and understood. Proponents of statistical process control take the perspective that the relationships between process variables are inherently probabilistic—a view that the relationships are not exact. SPC views the process as a cause-and-effect system that cannot be completely understood—one that will always have some degree of variation present.

There are also other differences. Automatic process control views the production process from a near-continuous, second-to-second perspective. It views the process as dynamic and events as causing chain reactions of other events throughout the system. Statistical process control has typically viewed processes from an hour-to-hour or week-to-week vantage point, with events examined as if the process were static—as if understanding steady-state characteristics were crucial to improving the process.

Clearly, there are a number of differences between automatic process control and statistical process control. Still, SPC has an important place in the process industries, especially as the features of automatic process control and statistical process control are blended with each other. This ILM presents the essential aspects of SPC with a focus on their application in the process industries.

## Exercises

2-1. How does the focus of statistical process control (SPC) differ from the focus of traditional statistical quality control (SQC)?

2-2. What are the two key questions in statistical process control?

2-3. Dr. Deming's chain of quality (Fig. 2-3) and his systems view (Fig. 2-4) both focus on the customer. Discuss briefly.

2-4. The idea that both the customer and the process have voices is discussed. What is the meaning of variation in each?

2-5. Give two definitions of quality. Discuss why the term quality has so many different meanings.

2-6. Every cost of quality (or lack of quality) can be grouped into one of four categories. Name them and give an example of each.

2-7. Statistical process control and automatic process control are clearly different. Name three important differences.

# Unit 3:
# Graphical Techniques for Data Collection and Presentation

# UNIT 3

## Graphical Techniques for Data Collection and Presentation

In order to meaningfully discuss quality-related problems, we must support the arguments with data. Well-presented data provides insight and serves as a basis for better problem understanding. This unit presents several graphical techniques to help organize and present data for analysis.

**Learning Objectives** — When you have completed this unit, you should:

A. Be able to present data in the form of a histogram, a cumulative frequency polygon, and on a run chart.

B. Know how and when to use three other graphical techniques for data analysis: the box plot, the dot plot, and the scatterplot.

### 3-1. Histogram

A histogram represents a simple way of grouping data by frequency of occurrence. In fact, histograms are sometimes referred to as frequency distributions.

Histograms are most easily described by example. A histogram describing the age distribution of a company's employees is shown in Fig. 3-1. Even a quick look at the histogram reveals that the company's employees tend to be older, although a sizable number are under 30. The gap in employee ages between 30 and 45 corresponds to a 15-year period during which few people were hired. The histogram in Fig. 3-2 shows clearly that the size of most orders is six or fewer different items. The histogram in Fig. 3-3 indicates that pipe welds tend to be between 0.50 and 0.70 inch wide and that it is equally likely for a weld to be wider or narrower than the average of about 0.60 inch.

Regardless of the data, histograms are usually able to show the patterns present. Fig. 3-1 shows a two-hump (bimodal) histogram. Fig. 3-2 shows a lopsided data pattern with a "tail" pointing to the right. Such a frequency distribution is said to be

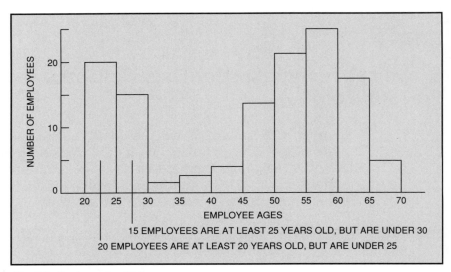

**Fig. 3-1. Employee Age Histogram**

"skewed" to the right. Fig. 3-3 shows that weld widths tend to be symmetric.

The histogram development process is simple. The data is subdivided into several intervals; the number of data points falling in each interval is counted; a histogram is then constructed with the height of individual bars equal to the count in that interval. An example is used to describe the

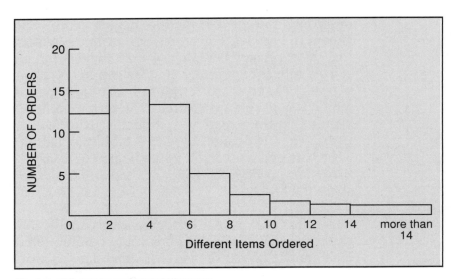

**Fig. 3-2. Different Items Ordered Histogram**

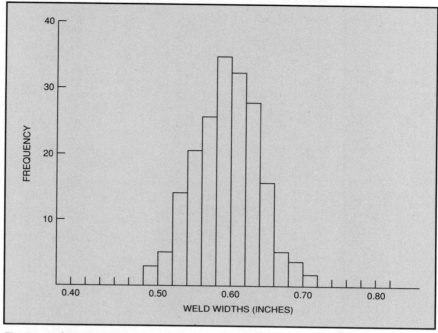

**Fig. 3-3. Weld Width Histogram**

development process in more detail. Table 3-1 shows 80 sulfur trioxide measurements (by percentage) taken during a one-month period from a chemical process, and Fig. 3-4 shows a histogram created from the data.

While little is known about the data after examining Table 3-1 (a typical scenario), considerably more is known after viewing

| | | | | |
|------|------|------|------|------|
| 15.8 | 16.0 | 15.7 | 15.9 | 16.4 |
| 15.7 | 15.8 | 15.7 | 15.6 | 15.9 |
| 15.7 | 15.8 | 15.7 | 15.7 | 16.2 |
| 15.7 | 15.7 | 15.7 | 15.8 | 15.8 |
| 15.3 | 16.0 | 15.5 | 15.6 | 16.1 |
| 16.1 | 15.8 | 15.8 | 14.4 | 16.3 |
| 15.7 | 15.8 | 15.6 | 15.8 | 16.0 |
| 15.7 | 15.7 | 15.5 | 15.8 | 15.6 |
| 15.9 | 16.0 | 15.7 | 15.9 | 16.3 |
| 15.7 | 15.5 | 15.7 | 16.4 | 15.5 |
| 15.7 | 15.8 | 15.8 | 15.5 | 16.0 |
| 15.8 | 15.6 | 15.5 | 15.8 | 15.7 |
| 15.4 | 16.0 | 15.2 | 15.9 | 16.1 |
| 15.7 | 15.8 | 15.7 | 14.4 | 15.9 |
| 15.5 | 15.8 | 15.1 | 15.8 | 16.0 |
| 15.6 | 15.7 | 15.6 | 15.8 | 15.6 |

**TABLE 3-1. Sulfur Trioxide Measurements**

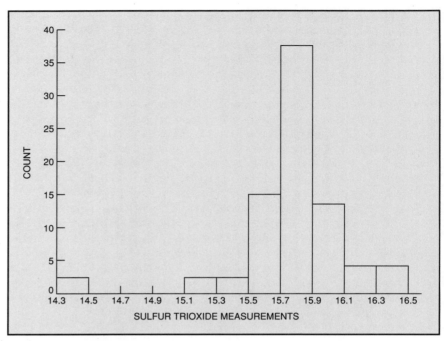

**Fig. 3-4. Histogram of Sulfur Trioxide Measurements**

the histogram in Fig. 3-4. It shows that, except for two measurements in the 14.2–14.4 interval, the data is concentrated around 15.8, is generally symmetric around 15.8, and has lows and highs ranging from about 15.1 to about 16.4.

A histogram can be constructed using the following steps:

*Step 1.* Decide on the number of intervals. There should be enough intervals to show the variability in the data without having so many intervals that the data appear to be sparsely distributed across the intervals.

Two rules of thumb are often applied to help decide on an appropriate number of intervals: (1) choose between 5 and 20 equal-sized intervals and (2) choose a number of intervals that is approximately equal to the square root of the number of observations. For the sulfur trioxide data of Table 3-1, since there are 80 measurements, we expect to have approximately nine equal-sized intervals (i.e., $\sqrt{80}$).

*Step 2.* Decide on the interval widths and on the locations of the intervals. As with the choice of the number of

| Number of Data Points | N = | 80 |
|---|---|---|
| Maximum Data Value | M = | 16.4 |
| Minimum Data Value | m = | 14.4 |
| Range (Maximum-Minimum) | M − m = | 2.0 |
| Approximate Number of Intervals | $\sqrt{N}$ = | 9 |
| Approximate Size of Intervals | (M − m)/$\sqrt{N}$ = | 0.22 |
| Convenient Interval Size | D = | 0.2 |
| Lowest Interval Boundary | | 14.3 |
| Highest Interval Boundary | | 16.4 |

**TABLE 3-2. Histogram Development Worksheet**

intervals, this is not an exact science. Approximate interval widths may be found by identifying the maximum and minimum values in the data and dividing the difference between them, called the range, by the approximate number of intervals chosen. Adjustments can then be made to convenient cutoff points. For the sulfur trioxide data, the high and low values are 16.4 and 14.4, respectively. Dividing their difference of 2.0 by 9 equals 0.22. Since an interval width of 0.22 is somewhat clumsy, an interval width of 0.20 was chosen. The lowest interval boundary is usually set at an appropriate cutoff point slightly less than the minimum value. For the sulfur trioxide data, the minimum value is 14.4 and the lowest interval boundary is set at 14.3. Table 3-2 shows a worksheet that summarizes the first two steps.

Step 3. Categorize the data. Table 3-3 shows the checksheet used to categorize the sulfur trioxide data prior to developing the histogram. Note that the approximate interval midpoints are given to help describe each

| Intervals | Interval "Midpoint" | Interval Frequency | Count |
|---|---|---|---|
| 14.3–14.4 | 14.4 | // | 2 |
| 14.5–14.6 | 14.6 | | 0 |
| 14.7–14.8 | 14.8 | | 0 |
| 14.9–15.0 | 15.0 | | 0 |
| 15.1–15.2 | 15.2 | // | 2 |
| 15.3–15.4 | 15.4 | // | 2 |
| 15.5–15.6 | 15.6 | 7H/ 7H/ 7H/ | 15 |
| 15.7–15.8 | 15.8 | 7H/ 7H/ 7H/ 7H/ 7H/ 7H/ 7H/ /// | 38 |
| 15.9–16.0 | 16.0 | 7H/ 7H/ /// | 13 |
| 16.1–16.2 | 16.2 | //// | 4 |
| 16.3–16.4 | 16.4 | //// | 4 |

**TABLE 3-3. Checksheet Used to Develop Histogram**

interval's location. In fact, the interval midpoints are sometimes shown on the histogram for additional clarity (and to facilitate preparation of the frequency polygon).

The intervals chosen should, in general, cover the entire range of data. When the data includes a few values well separated from the bulk of the measurements, it is common practice to leave the first and/or last intervals open ended to include the "outliers." For example, the histogram shown in Fig. 3-2 has an open-ended last interval.

In addition to showing the shape of the data, histograms are also useful in determining at least approximately the capability of a process to meet customer specifications. We say approximately because specification limits may fall within an interval rather than on an interval boundary. Fig. 3-5 shows the histogram of sulfur trioxide measurements originally presented in Fig. 3-4 with customer specification limits added. While the process is generally capable of meeting the customer's specifications, several measurements are outside specifications. (Process capability analysis is presented in detail in Unit 12.)

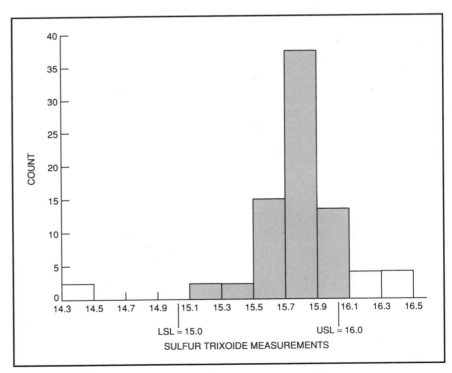

**Fig. 3-5. Histogram of Sulfur Trioxide Measurements with Customer Specification Limits**

| Intervals | Interval "Midpoint" | Interval Frequency | Cumulative | | |
|---|---|---|---|---|---|
| | | | Count | Count | % |
| 14.3–14.4 | 14.4 | // | 2 | 2 | 2.5 |
| 14.5–14.6 | 14.6 | | 0 | 2 | 2.5 |
| 14.7–14.8 | 14.8 | | 0 | 2 | 2.5 |
| 14.9–15.0 | 15.0 | | 0 | 2 | 2.5 |
| 15.1–15.2 | 15.2 | // | 2 | 4 | 5.0 |
| 15.3–15.4 | 15.4 | // | 2 | 6 | 7.5 |
| 15.5–15.6 | 15.6 | ⫫ ⫫ ⫫ | 15 | 21 | 26.3 |
| 15.7–15.8 | 15.8 | ⫫ ⫫ ⫫ ⫫ ⫫ ⫫ ⫫ /// | 38 | 59 | 73.8 |
| 15.9–16.0 | 16.0 | ⫫ ⫫ /// | 13 | 72 | 90.0 |
| 16.1–16.2 | 16.2 | //// | 4 | 76 | 95.0 |
| 16.3–16.4 | 16.4 | //// | 4 | 80 | 100.0 |

**TABLE 3-4. Checksheet Used to Develop Histogram (Cumulative Count and Percentage Columns Added)**

A closely related diagram, the cumulative frequency polygon (i.e., many sided figure), has one advantage over the histogram: it allows probability questions about the data to be answered more easily. The cumulative frequency polygon can be constructed directly from the checksheet by including two additional columns: a cumulative count (i.e., the count in each interval plus the count in all prior intervals) and a cumulative percentage. Table 3-4 shows the same figures presented in Table 3-3 with the cumulative count and cumulative percentage columns added. Fig. 3-6 shows the cumulative frequency polygon. Note that the points on the polygon are plotted above each interval's midpoint value.

By examining Fig. 3-6, it is apparent that over 25 percent of the measurements are 15.5 or less, nearly 75 percent are 15.7 or less, and 95 percent are 16.1 or less. Also, nearly 50 percent of the measurements are between 15.5 and 15.7, and about 90 percent of the measurements are between 15.1 and 16.1.

**Two Histogram Examples**

Fig. 3-7 shows a histogram of performance measurements made at the conclusion of a gasoline blending operation. The histogram shows an obvious gap to the left of the lower specification limit. Inspection of the process revealed the cause. When an unacceptable measurement followed the conclusion of the process, instructions called for the gasoline to be resampled. Because of the variation present in the measurement process, acceptable measurements or totally unacceptable ones often followed.

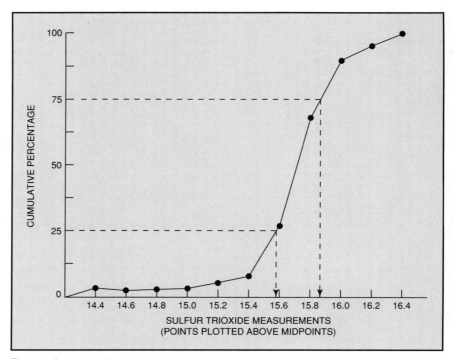

Fig. 3-6.  Cumulative Frequency Polygon of Sulfur Trioxide Measurements

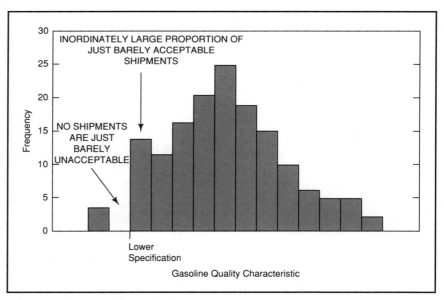

Fig. 3-7.  Histogram of 150 Gasoline Production Measurements

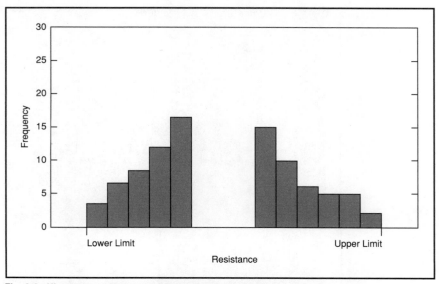

**Fig. 3-8. Histogram of Resistance Measurements on 87 Electrical Parts**

Fig. 3-8 shows a histogram based on the resistance measurement of 87 electrical parts received from a supplier. All values are inside specification limits, but the middle part of the histogram is missing. It appears that the supplier has sold the best components (i.e., those with less variation) to another company that has tighter specifications. This example shows the results of sorting production.

In both examples, the histograms, had they been fully formed, would likely have been symmetrical. Also, in both cases the oddities apparent in the data might likely have gone undetected without a histogram.

## 3-2. Run Chart

A run chart presents the same data as the histogram but shows the values plotted sequentially over time. The utility of a run chart lies in its ability to show time-dependent trends (gradually increasing or decreasing values), runs (consistently high or low values), shifts (sudden increase or decrease), and cycles (up-down-up-down pattern) that the histogram has no way of displaying. In fact, run charts typically look like control charts without control limits.

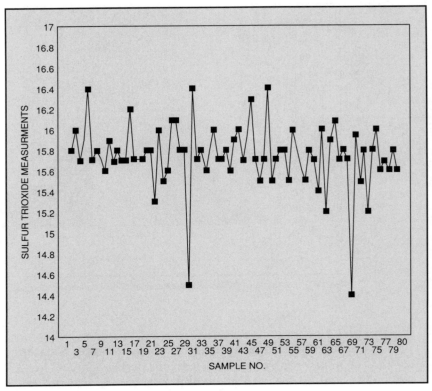

**Fig. 3-9. Run Chart of Sulfur Trioxide Measurements**

Run charts are usually constructed on individual measurements or counts but can obviously be plotted on other types of values as well (e.g., sums of values, averages of values, etc.). Fig. 3-9 shows the sulfur trioxide measurements presented in Table 3-1 plotted over time in row by row order. Except for two measurements of 14.4 (values 29 and 69), the process seems to be well behaved (i.e., no trends, runs, shifts, or cycles).

## 3-3. Box Plot

Box plots are lesser known but useful tools for comparing multiple sets of data (e.g., multiple histograms). They are composed of a rectangle (a box) whose top side corresponds to a frequency polygon's 75 percent mark and whose bottom side corresponds to a frequency polygon's 25 percent mark. A horizontal line within the box represents the data's middlemost value. Vertical lines, called "whiskers," are attached to the top and bottom of the box. The upper whisker ends at the data's cumulative 90 percent mark, while the lower whisker ends at

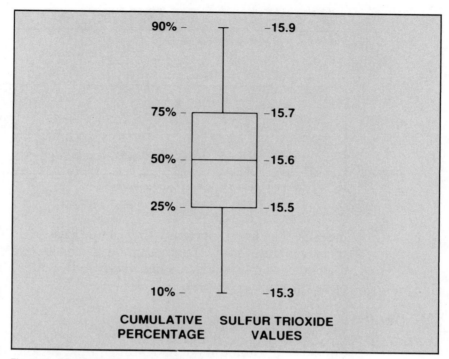

**Fig. 3-10.  Box Plot of Sulfur Trioxide Data**

the cumulative 10 percent mark. Fig. 3-10 shows a box plot created from the cumulative frequency polygon of the sulfur trioxide data.

Fig. 3-11 shows a series of box plots that compares the average daily yield of a production process over four successive

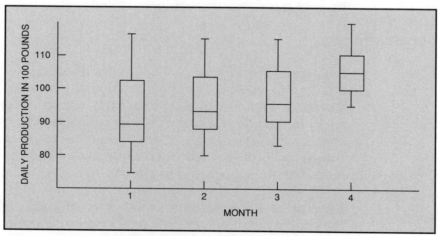

**Fig. 3-11.  Box Plots of Production Yield for Four Successive Months**

| 0.96 | 0.95 | 0.97 | 0.95 | 1.18 | 1.02 | 1.02 | 1.03 | 1.02 | 1.05 |

**TABLE 3-5. Ten Melt Index Measurements**

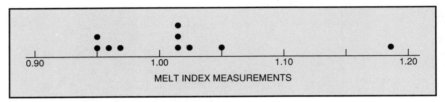

MELT INDEX MEASUREMENTS

**Fig. 3-12. Dot Plot of Ten Melt Index Measurements**

months. The box plots show that the process yield has steadily increased and that process variation has decreased (i.e., distance between whiskers has decreased), both clear indicators of an improving process.

## 3-4. Dot Plot

Considerable amounts of data are required to construct meaningful histograms (and box plots). Dot plots, however, can be constructed from only a few data points and, although not as instructive as histograms, can provide insight into a process. Table 3-5 shows 10 melt index (i.e., a polymer characteristic) measurements. Because of the small number of data values, it would be meaningless to construct a histogram. Instead, a dot plot is developed (Fig. 3-12). This simple plot shows that while most of the melt index values are clustered around 1.0, there is one outlier near 1.2. (Additional data is required for more extensive comments, such as symmetry, skewness, etc.)

## 3-5. Scatterplot

Scatterplots (sometimes called scatter diagrams or crossplots) are used to study the possible relationship between two variables. The horizontal axis (x axis) is used to represent one variable, and the vertical axis (y axis) is used to represent another. The resulting scatter of points indicates how closely the variables are related. A numeric measure of the relationship (correlation) is discussed in Unit 5.

**Example 3-1:** A customer wanted to determine how closely the results of laboratory tests performed by its primary supplier on a rubber product's key quality characteristic matched its own laboratory results. The ultimate objective was to determine whether the receiving company could rely on the supplier's test results or whether it was necessary to continue to conduct its own tests.

Twenty-one data pairs are shown in Table 3-6. A scatterplot of the data is shown in Fig. 3-13. Although the results from the two laboratories were not identical, the scatterplot shows a probable linear relationship. Low supplier lab values correspond to low customer lab values, while high supplier lab values correspond to high customer lab values. A bias is present, however. Results from the supplier's lab are consistently higher than results from the customer's lab. In addition, the differences seem to be greater as the measurement values increase. (This controversy was resolved when both parties agreed to have a third company recalibrate their instruments on a regular basis.)

| Shipment No. | Results, Supp. | Cust. | Shipment No. | Results, Supp. | Cust. | Shipment No. | Results, Supp. | Cust. |
|---|---|---|---|---|---|---|---|---|
| 1 | 3.36 | 3.25 | 8 | 4.05 | 3.65 | 15 | 3.46 | 3.35 |
| 2 | 4.18 | 3.75 | 9 | 3.46 | 3.55 | 16 | 4.17 | 3.95 |
| 3 | 3.55 | 3.67 | 10 | 4.29 | 3.85 | 17 | 3.65 | 3.45 |
| 4 | 4.45 | 3.85 | 11 | 3.65 | 3.65 | 18 | 4.45 | 3.95 |
| 5 | 3.65 | 3.75 | 12 | 4.45 | 4.05 | 19 | 3.88 | 3.53 |
| 6 | 4.55 | 3.95 | 13 | 3.95 | 3.75 | 20 | 4.59 | 4.15 |
| 7 | 3.95 | 3.95 | 14 | 4.65 | 4.05 | 21 | 4.35 | 3.65 |

TABLE 3-6. Twenty-One Pairs of Measurements on Key Rubber Quality Characteristic from Two Laboratories

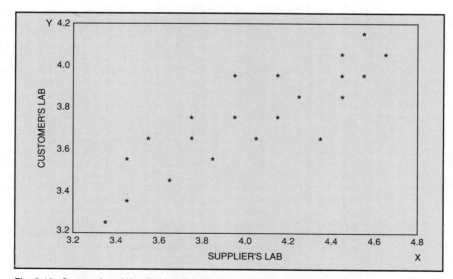

Fig. 3-13. Scatterplot of Key Rubber Quality Characteristic from Two Laboratories

**Example 3-2:**   The vapor pressure of gasoline can be measured via the Reid vapor pressure (RVP) test in two different ways: using an online analyzer and using a laboratory procedure. Federal regulations require the laboratory analysis, but the time required to obtain the results (usually over two hours) limits their value for online process control. Consequently, operations prefers to use the online analyzer's results to help control the process. There is, however, considerable concern with regard to the relationship between the results found using the two methods.

Table 3-7 shows 57 paired RVP measurements, one set of measurements produced in the plant laboratory and the other set produced by an online analyzer. Each measurement pair was based on samples taken from the same process at nearly the same time.

Fig. 3-14 shows a scatterplot of the paired RVP results. Several observations are possible:

    A.  The results appear to be generally related in most instances (i.e., as lab values increase, online analyzer values increase).

| No. | Lab | Online | No. | Lab | Online | No. | Lab | Online |
|-----|-----|--------|-----|-----|--------|-----|-----|--------|
| 1 | 8.6 | 8.7 | 21 | 8.9 | 8.8 | 41 | 8.7 | 8.7 |
| 2 | 8.8 | 9.0 | 22 | 8.5 | 8.8 | 42 | 8.5 | 9.0 |
| 3 | 9.0 | 9.1 | 23 | 8.6 | 9.2 | 43 | 8.8 | 9.1 |
| 4 | 8.5 | 9.1 | 24 | 8.9 | 8.6 | 44 | 8.6 | 9.1 |
| 5 | 8.7 | 9.1 | 25 | 8.6 | 9.4 | 45 | 8.6 | 8.6 |
| 6 | 9.1 | 9.2 | 26 | 8.8 | 9.4 | 46 | 8.3 | 8.9 |
| 7 | 9.1 | 9.2 | 27 | 8.5 | 8.9 | 47 | 8.4 | 9.0 |
| 8 | 9.2 | 9.2 | 28 | 8.7 | 8.7 | 48 | 8.0 | 8.2 |
| 9 | 8.9 | 9.2 | 29 | 7.8 | 8.8 | 49 | 8.8 | 7.7 |
| 10 | 9.1 | 9.2 | 30 | 8.0 | 8.8 | 50 | 8.3 | 7.6 |
| 11 | 9.0 | 9.2 | 31 | 8.5 | 8.9 | 51 | 9.5 | 7.5 |
| 12 | 8.8 | 9.0 | 32 | 8.4 | 9.0 | 52 | 7.8 | 9.2 |
| 13 | 8.8 | 9.2 | 33 | 8.6 | 9.0 | 53 | 8.3 | 9.1 |
| 14 | 9.1 | 9.2 | 34 | 8.5 | 9.0 | 54 | 8.3 | 8.5 |
| 15 | 9.2 | 9.6 | 35 | 8.5 | 8.9 | 55 | 8.7 | 8.4 |
| 16 | 9.3 | 9.5 | 36 | 8.0 | 8.5 | 56 | 8.8 | 8.3 |
| 17 | 8.8 | 9.0 | 37 | 8.0 | 8.4 | 57 | 8.8 | 8.3 |
| 18 | 8.5 | 9.2 | 38 | 8.0 | 8.4 | | | |
| 19 | 9.0 | 9.0 | 39 | 8.0 | 8.7 | | | |
| 20 | 7.5 | 8.9 | 40 | 8.5 | 8.6 | | | |

**TABLE 3-7.  Fifty-Seven Pairs of RVP Measurements**

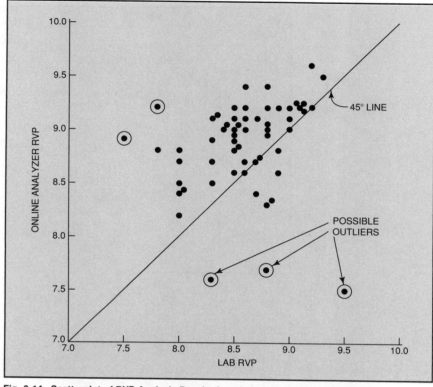

Fig. 3-14. Scatterplot of RVP Analysis Results from Laboratory and Online Analyzer

B.  After drawing a 45° line from the lower left corner to the upper right corner of the scatterplot, it is apparent that the online analyzer's results are consistently higher than the lab's results. (Note: A 45° line represents exact agreement since the horizontal and vertical scales are the same.)

C.  Several points (circled) are far out of line with the majority of values, indicating possible problems with the analyzer or the lab or both.

In both examples, the relationship between the two variables seems generally to be linear. Of course, relationships between two variables can take on an infinite variety of forms. The range of possibilities is shown in Fig. 3-15 with comments.

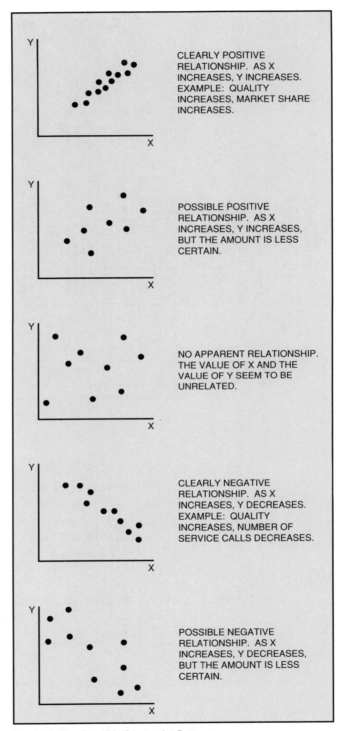

**Fig. 3-15. Five Possible Scatterplot Patterns**

# Exercises

3-1. The data in the table below represent percentage of budget spent on a variety of projects during the last several quarters. Based on the data shown, develop (a) a histogram, (b) a cumulative frequency polygon, and (c) a run chart. (d) Briefly discuss the results of each.

| Project No. | Percent of Budget | Project No. | Percent of Budget |
|---|---|---|---|
| 1 | 110 | 16 | 97 |
| 2 | 100 | 17 | 107 |
| 3 | 90 | 18 | 95 |
| 4 | 99 | 19 | 90 |
| 5 | 91 | 20 | 88 |
| 6 | 95 | 21 | 118 |
| 7 | 92 | 22 | 94 |
| 8 | 88 | 23 | 98 |
| 9 | 129 | 24 | 102 |
| 10 | 91 | 25 | 104 |
| 11 | 108 | 26 | 107 |
| 12 | 104 | 27 | 97 |
| 13 | 112 | 28 | 96 |
| 14 | 96 | 29 | 101 |
| 15 | 102 | 30 | 93 |

Project Budget Performance

3-2. The data in the table below represent the chlorine content in a polymer. Based on the data shown, develop (a) a histogram, (b) a cumulative frequency polygon, and (c) a run chart. (d) Briefly discuss the results of each one.

| Sample | Chlorine Content | Sample | Chlorine Content | Sample | Chorine Content |
|---|---|---|---|---|---|
| 1 | 36.4 | 16 | 36.6 | 31 | 36.6 |
| 2 | 36.6 | 17 | 36.0 | 32 | 36.8 |
| 3 | 36.3 | 18 | 37.1 | 33 | 36.4 |
| 4 | 35.6 | 19 | 36.6 | 34 | 36.9 |
| 5 | 35.1 | 20 | 36.5 | 35 | 35.8 |
| 6 | 35.1 | 21 | 36.8 | 36 | 37.0 |
| 7 | 35.3 | 22 | 37.1 | 37 | 34.8 |
| 8 | 36.0 | 23 | 37.0 | 38 | 35.5 |
| 9 | 36.1 | 24 | 36.7 | 39 | 36.5 |
| 10 | 34.5 | 25 | 36.1 | 40 | 36.5 |
| 11 | 36.4 | 26 | 36.1 | 41 | 36.2 |
| 12 | 36.1 | 27 | 36.6 | 42 | 35.1 |
| 13 | 36.6 | 28 | 36.1 | 43 | 35.5 |
| 14 | 36.5 | 29 | 36.5 | 44 | 35.0 |
| 15 | 36.7 | 30 | 36.5 | 45 | 35.3 |

Chlorine Content of a Polymer

3-3. The data in the table below represent melt index values for 150 samples of high-density polyethylene. Based on the data shown, (a) construct a histogram, (b) a cumulative frequency polygon, and (c) answer the following questions based on the cumulative frequency polygon:

(1) What value has about 25% of the values below it?
(2) What value has about 50% of the values below it?
(3) What value has about 90% of the values below it?
(4) Between what melt index values are the middlemost 50% of the values contained?
(5) Comment on any unusual characteristics present in the data.

| | | | | | | | |
|---|---|---|---|---|---|---|---|
| 1.062 | 0.972 | 1.085 | 1.105 | 0.985 | 1.022 | 0.910 | 0.997 |
| 1.030 | 1.057 | 1.018 | 1.059 | 1.024 | 1.007 | 1.063 | 0.975 |
| 1.002 | 1.072 | 1.161 | 0.928 | 1.085 | 0.968 | 1.048 | 1.003 |
| 1.022 | 1.000 | 1.153 | 1.055 | 1.022 | 1.033 | 1.102 | 1.092 |
| 1.035 | 1.057 | 0.930 | 0.985 | 1.140 | 1.042 | 0.908 | 0.912 |
| 0.978 | 0.987 | 1.107 | 1.027 | 0.983 | 1.077 | 0.980 | 1.166 |
| 1.034 | 1.032 | 1.042 | 1.027 | 0.954 | 0.997 | 1.075 | 1.123 |
| 0.980 | 0.931 | 1.041 | 0.923 | 1.090 | 1.022 | 1.118 | 0.992 |
| 1.065 | 1.005 | 0.983 | 0.946 | 1.122 | 1.151 | 1.023 | 1.097 |
| 0.967 | 1.062 | 1.020 | 1.030 | 1.013 | 1.000 | 1.128 | 1.033 |
| 0.945 | 1.082 | 1.143 | 1.087 | 0.957 | 1.003 | 1.023 | 1.135 |
| 0.985 | 0.930 | 1.050 | 1.066 | 0.980 | 1.047 | 0.989 | 1.073 |
| 1.050 | 0.933 | 0.963 | 0.965 | 1.048 | 1.069 | 1.086 | 1.012 |
| 1.017 | 0.979 | 1.145 | 1.005 | 1.003 | 0.998 | 1.111 | 1.080 |
| 1.115 | 1.008 | 1.005 | 1.088 | 1.051 | 1.027 | 1.040 | 1.077 |
| 1.158 | 0.942 | 1.023 | 0.999 | 1.002 | 1.003 | 1.067 | 1.038 |
| 1.093 | 1.007 | 0.953 | 1.069 | 1.008 | 0.969 | 1.035 | 1.017 |
| 1.045 | 1.024 | 1.046 | 0.957 | 1.005 | 1.054 | 0.975 | 0.985 |
| 1.034 | 1.022 | 1.077 | 1.043 | 1.058 | 1.024 | | |

**Melt Index Values for 150 Samples of High Density Polyethylene**

3-4. Consider the 20 sample pairs of melt index and temperature measurements shown in the table below. (a) Develop separate run charts for melt index values and for temperatures. (b) Plot both data characteristics in a scatterplot after coding the temperature as actual temperature minus 220 times 10 (e.g., 220.8 would be coded as 8). (c) Comment on your findings.

| No. | Melt Index | Temp. | No. | Melt Index | Temp. |
|---|---|---|---|---|---|
| 1 | 1.0 | 220.8 | 6 | 1.2 | 221.8 |
| 2 | 1.0 | 220.3 | 7 | 1.1 | 221.4 |
| 3 | 1.1 | 220.5 | 8 | 1.1 | 221.3 |
| 4 | 1.0 | 220.3 | 9 | 1.0 | 220.7 |
| 5 | 1.1 | 221.0 | 10 | 1.1 | 220.7 |

| No. | Melt Index | Temp. | No. | Melt Index | Temp. |
|-----|-----------|-------|-----|-----------|-------|
| 11 | 1.1 | 221.6 | 16 | 1.1 | 221.5 |
| 12 | 1.1 | 221.8 | 17 | 1.1 | 221.8 |
| 13 | 1.1 | 221.2 | 18 | 1.2 | 221.3 |
| 14 | 1.0 | 220.5 | 19 | 1.1 | 221.3 |
| 15 | 1.1 | 220.4 | 20 | 1.1 | 221.7 |

**Melt Index and Temperature (F°) Measurements**

3-5. *The table below gives the depth of nine wells and the average pollution level in parts per million of a hazardous material found in nearby well water. (a) Develop separate dot plots for each set of data. (b) Show the data in a scatterplot. (c) Briefly comment on your findings.*

| Location | Drill Hole Depth (feet) | Average Pollution Level |
|----------|------------------------|------------------------|
| 1 | 65 | 18 |
| 2 | 95 | 23 |
| 3 | 100 | 25 |
| 4 | 60 | 20 |
| 5 | 100 | 22 |
| 6 | 80 | 21 |
| 7 | 80 | 20 |
| 8 | 70 | 15 |

**Drill Hole Depth Versus Average Pollution Level**

3-6. *The data in the table below represent the flow index values (grams/10 minutes) for two laboratories based on samples from the same materials. (a) Develop histograms for each lab's data. (b) Develop a scatterplot. (c) Briefly comment on your findings.*

| No. | Flow Index Lab 1 | Flow Index Lab 2 | No. | Flow Index Lab 1 | Flow Index Lab 2 |
|-----|------------------|------------------|-----|------------------|------------------|
| 1 | 3.05 | 3.15 | 14 | 3.85 | 3.90 |
| 2 | 3.00 | 3.05 | 15 | 2.80 | 3.00 |
| 3 | 3.10 | 3.00 | 16 | 2.65 | 2.55 |
| 4 | 2.95 | 2.95 | 17 | 2.65 | 2.60 |
| 5 | 2.85 | 2.80 | 18 | 3.40 | 3.30 |
| 6 | 2.90 | 2.95 | 19 | 2.80 | 2.85 |
| 7 | 3.15 | 3.10 | 20 | 3.40 | 3.70 |
| 8 | 3.25 | 3.25 | 21 | 3.70 | 3.60 |
| 9 | 3.20 | 3.25 | 22 | 3.80 | 3.65 |
| 10 | 3.15 | 3.10 | 23 | 2.45 | 2.55 |
| 11 | 2.80 | 2.85 | 24 | 2.79 | 2.86 |
| 12 | 3.50 | 3.45 | 25 | 3.29 | 3.40 |
| 13 | 2.80 | 2.26 | | | |

**Flow Index Values**

3-7. The data in the table below indicate the failure times (in hours) for pump seals produced by two different companies. Develop a dot plot to present each set of data. Which company's seals seem to be better?

| Company A: | 909 | 1293 | 1601 | 1616 | 2012 | 2016 |
| | 2180 | 2201 | 2442 | | | |
| Company B: | 824 | 1082 | 1135 | 1308 | 1359 | 1372 |
| | 1401 | 1412 | 1601 | 1638 | 1640 | 1674 |
| | 1709 | 1805 | 1947 | 2208 | | |

**Seal Failure Times (Hours)**

3-8. In order to describe the relationship between float height and flow rate, 21 measurement pairs of a rotameter calibration test were collected. The data are shown in the table below. Present the data in a scatterplot and interpret your findings.

| x | y | x | y | x | y |
|---|---|---|---|---|---|
| 4 | 5.77 | 11 | 25.38 | 18 | 44.46 |
| 5 | 7.75 | 12 | 27.83 | 19 | 47.88 |
| 6 | 10.44 | 13 | 30.66 | 20 | 51.95 |
| 7 | 13.64 | 14 | 33.20 | 21 | 56.38 |
| 8 | 16.63 | 15 | 35.73 | 22 | 60.14 |
| 9 | 19.28 | 16 | 38.49 | 23 | 64.65 |
| 10 | 22.20 | 17 | 41.40 | 24 | 68.80 |

Note: x = float height (mm), y = flow rate of water (lbs/hr at 77°)
**Flow Rate versus Float Height**

3-9. The data in the table below represent the brine feed temperatures found in samples of chlorine and caustic. The data, in degrees Fahrenheit, were collected over a period of two months. Construct box plots for each month's data. Discuss your findings.

| | | April | | |
|---|---|---|---|---|
| 155 | 159 | 157 | 155 | 154 |
| 158 | 160 | 157 | 153 | 158 |
| 156 | 155 | 158 | 156 | 155 |
| 157 | 155 | 159 | 156 | 157 |

| | | May | | |
|---|---|---|---|---|
| 147 | 148 | 149 | 147 | 148 |
| 153 | 149 | 144 | 144 | 145 |
| 149 | 151 | 150 | 143 | 150 |
| 152 | 147 | 148 | 146 | 142 |

**Brine Feed Temperature (°F)**

3-10.  The data in the table below represent a measure of the amount of residual metal left on the catalyst from a cat-cracking unit over a period of about seven weeks. The amount of residual metal can reduce the unit's yield. Develop (a) a run chart and (b) a dot plot to describe the situation.

| Date | Residual Metal (ppm) |
|------|:--------------------:|
| Jun 28 | 981 |
| Jul 03 | 918 |
| Jul 07 | 907 |
| Jul 11 | 896 |
| Jul 14 | 967 |
| Jul 18 | 1026 |
| Jul 23 | 954 |
| Jul 29 | 995 |
| Aug 02 | 984 |
| Aug 04 | 1055 |
| Aug 08 | 1118 |
| Aug 11 | 1032 |
| Aug 15 | 1094 |

**Residual Metal**

# Unit 4:
# Graphical Techniques for Problem Solving

# UNIT 4

# Graphical Techniques for Problem Solving

Graphical techniques are widely used at all levels of business and industry. They are used to collect, summarize, and display data. This unit describes four simple graphical techniques that are helpful in problem solving: checksheets, Pareto diagrams, cause-and-effect diagrams, and flow charts.

**Learning Objectives** — When you have completed this unit, you should be able to use several graphical techniques effectively. In particular, you should:

A. Know how to construct and use a checksheet.

B. Know how to construct and use a Pareto diagram.

C. Know how to construct and use a cause-and-effect diagram.

D. Know how to construct and use a flowchart.

## 4-1. Checksheet

A checksheet is a simple tool that may be used to both collect (possibly for later use in a histogram, dot plot, or box plot) and present data. It can take on multiple forms, one being a simple tallysheet. Fig. 4-1 shows the results of an inspector's findings from three bottle production lots. The most frequently encountered problem was weight deviation.

Fig. 4-2 shows a modified version of the same tallysheet on which tallies are made vertically.

Location plots are checksheets combined with diagrams. Fig. 4-3 shows a location plot that divides a plant into nine logical work areas and shows (with an X) where emergency equipment maintenance was performed during the last quarter. Each X represents a separate emergency maintenance action.

Fig. 4-4 presents a variation of the same location plot with symbols used instead of X's to indicate the type of maintenance activity performed (i.e., pump or instrument).

| ITEM: | BOTTLE | DATE: | 7/10 |
| INSPECTOR: | WFB | LOT NUMBER: 001, 002, 003 | |

| TYPE OF DEFECT: | NUMBER |
| --- | --- |
| 1 AIR BUBBLE | ⊬⊬ ‖ |
| 2 WEIGHT DISTRIBUTION | ⊬⊬ ⊬⊬ ⊬⊬ |
| 3 DEFORMATION | ⊬⊬ ⊬⊬ |
| 4 COLOR | ‖‖ |
| TOTAL | *35* |

**Fig. 4-1. Simple Tallysheet**

Checksheets can be used in many situations. A storeroom supervisor realized that he was spending several hours each day answering similar questions. He first created a checksheet with abbreviated versions of the questions he could recall on the left-hand side. He then kept a tally on the number of times each question was asked, with new questions added to the

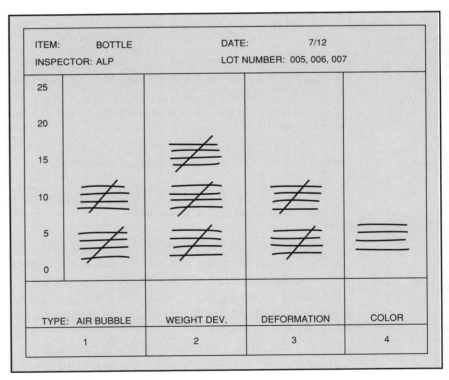

**Fig. 4-2. Modified Tallysheet**

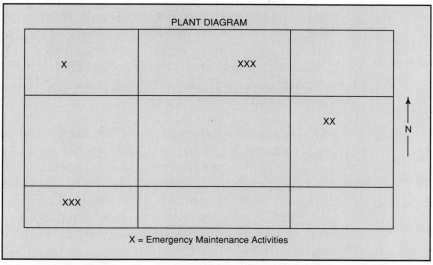

**Fig. 4-3. Location Plot Showing Emergency Maintenance Activities During Last Quarter**

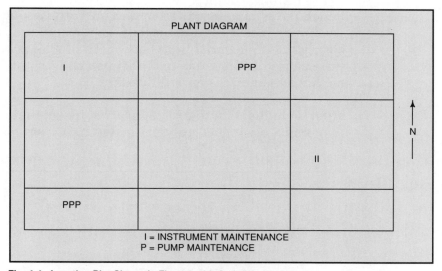

**Fig. 4-4. Location Plot Shown in Fig. 4-3 with Coded Symbols**

checksheet as they were asked. After maintaining the checksheet for a month, the supervisor developed and distributed a simple written document that answered each of the most frequently asked questions.

## 4-2. Pareto Diagram

Pareto diagrams can be used to help analyze quality-related problems by focusing attention on a few critical issues. The idea is that typically only a small number of causes result in most of the problems (sometimes referred to as the "80–20 rule"). As such, the Pareto diagram provides a simple means of displaying rank-ordered causes of problems, making it apparent which causes most frequently occur and providing a logical starting point for their solution.

Fig. 4-5 shows a Pareto diagram for numbers of polyethylene resin samples found to be outside specification limits. Four general possible cause areas, often referred to as the four M's, have been identified: material problems, machine problems, problems with the method, and worker-related (manpower) problems. A cursory examination of the diagram indicates that 30 of the nonconformities were caused by problems related to raw materials, while the other 20 were related to the other three categories.

Fig. 4-6 shows another version of the same Pareto diagram in which the nonconforming samples are further subdivided into weekly categories. While most of the nonconformities were clearly due to material problems, more problems in week 4 were caused by machine malfunctions and inappropriate methods than by material difficulties.

The Pareto diagram in Fig. 4-7 shows the amount (in millions of pounds) of off-spec polymer resin production resulting from

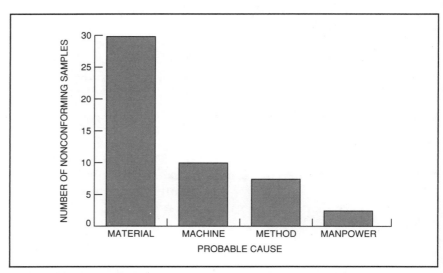

**Fig. 4-5. Pareto Diagram Categorizing Polyethylene Resin Nonconformities (One Month of Production)**

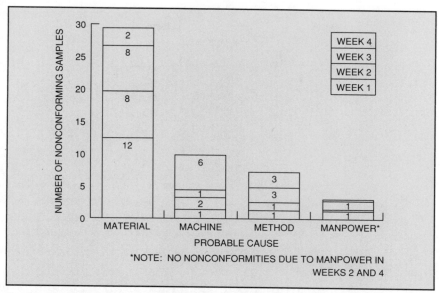

**Fig. 4-6. Pareto Diagram Categorizing Polyethylene Resin Nonconformities (Subdivided into Weeks)**

five major causes: unknown, transition, catalyst, instrument, and feeder. The segments in each bar show how much each reactor contributed to the total amount of off-spec product. Reactor D was clearly the largest contributor.

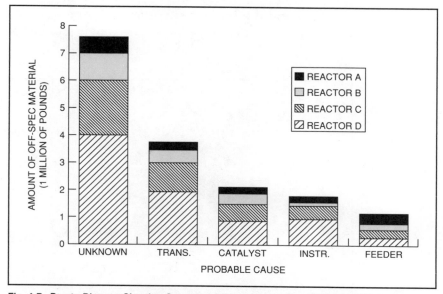

**Fig. 4-7. Pareto Diagram Showing Causes of Off-Spec Production (Subdivided by Reactor)**

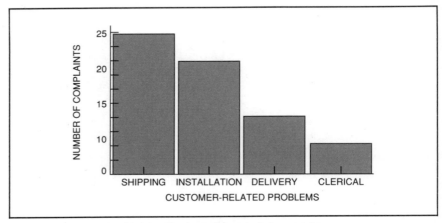

**Fig. 4-8. Pareto Diagram Showing Numbers of Customer Complaints**

Figures 4-8 through 4-12 show other variations of the Pareto diagram. Fig. 4-8 shows a Pareto diagram that categorizes field service customer complaints by number of complaints.

Fig. 4-9 shows that the most frequently occurring problems are not always the most costly. In Fig. 4-9, problems with installation dwarf the other customer-related problems in terms of measurable cost.

The Pareto diagram in Fig. 4-10 categorizes the causes related to supposedly repaired instruments. The problems include not recalibrating the instrument after repairing it, leaving a minor defect by not quite completing the repair job, simply not

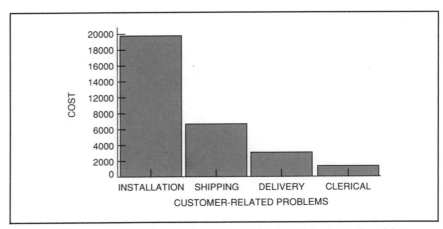

**Fig. 4-9. Pareto Diagram Showing Investment Required to Rectify Customer Complaints**

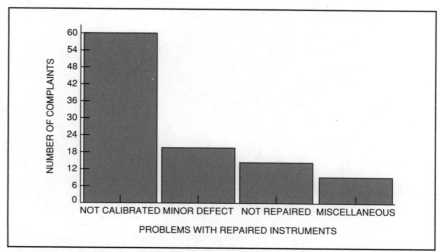

**Fig. 4-10. Pareto Diagram Showing Sources of Problems for Repaired Instruments**

repairing the instrument, and other miscellaneous complaints. Clearly, the most common problem was that the repaired instrument was not recalibrated before reissue.

Fig. 4-11 shows nonconformity totals before and after choosing a single-source supplier. Note that the categories of nonconformities (i.e., the order of the bars) changed. Only the number of problems with materials decreased. The diagrams are placed horizontally for ease of comparison.

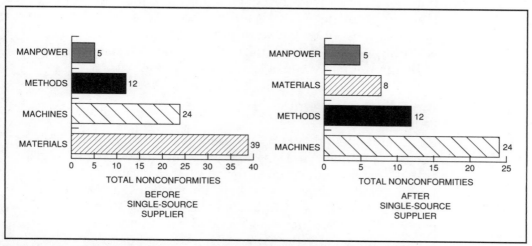

**Fig. 4-11. Pareto Diagram Showing Sources of Nonconformities before and after Choosing a Single-Source Supplier**

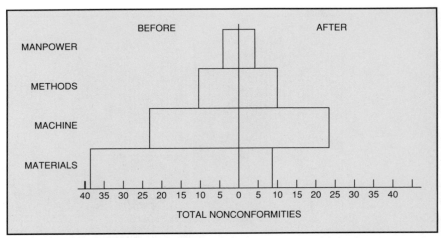

**Fig. 4-12. Modified Pareto Diagram Showing Sources of Nonconformities before and after Choosing a Single-Source Supplier**

Fig. 4-12 shows the same before and after nonconformity data in a modified Pareto diagram format. The "before" single-source supplier data is shown as a Pareto diagram whose scale increases to the left, while the "after" single-source supplier data is shown in corresponding categories with its scale increasing to the right.

Problem causes for an entire process may be subdivided in a linked manner using Pareto diagrams. Fig. 4-13 shows a situation in which most (i.e., 1.2 million pounds) off-spec products were due to material problems. Catalyst nonconformities were responsible for more than 50% of the material problems (i.e., 0.7 million pounds of the 1.2 million pounds), most of which were supplied by Supplier 1. In addition, most of the reactor problems took place at Reactor A, although the major cause is at present unknown.

## 4-3. Cause-and-Effect Diagram

Cause-and-effect diagrams are used to show relationships between problems and possible problem causes. They are also called "fishbone diagrams" (because of their shape) and "Ishikawa diagrams" (after their developer, Kaoru Ishikawa). The shape of the diagram lends itself well to collecting and categorizing ideas that are generated during or after brainstorming activities (since disjointed comments can be quickly and logically added to the diagram).

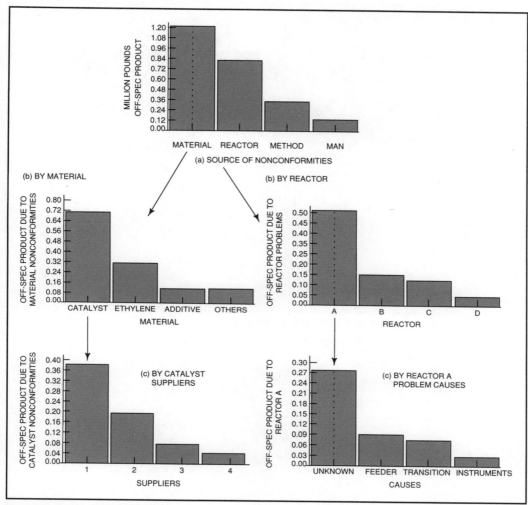

**Fig. 4-13. Linked Pareto Diagrams**

The general form of a cause-and-effect diagram is shown in Fig. 4-14. At the far right of the diagram, the effect (or problem) is presented (usually in a rectangle). Possible causes, subcauses, and sub-subcauses are then shown on arrows that eventually connect with the effect.

Developing a cause-and-effect diagram is a logical process. The first step is to identify the variable (problem) to be studied and place it at the diagram's far right. Next, major possible-cause areas are identified and placed on the diagram at the end of major fishbones emanating from the spine. (Note: One variation of this technique uses stick-on notes on a previously formed cause-and-effect structure.)

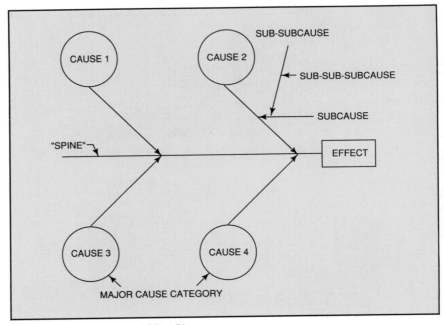

Fig. 4-14.  Generic Cause-and-Effect Diagram

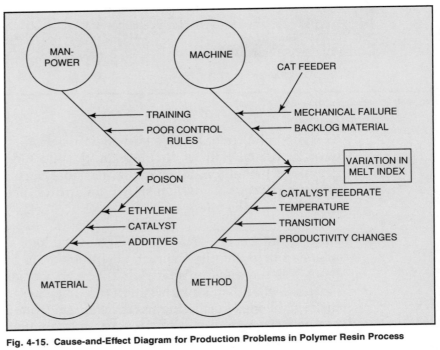

Fig. 4-15.  Cause-and-Effect Diagram for Production Problems in Polymer Resin Process

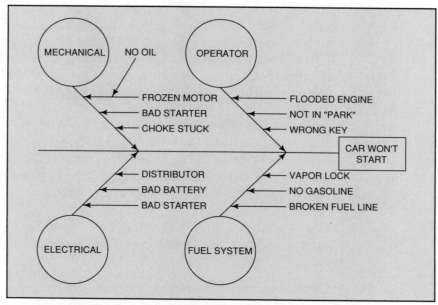

**Fig. 4-16. Cause-and-Effect Diagram for Car-Starting Problem**

Frequently, the four M's mentioned in the description of Pareto diagrams (i.e., manpower, machine, material, method) are used as starting points to help identify the major cause areas. Fig. 4-15 shows a cause-and-effect diagram for problems with a polymer resin production process. The problem identified is the variation present in the quality characteristic known as melt index. Possible causes are grouped under the four major headings: manpower, machine, material, method. A fifth category, environment, is also sometimes helpful as a possible major cause starting point. More specific causes, subcauses, sub-subcauses, and so forth that are related to each of the major headings are then shown on the diagram's fishbones.

Fig. 4-16 shows a simple cause-and-effect diagram for a car-starting problem. Four possible main causes are identified: mechanical, electrical, operator, and fuel system. Subcauses are then shown as fishbones connected to each major category.

## 4-4. Flowchart

Flowcharts represent still another simple graphical approach that is useful for problem solving, especially when the process results in a service rather than a product. A flowchart is a graphical method of describing and sequencing an operation's activities and processes. Traditionally, flowcharts have been used to describe computer programming logic, but flowcharts are also useful in describing other types of processes as well, especially when a process has a variety of possible options. (In fact, Figs. 2-1 and 2-2 are flowcharts that show the differences between product control and process control.)

Flowcharts are often developed using only a few symbols: (1) rectangles to indicate actions, (2) diamonds to indicate questions, (3) arrows to indicate directional flow, (4) small circles to serve as connectors (e.g., multiple pages), and (5) ovals to indicate starting and stopping points.

Fig. 4-17 shows a simple flowchart that describes a model process in which step 2 actions are repeated until they are correct.

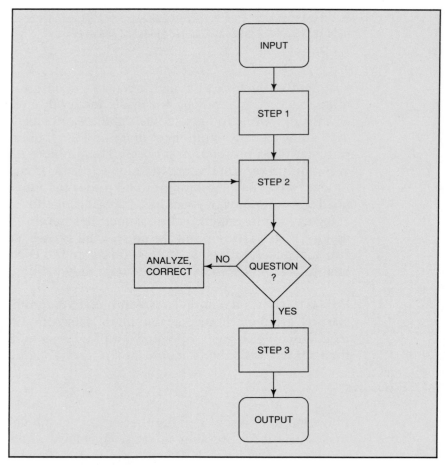

**Fig. 4-17. Model Process Flowchart**

Fig. 4-18 shows a flowchart that describes the agreed upon steps for the return of equipment used for maintenance activities. Note that a description of what is meant by ''large'' and ''small'' equipment is given on the flowchart.

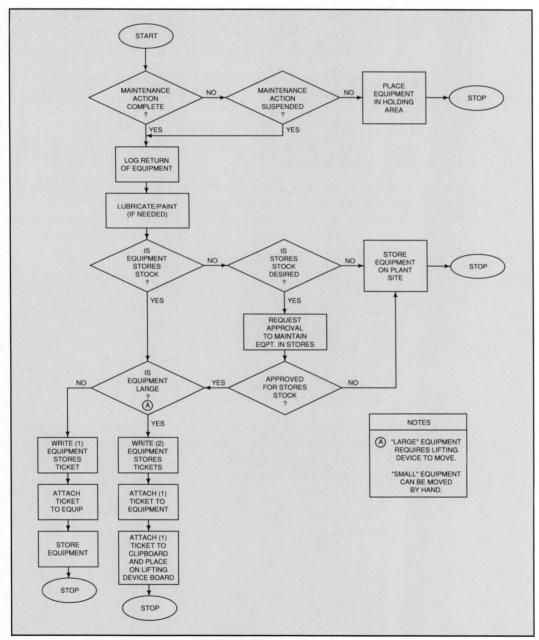

**Fig. 4-18. Flowchart for Return of Maintenance Equipment**

## Exercises

4-1. The data in the table below represent the number of nonconformities of various types found during the production of bottles on a weekly basis. One thousand bottles are produced each week. (a) Construct a Pareto diagram for the process ignoring the differentiation between weeks (i.e., use totals). (b) Split the data into weeks and construct four Pareto diagrams. Are there differences in what is implied by the two sets of charts?

| Week | Air Bubble | Weight Dev. | Deformation | Color |
|------|-----------|-------------|-------------|-------|
| 1 | 93 | 120 | 18 | 24 |
| 2 | 81 | 132 | 29 | 42 |
| 3 | 62 | 91 | 31 | 39 |
| 4 | 57 | 88 | 42 | 27 |

**Nonconformities in Bottle Production**

4-2. The data in the table below represent the number of work-related injuries reported monthly in a large chemical plant during a one-year period. Develop (a) a by-month Pareto diagram and (b) a by-quarter Pareto diagram to graphically describe the situation.

| Month | No. of Injuries | Month | No. of Injuries |
|-------|-----------------|-------|-----------------|
| Jan | 5 | Jul | 18 |
| Feb | 7 | Aug | 23 |
| Mar | 4 | Sep | 14 |
| Apr | 10 | Oct | 10 |
| May | 17 | Nov | 8 |
| Jun | 19 | Dec | 7 |

**Number of Work-Related Injuries**

4-3. The results of a one-calendar-year checksheet maintained on a variety of customer complaints regarding material produced by one production unit are shown in the table below. Develop a Pareto diagram that displays the data.

| Description of Complaint | Tally of Complaints |
|--------------------------|---------------------|
| Agglomeration | ʮʮ ʮʮ |
| Black Specks | ʮʮ ʮʮ ʮʮ ʮʮ /// |
| Brittleness | /// |
| Color | // |
| Contamination | ʮʮ /// |
| Mechanical | ʮʮ / |
| Processing | ʮʮ ʮʮ // |
| Shipping | //// |
| Other | /// |

**Customer Complaints Regarding Material During One Calendar Year**

4-4.  Suppose that you walk into your dark and empty house after returning from a trip, turn the light switch of the lamp beside the door to ON, and find that you are still in the dark. Construct a cause-and-effect diagram that focuses on the "problem" of NO LIGHT.

4-5.  Suppose that bicycles are commonly used for transportation in your plant and that a run chart maintained by maintenance shows that the number of flat tires seems to be increasing dramatically. Create a cause-and-effect diagram in an attempt to identify possible causes.

4-6.  Construct a flowchart for a process in your work environment that you are familiar with. For example, suppose that a request for a proposal arrives and it is not certain who should be assigned the project of leading the proposal development effort.

4-7.  Construct a flowchart that describes the process you use from the time you wake up until you leave your home each workday morning. (Recognize that resources you regard as reliable may or may not be reliable. For example, the newspaper may or may not arrive on time, there may or may not be bread in the pantry, etc.)

4-8.  Suppose that you are going on a business trip and must get three signatures before you can be issued a travel advance (for the amount of the trip). The three signatures are from (a) your immediate supervisor, (b) his supervisor, and (c) your organization's comptroller. The first signature must be that of your supervisor, but either of the next two signatures can be obtained next. After all three signatures have been obtained, you can get the travel advance from payroll. Construct a flowchart that describes the process.

# Unit 5:
# Descriptive Statistics

# UNIT 5

## Descriptive Statistics

The preceding two units examined a number of techniques for presenting and analyzing data graphically. This unit describes a variety of statistical measures used to describe data.

**Learning Objectives** — When you have completed this unit, you should:

    A. Know how to calculate and use three measures of central location (mean, median, mode).

    B. Know how to calculate and use three measures of variation (range, standard deviation, variance).

    C. Know how to calculate and use the coefficient of variation and the signal-to-noise ratio.

    D. Understand the concept of correlation and be able to calculate and interpret correlation coefficients.

    E. Understand the concept of autocorrelation and be able to compute and interpret autocorrelation coefficient values.

### 5-1. Parameters and Statistics

While parameters and statistics often share common names, they are fundamentally different. For example, the term "mean" could refer either to a parameter or to a statistic. Parameters are associated with populations (e.g., population mean); statistics are associated with samples taken from those populations (e.g., sample mean). Parameters represent true, but usually unknown, population values; statistics represent estimates of those population values based on sample results. For example, suppose that the true average age of employees in a company is 32.7 years. That a random sample of 10 employees might result in an average age of 31.0 rather than 32.7 should be no surprise.

While statistics are intended to estimate values of population parameters, the values are usually different. There are many reasons for the differences, including the fact that population parameters change. For example, the population of employee ages will be different in one year. Some new employees will be added to the company, some current employees will leave the company, and those who stay will all get one year older! As a result, population parameter values regarding employee ages will change. Samplers hope that by using sensible sampling techniques sample statistics will provide good approximations of current parameter values.

Confusion sometimes exists in differentiating between parameters and statistics of the same name. To clarify the differences, Greek letters are used to represent population parameters, while Arabic letters are used to represent sample statistics. For example, $\mu$ (mu) is used to represent the population mean, while $\bar{x}$ (pronounced x-bar) is used to represent the sample mean.

## 5-2. Measures of Central Location

If a company's typical employee age is to be described with a single value and that description must be based on a sample, how would the value be chosen? Similarly, if the quality of plastics taken from a plastic production process is measured by the melt index, how would the process melt index be estimated on the basis of a sample? Three statistics are most often used to answer such questions. They are the mean, the median, and the mode.

### Mean

The mean is the arithmetic average. If a single sample of n observations has values $x_1$, $x_2$, $x_3$, . . . , $x_n$, the sample mean $\bar{x}$ is

$$\bar{x} = \frac{(x_1 + x_2 + x_3 + \ldots + x_n)}{n}$$

or

$$\bar{x} = \sum_{i=1}^{n} \frac{x_i}{n}$$

For example, the sample mean melt index (MI), based on a single sample of five MI values (1.011, 1.017, 0.972, 0.910,

1.089), is

$$\overline{x} = \frac{(1.011 + 1.017 + 0.972 + 0.910 + 1.089)}{5}$$

$$= 1.000$$

The sample mean is the most widely used single descriptor of a population. It provides a good estimate of the central tendency of the population as long as the sample contains no extreme values (i.e., no outliers). For instance, suppose that during a 24-hour span, one five-minute stretch produced extremely high melt index values. Suppose further that a random sample of five happened to include a value from the poor quality five-minute stretch, a melt index value of 2.910. The resulting sample mean is

$$\overline{x} = \frac{(1.011 + 1.017 + 0.972 + 2.910 + 1.089)}{5}$$

$$= 1.400$$

Because of the single high value included in the calculation, this value is a poor estimate of the population mean melt index.

**Median**

The median is the middlemost number in a group of values when the values are ordered from low to high. For example, to obtain the median of the original melt index sample, we order the values from smallest to largest and pick the middlemost value.

0.910   (smallest)
0.972
1.011   median (middlemost value)
1.017
1.089   (largest)

Note: With an even number of values, the median is the average of the two middlemost numbers when the values are ordered from low to high.

The median, often abbreviated $\tilde{x}$, is easier to compute than the mean (particularly for small samples) and is less sensitive to outliers (since it focuses only on the values in the middle), but it ignores all but the middlemost values. As a result, the median is rarely used in statistical process control applications.

### Mode

A third (even less frequently used) measure of central tendency is the mode. Numerically, it is the most frequently occurring value; graphically, it is the peak in a distribution (e.g., histogram) of values. The mode is useful as a numeric measure when only a few different results are possible. For example, the mode of the sample 87, 88, 87, 89, 88, 86, 85, 88, 88, 85 is 88, since 88 occurs more than any other single value.

### Relationships between Measures of Central Location

How are the three ''location'' value estimates related? When are they the same (or similar), and when are they different? Fig. 5-1(a) shows a histogram skewed to the right. In this case, the mean is usually the largest and the median is usually larger than the mode. Fig. 5-1(b) shows a symmetric histogram. In this case, the mean, median, and mode are the same (or nearly the same). Fig. 5-1(c) shows a histogram skewed to the left. In this case, the mean is usually smallest, the median the next smallest, and the mode the largest of the three.

## 5-3. Measures of Variation

Measures of variation or dispersion (i.e., spread) provide a second indicator of the population's general form. Consider sample melt index readings taken from two similar processes. The data are presented in Table 5-1 and Fig. 5-2.

Both samples have the same mean, 1.000. But with even cursory inspection of Fig. 5-2, it is apparent that the two processes are quite different. The second process seems to have a much larger spread, indicating less process control. Measures of variation provide a numerical indication of the spread of the data. The three most frequently used measures of variation are the range, the variance, and the standard deviation.

| Process 1 | 0.910 | 0.972 | 1.011 | 1.017 | 1.089 |
|---|---|---|---|---|---|
| Process 2 | 0.730 | 0.850 | 1.050 | 1.140 | 1.230 |

TABLE 5-1. Samples of Melt Index Values from Two Processes

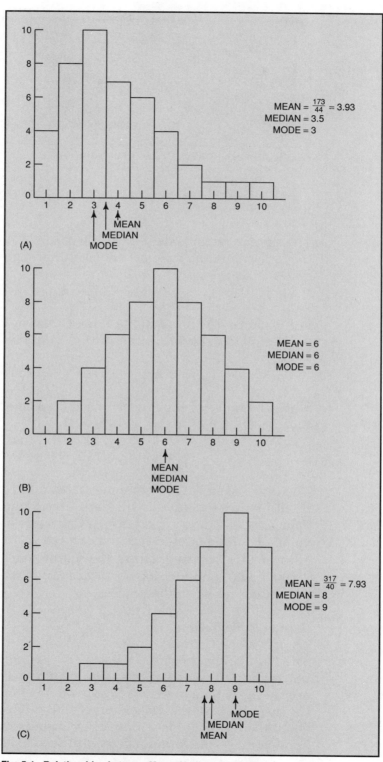

Fig. 5-1. Relationships between Mean, Median, and Mode

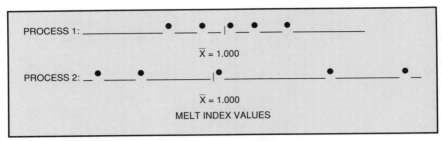

**Fig. 5-2. Dot Plot of Melt Index Values from Two Processes**

## Range

The sample range is defined as the absolute difference between the largest and the smallest values in the sample.

$$R = x_{max} - x_{min}$$

For instance, the range of the Process 1 sample shown in Table 5-1 (i.e., 0.910, 0.972, 1.011, 1.017, 1.089) is

$$1.089 - 0.910 = 0.179$$

while the range of the Process 2 sample shown in Table 5-1 (i.e., 0.730, 0.850, 1.050, 1.140, 1.230) is

$$1.230 - 0.730 = 0.500$$

The range is an easy to compute statistic but can be misleading if outliers are included in the data. For example, if melt index values for 364 days varied from a low value of 0.900 to a high value of 1.100 but on day 365 measured 2.900 (possibly because of a recording error), the sample range of 2.000 (i.e., 2.900–0.900) provides a poor indication of the variation generally present in the process.

## Standard Deviation

The most commonly used measure of variation is the standard deviation. This measure of spread may not be as intuitively appealing as the range, but it provides a meaningful measure of the magnitude of the dispersion of individual measurements about the mean and is widely used in statistical process control applications. The formula generally used to estimate the population standard deviation is:

$$s = \sqrt{\frac{1}{n-1}\left[\sum_{i=1}^{n}(x_i - \bar{x})^2\right]}$$

The standard deviation is *nearly* the square root of the average of the squared deviations about the mean. The result is that values more distant from the mean have considerably more impact on the standard deviation than values near the mean. Note that $n - 1$ rather than n is used in the denominator because it typically provides a better estimate of the population standard deviation. This has been confirmed through extensive experimentation.

The sample size n is sometimes used in the denominator rather than $n - 1$. For large samples, the two formulas yield almost identical results. For small samples the results may be quite different. Hand-held calculators often include both formulations. Of course, common sense indicates that population standard deviation estimates based on a single small sample are subject to considerable variation, regardless of the denominator chosen. Consider the Process 1 sample of five melt index values (1.011, 1.017, 0.972, 0.910, 1.089) examined earlier. The mean ($\bar{x}$) was computed as 1.000. The process standard deviation is then estimated as

$$s = \sqrt{\frac{(1.011-1)^2 + (1.017-1)^2 + (0.972-1)^2 + (0.910-1)^2 + (1.089-1)^2}{4}}$$

$$= 0.066$$

Since the standard deviation of 0.066 is relatively small in comparison to the individual values on which it is based, the implication is that the process deviation is relatively small.

**Relationship between Range and Standard Deviation**

Traditionally, the sample range has been used to estimate the process standard deviation in statistical process control calculations. Of course, this approach was initiated in the days before calculators were widely available. The approach is still used for two primary reasons: (1) the sample range is still easier to compute than the sample standard deviation and (2) there is a known theoretical relationship between the sample range and

| n | 2 | 3 | 4 | 5 |
|---|---|---|---|---|
| $d_2$ | 1.128 | 1.693 | 2.059 | 2.326 |
| n | 6 | 7 | 8 | 9 |
| $d_2$ | 2.534 | 2.704 | 2.847 | 2.97 |

**TABLE 5-2. $d_2$ Values Used to Estimate $\sigma$**

the population standard deviation. As a result, estimates of the true standard deviation $\sigma$ (sigma) may be calculated using the formula $s' = \overline{R}/d_2$, where $\overline{R}$ is the average sample range and $d_2$ is a function of n, the size of the individual samples (Table 5-2). (Note: The theoretical foundation of the relationship assumes that the data being sampled are normally distributed, but the calculation is widely and generally appropriately used regardless of the truth of that assumption.)

**Example 5-1:** Iodine is an important carbon black quality characteristic. To estimate the amount of variation in the iodine content of carbon black shipped, one sample of size n = 4 (i.e., four independent measurements comprise one sample) is taken each day during a 20-day period from the hopper cars used to transport the carbon black (Table 5-3).

| Day | $x_1$ | $x_2$ | $x_3$ | $x_4$ | R |
|---|---|---|---|---|---|
| 1 | 39.88 | 40.33 | 40.83 | 39.57 | 1.26 |
| 2 | 39.79 | 39.64 | 40.32 | 40.05 | 0.63 |
| 3 | 40.48 | 40.15 | 40.02 | 40.34 | 0.46 |
| 4 | 40.20 | 40.09 | 39.09 | 39.99 | 1.11 |
| 5 | 40.06 | 40.29 | 40.10 | 40.31 | 0.55 |
| 6 | 40.44 | 40.29 | 39.55 | 40.68 | 1.13 |
| 7 | 40.49 | 39.44 | 38.85 | 40.20 | 1.64 |
| 8 | 39.80 | 40.14 | 39.87 | 40.37 | 0.57 |
| 9 | 39.97 | 39.61 | 40.33 | 40.61 | 1.00 |
| 10 | 39.88 | 39.75 | 39.99 | 40.42 | 0.67 |
| 11 | 39.64 | 39.61 | 39.71 | 39.95 | 0.34 |
| 12 | 40.06 | 40.20 | 39.98 | 40.09 | 0.22 |
| 13 | 40.55 | 39.81 | 39.92 | 39.71 | 0.84 |
| 14 | 39.96 | 40.11 | 40.44 | 40.05 | 0.48 |
| 15 | 39.47 | 39.96 | 39.48 | 40.18 | 0.71 |
| 16 | 40.28 | 39.51 | 39.82 | 40.13 | 0.77 |
| 17 | 39.92 | 40.38 | 39.22 | 40.08 | 1.16 |
| 18 | 39.50 | 39.69 | 40.32 | 40.04 | 0.82 |
| 19 | 40.85 | 40.31 | 40.07 | 39.73 | 1.12 |
| 20 | 40.33 | 39.73 | 39.51 | 39.76 | 0.82 |
| | | | | $\overline{R} =$ | 0.82 |

**TABLE 5-3. Samples of Iodine Content in Carbon Black**

In the last column of Table 5-3, the sample ranges (largest value minus smallest value) for each of the 20 samples are given. The average of the sample ranges is $\overline{R}$ = 0.82. Since the sample size is n = 4, we use the conversion factor $d_2$ = 2.059 (Table 5-2). As such, the estimate of the true standard deviation $\sigma_x$ (i.e., sigma of the x's) is

$$s' = \overline{R}/d_2$$

$$= 0.82/2.059$$

$$= 0.40$$

This estimate is reliable only if the number of samples is large enough to obtain a stable estimate of the average range ($\overline{R}$). As a rule of thumb, at least 20 samples should be taken, with each sample having at least two values.

## Variance

The variance is another important measure of variation. It is simply the standard deviation squared. (The bad news is that variance units are "squared" values, such as the number of defects squared or the number of pounds squared, which often has no physical meaning.)

$$\text{Variance} = \sigma^2$$

In statistical process control, its importance stems from its use in calculating the standard deviation of a sum or difference. To determine the standard deviation of the sum (or difference) of two values, it is first necessary to add their variances and then take the square root of the total. Specifically, if x is a measurement with standard deviation $\sigma_x$ and y is a measurement with standard deviation $\sigma_y$, then the standard deviations of their sums and differences (i.e., x + y and x − y) are the same. That is,

$$\sigma_{x+y} = \sqrt{(\sigma_x^2 + \sigma_y^2)}$$

and

$$\sigma_{x-y} = \sqrt{(\sigma_x^2 + \sigma_y^2)}$$

The second relationship (summing $\sigma_x^2$ and $\sigma_y^2$ and taking the square root to obtain the standard deviation of the difference) is far from obvious but is nevertheless true. The following examples are intended to clarify the relationships.

**Example 5-2:** As stated above, carbon black is shipped in hopper cars. Suppose that the standard deviation of the weight of a single filled car is $\sigma_x = 50$ pounds. What is the standard deviation of the total weight of two filled hopper cars?

$$\sigma_{2x} = \sqrt{(\sigma_x^2 + \sigma_x^2)}$$
$$= \sqrt{(50^2 + 50^2)}$$
$$= \sqrt{5000}$$
$$= 70.7 \text{ pounds}$$

**Example 5-3:** Suppose that two sizes of hopper cars are used to transport carbon black: size A cars and size B cars. Size B cars are larger than size A cars and have larger standard deviations of the amount of weight they transport, $\sigma_A = 50$ and $\sigma_B = 70$ pounds. What is the standard deviation of the difference in the weight of the two sizes of hopper cars?

$$\sigma_{B-A} = \sqrt{(\sigma_B^2 + \sigma_A^2)}$$
$$= \sqrt{(50^2 + 70^2)}$$
$$= \sqrt{7400}$$
$$= 86 \text{ pounds}$$

## 5-4. Coefficient of Variation and Signal-to-Noise Ratio

The standard deviation is meaningful only in comparison with other standard deviations or in comparison with its associated mean. For instance, a process standard deviation of 1 minute seems (by itself) to be neither good nor bad. However, if it is learned that the typical standard deviation for such processes is 10 minutes, the 1-minute standard deviation suddenly seems quite good. Similarly, a process standard deviation of 1 seems relatively small when the process mean is 100. The same standard deviation appears to be quite large when the process mean is 1, however. Two related measures, the coefficient of variation and the signal-to-noise ratio, help to quantify the relationship between the mean and the standard deviation.

The coefficient of variation is defined as the sample standard deviation divided by the sample mean. The formula is shown below.

$$v = s/\bar{x}$$

This value is usually expressed in percentage form. For example, if the sample standard deviation is 10 and the sample mean is 50, the coefficient of variation is 20% (i.e., $10/50 \times 100$).

The signal-to-noise ratio (SN) is defined as the reciprocal of the coefficient of variation. That is, it is the sample mean divided by the sample standard deviation.

$$SN = 1/v = \bar{x}/s$$

The signal-to-noise ratio is sometimes used in statistical process control as an indicator of process performance. If closeness to target (not just adherence to specifications) is the objective, then the ideal is obviously for the signal-to-noise ratio to be large. The so-called loss function (proposed by Genichi Taguchi) amplifies the idea that the farther the product is from target, the larger the "loss." The loss function is defined as follows:

$$Loss(x) = cost\ (x - target)^2$$

where x is the actual measurement, target is the value aimed at, and "cost" is a constant that is dependent on the particular process. The idea of cost in this situation is to some degree relative. For example, a nut and a bolt may both be produced within specifications but well away from their target values. As such, the nut and bolt may fit together loosely, possibly resulting in a rattle or eventual failure. As such, the loss is a function of the cost estimate and the (square of the) deviation from target. Suppose that for a particular process, cost = $100 and target = 11.5 inch. If the actual x = 13.5 inch, loss =

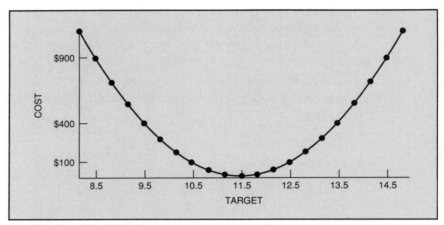

**Fig. 5-3. Quadratic Loss Function**

$(100)(13.5 - 11.5)^2 = \$400$. On the other hand, if the actual x
$= 12.5$ inch, loss $= (100)(12.5 - 11.5)^2 = \$100$. The loss
function for this situation is shown in Fig. 5-3.

While there is considerable disagreement regarding the
mathematical accuracy of Taguchi's loss function, there is no
arguing that processes with smaller variation are generally
better than processes with larger variation.

## 5-5. Coding

Many statistical process control applications involve the
recording of numbers having several digits (e.g., 39,356.18
pounds). This results in tedious computations if parameter
estimates must be computed by hand. It is often convenient to
simplify numbers by coding them in some way. The most
common coding method is to subtract a location value from
each observation and multiply (or divide) the result by a scale
value. The location value may be any number, but it is often
appropriate to choose the average value, the target value, or a
specification value. The scale value may be any value that
results in the coded data being easy to work with.

**Example 5-4:** Suppose that the temperature of high density
polyethylene is measured during production and that the
temperature range is 220 ± 1°F. Process adjustments are made

in increments of 0.1°F. If we code the temperatures by
subtracting 220 from each one and multiplying by 10, a
temperature of 220.7 becomes 7 (i.e., $(220.7 - 220) \times 10 = 7$).

## 5-6. Correlation

Correlation is a measure of the strength of the relationship
between two variables. Correlation is indicated graphically by
the spread of the data points around a fitted straight line (i.e., a
straight line that indicates the trend of the data). Correlation
was shown graphically in the last unit when scatterplots were
discussed. Fig. 5-4 shows scatterplots that indicate strong and
weak correlations between two variables. In general, the closer
the points are to the fitted line, the stronger the correlation.

The strength of the correlation between the two variables, x and
y, may be expressed numerically. This numeric measure of the
relationship is known as the correlation coefficient, $r_{xy}$, and
may be computed as

$$r_{xy} = \frac{1}{n-1} \sum_{i=1}^{n} \left[ \frac{x_i - \bar{x}}{s_x} \right] \left[ \frac{y_i - \bar{y}}{s_y} \right]$$

$$= \frac{1}{n-1} \sum_{i=1}^{n} \frac{(x_i - \bar{x})(y_i - \bar{y})}{s_x s_y}$$

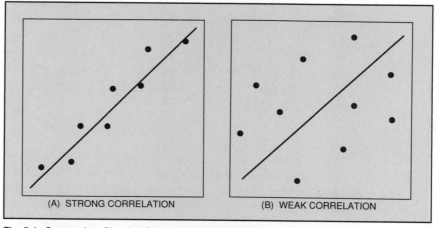

(A) STRONG CORRELATION          (B) WEAK CORRELATION

**Fig. 5-4. Scatterplots Showing Strong and Weak Correlations**

As in the case of the sample standard deviation, $n - 1$ rather than n is used in the denominator to reduce (on the average) the degree to which the estimate deviates from the true correlation coefficient. The equation ensures that the result is unit-free and that all $r_{xy}$ lie between $-1$ and $+1$.

In Fig. 5-5(a), horizontal and vertical lines mark $\bar{y}$ and $\bar{x}$. These lines subdivide the data area into four regions, i.e., I, II, III, IV. Note that the product $(x_i - \bar{x})(y_i - \bar{y})$ is positive in region II, since for all these points $(x_i - x) > 0$ and $(y_i - \bar{y}) > 0$. Similarly, for region III, all $(x_i - \bar{x})(y_i - \bar{y})$ products are positive since $(x_i - \bar{x}) < 0$ and $(y_i - \bar{y}) < 0$. Similarly, all products $(x_i - \bar{x})(y_i - \bar{y})$ in regions I and IV are negative. The idea, as shown in Fig. 5-5(b), is that if the majority of points are in regions II and III, the data trends upward and the resulting correlation coefficient is positive. If the data points fall mainly in regions I and IV, the data slopes downward and the resulting correlation coefficient is negative.

When the correlation coefficient has a value of $+1$, the two variables are said to be perfectly positively correlated and the plotted points all fall on a straight line with an upward slope (Fig. 5-6(a)). When the correlation coefficient has a value of $-1$, the two variables are said to be perfectly negatively correlated and the plotted points all fall on a straight line with a downward slope [Fig. 5-6(b)].

When the correlation coefficient for the two variables has a value of 0, the two variables are said to be uncorrelated. In a scatterplot (Fig. 5-7), if the correlation coefficient is 0, the plotted points are randomly distributed, showing no general trend. (In reality, even if two variables are uncorrelated, $r_{xy}$ will not be exactly zero.)

As a rule of thumb, correlation coefficients of 0.80 or more (or $-0.80$ or less) indicate significant correlation and correlation coefficients of 0.20 or less (or $-0.20$ or more) indicate no significant correlation. Correlation coefficients between those values are less conclusive.

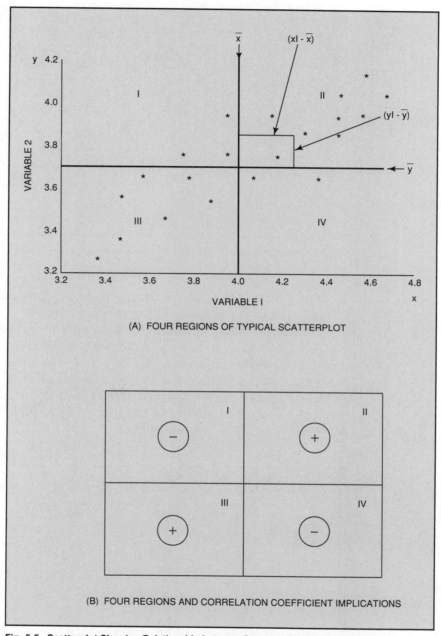

**Fig. 5-5. Scatterplot Showing Relationship between Data and Correlation Coefficient**

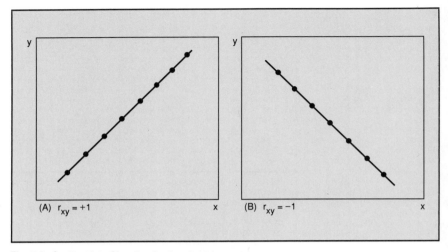

**Fig. 5-6. Scatterplots Showing Perfect Positive and Negative Correlation**

**Example 5-5:** DBP is an important carbon black quality characteristic. As a result, DBP measurements for finished carbon black (FCB) are maintained. In an attempt to obtain an early indication of process performance, DBP measurements are also taken at the smoke header (SH). The way the process is set up, two reactors feed into a single smoke header. However, it is not clear that the DBP measurements taken at the SH tell anything about the quality of the finished product. A correlation study was undertaken.

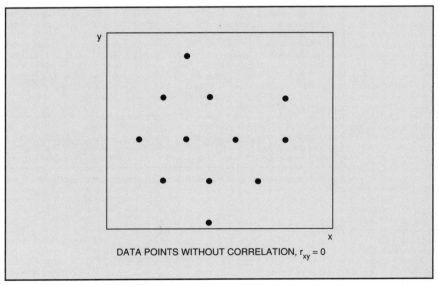

**Fig. 5-7. Scatterplot Showing No Correlation**

| Sample No. | $x_i$ (SH) | $y_i$ (FCB) | $(x_i - \bar{x})$ | $(y_i - \bar{y})$ | $(x_i - \bar{x})(y_i - \bar{y})$ |
|---|---|---|---|---|---|
| 1 | 94.8 | 90.5 | −0.35 | 0.93 | −0.32 |
| 2 | 94.8 | 91.1 | −0.35 | 1.53 | −0.53 |
| 3 | 94.2 | 89.1 | −0.95 | −0.47 | 0.45 |
| 4 | 94.4 | 89.2 | −0.75 | −0.37 | 0.28 |
| 5 | 93.4 | 89.3 | −1.75 | −0.27 | 0.48 |
| 6 | 94.2 | 89.2 | −0.95 | −0.37 | 0.35 |
| 7 | 94.6 | 87.3 | −0.55 | −2.27 | 1.24 |
| 8 | 96.6 | 88.2 | 1.45 | −1.37 | −2.00 |
| 9 | 96.3 | 89.7 | 1.15 | 0.13 | 0.15 |
| 10 | 96.6 | 91.1 | 1.45 | 1.53 | 2.22 |
| 11 | 96.7 | 90.6 | 1.55 | 1.03 | 1.60 |
| Totals | 1046.6 | 985.3 | | | 3.92 |

$$\bar{x} = 1046.6/11 = 95.15, \quad \bar{y} = 985.3/11 = 89.57$$

**TABLE 5-4. Sample DBP Measurements**

The correlation coefficient between the DBP measurements taken at the SH and the DBP measurements of finished carbon black is computed as shown in Table 5-4 and a scatterplot of the data is shown in Fig. 5-8. The DBP measurements at the

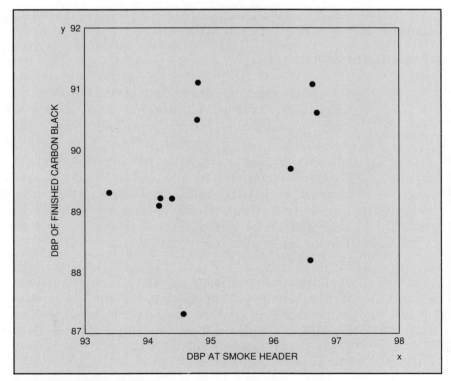

**Fig. 5-8. Scatterplot of DBP Data**

smoke header are denoted as $x_i$ and the DBP measurements of finished carbon black are denoted as $y_i$.

$$s_x = \sqrt{\frac{1}{11 - 1}\left[\sum_{i=1}^{11}(x_i - 95.15)^2\right]} = 1.18$$

$$s_y = \sqrt{\frac{1}{11 - 1}\left[\sum_{i=1}^{11}(y_i - 89.57)^2\right]} = 1.19$$

$$r_{xy} = \frac{1}{n - 1}\sum_{i=1}^{n}\frac{(x_i - \bar{x})(y_i - \bar{y})}{s_x s_y}$$

$$= \frac{(1/10)(3.92)}{(1.18 \times 1.19)}$$

$$= 0.28$$

The correlation coefficient of $r_{xy} = 0.28$ and the scatterplot indicate that the DBP measurements taken at the smoke header are at best only weakly related to the DBP measurements of finished carbon black.

## 5-7. Autocorrelation

In process control, when observations are recorded and plotted sequentially versus time, the chart developed is called a run chart (presented in Unit 3; also called a time series). Run chart values based on measurements taken from chemical processes often exhibit cyclic variation (such as that shown in Fig. 5-9); that is, time-ordered results tend to trend upward, then downward, then upward and so forth, rather than moving randomly. In other words, measurements taken at time t often seem to be related to measurements taken at time $t - k$ or time $t + k$.

A statistic used to measure the relationship between measurements within the time-ordered data is the autocorrelation coefficient, a special form of the correlation coefficient. Autocorrelation measures the correlation between observations taken at regular intervals, say, between observation $x_t$ at time t and observation $x_{t+k}$ at time $t + k$.

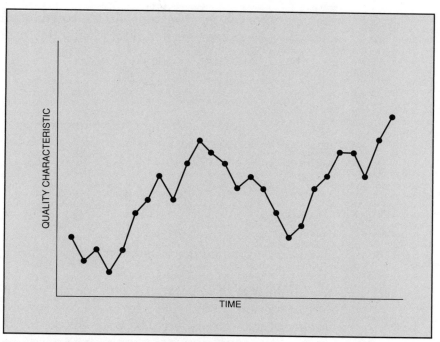

**Fig. 5-9. Run Chart Showing Autocorrelated Process**

For instance, if melt index (MI) measurements from a high-density polyethylene process are recorded every hour, the autocorrelation for "lag 1" is the correlation between MI values taken one hour apart. The autocorrelation for "lag 2" is the correlation between MI values taken two hours apart, i.e., between MI at 1 p.m. and MI at 3 p.m., between MI at 2 p.m. and MI at 4 p.m., etc.

If a strong autocorrelation exists between measurement values taken at some interval k, knowing an observation's value at time t will help to predict the observation value at time t + k. That is, if there is a strong (positive) autocorrelation between MI values taken two hours apart, then knowing that the MI value was high at 1 pm allows a prediction that the MI value at 3 pm is likely to be high as well. If there is no autocorrelation present, knowing a measurement value $x_t$ will not help to predict future measurement values.

Autocorrelation values can be computed for various time lags (i.e., k = 1, 2, 3, etc.). For instance, the autocorrelation coefficient for lag one (i.e., correlation between observations one time period apart) is computed using the formula

$$r_1 = \frac{1}{n-1} \sum_{t=1}^{n-1} \frac{(x_t - \overline{x})(x_{t+1} - \overline{x})}{s^2}$$

Like the correlation coefficient, the autocorrelation coefficient has a value between $-1$ and $+1$. In fact, the autocorrelation coefficient for any time interval k is defined by

$$r_k = \frac{1}{n-1} \sum_{t=1}^{n-k} \frac{(x_t - \overline{x})(x_{t+k} - \overline{x})}{s^2}$$

This is called the autocorrelation coefficient for lag k.

How much autocorrelation is a lot? As a rule of thumb, autocorrelation coefficients within $\pm 2/\sqrt{n}$, where n is the number of data points, are usually not considered significant. Since $\pm 2/\sqrt{n}$ corresponds roughly to a two-sigma interval, the rule of thumb uses two standard deviations as cutoff points in deciding whether or not a true autocorrelation coefficient is other than zero.

**Example 5-6:** Data was collected on a key quality characteristic for a rubber product (Table 5-5). A run chart (Fig. 5-10) shows that some degree of cycling has occurred, indicating that autocorrelation may be present in the process.

| Time | x | Time | x | Time | x | Time | x |
|------|-----|------|-----|------|-----|------|-----|
| 2 p.m. | 579 | 2 p.m. | 583 | 2 p.m. | 592 | 2 p.m. | 609 |
| 4 p.m. | 613 | 4 p.m. | 588 | 4 p.m. | 598 | 4 p.m. | 606 |
| 6 p.m. | 608 | 6 p.m. | 594 | 6 p.m. | 600 | 6 p.m. | 601 |
| 8 p.m. | 605 | 8 p.m. | 594 | 8 p.m. | 598 | 8 p.m. | 596 |
| 10 p.m. | 612 | 10 p.m. | 591 | 10 p.m. | 602 | 10 p.m. | 597 |
| 12 a.m. | 610 | 12 a.m. | 598 | 12 a.m. | 605 | 12 a.m. | 601 |
| 2 a.m. | 596 | 2 a.m. | 588 | 2 a.m. | 601 | 2 a.m. | 594 |
| 4 a.m. | 602 | 4 a.m. | 581 | 4 a.m. | 607 | 4 a.m. | 603 |
| 6 a.m. | 596 | 6 a.m. | 591 | 6 a.m. | 604 | 6 a.m. | 611 |
| 8 a.m. | 590 | 8 a.m. | 607 | 8 a.m. | 611 | 8 a.m. | 609 |
| 10 a.m. | 592 | 10 a.m. | 600 | 10 a.m. | 609 | 10 a.m. | 612 |
| 12 p.m. | 596 | 12 p.m. | 587 | 12 p.m. | 603 | | |

$$\overline{x} = 599.0$$
$$s_x = 8.7$$

**TABLE 5-5. Data for Key Quality Characteristic of a Rubber Product**

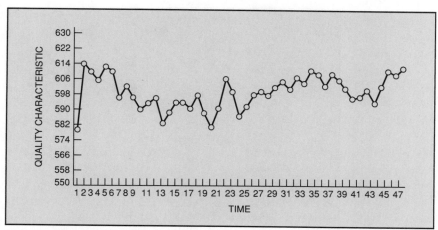

**Fig. 5-10. Run Chart for Rubber Data**

The decision was made to compute the autocorrelation coefficient for lag = 1. Step one is to compute the sum of the products $(x_t - \bar{x})(x_{t+1} - \bar{x})$. Table 5-6 shows the first five calculations. The scatterplot in Fig. 5-11 shows that there is at least some relationship between consecutive readings (i.e., not completely random).

The sum of the products for all 46 pairs of values is 1598, so the average is 1598/46 = 34.7. The autocorrelation for lag = 1 is then

$$r_1 = \frac{1}{n-1} \sum \frac{(x_t - \bar{x})(x_{t+1} - \bar{x})}{s^2}$$

$$= \frac{1}{46} \frac{(1598)}{(8.7)^2}$$

$$= \frac{34.7}{(8.7)^2}$$

$$= 0.46$$

| | $x_{t+1} - \bar{x}$ | $x_t - x$ | $(x_t - \bar{x})(x_{t+1} - \bar{x})$ |
|---|---|---|---|
| | | t | |
| 1 | 613 − 599 = 14 | 579 − 599 = −20 | −20 × 14 = −280 |
| 2 | 608 − 599 = 9 | 613 − 599 = 14 | 14 × 9 = 126 |
| 3 | 605 − 599 = 6 | 608 − 599 = 9 | 9 × 6 = 54 |
| 4 | 612 − 599 = 13 | 605 − 599 = 6 | 6 × 13 = 78 |
| 5 | 610 − 599 = 11 | 612 − 599 = 13 | 13 × 11 = 143 |

**TABLE 5-6. Sample Computations Leading to an Autocorrelation with Lag = 1**

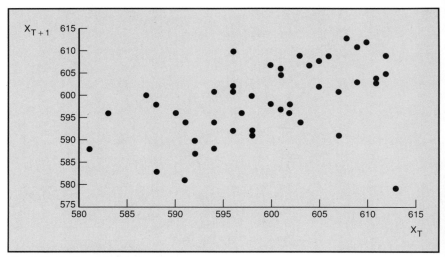

**Fig. 5-11. Scatterplot of Rubber Data**

This autocorrelation value indicates that there is a relationship between measurements taken two hours apart, but that the relationship is far from exact. Based on the rule of thumb for significance, described above, the limits to determine significance are $\pm 2/\sqrt{n} = \pm 2/\sqrt{(47)} = \pm 0.29$. Since for lag = 1, $r_1 = 0.46$, the autocorrelation present is significant.

Using the same procedure described above, but with lags of 2, 3, and 4, autocorrelation values $r_2 = 0.26$, $r_3 = 0.31$, and $r_4 = 0.21$ are found. All four autocorrelation coefficients are plotted for comparison in Fig. 5-12. Using the 0.29 figure as the cutoff, there is significant autocorrelation only for lag = 1 and lag = 3.

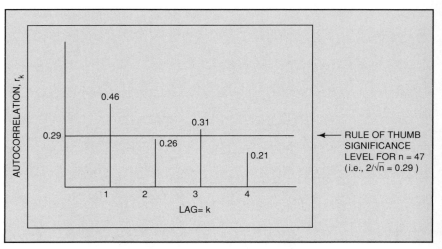

**Fig. 5-12. Comparison of Autocorrelation Coefficients for Rubber Data**

Although the lag = 3 value is an exception in the rubber data case, autocorrelation tends generally to decrease as the time between observations increases; that is, in general, the further apart observations are taken, the smaller is the association between the resulting values.

# Exercises

5-1. *Sample measurements of the percentage of sulfur trioxide in a mixed powder were taken over a one-month period (see table below). (a) For each of the 16 samples of five observations each (n = 5), calculate the mean, the range, the standard deviation, the signal-to-noise ratio, and the coefficient of variation. (b) Compute the average range and average standard deviation. (c) Estimate the standard deviation using the average range and compare it with the computed average standard deviation.*

| Sample | Sulfur Trioxide Percentages | | | | |
|--------|------|------|------|------|------|
| 1 | 15.8 | 16.0 | 15.7 | 15.9 | 16.4 |
| 2 | 15.7 | 15.8 | 15.7 | 15.6 | 15.9 |
| 3 | 15.7 | 15.8 | 15.7 | 15.7 | 16.2 |
| 4 | 15.7 | 15.7 | 15.7 | 15.8 | 15.8 |
| 5 | 15.3 | 16.0 | 15.5 | 15.6 | 16.1 |
| 6 | 16.1 | 15.8 | 15.8 | 14.4 | 16.3 |
| 7 | 15.7 | 15.8 | 15.6 | 15.8 | 16.0 |
| 8 | 15.7 | 15.7 | 15.5 | 15.8 | 15.6 |
| 9 | 15.9 | 16.0 | 15.7 | 15.9 | 16.3 |
| 10 | 15.7 | 15.5 | 15.7 | 16.4 | 15.5 |
| 11 | 15.7 | 15.8 | 15.8 | 15.5 | 16.0 |
| 12 | 15.8 | 15.6 | 15.9 | 15.8 | 15.7 |
| 13 | 15.4 | 16.0 | 15.2 | 15.9 | 16.1 |
| 14 | 15.7 | 15.8 | 15.7 | 14.4 | 15.9 |
| 15 | 15.5 | 15.8 | 15.1 | 15.8 | 16.0 |
| 16 | 15.6 | 15.7 | 15.6 | 15.8 | 15.6 |

Sulfur Trioxide Percentages

5-2. *Consider the 20 sample pairs of melt index (MI) and temperature (T) measurements shown in the table below. (a) Calculate a mean and standard deviation for both MI and T values, (b) develop a scatterplot diagram, (c) calculate the correlation coefficient between MI and T, and (d) interpret your findings.*

| Sample | MI | T | Sample | MI | T |
|--------|------|-------|--------|------|-------|
| 1 | 1.03 | 220.8 | 11 | 1.12 | 221.6 |
| 2 | 0.97 | 220.3 | 12 | 1.14 | 221.8 |
| 3 | 1.08 | 220.5 | 13 | 1.12 | 221.2 |
| 4 | 1.00 | 220.3 | 14 | 1.00 | 220.5 |
| 5 | 1.05 | 221.0 | 15 | 1.08 | 220.4 |
| 6 | 1.15 | 221.8 | 16 | 1.08 | 221.5 |
| 7 | 1.07 | 221.4 | 17 | 1.13 | 221.8 |
| 8 | 1.11 | 221.3 | 18 | 1.16 | 221.3 |
| 9 | 1.04 | 220.7 | 19 | 1.08 | 221.3 |
| 10 | 1.06 | 220.7 | 20 | 1.13 | 221.7 |

**Paired Melt Index and Temperature Measurements**

5-3. *Using the parameter values for the four populations shown in table below, determine whether the population's distribution is symmetrical, skewed left, or skewed right.*

| Population | Mean | Mode | Median |
|-----------|------|------|--------|
| 1 | 10.5 | 9.5 | 10.0 |
| 2 | 3.5 | 4.5 | 4.0 |
| 3 | 3.5 | 3.5 | 3.5 |
| 4 | 7.0 | 9.0 | 8.0 |

**Parameter Values for Four Populations**

5-4. *The data in the following table indicate the failure times (in hours) for supposedly identical seals produced by two different companies. For each company's seals, calculate (a) the mean, median, and mode, (b) the range, standard deviation, and variance, and (c) the coefficient of variation and the signal-to-noise ratio. (d) Interpret your findings.*

| Seals from Company A | 909 | 1293 | 1601 | 1616 | 2012 | 2016 |
|----------------------|------|------|------|------|------|------|
| | 2180 | 2201 | 2442 | | | |
| Seals from Company B | 824 | 1082 | 1135 | 1308 | 1359 | 1372 |
| | 1401 | 1412 | 1601 | 1638 | 1641 | 1674 |
| | 1709 | 1805 | 1947 | 2208 | | |

**Seal Failure Times (hours)**

5-5. *During the course of a single day, hundreds of units of a plastic product are produced by an injection molding process. Five times during the day, random samples of five parts are taken and analyzed. Part shrinkage in*

percentage by weight is measured for each of the parts.
The table below shows the results of one day's
measurements. (a) For each sample, compute the sample
mean $\bar{x}$, the sample standard deviation s, and the sample
range R. (b) Compute the average sample range $\bar{R}$ and
estimate the standard deviation for the process using the
average range.

| Sample | Part Shrinkage | | | | | $\bar{x}$ | R | s |
|---|---|---|---|---|---|---|---|---|
| 1 | 9.30 | 9.60 | 9.00 | 10.80 | 11.10 | | | |
| 2 | 9.00 | 12.30 | 10.80 | 10.50 | 9.60 | | | |
| 3 | 8.70 | 10.80 | 11.10 | 9.00 | 9.90 | | | |
| 4 | 10.20 | 9.00 | 9.00 | 11.40 | 10.80 | | | |
| 5 | 11.70 | 11.40 | 10.20 | 9.60 | 11.10 | | | |

**Part Shrinkage**

5-6. The following table shows the percentage of iodine ($I_2$)
present in a carbon black production process. The
measurements were made over the span of several days
at two hour intervals. (a) Plot the data in run chart form.
(b) Plot the data using a lag of 1 period in a scatterplot.
Does it appear that autocorrelation is present in the
process? (c) Compute the autocorrelation coefficients for
lags of 1, 2, and 3. (d) Using the rule-of-thumb criteria
discussed in the unit, are any of the autocorrelation
coefficients significant?

| Time | $I_2$ | Time | $I_2$ | Time | $I_2$ |
|---|---|---|---|---|---|
| 11 p.m. | 41.2 | 5 a.m. | 42.1 | 11 a.m. | 41.0 |
| 1 a.m. | 41.2 | 7 a.m. | 42.0 | 1 p.m. | 42.2 |
| 3 a.m. | 40.0 | 9 a.m. | 39.6 | 3 p.m. | 41.0 |
| 5 a.m. | 40.0 | 11 a.m. | 42.6 | 5 p.m. | 42.2 |
| 7 a.m. | 41.2 | 1 p.m. | 42.0 | 7 p.m. | 42.3 |
| 9 a.m. | 41.4 | 3 p.m. | 40.8 | 9 p.m. | 42.2 |
| 11 a.m. | 41.4 | 5 p.m. | 41.4 | 11 p.m. | 40.1 |
| 1 p.m. | 42.0 | 7 p.m. | 40.9 | 1 a.m. | 39.9 |
| 3 p.m. | 40.9 | 9 p.m. | 39.8 | 3 a.m. | 41.4 |
| 5 p.m. | 42.6 | 11 p.m. | 40.8 | 5 a.m. | 41.5 |
| 7 p.m. | 42.1 | 1 a.m. | 42.0 | 7 a.m. | 40.2 |
| 9 p.m. | 42.6 | 3 a.m. | 41.4 | 9 a.m. | 38.5 |
| 11 p.m. | 41.4 | 5 a.m. | 42.0 | 7 a.m. | 38.5 |
| 1 a.m. | 42.6 | 7 a.m. | 42.6 | | |
| 3 a.m. | 40.9 | 9 a.m. | 42.8 | | |

**Iodine Content in Carbon Black Process**

5-7. In a high-density polyethylene process, three bottles of color stabilizer are added to the process each hour. If the standard deviation of the amount of stabilizer in an individual bottle is 0.07 ounce, what is the standard deviation of the total amount of stabilizer added to the process each hour?

5-8. Component A fits into component B. The critical outer dimension of component A has a mean of 40 mm and a standard deviation of 0.4 mm. Component B has a critical inner dimension with mean 40.57 mm and a standard deviation of 0.4 mm. (a) What is the standard deviation of the difference between the inner and outer dimensions of the pairs of fitted pieces? (b) In what proportion of the cases do you expect a problem with the fit? Assume that the components are chosen at random.

5-9. A polymer is transported in hopper cars. The average weight of a loaded hopper car is 226,000 pounds with a standard deviation of 100 pounds. What are the mean and standard deviation of 10 shipments?

5-10. The data shown in the following table represent a measure of the amount of residual metal left on the catalyst from a cat-cracking unit over a period of about seven weeks. The amount of residual metal can reduce the unit's yield. (a) Develop a run chart on the residual metal and (b) compute the autocorrelation coefficient for a lag of one.

| Date | Residual Metal (ppm) |
| --- | --- |
| Jun 28 | 981 |
| Jul 03 | 918 |
| Jul 07 | 907 |
| Jul 11 | 896 |
| Jul 14 | 967 |
| Jul 18 | 1026 |
| Jul 23 | 954 |
| Jul 29 | 995 |
| Aug 02 | 984 |
| Aug 04 | 1055 |
| Aug 08 | 1118 |
| Aug 11 | 1032 |
| Aug 15 | 1094 |

Residual Metal (Cat-Cracking Process)

5-11.  Consider the 40 consecutive sample melt index measurements (data recorded in column order) taken from a high-density polyethylene process and shown in the table below. (a) Plot the data on a run chart and (b) compute the autocorrelation coefficient for a lag of one period.

| | | | | | | | |
|------|------|------|------|------|------|------|------|
| 1.00 | 1.02 | 1.09 | 1.09 | 1.12 | 0.95 | 1.17 | 1.01 |
| 1.02 | 1.06 | 1.06 | 1.17 | 1.11 | 0.91 | 1.15 | 1.06 |
| 1.04 | 1.09 | 1.04 | 1.11 | 1.09 | 1.05 | 1.14 | 1.10 |
| 1.03 | 1.11 | 1.04 | 1.14 | 0.98 | 1.10 | 1.11 | 1.16 |
| 1.03 | 1.13 | 1.02 | 1.17 | 1.00 | 1.12 | 1.07 | 1.11 |

**Melt Index Measurements**

# Unit 6: The Normal Distribution and Its Applications

# Unit 6

# The Normal Distribution and Its Applications

The most important probability distribution in all of statistical process control is the normal distribution. Because of its importance, the normal distribution and a closely related concept, the central limit theorem, are discussed in detail in this unit.

**Learning Objectives** — When you have completed this unit, you should:

   A. Know the characteristics of the normal distribution.

   B. Know how to make probability calculations based on the normal distribution.

   C. Know how to determine whether or not data is from a normally distributed process using a normal probability plot.

   D. Understand the concepts known as the central limit theorem and be able to apply them to help analyze quality data.

## 6-1. The Normal Distribution

The normal distribution is a continuous, symmetric, bell-shaped distribution having a range that includes all real numbers and two parameters: the mean $\mu$ and the standard deviation $\sigma$ (Fig. 6-1).

Although all normal distributions are continuous, symmetric, and bell-shaped, the normal distribution's form has an infinite number of variations. Fig. 6-2 shows three, all having the same mean value but with different standard deviations.

The normal distribution is unusual in that it has completely predictable proportions of its total area within one, two, and three standard deviations of the mean, regardless of the magnitude of the standard deviation. Fig. 6-3 shows a generic normal distribution and the percentages of the total area within one, two, and three standard deviations of the mean (i.e.,

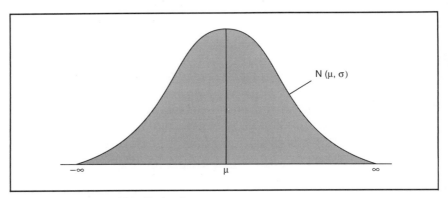

**Fig. 6-1. Typical Normal Distribution Form**

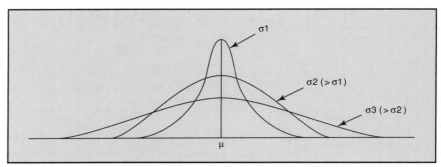

**Fig. 6-2. Three Variations of the Normal Distribution**

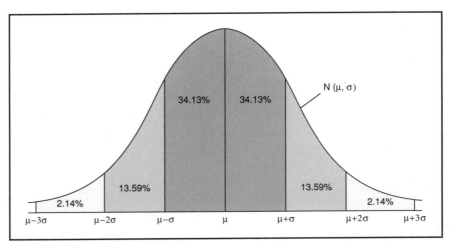

**Fig. 6-3. Relationships between the Number of Standard Deviations and Area for All Variations of the Normal Distribution**

68.26% within $\pm 1\sigma$, 95.44% within $\pm 2\sigma$, and 99.73% within $\pm 3\sigma$).

Conceptually, the area under the normal curve from minus infinity to any value x can be interpreted as the percentage of observations expected to be less than x. In other words, the probability that a normally distributed random variable X will take on a value less than x is given by the area under the curve from negative infinity to x. Standard naming conventions use uppercase letters to represent random variables and lowercase letters to represent individual values. As such, $Pr(X \leq x)$ is written to mean the probability that X is less than or equal to x (Fig. 6-4).

The random variable X may represent any measurement (i.e., melt index, density, weight, height, length, etc.). For example, suppose that a sample of high-density polyethylene is taken at 3 p.m. and the melt index measured as 1.05. Assume that the melt index is a normally distributed process characteristic. This means that if melt index measurements are taken over a long period of time and the values plotted, the distribution of values will be normally distributed. The probability that the melt index is less than or equal to 1.05 is calculated by finding the area under the normal curve to the left of 1.05. Suppose that $Pr(X \leq 1.05) = 0.90$. This means that (1) approximately 90% of the samples taken from the distribution will have a value below 1.05 and (2) the chance of observing a melt index of 1.05 or less in the next sample is 90%.

But how is the area under a normal curve computed? The first step is to convert the variable's value to "standard normal

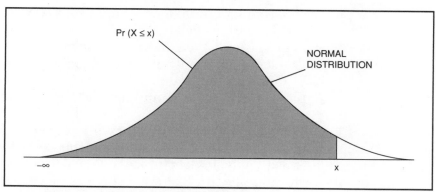

**Fig. 6-4. $Pr(X \leq x)$ Represented by the Shaded Area**

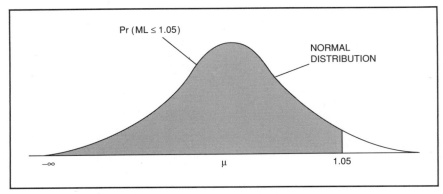

**Fig. 6-5. Probability of Observing a Melt Index Equal to or Less than 1.05**

form." Fortunately, this is a simple process. Variable values from all normal distributions may be transformed into standard normal variable values by using the standardizing transformation shown below:

$$Z = (X - \mu_x)/\sigma_x$$

Of course, when parameter values are unknown, sample statistics are used in their places, so that

$$Z = (X - \bar{x})/s$$

(Note: Z represents a variable from the standard normal distribution. The standard normal distribution is a normal distribution whose mean $\mu = 0$ and whose standard deviation $\sigma = 1$.) This transformation step is necessary because areas under typical normal curves cannot be found by usual means (i.e., by standard integration techniques). Fortunately, areas under the standard normal curve are well known and have been tabulated for various values of Z. As a result, step two, the process of finding a probability associated with the transformed variable's value, is simply a matter of looking up the probability corresponding to Z in the standard normal table. Examples throughout this unit demonstrate the process.

**Example 6-1:** The checksheet shown in Table 6-1 represents a summary of 150 melt index measurements collected from a high-density polyethylene process. (Note: The complete set of data was presented in Exercise 5-1.). Fig. 6-6 shows the accompanying histogram.

| Intervals | "Midpoint" | Interval Frequency | Count |
|---|---|---|---|
| 0.901–0.920 | 0.910 | /// | 3 |
| 0.921–0.940 | 0.930 | 卌 / | 6 |
| 0.941–0.960 | 0.950 | 卌 // | 7 |
| 0.961–0.980 | 0.970 | 卌 卌 // | 12 |
| 0.981–1.000 | 0.990 | 卌 卌 卌 / | 16 |
| 1.001–1.020 | 1.010 | 卌 卌 卌 卌 | 20 |
| 1.021–1.040 | 1.030 | 卌 卌 卌 卌 卌 | 25 |
| 1.041–1.060 | 1.050 | 卌 卌 卌 /// | 18 |
| 1.061–1.080 | 1.070 | 卌 卌 卌 | 15 |
| 1.081–1.100 | 1.090 | 卌 卌 | 10 |
| 1.101–1.120 | 1.110 | 卌 / | 6 |
| 1.121–1.140 | 1.130 | 卌 | 5 |
| 1.141–1.160 | 1.150 | 卌 | 5 |
| 1.161–1.180 | 1.170 | // | 2 |

Sample statistics: $\bar{x} = 1.0303$ and
$s = 0.0573$

**TABLE 6-1. Checksheet Used to Develop Melt Index Histogram**

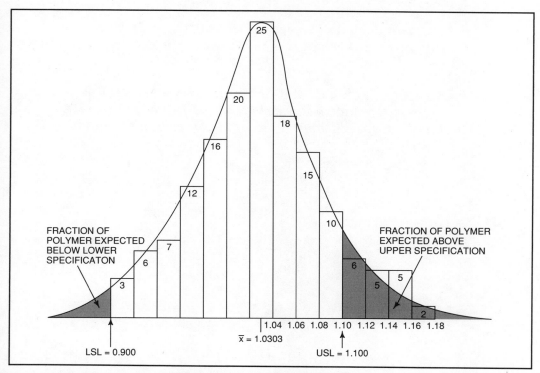

**Fig. 6-6. Approximate Normal Distribution Based on Histogram of Melt Index Data**

Suppose that the lower and upper specification limits (LSL and USL) are 0.900–1.100. What proportion of polymers have melt index values outside the specification limits? From Table 6-1, it is possible to estimate this proportion by counting the number of values below 0.900 (there are none) and above 1.100 (there are 18) and dividing by 150. Using this approach, the estimate of the probability of getting a melt index value outside the specification limits is $\frac{18}{150}$ or 12%.

If the melt index measurements are assumed to be approximately normally distributed, it is also possible to obtain an estimate using only the sample mean, the sample standard deviation, and knowledge of the normal distribution. Thus, we avoid constructing a histogram or checksheet. Although the normality assumption is admittedly subjective, based on the histogram's shape, it appears to be a reasonable one. (Note: In the next section, a formalized graphical approach known as normal probability plots is discussed. This technique helps determine whether or not data is from a normal population.)

Fig. 6-7 shows a normal approximation of the melt index's frequency distribution based on the sample mean and sample standard deviation values calculated. The estimated proportions of values above and below the specification limits are indicated.

To compute the probabilities in the marked areas, it is necessary to follow the steps outlined earlier in this section. First, the specification limits are expressed in standardized units.

$$Z_L = \frac{LSL - mean}{Standard\ deviation}$$

$$= \frac{(0.9 - 1.0303)}{0.0573}$$

$$= -2.27$$

$$Z_U = \frac{USL - mean}{Standard\ deviation}$$

$$= \frac{(1.1 - 1.0303)}{0.0573}$$

$$= 1.22$$

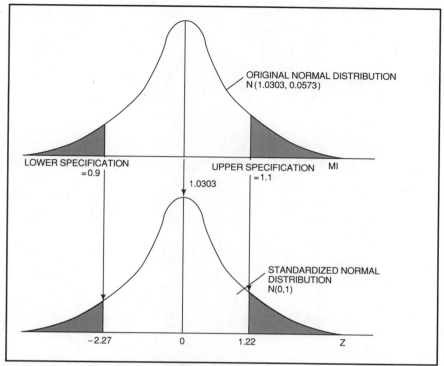

**Fig. 6-7. Normal Approximation of the Melt Index Data**

If X represents the melt index variable, then $Z = (X - \bar{x})/s$, and the fraction outside the specification limits is given by

$$Pr(X \leq 0.9) + Pr(X \geq 1.1) = Pr(Z \leq -2.27) + Pr(Z \geq 1.22)$$

From Table B-1 (Appendix B) we obtain the area under the normal curve less than $Z = -2.27$ and the area under the curve greater than $Z = 1.22$. An excerpt of Table B-1 is shown in Table 6-2. Using either table, the two probability values can be found.

$$Pr(Z \leq -2.27) = 0.0116 \text{ (or 1.16\%)}$$

and

$$Pr(Z \geq 1.22) = 1 - Pr(Z \leq 1.22)$$
$$= 1 - 0.8888$$
$$= 0.1112 \text{ (or 11.12\%)}$$

| Z | 0.09 | 0.08 | 0.07 | 0.06 | 0.05 | 0.04 | 0.03 | 0.02 | 0.01 | 0.00 |
|---|---|---|---|---|---|---|---|---|---|---|
| -3.5 | 0.00017 | 0.00017 | 0.00018 | 0.00019 | 0.00019 | 0.00020 | 0.00021 | 0.00022 | 0.00022 | 0.00023 |
| . | | | | | | | | | | |
| . | | | | | | | | | | |
| -2.2 | 0.0110 | 0.0113 | 0.0116 | 0.0119 | 0.0122 | 0.0125 | 0.0129 | 0.0132 | 0.0136 | 0.0139 |
| . | | | for $Z = -2.27$ | | | | | | | |
| . | | | | | | | | | | |
| -0.1 | 0.4247 | 0.4286 | 0.4325 | 0.4364 | 0.4404 | 0.4443 | 0.4483 | 0.4522 | 0.4562 | 0.4602 |
| -0.0 | 0.4641 | 0.4681 | 0.4721 | 0.4761 | 0.4801 | 0.4840 | 0.4880 | 0.4920 | 0.4960 | 0.5000 |

| Z | 0.00 | 0.01 | 0.02 | 0.03 | 0.04 | 0.05 | 0.06 | 0.07 | 0.08 | 0.09 |
|---|---|---|---|---|---|---|---|---|---|---|
| 0.0 | 0.5000 | 0.5040 | 0.5080 | 0.5120 | 0.5160 | 0.5199 | 0.5239 | 0.5279 | 0.5319 | 0.5359 |
| 0.1 | 0.5398 | 0.5438 | 0.5478 | 0.5517 | 0.5557 | 0.5596 | 0.5636 | 0.5675 | 0.5714 | 0.5753 |
| . | | | for $Z = 1.22$ | | | | | | | |
| . | | | | | | | | | | |
| 1.2 | 0.8849 | 0.8869 | 0.8888 | 0.8907 | 0.8925 | 0.8944 | 0.8962 | 0.8980 | 0.8997 | 0.9015 |
| . | | | | | | | | | | |
| . | | | | | | | | | | |
| 3.5 | 0.99977 | 0.99978 | 0.99978 | 0.99979 | 0.99980 | 0.99981 | 0.99981 | 0.99982 | 0.99983 | 0.99983 |

(Notes: (1) Areas under curve from $-\infty$ to Z.
(2) Headings in top part of this table are shown in reverse order in Appendix B-1.

**TABLE 6-2. Excerpt from Normal Probability Table B-1**

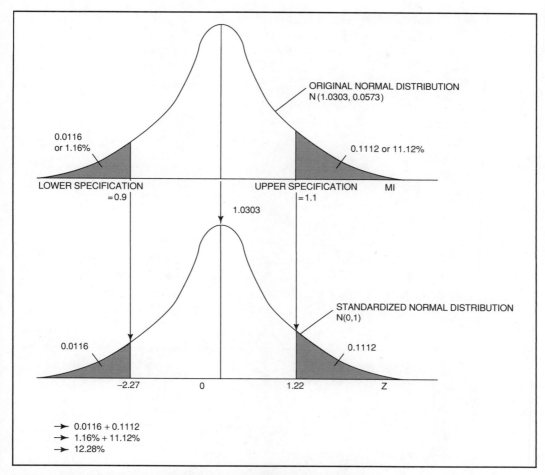

Fig. 6-8. Expected Proportions of Melt Index Values Outside Specifications

These proportions are marked on both the normal curves shown in Fig. 6-8. Note that the top part of Fig. 6-8 shows a normal distribution with mean 1.0303 and standard deviation 0.0573, while the bottom part of Fig. 6-8 shows the standard normal distribution equivalent.

The sum of the two probabilities is 0.1228 (i.e., 0.0116 + 0.1112). Therefore, approximately 12.28% of the melt index values will be outside specifications, a figure very near the 12% value based on the frequency table.

**Example 6-2:** Suppose a large sample with mean $\bar{x} = 10$ and standard deviation $s = 2$ is taken from a process having an approximately normally distributed quality characteristic.

Suppose that the upper limit is the product's key specification limit and that it is set at 13. What fraction of products may be expected to be inside the upper specification limit?

The first step is to compute the standardized equivalent of the specification limit value:

$$Z_U = \frac{(USL - \bar{x})}{s}$$

$$= \frac{(13 - 10)}{2}$$

$$= 1.5$$

The 1.5 Z value means that the upper specification limit of 13 lies 1.5 standard deviations above the mean. The probability of obtaining a measurement less than 1.5 standard deviations above the mean is the same for all normal distributions. Fig.

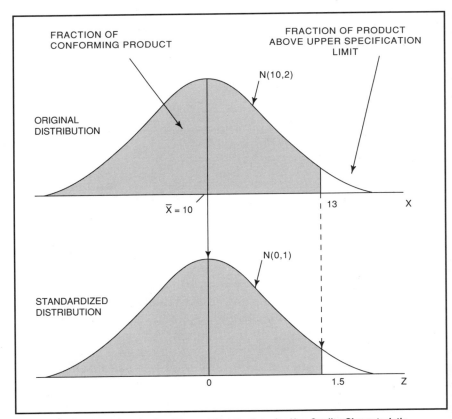

**Fig. 6-9. Original and Standardized Normal Distributions for Key Quality Characteristic**

| Z | 0.00 | 0.01 | 0.02 | 0.03 | 0.04 | 0.05 | 0.06 | 0.07 | 0.08 | 0.09 |
|---|------|------|------|------|------|------|------|------|------|------|
| 0.0 | 0.5000 | 0.5040 | 0.5080 | 0.5120 | 0.5160 | 0.5199 | 0.5239 | 0.5279 | 0.5319 | 0.5359 |
| 0.1 | 0.5398 | 0.5438 | 0.5478 | 0.5517 | 0.5557 | 0.5596 | 0.5636 | 0.5675 | 0.5714 | 0.5753 |
| . | . | . | . | . | . | . | . | . | . | . |
| 1.2 | 0.8849 | 0.8869 | 0.8888 | 0.8907 | 0.8925 | 0.8944 | 0.8962 | 0.8980 | 0.8997 | 0.9015 |
| . | . | | | | | | | | | |
| 1.5 | 0.9332 | 0.9345 | 0.9357 | 0.9370 | 0.9382 | 0.9394 | 0.9406 | 0.9418 | 0.9429 | 0.9441 |
| 1.6 | 0.9452 | 0.9463 | 0.9474 | 0.9484 | 0.9495 | 0.9505 | 0.9515 | 0.9525 | 0.9535 | 0.9545 |
| . | . | | | | | | | | | |
| 3.4 | 0.9997 | 0.9997 | 0.9997 | 0.9997 | 0.9997 | 0.9997 | 0.9997 | 0.9997 | 0.9997 | 0.9998 |
| 3.5 | 0.9998 | 0.9998 | 0.9998 | 0.9998 | 0.9998 | 0.9998 | 0.9998 | 0.9998 | 0.9998 | 0.9998 |

**TABLE 6-3. Excerpt from Normal Probability Table (from Appendix Table B-1)**

6-9 shows the original normal distribution and the equivalent standardized normal distribution for the situation described.

The second step is to determine the probability that a product's quality characteristic will be less than 13 by locating the standard normal value of 1.50 in Table B-1 or in the Table 6-3 excerpt.

$$Pr(X < 13) = Pr(Z < 1.5) = 0.9332 = 93.32\%$$

In other words, unless the process changes, the quality characteristic for approximately 93% of its output will be inside the upper specification limit.

**Example 6-3:** Suppose that pump repair times are approximately normally distributed. Examination of pump repair time data resulted in the following sample statistics: $\bar{x} = 4.5$ hours and $s = 0.5$ hours. Suppose that management wants to set a pump repair time standard at a value that can be met 90% of the time. At what value should the standard be set?

This is, of course, the same problem that was solved earlier but is approached from a different perspective. To find the repair time standard, first find the standardized Z value that corresponds to a 90% or less probability. From Table B-1 or

Table 6-3, the Z value is approximately Z = 1.28. Then,

$$Z_U = \frac{(USL - \bar{x})}{s}$$

$$1.28 = \frac{(USL - 4.5)}{0.5}$$

so that

$$USL = 4.5 + (0.5)(1.28)$$

$$= 5.14 \text{ hours}$$

The result shows that if the repair time standard is set at 5.14 hours, 90% of the repair times will be completed within that time span.

## 6-2. Normal Probability Plots

In practice, whether or not a quality characteristic is truly normally distributed is rarely obvious. In addition, because a number of quality-related techniques are based on the normality assumption, it is frequently important to know whether or not a quality characteristic is normally distributed.

In addition to the subjective examination of a data set's histogram, another method of determining whether or not a sample is from a normally distributed population makes use of a special type of paper known as normal probability paper (Appendix B, Figure B-1). Sample data are plotted on the special paper. If the points lie along a straight line, the data are from a normal probability distribution. If the points do not lie along a straight line, the data are not normally distributed.

The normal probability plot technique is useful in a number of circumstances: (1) to determine whether or not sample data exhibit the characteristics of a normal distribution; (2) to compare independent sets of data to see if they are all from the same normal population; and (3) to estimate process parameter values (mean, standard deviation).

Fig. 6-10 shows both a histogram and a cumulative frequency polygon based on normally distributed data. Fig. 6-11 shows the same data as it would appear on a normal probability plot.

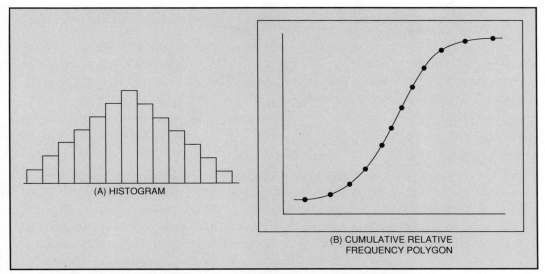

**Fig. 6-10. Histogram and Cumulative Frequency Polygon of Normally Distributed Data**

The process of creating a probability plot is summarized in the following six steps:

1. Order the n observations (i.e., $x_1$, $x_2$, . . . , $x_n$) from smallest to largest.

2. Assign a rank to each value. Assign the smallest value a rank of 1, the second smallest value a rank of 2, and so forth. Finally, assign the largest value a rank of n.

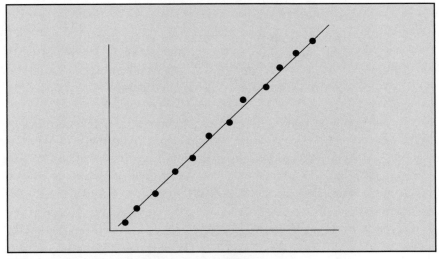

**Fig. 6-11. Normal Probability Plot of Normally Distributed Data**

3. Obtain probability plotting positions $F_i$ using the formula shown below (or from Table B-2)

$$F_i = \frac{100(i - \frac{3}{8})}{n + \frac{1}{4}}$$

$$= \frac{100(i - 0.375)}{n + 0.25}$$

where i is the rank assigned and n is the total number of observations. (Note: The formula for $F_i$ is actually not as formidable as it at first appears. In fact, it is only a slight variation of $100(i/n)$. The modification is to ensure that the nth plotting point does not equal 100%. Other variations of the plotting point formula are sometimes used to compute plotting positions, including $F_i = 100i/(n + 1)$ and $F_i = 100(i - 0.5)/n$. The formula chosen is considered the best for the normal distribution.)

4. Plot the points $(x_i, F_i)$ on normal probability paper.

5. Draw a straight line through the set of plotted points, generally following the trend of the data.

6. Assess whether or not the data are from a normal distribution by observation, depending on whether or not the points generally fall along the straight line drawn.

**Example 6-5:** In determining whether or not the 10 melt index values shown in Table 6-4 are from a normal distribution, a dot plot of the data (Fig. 6-12) is inconclusive and there are too few points for a meaningful histogram.

A normal probability plot may help to make the determination. The first step is to order the sample values from smallest to largest and then assign each value a rank. The plotting positions are obtained next. Table 6-5 shows the ordered ten melt index values, their ranks, and their associated plotting

| 0.76 | 1.00 | 0.83 | 0.86 | 1.04 |
| 0.90 | 1.11 | 0.92 | 0.95 | 0.98 |

**TABLE 6-4. Ten Melt Index Values**

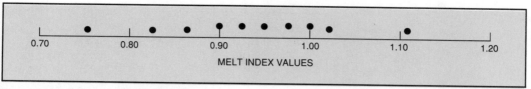

Fig. 6-12. Dot Plot of Ten Melt Index Values

| Rank | 1 | 2 | 3 | 4 | 5 | 6 | 7 | 8 | 9 | 10 |
|---|---|---|---|---|---|---|---|---|---|---|
| $x_i$ | 0.76 | 0.83 | 0.86 | 0.90 | 0.92 | 0.95 | 0.98 | 1.00 | 1.04 | 1.11 |
| $F_i$ | 6.1 | 15.9 | 25.6 | 35.4 | 45.1 | 54.9 | 64.6 | 74.4 | 84.1 | 93.9 |

TABLE 6-5. Melt Index Values in Low-to-High Order and Their Plotting Positions

position values. Calculations for the first three plotting positions F1, F2, and F3 are shown below.

$$F_1 = 100(1 - \tfrac{3}{8})/(10 + \tfrac{1}{4})$$

$$= 100(\tfrac{5}{8})/(\tfrac{41}{4})$$

$$= 6.1$$

$$F_2 = 100(2 - \tfrac{3}{8})/(10 + \tfrac{1}{4})$$

$$= 100(\tfrac{13}{8})/(\tfrac{41}{4})$$

$$= 15.9$$

$$F_3 = 100(3 - \tfrac{3}{8})/(10 + \tfrac{1}{4})$$

$$= 100(\tfrac{21}{8})/(\tfrac{41}{4})$$

$$= 25.6$$

The coordinate pairs $(x_i, F_i)$ are then plotted on normal probability paper. The results are shown in Fig. 6-13. Since a straight line closely follows the set of points, it is reasonable to assume that the data are from a normally distributed population.

A few rules of thumb may also be helpful in determining whether or not data values are from a normal distribution: (1) since the normal distribution is symmetric, the sample mean, median, and mode should be nearly the same; (2) approximately two-thirds (68%) of the data values should be within $\pm 1$ standard deviation of the sample mean; and, (3) approximately 19 out of 20 data points (95%) should be within $\pm 2$ standard deviations of the sample mean.

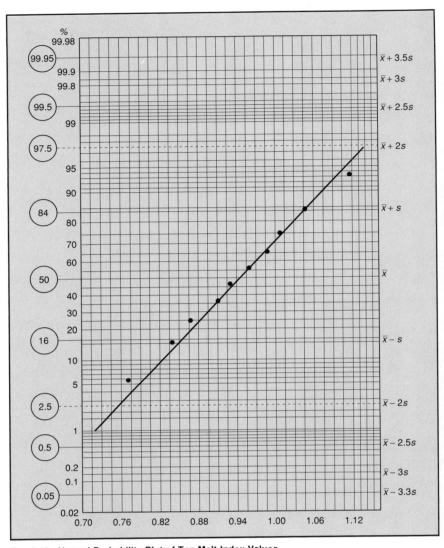

**Fig. 6-13. Normal Probability Plot of Ten Melt Index Values**

Estimates of the distribution's mean and standard deviation can be obtained directly from the plot (Fig. 6-14). The mean corresponds to the x value at the plot's 50 percent mark. For the melt index data, this is approximately 0.94. Since approximately 68% of normally distributed values are within $\pm 1$ standard deviation of the mean, one standard deviation may be estimated by subtracting the 16% value from the 84% value and dividing by 2. For the melt index data, the 84% value is approximately 1.05 and the 16% value is approximately 0.84, so the standard deviation is approximately $(1.04 - 0.83)/2 =$

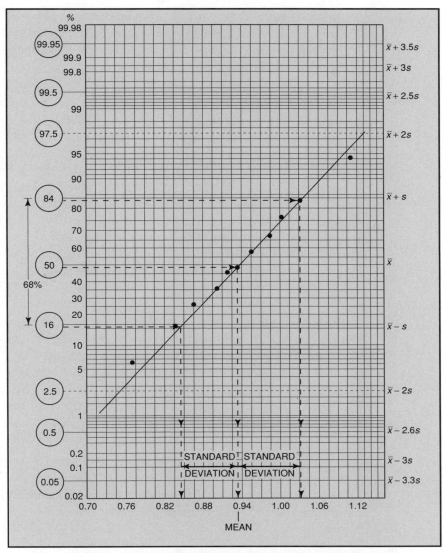

**Fig. 6-14. Normal Probability Plot of Ten Melt Index Values Showing Markings to Estimate Mean and Standard Deviation**

$(0.21/2) = 0.105$. (Note: Calculations of the mean and standard deviation using the 10 melt index values yield $\bar{x} = 0.94$ and $s = 0.105$.)

## 6-3. The Central Limit Theorem

The central limit theorem is important in a variety of statistical process control applications. It is introduced by way of an example.

**Example 6-6:** Suppose that five individual samples, each of size n = 4, are drawn from a polyethylene resin production process whose quality characteristic is approximately normally distributed (Table 6-6).

Sample statistics on both the individual values and on the averages are computed as follows: (1) By treating the 20 melt index values as one large sample and using the standard formulas for the mean and standard deviation, the overall sample mean is $\bar{x} = 10.18$ and the overall sample standard deviation is $s_x = 0.88$ (i.e., the sample-based standard deviation of the x's is 0.88). (2) By computing an average value for each of the five samples (results shown in the last column of Table 6-6) and treating these five values as data points in a single sample, the sample mean is $\bar{\bar{x}} = 10.18$ (i.e., the mean of the means) and the sample standard deviation $s_{\bar{x}} = 0.43$ (i.e., the sample-based standard deviation of the $\bar{x}$'s is 0.43).

These two approaches represent two important perspectives regarding data. The first deals with individual data points, while the second deals with sample averages. The means for both the individual measurements and for the sample averages are the same (i.e., both are 10.18), while the standard deviation of the averages (0.43) is noticeably smaller than the standard deviation of the individual values (0.88).

In fact, a proven relationship exists between the true standard deviation of individual values $\sigma_x$ and the true standard deviation of the average values $\sigma_{\bar{x}}$ (sometimes called the standard error). The relationship is shown below in algebraic form.

$$\sigma_{\bar{x}} = \sigma_x / \sqrt{n}$$

| Sample No. | Individual Values | | | | Sample Averages |
|---|---|---|---|---|---|
| 1 | 9.7 | 10.9 | 9.5 | 9.7 | 9.95 |
| 2 | 10.1 | 7.9 | 10.7 | 10.9 | 9.90 |
| 3 | 10.2 | 11.4 | 10.7 | 11.4 | 10.93 |
| 4 | 9.7 | 9.5 | 11.2 | 10.2 | 10.15 |
| 5 | 9.1 | 10.0 | 9.7 | 11.1 | 9.98 |

TABLE 6-6. Normally Distributed Individual and Average Values from Polyethylene Resin Production Process

where n is the sample size. The relationship may be approximated by

$$\hat{\sigma}_{\bar{x}} = s_x/\sqrt{n}.$$

For this set of data based on five samples of size n = 4 measurements each, $\hat{\sigma}_{\bar{x}} = 0.88/\sqrt{4} = 0.88/2 = 0.44$. This is very close to the standard deviation of the averages, $s_{\bar{x}}$ of 0.43, calculated directly from the five averages. The relationship between the two distributions is shown in Fig. 6-15.

Both curves shown in Fig. 6-15 appear to be normally distributed, although the variation present in the $\bar{x}$ curve is clearly less. In practice, however, individual values may or may not be normally distributed. For example, many processing industry measurements do not follow the normal form. Regardless of the form of the individual measurements, however, the distribution of the $\bar{x}$ values will in almost all circumstances be approximately normal.

This amazing statement, known as the central limit theorem, is one of the foundations of control charting (as will be seen in subsequent units). It states that for sufficiently large sample sizes, the distribution of the sample mean (i.e., $\bar{x}$) will be approximately normally distributed, regardless of the form of the distribution of the individual values on which the average calculations are based. (In practice, the sample size may be as small as n = 2, if the distribution is symmetric, but is almost always true for n = 4 or more.) It further states that the $\bar{x}$ distribution will have the same mean $\mu_{\bar{x}}$ as the mean $\mu_x$ of the population of individual (i.e., x) values and a standard deviation $\sigma_{\bar{x}}$ equal to the standard deviation of the population of

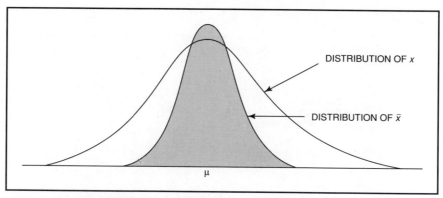

Fig. 6-15. Distributions of Individual Values and Average Values

individual values $\sigma_x$ divided by the square root of n, the number of measurements in each sample.

**Example 6-7:** In a large production plant, maintenance inspectors routinely check plant machinery. Each week they are given a list of machinery to inspect. In an attempt to determine how long the list should be, 24 inspectors were asked to record (to the nearest minute) the time they spent inspecting five randomly selected pieces of machinery from their list. Table 6-7 shows the results. Table 6-8 shows a checksheet that

| Insp. No. | Inspection Times | | | | | |
|---|---|---|---|---|---|---|
| | $x_1$ | $x_2$ | $x_3$ | $x_4$ | $x_5$ | $\bar{x}$ |
| 1 | 6 | 2 | 6 | 3 | 3 | 4.0 |
| 2 | 2 | 1 | 5 | 3 | 6 | 3.4 |
| 3 | 4 | 6 | 1 | 1 | 4 | 3.2 |
| 4 | 1 | 2 | 5 | 1 | 6 | 3.0 |
| 5 | 1 | 3 | 6 | 4 | 6 | 4.0 |
| 6 | 2 | 6 | 6 | 4 | 4 | 4.4 |
| 7 | 5 | 2 | 1 | 3 | 5 | 3.4 |
| 8 | 2 | 1 | 4 | 6 | 5 | 3.6 |
| 9 | 1 | 2 | 5 | 2 | 4 | 2.8 |
| 10 | 6 | 3 | 1 | 5 | 2 | 3.4 |
| 11 | 1 | 2 | 6 | 5 | 2 | 3.2 |
| 12 | 6 | 2 | 1 | 3 | 1 | 2.6 |
| 13 | 6 | 3 | 5 | 6 | 3 | 4.6 |
| 14 | 6 | 6 | 4 | 2 | 3 | 4.2 |
| 15 | 5 | 1 | 6 | 2 | 3 | 4.2 |
| 16 | 5 | 5 | 2 | 2 | 4 | 3.6 |
| 17 | 1 | 5 | 2 | 1 | 4 | 2.6 |
| 18 | 5 | 4 | 2 | 1 | 5 | 3.4 |
| 19 | 4 | 2 | 5 | 3 | 6 | 4.0 |
| 20 | 3 | 1 | 3 | 4 | 4 | 3.0 |
| 21 | 4 | 6 | 4 | 5 | 2 | 4.2 |
| 22 | 5 | 3 | 4 | 2 | 4 | 3.6 |
| 23 | 3 | 6 | 1 | 1 | 2 | 2.6 |
| 24 | 1 | 5 | 3 | 4 | 4 | 3.4 |

**TABLE 6-7. Inspection Time Data**

| Interval (Minutes) | Interval Frequency | Frequency Total |
|---|---|---|
| 1 | 𝍷𝍷𝍷 𝍷𝍷𝍷 𝍷𝍷𝍷 𝍷𝍷𝍷 | 20 |
| 2 | 𝍷𝍷𝍷 𝍷𝍷𝍷 𝍷𝍷𝍷 𝍷𝍷𝍷 // | 22 |
| 3 | 𝍷𝍷𝍷 𝍷𝍷𝍷 𝍷𝍷𝍷 / | 16 |
| 4 | 𝍷𝍷𝍷 𝍷𝍷𝍷 𝍷𝍷𝍷 /// | 18 |
| 5 | 𝍷𝍷𝍷 𝍷𝍷𝍷 𝍷𝍷𝍷 // | 17 |
| 6 | 𝍷𝍷𝍷 𝍷𝍷𝍷 𝍷𝍷𝍷 𝍷𝍷𝍷 // | 22 |

**TABLE 6-8. Checksheet of Individual Inspection Times**

| Interval of Averages | Interval Frequency | Frequency Total |
|---|---|---|
| 2.26–2.75 | /// | 3 |
| 2.76–3.25 | ᵗᴴᴴ | 5 |
| 3.26–3.75 | ᵗᴴᴴ /// | 8 |
| 3.76–4.25 | ᵗᴴᴴ | 5 |
| 4.26–4.75 | /// | 3 |

Note: All $\bar{x}$ values are calculated to one decimal place.

**TABLE 6-9. Checksheet of Average Inspection Times**

categorizes individual inspection times. Table 6-9 shows a checksheet categorizing average inspection times.

Fig. 6-16 shows histograms of both the individual inspection times and the average inspection times. The histogram of individual inspection times is nearly flat, indicating an

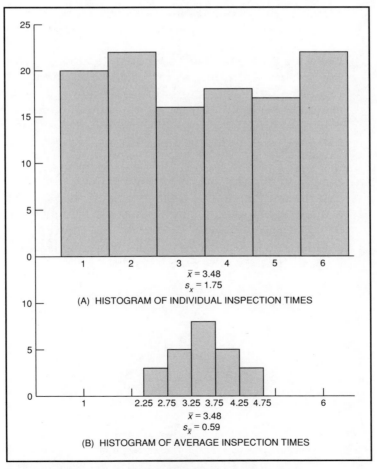

$\bar{x} = 3.48$
$s_x = 1.75$

(A) HISTOGRAM OF INDIVIDUAL INSPECTION TIMES

$\bar{x} = 3.48$
$s_{\bar{x}} = 0.59$

(B) HISTOGRAM OF AVERAGE INSPECTION TIMES

**Fig. 6-16. Histograms of Individual and Average Inspection Times**

approximately uniformly distributed characteristic. However, the average inspection times $\overline{x}$ (based on samples of size n = 5) of individual inspectors follow a bell-shaped pattern, indicating an approximately normal pattern.

The mean inspection time is 3.48 minutes. The standard deviation of the individual inspection times is $s_x = 1.75$ and the standard deviation of the 24 $\overline{x}$ values is $s_{\overline{x}} = 0.59$. The value of $s_{\overline{x}}$ using the central limit theorem is $s_x/\sqrt{n} = 1.75/\sqrt{5} = 0.78$. Clearly the $s_{\overline{x}}$ value calculated from the 24 sample means is somewhat different from the $s_{\overline{x}}$ value obtained using the central limit theorem. It is unrealistic, however, to expect accuracy to two decimal places when individual inspection times are integer-valued and the total number of averages is relatively small (only two decimal places when individual inspection times are integer-valued and the total number of averages is relatively small, only 24 in this case). Still, the two estimates are relatively close.

---

**Example 6-8:** Sampling over an extended period of time when the process is running as expected has shown that an important process quality characteristic has an average value of 100 and a standard deviation of 8. A single sample of size n = 4 is taken from the process. The sample mean is 92. Is there reason to believe that the process mean has shifted?

Since the distribution of average values is normally distributed (because of the central limit theorem), the probability of finding a single sample value of 92 when the true mean is still 100 can be calculated by using the normal distribution. Step one is to standardize the variable's value. Step two is to calculate the probability using the normal tables.

$$Z = \frac{\overline{X} - \mu_{\overline{x}}}{\sigma_{\overline{x}}}$$

$$= \frac{(\overline{X} - \mu_x)}{\left(\dfrac{\sigma_x}{\sqrt{n}}\right)}$$

$$= \frac{(92 - 100)}{\left(\dfrac{8}{\sqrt{4}}\right)}$$

$$= -2$$

$$\Rightarrow \Pr(\overline{X} \leq 92) = \Pr(Z \leq -2)$$

$$= 0.02275 \qquad \text{(using Table B-1)}$$

$$= 2.3\%$$

The calculations show that there is only about a 2% chance that an $\overline{x}$ value of 92 or less would occur based on a sample of size $n = 4$ when the true mean of the distribution of individual values is 100. As such, there is some reason for concern.

## Exercises

6-1. Based on 100 polymer resin samples taken from an approximately normally distributed process, the mean melt index is estimated as 9.5 and the standard deviation estimated as 0.8. What percentage of resins produced will have a melt index above 11.0? Below 9.0?

6-2. Diaphragm seals used to prevent fluid seepage are received from two suppliers. The target diameter is 32 mm, with specifications of 32 ± 0.1 mm. The process mean and standard deviation of products from supplier A are 32.02 mm and 0.05 mm, respectively. The process mean and standard deviation of products from supplier B are 32.0 mm and 0.06 mm, respectively. Which supplier has the better quality in terms of percent of nonconforming seals?

6-3. Consider the situation described in Exercise 6-2. Suppose that the diameter of one seal from supplier A is measured and found to have a diameter of 32.13 mm. What would you conclude about the process from that result?

6-4. Consider the quality-related measurements for 12 successive individual samples shown in the table below (or the following table). (a) Construct a normal probability plot to determine whether or not the sample comes from a normally distributed population. (b) Using the plot, estimate the mean and standard deviation of the distribution.

| 0.94 | 0.98 | 0.96 | 1.05 | 0.97 | 0.97 |
| 0.93 | 0.90 | 0.87 | 0.91 | 0.91 | 0.92 |

6-5. Measurements based on samples taken from two processes are shown in the table below. Develop two normal probability plots, one based on each set of data. What can you conclude about the two processes?

**Process A:**

| | | | | | |
|---|---|---|---|---|---|
| 0.96 | 0.98 | 0.99 | 1.00 | 1.02 | 1.02 |
| 1.03 | 1.05 | 1.06 | 1.07 | 1.09 | 1.12 |

**Process B:**

| | | | | | |
|---|---|---|---|---|---|
| 1.01 | 1.03 | 1.03 | 1.03 | 1.04 | 1.04 |
| 1.04 | 1.05 | 1.06 | 1.06 | 1.07 | 1.08 |

6-6. Suppose that a process yield measured in grams is normally distributed with mean 1550 and standard deviation 50. In a run of 100 individual measurements, how many would you expect, on the average, (a) below 1550? (b) above 1650? (c) between 1525 and 1575? (d) above 1470?

6-7. Suppose that a process has an average performance value of 101.7 and a standard deviation of 11.5. Samples of $n = 4$ measurements each are taken from the process at regular intervals. (a) What is the probability that the next sample average will be above 113? (b) Below 99? (c) Equal to exactly 101.7? (d) Find a lower limit below which not more than 9 out of 500 sample averages will fall.

6-8. Outside diameter measurements of a particular type of bushing are normally distributed with a mean of 2 inch and a standard deviation of 0.003 inch. (a) Find a lower limit such that only 3% of the bushings will have a diameter below it. (b) Determine symmetrical limits about the mean such that only 10% of the bushings will have diameters outside these limits. (c) What is the probability that the diameter of a single, randomly chosen bushing will be between 1.994 and 2.006 inch?

6-9. In order to check a process for control, samples of size n = 4 are taken from each of five randomly chosen batches. Resulting calculations show that $\bar{\bar{x}} = 1.5$ and $\bar{R} = 0.006$. (a) Assuming that the $\bar{x}$ distribution is normal, within what limits would you expect all five samples averages to fall (i.e., $\pm 3$ standard deviation limits)? (b) Assuming that the $\bar{x}$ distribution is normal, approximately what specification limits should be set so

that 95% of the individual items will meet the
specifications?

6-10. A process (i.e., individual) measurement follows a
normally distributed pattern, has a true mean of $\mu_x =$
758 and a standard deviation of $\sigma_x = 19.4$. If the
specification limits are 700 and 800, what percent of
production can be expected to be outside the
specification limits?

6-11. An extensive study of flow index values of products from
four parallel product streams yielded the results shown
in the table below. The flow index specification limits are
$1.500 \pm 0.005$. Assuming that the measurement is
approximately normally distributed, which process
produces the smallest proportion of products outside
specifications?

| Process | Average Flow Index Measurement | Standard Deviation of Flow Index Measurements |
|---------|--------------------------------|-----------------------------------------------|
| 1 | 1.495 | 0.0007 |
| 2 | 1.502 | 0.0010 |
| 3 | 1.500 | 0.0020 |
| 4 | 1.498 | 0.0003 |

# Unit 7: Basics of Control Charting

# Unit 7

# Basics of Control Charting

This unit is intended as an introduction to the process of control charting. Emphasis is placed on describing the elements involved in developing and using control charts. Subsequent units describe the control charting process in more detail.

**Learning Objectives** — When you have completed this unit, you should:

A. Know what is meant by statistically in-control and statistically out-of-control processes and how control charts help to monitor them.

B. Know the purposes of the two primary components of a control chart (the centerline and the control limits) and know generally how they are determined.

C. Understand the issues related to three key control chart sampling issues: sample size, sample frequency, and rational subgrouping.

## 7-1. In-Control and Out-of-Control Processes

Every production process exhibits variability. This variability may or may not be minor and may be due to a variety of possible causes. Some of the causes are a natural part of the process. For example, in the chemical processing industry, minor differences in raw materials, changes in the ambient temperature, or differences in operator skill levels may result in process variation. Generally, causes such as these have a relatively minor impact on the results of the process. As such, they are referred to as common (or random) causes.

Other causes have larger impacts on process variation. For example, a miscalibrated instrument, an inappropriate policy for changing parameter settings in a continuous process, or major raw material differences may each result in considerable process variation. Causes such as these are referred to as special causes.

A process having only common causes of variation present is said to be in control or, more accurately, in statistical control.

A process with one or more special causes present (in addition to the inevitable common causes of variation) is said to be out of control. Stated in another way, as long as the behavior of a process is stable and consistent, the process is in control. When the behavior of the process is erratic and inconsistent, the process is out of control.

It is common sense to eliminate the major causes of variation as quickly as possible. To do so, however, requires that the special causes be identified. Control charts are used to point out the presence of special causes of variation, but they do not usually show the source of the special cause itself. Identification of the special cause always requires thought and often requires follow-up study.

Special causes can often be corrected at the process. For example, once an instrument is recognized as being out of calibration, it can typically be recalibrated at the request of the operator. Common causes are system faults that typically cannot be corrected without the attention of management. For example, variation in raw materials can be reduced only by improvements in the supplier's production process, which requires management intervention.

In-control processes exhibit stable variation patterns. Fig. 7-1 shows a run chart of an in-control process. Fig. 7-2 shows several snapshots of the same process over time. The sketches emphasize that both the process mean and the process variation are nearly constant over time. The sketches also indicate that the quality characteristic is approximately normally distributed, a not uncommon situation for in-control processes.

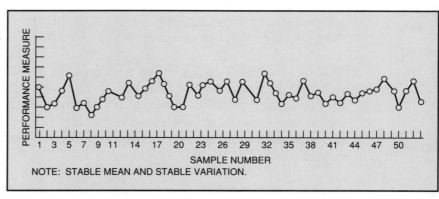

**Fig. 7-1. Run Chart for In-Control Process**

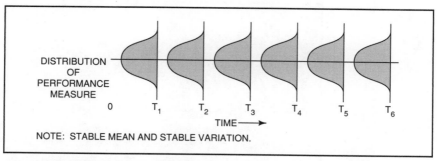

DISTRIBUTION
OF
PERFORMANCE
MEASURE

0       T$_1$        T$_2$        T$_3$        T$_4$        T$_5$        T$_6$

TIME⟶

NOTE: STABLE MEAN AND STABLE VARIATION.

**Fig. 7-2. Snapshots of In-Control Process**

Fig. 7-3 presents run charts for five out-of-control processes. Fig. 7-3(a) shows a process with relatively constant variation, but with an upward shift in the mean. (Note that the process may be "in control" at the higher level, after the process shift has occurred, but is definitely "out of control" with regard to the original setting of the mean.) Fig. 7-3(b) shows a process with relatively constant variation but with multiple shifts in the mean. Fig. 7-3(c) shows a process with stable variation but with a mean that is trending upward. Fig. 7-3(d) shows a process whose mean is relatively constant but whose variation increases over time. Fig. 7-3(e) shows a process with both changing mean and changing variation. Fig. 7-4 shows the same five situations using snapshot sketches of the processes.

Knowing that a process is in control does not guarantee that it is producing product within the specification limits. Specifications are generally set based on need (or perceived need), not on process capability. However, if the process is capable of producing within-specification products and has been doing so for some period of time, an in-control process does imply that the within-specification output is probably continuing and that no significant outside influences (i.e., special causes of variation) are acting on the process.

## 7-2. The Control Chart

Control charts provide guidelines regarding in-control and out-of-control processes; they indicate when to try to locate special causes of variation and when not to. The charts can be set up in several ways and on a variety of performance measures (e.g., on individual estimates, sample means, sample ranges, proportion of nonconforming products, etc.).

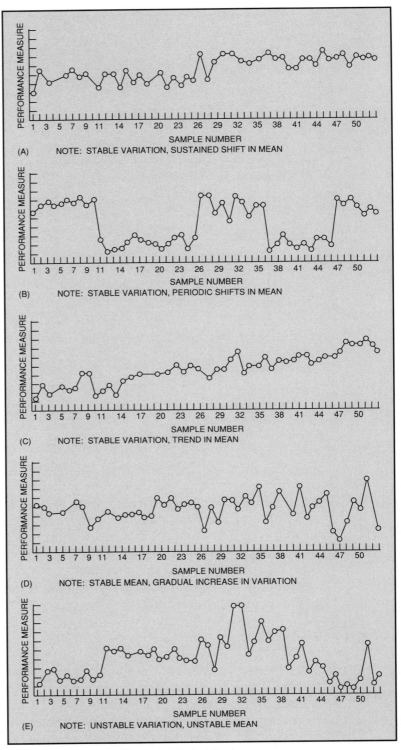

**Fig. 7-3. Run Charts for Five Out-of-Control Processes**

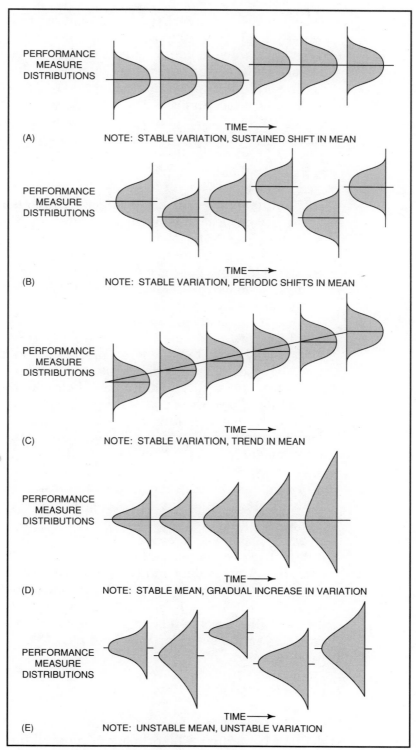

**Fig. 7-4. Snapshots of Five Out-of-Control Processes**

There is always some chance of misinterpreting what is actually happening in a process. In deciding what performance measures and what control charts to use, the goal is to strike a balance between the consequences of two kinds of errors: (1) finding an indication of trouble that does not exist and (2) not finding an indication of trouble that does exist. The first type of error (false signal) is referred to as a Type I error, while the second type of trouble (lack of signal) is known as a Type II error. Where control limits are set directly influences the probability that each type of error will occur.

The familiar concentric circle target is presented to further clarify the purpose of control charts. Fig. 7-5 shows four such targets. In Fig. 7-5(a), the holes are scattered but seem to be centered well away from the target's center—an indication of a process with both poor accuracy and poor precision. In Fig. 7-5(b), the holes are all around the bull's eye but not consistently close to it. This indicates a process exhibiting accuracy (i.e., average is good) but not precision (i.e., range is large). In Fig. 7-5(c), the holes are well away from the bull's eye but are tightly bunched—an indication of a process with precision (i.e., range is small) but not accuracy (i.e., average is poor). In Fig. 7-5(d), the holes are all close to the bull's eye, an indication of a process possessing both accuracy (i.e., appropriate average) and precision (i.e., small range). Control charts are intended to help differentiate processes with accuracy and precision from those with only one or neither.

A typical control chart recording and presentation form is shown in Fig. 7-6 for sample averages and sample ranges. (Note: Of course, control charts for other performance measures, such as the proportion defective, would look slightly different.) In the upper part of the form, space is provided for recording process data and sampling results. The lower part of the form features grids for plotting the characteristic or characteristics being monitored. An event log is also provided for recording process-related settings and events. The data collected in the event log may later help to pinpoint problems in the process.

### Centerline

The first step in the process of setting up a control chart is to define a centerline. The primary purpose of the centerline is to

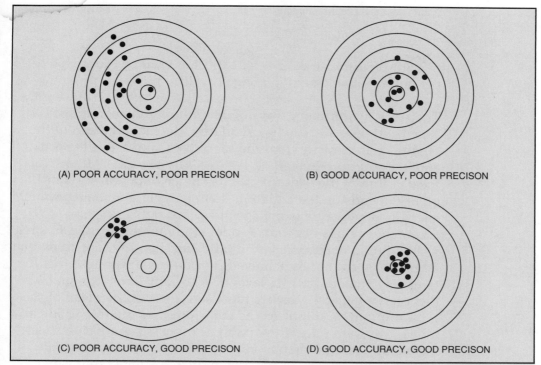

Fig. 7-5. **Target: Concepts of Precision and Accuracy**

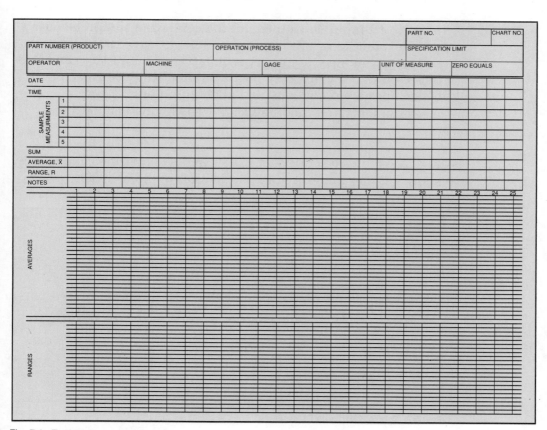

Fig. 7-6. **Typical Control Chart Form**

provide a reference value—an expected or hoped for value of the quality characteristic being charted.

There are two primary ways of determining the centerline: (1) The usual procedure is by calculating the overall mean of the quality characteristic from the set of data values available; (2) another appropriate method is to use the process "target" (or ideal) value as the centerline. The choice of one method or the other depends on the situation. For example, for some products a single target value is not specified. Instead, a range of acceptable values is given. A pilot study might be used in such a situation to determine an initial centerline. In other cases, the target value cannot be achieved. For instance, suppose that the target is a material purity level of 100%. In situations such as this one, it generally makes more sense to use the mean of the present production process as the centerline and to periodically move it upward (closer to 100%) as process improvements are made. On the other hand, a target value is more appropriate in certain situations, such as when only a few data points are available or when the process can easily be adjusted to target.

Ideally, a computed estimate of the centerline should be based on a substantial number of measurements (say, 100). Otherwise, the centerline may not be representative of the process and false out-of-control signals may result. In practice, however, centerlines are often constructed based on only a few measurements and modified as more is learned about the process.

Fig. 7-7 shows a set of data values and a centerline. The values show a minor amount of variation around the centerline.

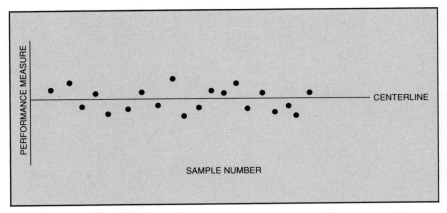

**Fig. 7-7. Control Chart with Centerline**

Subsequent units discuss the details associated with developing and interpreting values with respect to the centerline.

Recall that the objective of a control chart is to help determine whether the process is in or out of statistical control. This definition does not say that the process must produce at target in order to be in control. Rather, the implication is that for a process to be considered in statistical control, it should be able to maintain a consistent quality level.

### Control Limits

Once the centerline is specified, the control limits may be calculated. Control limits are used as a basis for judging the significance of the variation of some quality characteristic from sample to sample, from lot to lot, or from time to time. In other words, they provide guidelines for deciding when a production process is in or out of statistical control. The most basic rule of control charting is that points falling outside the control limits indicate that the process is probably out of control. Fig. 7-8 shows the data pictured in Fig. 7-7, but also includes control limits.

Control limits are typically placed three standard deviations above and three standard deviations below the centerline, with the standard deviation of the characteristic being plotted computed from process data.

There are two reasons for using three standard deviation control limits: (1) Three standard deviation control limits are used because of the characteristics of the normal distribution.

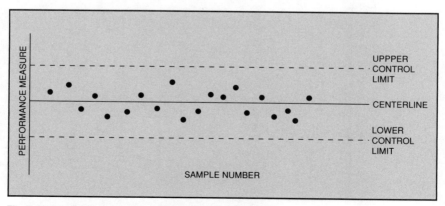

**Fig. 7-8. Control Chart with Centerline and Control Limits**

(It was mentioned earlier in this unit that in-control quality characteristics frequently follow a normally distributed pattern.) By setting the limits ±3 standard deviations from the centerline, no action is taken unless there is a clear sign that something is wrong. In fact, because 99.73% of the area is within ±3 standard deviations of the normal distribution's mean, a Type I error (i.e., false signal/possibility of overcontrol) is made only about 0.27% of the time. (2) Three standard deviation control limits are used for simplicity. For example, one reasonable alternative might be to set control limits that correspond to a 1.00% Type I error probability. If that were done, control limits would be set at ±2.575 standard deviations instead of ±3 sigma. Still, there is nothing magical about three-sigma limits. If the concern is primarily to find all potential trouble spots quickly, even if that requires following up on a number of false leads, it may be preferable to set narrower control limits (say, at ±2 standard deviations). Fig. 7-9 shows the relationship between the three standard deviation control limits and the normal distribution.

What can go wrong in the control charting process? The answer is that a number of things can. (Unit 11, Issues In Control Charting, deals with this question in more detail.) One of the most common errors is the use of an inappropriate estimate of

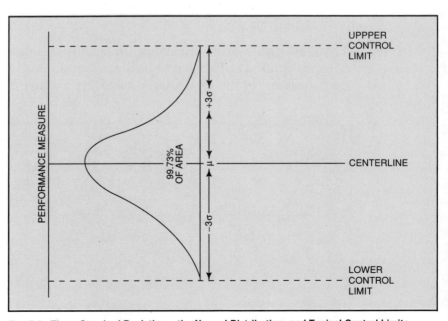

**Fig. 7-9. Three Standard Deviations, the Normal Distribution, and Typical Control Limits**

the process standard deviation for the characteristic being plotted. For example, if multiple measurements are taken from a gasoline production process at nearly the same point in time, the variation exhibited by these measurements is likely to be very small since gasoline tends to be homogeneous. If the process standard deviation is estimated using such data, the control limits will almost undoubtedly be too narrow. Other possible control charting issues concern choices of sample size, sampling frequency, and rational subgrouping.

## 7-3. Sampling

### Sample Size

The choice of sample size is obviously important. For instance, if the quality of rubber seals is to be monitored, how many seals should be chosen each time a sample is taken to obtain an appropriate indicator of process performance? From a statistical point of view, the larger the sample size, the better; from an economical point of view, the smaller the sample size, the better. In practice, what usually happens is a compromise.

Samples of sizes 4 to 6 are common in the parts industry. Selecting sample sizes for continuous processes in the chemical, hydrocarbon processing, and pulp and paper industries is a different matter, however. Chemical composition analysis is often time-consuming and costly. Therefore, sample sizes in process industries are usually relatively small. In many cases, samples of size $n = 1$ are taken.

In the process industry, unlike the parts industry, each sample is often taken from a homogeneous mixture rather than from a group of individual components. For example, in one plastics plant, in an attempt to monitor the quality of outgoing product, pellets are taken from each compartment of the hopper cars used to transport them, mixed, divided into five groups (i.e., $n = 5$), and then analyzed. Unfortunately, this provides little information about process variation at any one time, since the pellets in different compartments were likely produced at different times. In addition, since the pellets are mixed, one would also expect that the measurement results would be nearly identical, which means that there is little incentive to choose a sample size larger than $n = 1$.

On the other hand, if measurement error is present in the measurement process, multiple measurements of essentially the same material may be necessary. This serves two purposes: (1) the degree of measurement error can be determined, and (2) it allows a sample mean value to be monitored (plotted) as if it were an individual value. In the plastics plant example, if laboratory results of the mixed groups of pellets are significantly different, the differences are primarily attributable to measurement error rather than to process variation. In this case, it is necessary to analyze multiple batches and average the results in order to obtain a single measure of outgoing quality.

A similar situation has been observed in a gasoline blending operation. Gasoline samples are "caught" in one or more small bottles every four hours, and the gasoline's octane rating is measured in the laboratory. One would expect that multiple measurements of the octane rating that are based on gasoline blended in a particular unit at approximately the same point in time would all be the same. Unfortunately, because of variation in the laboratory measurement procedure, the octane rating on similar "samples" can vary significantly (say, from 89.0 to 90.0). In this case, it is necessary to analyze multiple bottles of gasoline (at least two) and average the results in order to obtain a single octane rating measurement appropriate for plotting.

### Sample Frequency

How frequently should samples be taken? On the one hand, since it is important to know when process changes occur, frequent samples make sense. Obviously, if the interval between samples is too long, the process could change markedly and perhaps several times between samples, resulting in large quantities of out-of-spec production. On the other hand, if the interval between samples is very short and the process is generally stable, taking and analyzing frequent samples is both time-consuming and unnecessary.

Appropriate sampling intervals in the process industries depend on the dynamics (time relationships) of the processes themselves, on what are called process dead times and time constants (Fig. 7-10). Once there is a change in the value of a process variable (either intentionally or unintentionally), there may be a period of time when no measurable change occurs in the process' performance measure. This is called dead time.

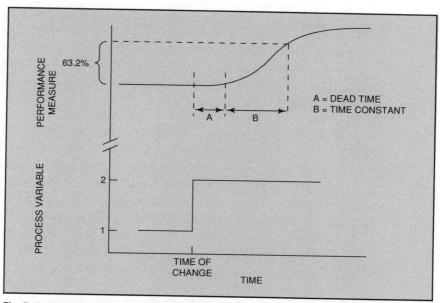

Fig. 7-10. Relationship between Process Changes and Performance Measure Changes in the Process Industry

Once the dead time ends, the process performance measure begins to change, but considerable time may pass before the change is complete. The time constant is the amount of time required to realize approximately two-thirds (63.2% to be exact) of the ultimate change in the performance measurement once the dead time, if any, has ended.

For instance, in processes involving a chemical reaction and the mixing of components, process time constants of 10 to 20 minutes are common—and ones of 2 to 4 hours are not unheard of. It is unnecessary to sample more frequently than the process constant time period. In general, a process should be sampled at intervals that allow the recognition of significant process changes and provide ample reaction time. In some cases, experimentation may be needed to arrive at a satisfactory sampling interval.

Online analyzers that produce near-continuous readings provide a partial solution. There is a danger in over-reliance on the online devices, however, because instruments sometimes go out of calibration or break. As a result, their values must be checked against some other reliable measure at regular intervals. For example, operators may base operating decisions on values produced by online analyzers but should also

consider the results of periodic samples produced by the
laboratory (say, every four hours) in order to verify that the
online analyzers have maintained their accuracy and
repeatability. Also, samples of known composition (so-called
"standards") are used to periodically calibrate the online
devices.

## Rational Subgroups

A rational subgroup is a sample composed of items as
homogeneous as the process will permit with respect to the
variability being studied. For example, a rational subgroup
might be composed of items whose feedstock is from a single
supplier or items from a single shift and single processing unit.
(Note: In statistical process control applications, the terms
subgroup and sample have the same meaning—a selection of
one or more items taken from a process. For example, a
subgroup of size n = 5 and a sample of size n = 5 refer to the
same thing—a collection of five items or specimens taken from
a process. Confusion sometimes arises when an individual item
or specimen is referred to inappropriately as a sample.)

Rational subgrouping is intended to result in collections of
items with only common cause variation within groups of n
measurements (i.e., sample size = n) and special cause
variation (if it exists) between groups. That is, if rational
subgrouping is done properly and the process is in control, the
variation within an individual sample will be due entirely to
common causes. Observations within the same sample should
have a number of important common factors (e.g., output from
a single shift on a single machine run by a single operator).

Subgroups should be selected to represent possible or
suspected differences in the processes that produced them. For
instance, subgroups (samples) might be selected for both the
day and night shifts, before and after changes of raw materials,
before and after lunch, etc.

If samples are not based on rational subgroups and special
causes are present in the process, control charts whose
monitored characteristic is the average of multiple
measurements (sample size n > 1) may present misleading
results. For example, hourly measurements are shown in Fig.
7-11 and 7-12. The plotted points in the two figures are
identical. Assume, however, that it is not feasible to sample the

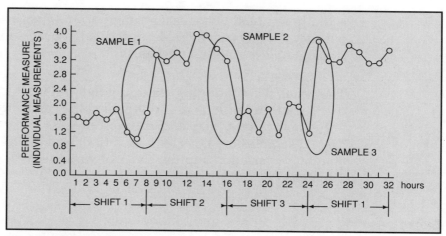

Fig. 7-11. **Nonrational Subgrouping**

process on an hourly basis. As such, the analyst is not privy to all of the information that can be seen by examining the hourly plots.

Fig. 7-11 represents the nonrational subgrouping case. Each sample of size n = 3 includes items from two shifts. The sampling results indicate that the process mean is stable and that process variation is constant (although large), neither of which are true. Fig. 7-12 represents the rational subgrouping case. Each item in the sample of size n = 3 is taken during a single shift rather than during overlapping shifts. The sampling results show that variation of the quality characteristic is

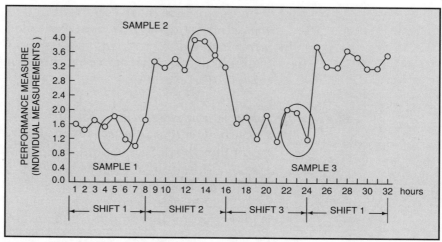

Fig. 7-12. **Rational Subgrouping**

actually minimal within each subgroup (i.e., within each shift) but that there is considerable variation between subgroups (i.e., considerable variation between shifts).

The rational subgrouping results shown in Fig. 7-12 indicate that something unique to individual shifts (probably the actions of the operators) is a special cause of process variation. In this case, if samples are not based on rational subgroups, both the amount of variation and the cause of variation will go undetected.

## Exercises

7-1.   (a) Describe some possible common and special causes of variation for a process you are familiar with. (Note: While the process could be ''work'' related, it need not be. For example, yard mowing, meal presentation, and doing homework are three ''non-work'' related processes having considerable variation.)

(b) How can common cause variation be statistically described?

(c) What is the purpose of a control chart?

(d) Describe two ways the centerline of a control chart is determined?

(e) Why are control limits set at $\pm 3\sigma$?

(f) What factors are important in determining the sample size used in the development of a control chart? Give an example.

(g) What factors are most important in determining the sampling frequency? Give an example.

(h) What is meant by rational subgrouping? Give an example of how rational subgrouping might prevent misleading results.

7-2.   (a) When is a process said to be ''in statistical control?''

(b) Does the fact that a process is in statistical control mean that the products produced will be within specification limits? Discuss briefly.

(c) What is a ''false signal?'' Give an example of how a false signal might occur.

(d) With regard to the sampling and control charting process, what is meant by a ''lack of signal?'' Give an example in which a lack of signal might occur.

7-3.  (a) What is meant by "common cause" variation? Give an example.
      (b) What is meant by "special cause" variation? Give an example.
      (c) In general, who must correct (or improve) the common cause variation inherent in a process? Give an example.
      (d) In general, who must correct (or improve) the special cause variation that occurs in a process? Give an example.

7-4.  (a) How do you know when only common-cause variation is present in a process?
      (b) As an operator, what should you do when you realize that only common-cause variation is present in a process and that the process is producing products within specification limits?
      (c) Same question as (b), but suppose the process is producing out-of-spec products a significant portion of the time.
      (d) What is the probability that an in-control (normally distributed) process will produce sample values outside 3-sigma control limits? Outside 2-sigma control limits?
      (e) What is an "event log?" Describe how one should be used in conjunction with a control chart.

# Unit 8:
# Control Charts for Individual Measurements

# UNIT 8

## Control Charts for Individual Measurements

Charts for individual measurements are generally reserved for quality characteristics for which it is impractical or unreasonable to take multiple observations (i.e., multiple items) at the time the sample is taken. This unit discusses two control charts that are useful in such cases.

**Learning Objectives — When you have completed this unit, you should:**

A. Be able to set up and analyze a moving range chart (i.e., an $R_m$ chart).

B. Be able to set up and analyze a control chart for individual measurements (i.e., an x chart).

## 8-1. Introduction

An individuals chart (or x chart) is a control chart on which single measurements of a quality characteristic are plotted (e.g., individual temperature or pressure measurements). Developed by William Shewhart in the 1920s, single measurements are typically used when it is difficult, impractical, or uneconomical to obtain multiple measurements during a short period of time (e.g., destructive testing) or when multiple measurements are essentially the same as a single measurement (e.g., when a mixture is homogeneous). Under these conditions, control charts based on multiple measurements, namely $\bar{x}$ and R charts (Unit 9), are inappropriate. When process control is based on individual measurements, the x chart is frequently used along with an accompanying moving range chart.

While using an individuals chart is much the same as using other types of control charts, there are differences: (1) There is the obvious problem of estimating the process variation; that is, how does one determine process variation at each sample point from only one measurement? The approach typically used is to estimate the process variation based on a moving range, usually a two-period moving range. (2) Since individual values are sometimes nonnormal (e.g., skewed), probability estimates based on normal distribution assumptions may not be appropriate. (3) Charts based on single-value samples are not as sensitive to process changes as charts based on multi-value samples. Since single data points generally yield less information about a process than multiple readings, there is a smaller chance that single-value samples will indicate an out-of-control condition at the time it occurs than will multi-value samples. (4) It usually takes longer to establish reliable control limits for individual measurement charts than for multiple measurement charts even when the process is in control, since each sample yields only one value.

Nevertheless, x charts and moving range charts are often used, especially in the chemical, pulp and paper, refining, and hydrocarbon processing industries. In fact, because control limits for the individuals chart require an estimate of the process standard deviation, development of the moving range chart should precede the individuals chart; that is, an estimate of the process standard deviation is appropriate only after it has been established that the process variation is stable. When the moving ranges are in control, the process variation can be estimated and the control limits for the individuals chart calculated. Of course, individual measurements can be plotted on a chart without control limits (i.e., a run chart) from the outset, but control limits should not be drawn until the process variation is in control.

The process of creating and using both the moving range chart and the individuals charts can be summarized as follows:

1.  Select the process characteristic to be monitored.

2.  Determine an appropriate sampling interval and collect a sufficient number of trial values to develop a moving range chart. In practice, at least 20 observations should be collected.

3.  Calculate the centerline and control limits for the moving range chart (using the guidelines described in the next section) and plot the trial observations on the chart. (An accompanying run chart of individual values may also be set up at this time, but control limits should not be drawn.)

4.  Examine the points on the moving range chart for variation due to special causes (indicated by values outside the control limits and other abnormal tendencies) and take

action as necessary to bring the process variation into control.

5.  Once the moving range chart indicates that only common cause variation is present, extend the chart's limits into the future as a guide for future observations, then compute the centerline and control limits for the individuals chart. Ideally, these control limits would be based on 100 or more measurements.

6.  Plot the individual values used earlier to develop the moving range chart on the individuals chart and examine the plotted points for indications of process irregularities. (a) Are all the values plotted within the control limits? (b) Is the process average satisfactorily centered? (c) Is the process spread inappropriately large? (d) Are there measurements outside the specification limits?

7.  Take action as necessary to bring the process into control and to correct problems. When the individual measurements are in control, extend the control limits as a guide for future observations and process control.

## 8-2.  Moving Range Chart ($R_m$ Chart)

The moving range chart is primarily used to identify the presence of special causes of variation in the process. It is also used to establish the level of variation present in an in-control process (so that an estimate of the process standard deviation can be made). It consists of a centerline and a pair of control limits. In practice, however, only the upper control limit has any meaning since the lower control limit is generally 0.00. This is because ranges (by definition) cannot be negative and because moving range calculations are almost always based on only a few moving periods (typically two).

The two-period moving range is the simplest (and most widely used) moving range. It is defined as the absolute value of the difference between the values of successive individual observations. For example, suppose that five consecutive observations are 10, 15, 13, 16, and 12. The four consecutive pairs of values are (10, 15), (15, 13), (13, 16), and (16, 12). The four associated moving range values are 5, 2, 3, and 4. (Note: There will always be one fewer two-period moving range value than there are data points.)

Of course, moving ranges can be based on groups of consecutive observations larger than two. For example, consider the same five observations but with a moving range subset size of three (also called, "three-period moving range"). As such, the three subsets are (10, 15, 13), (15, 13, 16), and (13, 16, 12) and the three associated moving ranges are 5, 3, and 4. If the subset size had been four (i.e., (10, 15, 13, 16) and (15, 13, 16, 12)), the two four-period moving ranges for the group of five observations would be 6 and 4.

Generally, measurements from two consecutive periods are used to compute moving ranges. The advantages are simplicity and the fact that estimates of process variation are based on more recent data. If a two-period moving range is used, the individual moving ranges for k observations are

$$R_{mi} = |x_i - x_{i-1}|$$

where i = 2, 3, 4, . . . , k. The two-period average moving range is typically used as the moving range chart's centerline and is computed as

$$\overline{R}_m = \sum_{i=1}^{k-1} \frac{R_{mi}}{(k-1)}$$

The control limits for the moving range chart employ the same factors (Table 8-1) used in computing the limits of the range chart (discussed in Unit 10). Note that even though the measurements are sampled individually, it is the number of readings grouped together to form the moving range (e.g.,

| Subgroup Size | Ranges | | Standard Deviation | |
|---|---|---|---|---|
| n | $D_3$ | $D_4$ | $d_2$ | $E_2$ |
| 2 | 0.000 | 3.268 | 1.128 | 2.660 |
| 3 | 0.000 | 2.574 | 1.693 | 1.772 |
| 4 | 0.000 | 2.282 | 2.059 | 1.457 |
| 5 | 0.000 | 2.115 | 2.326 | 1.290 |
| 6 | 0.000 | 2.004 | 2.534 | 1.184 |
| 7 | 0.076 | 1.924 | 2.704 | 1.109 |
| 8 | 0.136 | 1.864 | 2.847 | 1.054 |
| 9 | 0.184 | 1.816 | 2.970 | 1.010 |
| 10 | 0.223 | 1.777 | 3.078 | 0.975 |

Note: $E_2$ is used later in the unit in developing individuals chart control limits. Note that $E_2 = 3/d_2$.
**TABLE 8-1. Factors Used in Computing Individuals and Moving Range Control Limits**

n = 2 for a two-period moving range) that determines the nominal sample size or, as it indicated in Table 8-1, the "subgroup size." The general forms for the control limit calculations are shown below.

$$UCL_{MR} = D_4\overline{R}_m$$

$$LCL_{MR} = D_3\overline{R}_m$$

Since the moving range is usually based on a subset of size two, the factors $D_3 = 0.000$ and $D_4 = 3.268$ are almost always used. In practice, this means that the upper and lower control limits for the moving range chart are

$$UCL_{MR} = 3.268\overline{R}_m$$

$$LCL_{MR} = 0.000$$

It is important to recognize that the factors shown in Table 8-1 are based on the assumptions that the individual measurements are independent (i.e., not strongly autocorrelated) and normally distributed. Ramifications of violating these assumptions are discussed in more detail in this unit's Summary.

**Example 8-1:** Consider 47 individual measurements of a quality characteristic where one measurement is taken every 12 hours during the production of rubber. Individual measurements of the characteristic are appropriate because the molten rubber is homogeneous during most of the production process (i.e., multiple measurements taken at the same time tend to be identical). The target value for the characteristic (which will be referred to as R1) is 4400 units and the specification limits are 4400 ± 1000 units. Table 8-2 shows the values observed during a 3-1/2 week period.

Is the rubber production process in control? The question must be answered in stages. First, since it is necessary to monitor the process based on the results of individual measurements, an individuals chart/moving range chart pair is selected for use. The following steps describe the implementation of a two-period moving range chart for the process. An individuals chart for the same process, which can be employed once the process variation has been estimated, is described in the next section.

| Time | Week | | | |
|---|---|---|---|---|
| | 1 | 2 | 3 | 4 |
| 6 a.m. | 4471 | 4162 | 4371 | 4684 |
| 6 p.m. | 4438 | 4473 | 4277 | 4257 |
| 6 a.m. | 4454 | 4616 | 4102 | 4327 |
| 6 p.m. | 4325 | 4530 | 4527 | 4476 |
| 6 a.m. | 4335 | 4102 | 4173 | 4495 |
| 6 p.m. | 4541 | 4412 | 4374 | |
| 6 a.m. | 4183 | 4354 | 4403 | |
| 6 p.m. | 4514 | 4446 | 4512 | |
| 6 a.m. | 4626 | 4191 | 4023 | |
| 6 p.m. | 4519 | 4732 | 4102 | |
| 6 a.m. | 4541 | 4247 | 4677 | |
| 6 p.m. | 4518 | 4685 | 4556 | |
| 6 a.m. | 4322 | 4482 | 4483 | |
| 6 p.m. | 3725 | 4057 | 4596 | |

**TABLE 8-2. Individual R1 Measurements**

1. The first step is to compute the two-period moving range values. These are shown in Table 8-3. For example, $|x_2 - x_1| = |4438 - 4471| = 33$ and $|x_3 - x_2| = |4454 - 4438| = 16$. The average moving range is shown at the bottom of Table 8-3. It is the sum of the individual moving ranges divided by the total number of moving ranges (i.e., $\overline{R}_m = (33 + 16 + 129 + \ldots + 19)/46 = 223$).

2. The centerline and control limits are computed based on the average moving range and the corresponding $D_4$ and $D_3$ values. Since the moving ranges are based on measurements

| Day/ Time | Week 1 | Moving Range | Week 2 | Moving Range | Week 3 | Moving Range | Week 4 | Moving Range |
|---|---|---|---|---|---|---|---|---|
| 1–6 a.m. | 4471 | — | 4162 | 437 | 4371 | 314 | 4684 | 88 |
| 1–6 p.m. | 4438 | 33 | 4473 | 311 | 4277 | 94 | 4257 | 427 |
| 2–6 a.m. | 4454 | 16 | 4616 | 143 | 4102 | 175 | 4327 | 70 |
| 2–6 p.m. | 4325 | 129 | 4530 | 96 | 4527 | 425 | 4476 | 149 |
| 3–6 a.m. | 4335 | 10 | 4102 | 428 | 4173 | 354 | 4495 | 19 |
| 3–6 p.m. | 4541 | 206 | 4412 | 310 | 4374 | 201 | | |
| 4–6 a.m. | 4183 | 358 | 4354 | 58 | 4403 | 29 | | |
| 4–6 p.m. | 4514 | 331 | 4446 | 92 | 4512 | 109 | | |
| 5–6 a.m. | 4626 | 112 | 4191 | 255 | 4023 | 489 | | |
| 5–6 p.m. | 4519 | 107 | 4732 | 541 | 4102 | 79 | | |
| 6–6 a.m. | 4541 | 22 | 4247 | 485 | 4677 | 575 | | |
| 6–6 p.m. | 4518 | 23 | 4685 | 438 | 4556 | 121 | | |
| 7–6 a.m. | 4322 | 196 | 4482 | 203 | 4483 | 73 | | |
| 7–6 p.m. | 3725 | 597 | 4057 | 425 | 4596 | 113 | | |

$\bar{x} = 206,424/47$     $\overline{R}_m = 10,258/46$
   $= 4,392$          $= 223$

**TABLE 8-3. Individual R1 Measurements and Two-Period Moving Ranges**

in two consecutive periods (i.e., n = 2), the factors $D_4$ = 3.268 and $D_3$ = 0.000 from Table 8-1 are used.

Centerline:

$$\overline{R}_m = 223$$

Control Limits:

$$UCL_{MR} = 3.268(223)$$
$$= 728.6$$
$$LCL_{MR} = 0.0$$

3. The centerline and control limits are then plotted along with the individual moving range values (Fig. 8-1).

4. Once the individual moving ranges are plotted, the chart can be analyzed. There are no points outside the control limits and no other obvious signs of inconsistent process activity (such as 10 consecutive increasing measurements), indicating a stable process. As such, since the process variation appears to be in control, an estimate of the process standard deviation based on the average moving range can be found.

If the two-period moving range chart had indicated an out-of-control condition, it would have been necessary to determine the cause of variation and then make appropriate control chart or process adjustments before estimating the process standard deviation. For example, suppose that a single measurement had been recorded improperly and that this error had caused two moving ranges to fall above the

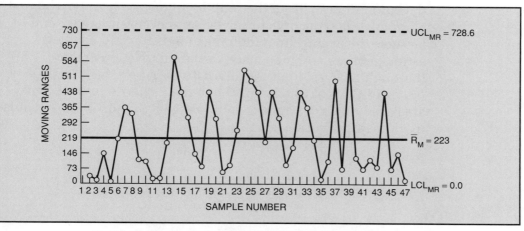

Fig. 8-1. Moving Range Chart for Rubber Product Characteristic

upper control limit. It would be necessary to correct that measurement, recalculate the two moving range values that include the corrected value, recalculate the moving range chart's centerline and control limits, and then reevaluate the process variation in light of the new information. On the other hand, suppose that an out-of-control condition on the moving range chart led to the discovery of a special cause of process variation (e.g., a change in an inappropriate process control rule). Additional data must be collected and the moving range chart's centerline and control limits recomputed, based on the new data, before control can be established.

## 8-3. Individuals Chart (x Chart)

Once the moving range chart indicates that the process variation is in control, an estimate of the process standard deviation $\sigma_x$ can be calculated. Control limits for an individuals chart can then be set up. Three-sigma control limits for the individuals chart are

$$UCL_x = \mu_x + 3\sigma_x$$

$$LCL_x = \mu_x - 3\sigma_x$$

Either the process target value or the sample mean of the individual measurements, whichever is more appropriate, is used to estimate $\mu_x$. The process standard deviation $\sigma_x$ is estimated using one of two approaches: (1) calculate an estimate of the standard deviation based on the average of the moving ranges, or (2) calculate an estimate of the standard deviation directly from the individual measurements. The first alternative is typically chosen because of its simplicity and because the average moving range tends to yield a better estimate of the common cause variation. (Note: A more thorough discussion of the alternatives is presented in Unit 11, Issues in Control Charting.) When the x chart's control limits are based on the average moving range $\overline{R}_m$ (and $\overline{x}$), the formulas used are as follows:

$$\begin{aligned}
UCL_x &= \mu_x + 3\sigma_x \\
&= \overline{x} + 3\overline{R}_m/d_2 \\
&= \overline{x} + (3/d_2)\overline{R}_m \\
&= \overline{x} + E_2\overline{R}_m
\end{aligned}$$

where $E_2 = 3/d_2$

$$LCL_x = \mu_x - 3\sigma_x$$
$$= \overline{x} - 3\overline{R}_m/d_2$$
$$= \overline{x} - (3/d_2)\overline{R}_m$$
$$= \overline{x} - E_2\overline{R}_m$$

where $d_2$ and, consequently, $E_2$ depend on the number of periods used in computing the individual moving ranges. Both factors are presented in Table 8-1. Since it is common practice to use the two-period moving range, the x chart's three-sigma control limits are usually shown as

$$UCL_x = \overline{x} + 2.66\,\overline{R}_m$$
$$LCL_x = \overline{x} - 2.66\,\overline{R}_m$$

(Note: Since $E_2 = 3/d_2$, for a 2-period moving range, $d_2 = 1.128$ and $E_2 = 3/1.128 = 2.66$.)

**Example 8-1 (Continued):**

Since the two-period moving range chart indicated that the rubber product's process variation is in control, the process standard deviation can be estimated from the process data and control limits for the individuals chart can be set up.

1. The first step is to set the control chart's centerline. Either the process target value (i.e., 4400 units) or the overall sample mean (i.e., $\overline{x} = 4392$, from Table 9-3) can be used as the centerline. Since the initial concern is process control rather than the production level attained, the overall sample mean is chosen for use.

2. The control limits are set next. The estimate of the process standard deviation is based on the average moving range (i.e., $\overline{R}_m = 223$, from Table 8-3). The average moving range was developed from two-period moving ranges. Therefore, $d_2 = 1.128$ and $E_2 = 2.66$.

Centerline:

$$\overline{x} = 4392$$

Control Limits:

$$UCL_x = 4392 + (3/d_2)\overline{R}_m$$

$$= 4392 + (3/1.128)(223)$$

$$= 4392 + 2.66(223)$$

$$= 4392 + 593$$

$$= 4985$$

$$LCL_x = 4392 - 2.66(223)$$

$$= 4392 - 593$$

$$= 3799$$

3. The centerline and control limits are then plotted along with the 47 individual values. The x chart is shown in the upper part of Fig. 8-2. The lower part of Fig. 8-2 shows the same moving range chart originally presented in Fig. 8-1.

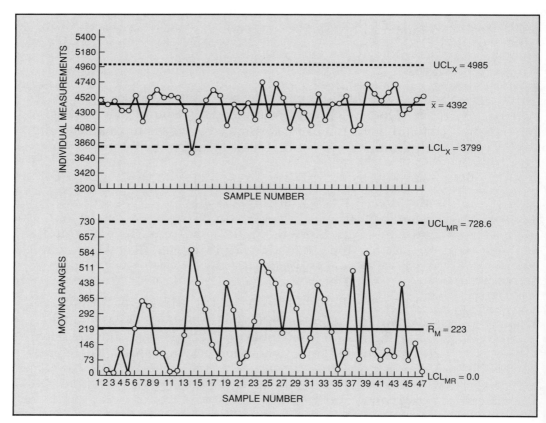

**Fig. 8-2. Individuals Chart and Moving Range Chart for Rubber Product Characteristic**

4. Once the centerline and control limits are in place, the measurements on the individuals chart can be analyzed. The 14th individual value (3725) falls below the lower control limit. As a result of follow-up efforts, it was found that the measurement should have been recorded as 4725. All the other x values are within the control limits and seem to exhibit in-control characteristics.

5. Replacing the 3725 value with 4725, recalculating the two affected moving range values, and recalculating the moving range chart's centerline and control limits yield the following:

Centerline:

$$\overline{R}_m = 10{,}190/46 = 221.5$$

Control Limits:

$$UCL_{MR} = 3.268(221.5)$$

$$= 723.9$$

$$LCL_{MR} = 0.0$$

An examination of the moving ranges (Fig. 8-3) indicates that no points fall outside the control limits and that no other nonrandom patterns (such as a trend or zig-zag pattern) are present.

6. A revised x chart is then set up. Calculations are given below and the revised x chart is shown in Fig. 8-3.

$$\overline{x} = 207{,}424/47 = 4413.3, \overline{R}_m = 221.5$$

Centerline:

$$\overline{x} = 4413.3$$

Control Limits:

$$UCL_x = 4413.3 + 2.66(221.5)$$

$$= 5002.5$$

$$LCL_x = 4413.3 - 2.66(221.5)$$

$$= 3824.1$$

Upon examining Fig. 8-3, several encouraging characteristics are apparent: (1) all values are within the

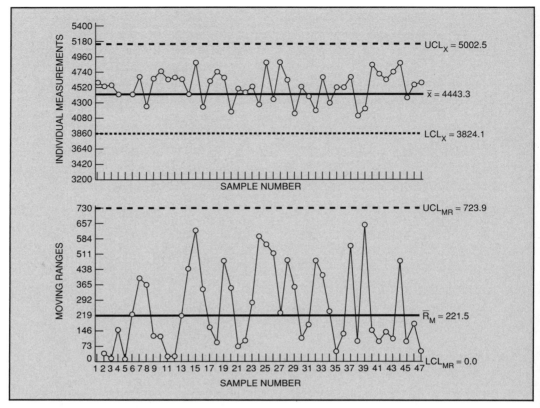

**Fig. 8-3. Revised Individuals Chart and Moving Range Chart for Rubber Product Characteristic**

control limits; (2) no obvious nonrandom patterns or dramatic inconsistencies are present; (3) the process average, although not exactly 4400, is nearly centered; (4) the process spread seems to be relatively small in comparison to the control limits; and, (5) there are no points outside the specification limits (i.e., all points are less than 5400 and greater than 3400).

7. Since the process is now in statistical control, the control limits on both charts can be extended for continued process monitoring.

**Example 8-2:** Table 8-4 shows individual melt index measurements taken every two hours on resins produced in a polymer production process. Individuals and moving range control charts are chosen to monitor the process because the mixtures from which the samples are taken tend to be homogeneous during relatively short time periods (e.g., 2 hours).

| Sample Number | MI Value | Sample Number | MI Value | Sample Number | MI Value | Sample Number | MI Value |
|---|---|---|---|---|---|---|---|
| 1 | 0.58 | 11 | 0.60 | 21 | 0.59 | 31 | 0.59 |
| 2 | 0.62 | 12 | 0.58 | 22 | 0.58 | 32 | 0.56 |
| 3 | 0.62 | 13 | 0.62 | 23 | 0.58 | 33 | 0.58 |
| 4 | 0.57 | 14 | 0.72 | 24 | 0.57 | 34 | 0.59 |
| 5 | 0.52 | 15 | 0.62 | 25 | 0.57 | 35 | 0.65 |
| 6 | 0.58 | 16 | 0.58 | 26 | 0.58 | 36 | 0.74 |
| 7 | 0.57 | 17 | 0.57 | 27 | 0.61 | 37 | 0.78 |
| 8 | 0.57 | 18 | 0.58 | 28 | 0.60 | 38 | 0.75 |
| 9 | 0.58 | 19 | 0.57 | 29 | 0.62 | 39 | 0.76 |
| 10 | 0.58 | 20 | 0.58 | 30 | 0.60 | 40 | 0.70 |

TABLE 8-4. Melt Index Measurements Taken at Two-Hour Intervals

The melt index target value for the process is 0.58. The process may be adjusted to achieve the target by changing the reactor temperature. Also, as the result of data collected from other "identical" polymer production processes, the average two-period moving range is known to be $\overline{R}_m = 0.035$. (Results from "identical" processes are used to set $\overline{R}_m$ rather than the data in Table 8-4 since the capability of this process is not uncertain.)

The general procedure used to set up control charts for the process is, of course, the same as described earlier. However, since the centerline is based on a target value and the process standard deviation is estimated from historic values (rather than from the sample of 40 values), some of the steps shown earlier in Example 8-1 may be omitted. The centerline and control limits for the moving range chart are set first.

Centerline:

$$\overline{R}_m = 0.035$$

Control Limits:

$$UCL_{MR} = 3.268\ \overline{R}_m$$

$$= 3.268(0.035)$$

$$= 0.115$$

$$LCL_{MR} = 0.0$$

The 39 moving ranges (not shown in Table 8-4) are plotted along with a centerline and control limits in the lower part of Fig. 8-4. The process variation appears to be stable. In fact, the series of moving ranges from sample 17 through sample 34 all exhibit values below the centerline, a possible indicator of too little variation (e.g., analyzer broken at acceptable value). Such

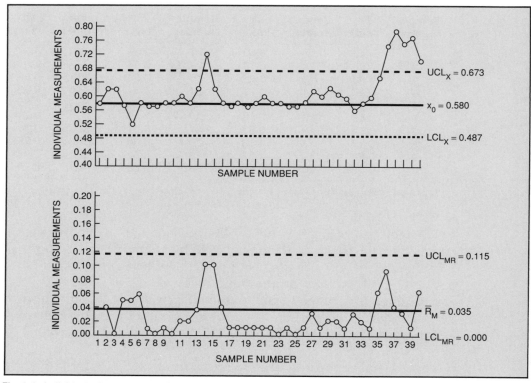

**Fig. 8-4. Individuals Chart and Moving Range Chart for Polymer Production Process**

a sequence is called a "run," and represents one example of a nonnormal pattern. A follow-up study revealed no abnormal occurrences, however. This is not surprising since the distribution of moving ranges is usually skewed with the bulk of the moving ranges clustered near zero.

Next, the control limits for the individuals chart are set. The target melt index value $x_0 = 0.58$ is used as the centerline. The x chart is shown in the upper part of Figure 8-4.

Centerline:

$$x_0 = 0.58$$

Control Limits:

$$UCL_x = x_0 + 2.66\overline{R}_m$$

$$= 0.58 + 2.66(0.035)$$

$$= 0.58 + 0.093$$

$$= 0.673$$

$$LCL_x = x_0 - 2.66\overline{R}_m$$

$$= 0.58 + 2.66(0.035)$$

$$= 0.58 + 0.093$$

$$= 0.673$$

Again, $E_2 = 2.66$ was chosen since a two-period moving range was used to estimate the process variation.

The melt index values for samples 14 and 36 through 40 fall outside the control limits. It was found that the large sample melt index value of sample 14 was the result of a measurement error, but the melt index values recorded for samples 36 through 40 signaled a shift in the process average due to a special cause. A process modification (temperature adjustment in the reactor) was made and the process was brought under control. Since neither the centerlines nor control limits for either chart were based on the Table 8-4 results, no adjustments to the control charts were necessary.

The decision to leave the control limits unchanged after an out-of-control sequence has been identified is appropriate in this case. However, if the centerline and control limits had been developed based on the process data shown in Table 8-3 and an out-of-control sequence occurred, the out-of-control points would have been omitted and a new set of centerlines and control limits for both the $R_m$ and x charts would have been calculated based on the remaining data. This important, iterative sequence is demonstrated several times in subsequent units.

## 8-4. Summary

The x chart's control limits are based on the assumption that the measurements when plotted will be normally distributed if the process is in control. Frequently, particularly in the process industries, this assumption is not true. When this is the case, consideration should be given to using some other type of control chart, such as a CUSUM chart (Unit 13) or some type of moving average chart (Unit 14). Both of these alternative chart types can be based on individual measurements but group the measurements in some way, at least partially to compensate for the lack of normality. This usually has a normalizing effect on the points plotted (because of the central limit theorem) and frequently results in a more effective monitoring process.

In this unit and in Unit 9, out-of-control decisions are based primarily on three-sigma control limit criteria; that is, only when a point falls outside the three-sigma control limits are special causes of variation looked for. This rather simplistic approach is usually adequate for avoiding overcontrol (a so-called Type I error) and is sufficient for the examples in this unit, but it often overlooks more subtle special causes of variation. In Unit 10, the three-sigma criteria are enhanced by the addition of several reliable rules of thumb to help identify nonrandom patterns (i.e., zone rules, run rules).

In practice, x charts are sometimes applied without accompanying $R_m$ charts. The reasoning behind this is that, since individual measurements are already plotted on the x chart, sudden process shifts (i.e., spikes) will appear on it and the moving range chart is therefore unnecessary. While this is often true, there are situations in which the moving range chart will provide an out-of-control signal that the x chart overlooks. For example, if one measurement well below the mean (but above the lower control limit) is followed by a second measurement well above the mean (but below the upper control limit), the x chart gives no out-of-control signal, while the $R_m$ chart might appropriately provide an out-of-control indication. For this reason, especially since the additional effort is minimal, it is a good practice to accompany the x chart with a moving range chart.

## Exercises

8-1. The following sample measurements were taken from a process known to be in statistical control: 42, 52, 64, 45, 53, 56, 70, 49, 62. Compute preliminary estimates of the upper and lower control limits for both a two-period moving range chart and an individuals chart used to monitor the process.

8-2. The spread of individual observations taken from a normal distribution may be best approximated by which of the following formulas? (a) $6\overline{R}_m/d_2$, (b) $2A_2\overline{R}_m$, (c) $\overline{R}_m/d_2$, or (d) $D_4\overline{R}_m$.

8-3. Explain the meanings and functions of the three factors 9(i.e., $d_2$, $E_2$, and $D_4$) commonly used in setting up individuals and moving range charts.

8-4. The table below shows 30 individual measurements of an additive for a high density polyethylene resin and the corresponding two-period moving ranges. The measurement x is in parts per million (ppm). Construct a two-period moving range chart and, once the variation is in control, an individuals chart for the process. Discuss your findings.

| Sample No. | x | $R_m$ | Sample No. | x | $R_m$ | Sample No. | x | $R_m$ |
|---|---|---|---|---|---|---|---|---|
| 1 | 950 | — | 11 | 915 | 64 | 21 | 971 | 47 |
| 2 | 947 | 3 | 12 | 906 | 9 | 22 | 936 | 35 |
| 3 | 949 | 3 | 13 | 948 | 42 | 23 | 916 | 20 |
| 4 | 878 | 71 | 14 | 972 | 24 | 24 | 945 | 29 |
| 5 | 953 | 75 | 15 | 975 | 3 | 25 | 969 | 24 |
| 6 | 956 | 3 | 16 | 978 | 3 | 25 | 985 | 16 |
| 7 | 977 | 21 | 17 | 929 | 49 | 27 | 896 | 89 |
| 8 | 956 | 21 | 18 | 950 | 21 | 28 | 932 | 35 |
| 9 | 922 | 34 | 19 | 941 | 9 | 29 | 939 | 7 |
| 10 | 979 | 57 | 20 | 924 | 17 | 30 | 937 | 2 |
| SUM | 9467 | 287 | | 9438 | 241 | | 9426 | 305 |

**Additive Measurements**

8-5. For the purpose of lab-instrument calibration control, data values were collected over a 20-day period. At the beginning of each shift, one measurement was made on a standard material using the instrument. The measurements are shown below, along with two-period moving range values. Set up and plot a two-period moving range chart and, once the variation is in control, an individuals chart for the process. Discuss your findings.

| Day | $x_1$ | $R_m$ | $x_2$ | $R_m$ | $x_3$ | $R_m$ |
|---|---|---|---|---|---|---|
| 1 | 0.98 | — | 0.96 | 0.02 | 0.96 | 0.00 |
| 2 | 1.02 | 0.06 | 0.92 | 0.10 | 0.92 | 0.00 |
| 3 | 1.00 | 0.08 | 1.05 | 0.05 | 1.04 | 0.01 |
| 4 | 1.03 | 0.01 | 1.04 | 0.01 | 0.98 | 0.06 |
| 5 | 0.92 | 0.06 | 1.09 | 0.17 | 0.96 | 0.13 |
| 6 | 1.06 | 0.10 | 0.98 | 0.08 | 1.05 | 0.07 |
| 7 | 0.97 | 0.08 | 0.99 | 0.02 | 0.99 | 0.00 |
| 8 | 0.99 | 0.00 | 1.02 | 0.03 | 1.01 | 0.01 |
| 9 | 1.04 | 0.03 | 0.95 | 0.09 | 0.90 | 0.05 |
| 10 | 0.86 | 0.04 | 0.85 | 0.01 | 0.83 | 0.02 |

**Standard Material Measurements**

8-6. The data shown below represent the percentage of budget spent on a variety of projects during the last several quarters. Construct a two-period moving range chart to monitor project expenditures and, once the variation is in control, an individuals chart as well. Briefly discuss your findings.

| Project No. | Percent of Budget | Project No. | Percent of Budget |
|---|---|---|---|
| 1 | 110 | 16 | 97 |
| 2 | 100 | 17 | 107 |
| 3 | 90 | 18 | 95 |
| 4 | 99 | 19 | 90 |
| 5 | 91 | 20 | 88 |
| 6 | 95 | 21 | 118 |
| 7 | 92 | 22 | 94 |
| 8 | 88 | 23 | 98 |
| 9 | 129 | 24 | 102 |
| 10 | 91 | 25 | 104 |
| 11 | 108 | 26 | 107 |
| 12 | 104 | 27 | 97 |
| 13 | 112 | 28 | 96 |
| 14 | 96 | 29 | 101 |
| 15 | 102 | 30 | 93 |

Project Budget Performance

8-7. The following data represent the chlorine content in a polymer. Construct a two-period moving range chart to monitor chlorine content and, once the variation is in control, an individuals chart as well. Use the chlorine target value of 36.5 as the x chart's centerline. Is the process in control? Briefly discuss your findings.

| Sample | Chlorine Content | Sample | Chlorine Content | Sample | Chlorine Content |
|---|---|---|---|---|---|
| 1 | 36.4 | 16 | 36.6 | 31 | 36.6 |
| 2 | 36.6 | 17 | 36.0 | 32 | 36.8 |
| 3 | 36.3 | 18 | 37.1 | 33 | 36.4 |
| 4 | 35.6 | 19 | 36.6 | 34 | 36.9 |
| 5 | 35.1 | 20 | 36.5 | 35 | 35.8 |
| 6 | 35.1 | 21 | 36.8 | 36 | 37.0 |
| 7 | 35.3 | 22 | 37.1 | 37 | 34.8 |
| 8 | 36.0 | 23 | 37.0 | 38 | 35.5 |
| 9 | 36.1 | 24 | 36.7 | 39 | 36.5 |
| 10 | 34.5 | 25 | 36.1 | 40 | 36.5 |
| 11 | 36.4 | 26 | 36.1 | 41 | 36.2 |
| 12 | 36.1 | 27 | 36.6 | 42 | 35.1 |
| 13 | 36.6 | 28 | 36.1 | 43 | 35.5 |
| 14 | 36.5 | 29 | 36.5 | 44 | 35.0 |
| 15 | 36.7 | 30 | 36.5 | 45 | 35.3 |

Chlorine Content of a Polymer

8-8. The data shown below represent the flow index values (grams/10 minutes) for two laboratories based on samples from the same materials. (a) Construct one two-period moving range chart for each lab's process. Terminate the control charting process after the initial moving range values have been plotted. Are both processes in control? Briefly discuss your findings. (b) Compute differences in flow index values for each sample (e.g., $3.05 - 3.15 = -0.10$) and construct a two-period moving range chart and an x chart based on these differences. Plot appropriate values on each chart and comment on your findings.

| No. | Flow Index Lab 1 | Flow Index Lab 2 | No. | Flow Index Lab 1 | Flow Index Lab 2 |
|-----|------|------|-----|------|------|
| 1 | 3.05 | 3.15 | 14 | 3.85 | 3.90 |
| 2 | 3.00 | 3.05 | 15 | 2.80 | 3.00 |
| 3 | 3.10 | 3.00 | 16 | 2.65 | 2.55 |
| 4 | 2.95 | 2.95 | 17 | 2.65 | 2.60 |
| 5 | 2.85 | 2.80 | 18 | 3.40 | 3.30 |
| 6 | 2.90 | 2.95 | 19 | 2.80 | 2.85 |
| 7 | 3.15 | 3.10 | 20 | 3.40 | 3.70 |
| 8 | 3.25 | 3.25 | 21 | 3.70 | 3.60 |
| 9 | 3.20 | 3.25 | 22 | 3.80 | 3.65 |
| 10 | 3.15 | 3.10 | 23 | 2.45 | 2.55 |
| 11 | 2.80 | 2.85 | 24 | 2.79 | 2.86 |
| 12 | 3.50 | 3.45 | 25 | 3.29 | 3.40 |
| 13 | 2.80 | 2.26 | | | |

Flow Index Values

# Unit 9:
# Control Charts for Averages and Ranges

# UNIT 9

## Control Charts for Averages and Ranges

Control charts for sample averages and sample ranges (i.e., $\bar{x}$ and R charts) are probably the most widely used of all control charts in the discrete manufacturing (i.e., parts) industry. They are appropriate when multiple measurements at each sampling point provide independent measures of process performance. The two charts are used together because they are able to detect different kinds of process changes. This unit describes both types of charts.

**Learning Objectives** — When you have completed this unit, you should:

A. Be able to set up and analyze an R chart.

B. Be able to set up and analyze an $\bar{x}$ chart.

C. Know what a standardized control chart is, when one is appropriate, and how such a chart is developed.

## 9-1. Introduction

The $\bar{x}$ chart is intended to help monitor and control the location of the process (i.e., the process mean), while the R chart is to help monitor and control the spread of the process (i.e., the process variation). The two charts are usually used together. Because development of the $\bar{x}$ chart's control limits requires a stable estimate of the process standard deviation, however, control of the process variation should be established first, that is, $\bar{x}$ chart control limits should not be set up until the R chart indicates that the process variation is stable.

As mentioned above, $\bar{x}$ and R charts are often used when multiple measurements at each sampling point provide independent (i.e., non-autocorrelated) measures of process performance. For example, suppose a process produces 20 batches of a chemical compound each hour and that five of those batches are selected at random for testing. Each batch results in an independent measure of process performance. By summing the five measurements and dividing by five, an estimate of the process mean at that point in time is found. By subtracting the smallest measurement value from the largest measurement value in each sample, an estimate of the process variation (i.e., the sample range) is found.

It is important to recognize that multiple measurements do not always mean multiple independent measures. For example, suppose a gasoline production process is sampled each hour by filling five bottles with gasoline. In this case, because the gasoline is homogeneous, the five measurements essentially represent one measurement duplicated five times. In this case, charts for individual measurements, such as x and $R_m$ charts (discussed in Unit 8), are more appropriate.

Charts based on multiple measurements are preferred over charts based on individual measurements for at least two reasons: (1) Control charts based on multiple measurements are more sensitive to changes in the process than control charts based on individual measurements. (2) The central limit theorem (discussed in Unit 6) states that the distribution of average values is normally distributed regardless of the distribution of individual measurements. The normality "guarantee" allows probability estimates to be made regarding the process mean. The remainder of this unit describes two control charts based on multiple measurements: $\bar{x}$ charts and R charts.

## 9-2. Range Chart (R Chart)

The first step in developing an R chart is to decide on the quality characteristic to be monitored, the sample size, and the sampling interval. The process then consists of establishing a centerline and three standard deviation control limits. The centerline is usually set using the average range $\bar{R}$. Three-sigma control limits are set, using the following relationships:

$$UCL_R = D_4\bar{R}$$

$$UCL_R = D_3\bar{R}$$

The $D_3$ and $D_4$ values are shown in Table 9-1 for only n = 2, 3, . . . , 10, since sample sizes larger than 10 are rarely used. Note that for small samples, only the upper control limit is meaningful (i.e., $D_3$ is 0.000 for n = 1, 2, . . . , 6). This is another way of saying that the sample range distribution is

| Sample Size, n | $A_2$ | $D_3$ | $D_4$ | $d_2$ |
|---|---|---|---|---|
| 2 | 1.880 | 0.0 | 3.268 | 1.128 |
| 3 | 1.023 | 0.0 | 2.574 | 1.693 |
| 4 | 0.729 | 0.0 | 2.282 | 2.059 |
| 5 | 0.577 | 0.0 | 2.115 | 2.326 |
| 6 | 0.483 | 0.0 | 2.004 | 2.534 |
| 7 | 0.419 | 0.076 | 1.924 | 2.704 |
| 8 | 0.373 | 0.136 | 1.864 | 2.847 |
| 9 | 0.337 | 0.184 | 1.816 | 2.970 |
| 10 | 0.308 | 0.223 | 1.777 | 3.078 |

Note: The factor $A_2$ is used in constructing control limits for $\bar{x}$ charts; $D_3$ and $D_4$ are used in constructing control limits for R charts; $d_2$ is used in computing estimates of the process standard deviation based on the average range (i.e., $\hat{\sigma}_x = \bar{R}/d_2$).

**TABLE 9-1. Factors Used in Computing $\bar{x}$ Chart and R Chart Control Limits**

skewed to the right for small sample sizes. For example, suppose process samples of size n = 5 are taken each hour. Samples taken over a two-week period have an average range of 10 (i.e., $\bar{R}$ = 10). Since n = 5, $D_3$ = 0 and $D_4$ = 2.115 are used, so that the R chart's control limits are

$$\text{UCL}_R = D_4\bar{R}$$

$$= (2.115)10$$

$$= 21.15$$

$$\text{LCL}_R = D_3\bar{R}$$

$$= (0.0)10$$

$$= 0.00$$

The simplicity of the formulas makes the actual process of developing $\bar{x}$ and R charts extremely easy. The challenge, however, is to apply the control charts thoughtfully. As a part of the application process, it is important that trial samples be used in validating the control charts before they are used for any type of process control. These trial values are used to determine whether or not special cause variation is present at the beginning of the control charting process. If special causes are present, the process is not yet in statistical control, the control limits for the $\bar{x}$ and R charts are useless for maintaining further control. Only if both the $\bar{x}$ and R charts indicate an in-control process during the trial period should the charts be applied to the actual process.

## 9-3.  Average Chart ($\bar{x}$ Chart)

Sample means (sample averages) are plotted on $\bar{x}$ charts. The control limits for the $\bar{x}$ chart require a meaningful estimate of the process standard deviation. This requires that the process variation, as exhibited on an R chart, be in statistical control. This section describes the development of the $\bar{x}$ chart by assuming that the process variation is already in statistical control.

In fact, $\bar{x}$ values are sometimes plotted on the control chart grid before the control limits are drawn (i.e., a run chart of sample means). The only real disadvantage of plotting the $\bar{x}$ values before setting the control limits is that an inappropriate scale may be chosen for use on the vertical axis of the chart.

Given that the process characteristic to be measured, the sampling interval, and the sample size have been decided on, the next step is to either set the centerline based on some target value or to collect enough measurements (ideally, 100 or more) so that an estimate of the process centerline can be developed with some degree of confidence. In this case, the process mean is estimated by the overall mean (i.e., the average of the averages, called x-bar-bar).

$$\bar{\bar{x}} = (\bar{x}_1 + \bar{x}_2 + \ldots + \bar{x}_m)/m$$

where $\bar{x}_1$, $\bar{x}_2$, etc. represent the individual sample means and m represents the number of sample means found.

Next, the control limits can be calculated and drawn on the chart. If a known value of the process standard deviation (possibly from an "identical" current process) is available, three-sigma (i.e., $\pm 3$ standard deviations) upper and lower control limits for the $\bar{x}$ chart can be calculated as follows:

$$\text{UCL}_{\bar{x}} = \bar{\bar{x}} + 3\sigma_x/\sqrt{n}$$

$$\text{LCL}_{\bar{x}} = \bar{\bar{x}} - 3\sigma_x/\sqrt{n}$$

where $\sigma_x$ is the known process standard deviation for the quality characteristic being measured and n is the size (i.e., the number of measurements) of individual samples. For example, if the process target value is 12, the known process standard deviation is $\sigma_x = 2.8$, and each sample mean is based on a sample of size n = 6, the control limits for the $\bar{x}$ chart are

$$\text{UCL}_{\bar{x}} = 12 + 3(2.8)/\sqrt{6}$$

$$= 12 + 3(2.8)/(2.45)$$

$$= 12 + 3.43$$

$$= 15.43$$

$$\text{LCL}_{\bar{x}} = 12 - 3(2.8)/\sqrt{6}$$

$$= 12 - 3(2.8)/(2.45)$$

$$= 12 - 3.43$$

$$= 8.57$$

The above approach assumes that the process standard deviation is known. Since this is usually not the case, it is necessary to estimate it. Of course, it is important that this estimate not include special cause variation or be based on nonrational subgroups, since the inclusion of special cause variation or measurements from nonrational subgroups typically results in an overestimate of the process standard deviation. For these reasons, it is usually inappropriate to estimate the process standard deviation based on an estimate of the overall process mean $\bar{\bar{x}}$ and the traditional standard deviation formula shown below. (Note: In the formula shown below, N = mn, where m represents the number of samples and n represents the sample size, the number of measurements in each sample.)

$$s = \sqrt{\Sigma(x_i - \bar{\bar{x}})^2/(N - 1)}$$

Fortunately, other approaches are available. Assuming that the R chart shows that the process variation is in control, the average range can be used to obtain a reliable estimate of the process standard deviation. If the R chart shows that process variation is not in control, calculation of an estimate of the process standard deviation and subsequent use of the $\bar{x}$ chart should be delayed until the process variation is brought into control. Why this is important will become obvious in the next few paragraphs. Let $R_1, R_2, \ldots, R_m$ represent the individual ranges from the m samples. Each sample range represents an independent measure of the process variation. The average range is then

$$\bar{R} = (R_1 + R_2 + \ldots + R_m)/m$$

An estimate of the process standard deviation $\sigma_x$ is then

$$\hat{\sigma}_x = \overline{R}/d_2$$

where $d_2$ is a factor dependent on the sample size n. (Recall that $d_2$ values for sample sizes 2 through 10 are shown in Table 9-1.) The upper and lower control limits of the $\overline{x}$ chart can then be written as

$$UCL_{\overline{x}} = \overline{\overline{x}} + 3\hat{\sigma}_x/\sqrt{n}$$
$$= \overline{\overline{x}} + 3\overline{R}/(d_2\sqrt{n})$$
$$LCL_{\overline{x}} = \overline{\overline{x}} - 3\hat{\sigma}_x/\sqrt{n}$$
$$= \overline{\overline{x}} - 3\overline{R}/(d_2\sqrt{n})$$

For convenience, the constant $A_2$, which stands for $3/(d_2\sqrt{n})$, has been tabulated (Table 9-1), so that the $\overline{x}$ chart control limits can be written as

$$UCL_{\overline{x}} = \overline{\overline{x}} + A_2\overline{R}$$
$$LCL_{\overline{x}} = \overline{\overline{x}} - A_2\overline{R}$$

Once the control limits are in place, the sample means can then be plotted and judgments made regarding the process.

**Example 9-1:** Suppose that a process is to be monitored by taking samples of size n = 6 during every shift and measuring the results. Two shifts are worked each day. The findings for the first five days (10 samples) are shown in Table 9-2. (Note: Ideally, control chart parameter estimates should be based on 100 or more data points from 20 or more samples, but for simplicity only 60 data points and 10 samples are used in this example.)

Based on the data shown in Table 9-2 (average range $\overline{R}$ = 5 and sample size n = 6), the R chart's centerline and control limits are

Centerline:

$$\overline{R} = 5$$

| Sample Number | $x_1$ | $x_2$ | $x_3$ | $x_4$ | $x_5$ | $x_6$ | $\bar{x}$ | R |
|---|---|---|---|---|---|---|---|---|
| 1 | 9 | 9 | 8 | 4 | 8 | 7 | 7 | 5 |
| 2 | 8 | 9 | 9 | 8 | 8 | 6 | 8 | 3 |
| 3 | 6 | 2 | 8 | 7 | 7 | 6 | 6 | 6 |
| 4 | 4 | 8 | 6 | 7 | 8 | 9 | 7 | 5 |
| 5 | 6 | 7 | 4 | 8 | 10 | 7 | 7 | 6 |
| 6 | 3 | 10 | 6 | 9 | 3 | 5 | 6 | 7 |
| 7 | 8 | 8 | 5 | 10 | 9 | 8 | 8 | 5 |
| 8 | 8 | 7 | 4 | 8 | 8 | 7 | 7 | 4 |
| 9 | 7 | 8 | 8 | 9 | 11 | 5 | 8 | 6 |
| 10 | 6 | 7 | 7 | 6 | 4 | 6 | 6 | 3 |

$$\text{Totals} = 70 \qquad 50$$
$$\bar{\bar{x}} = 7$$
$$\bar{R} = 5$$

**TABLE 9-2. Sampling Results**

Control Limits:

$$UCL_R = D_4\bar{R}$$

$$= (2.004)(5) \qquad (D_4 = 2.004 \text{ for } n = 6)$$

$$= 10.02$$

$$LCL_R = D_3\bar{R}$$

$$= (0.000)(5) \qquad (D_3 = 0.000 \text{ for } n = 6)$$

$$= 0.00$$

Fig. 9-1 shows the R chart with all 10 sample ranges plotted. Since no points fall outside the control limits and no obvious nonrandom patterns are present, the process variation appears to be stable. Therefore, an $\bar{x}$ chart can be set up.

Based on the data in Table 9-2, $\bar{\bar{x}} = 7$. Since n = 6, $A_2$ is 0.483. (Note: The reader can double check this: $A_2 = 3/(d_2\sqrt{n})$ $= 3/(2.534\sqrt{6})$.) Therefore, the $\bar{x}$ chart's centerline and control limits are

Centerline:

$$\bar{\bar{x}} = 7$$

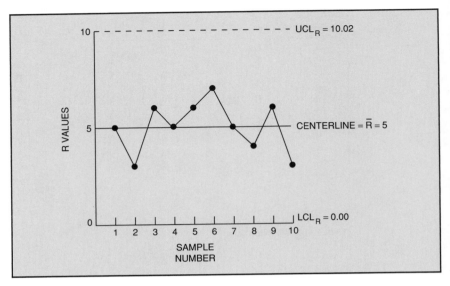

**Fig. 9-1. Range Chart**

Control Limits:

$$UCL_{\bar{x}} = \bar{\bar{x}} + A_2\bar{R}$$

$$= 7 + (0.483)(5)$$

$$= 7 + 2.415$$

$$= 9.415$$

$$LCL_{\bar{x}} = \bar{\bar{x}} - A_2\bar{R}$$

$$= 7 - (0.483)(5)$$

$$= 7 - 2.415$$

$$= 4.585$$

Fig. 9-2 shows the $\bar{x}$ chart with the 10 $\bar{x}$ values plotted. Since all 10 $\bar{x}$ values are within the control limits and since no obvious nonrandom patterns are present, it appears that the process mean is also in control. Since both the R and $\bar{x}$ charts show that the process is in control, the centerlines and control limits on each chart can be extended for continued process monitoring.

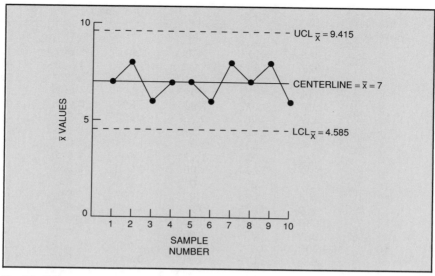

**Fig. 9-2. x̄ Chart**

**Example 9-2:** Suppose that process engineers in the plastics industry are interested in using the melt index (MI) to control the production of high-density polyethylene. The process specification for the melt index of this specific polyethylene is $1.00 \pm 0.10$. One hundred melt index measurements were taken in 20 samples of five measurements each, with each sample's measurements representing a different production batch. The goal is to develop meaningful x̄ and R charts to help monitor the production process. The steps are shown below:

1. The first step is to accurately record the trial MI values. The values are shown in the last five columns of Table 9-3 under the headings $x_1, x_2, \ldots, x_5$. The sample size n = 5.

2. Next, the averages and ranges for each sample are computed, as well as the overall mean and the average range. These values are shown in columns 2 and 3 of Table 9-3. The overall mean is $\overline{\overline{x}} = 1.004$ and the average range is $\overline{R} = 0.057$ (bottom of Table 9-3).

3. The next step is to define the R chart's centerline and control limits, include them on the R chart grid, and plot

| Sample Number | Melt Index Values | | | | | | |
|:---:|:---:|:---:|:---:|:---:|:---:|:---:|:---:|
| | $\bar{x}$ | R | $x_1$ | $x_2$ | $x_3$ | $x_4$ | $x_5$ |
| 1 | 0.995 | 0.074 | 1.033 | 0.988 | 1.007 | 0.990 | 0.959 |
| 2 | 1.022 | 0.049 | 1.039 | 0.999 | 1.048 | 1.004 | 1.020 |
| 3 | 1.000 | 0.038 | 1.010 | 0.998 | 1.017 | 0.979 | 0.998 |
| 4 | 1.014 | 0.020 | 1.015 | 1.026 | 1.007 | 1.006 | 1.013 |
| 5 | 1.006 | 0.047 | 0.995 | 1.004 | 0.998 | 1.039 | 0.992 |
| 6 | 1.003 | 0.075 | 0.967 | 1.002 | 0.975 | 1.042 | 1.031 |
| 7 | 1.018 | 0.124 | 1.033 | 1.073 | 0.998 | 0.949 | 1.039 |
| 8 | 1.016 | 0.035 | 1.014 | 1.001 | 1.013 | 1.015 | 1.036 |
| 9 | 1.032 | 0.038 | 1.051 | 1.035 | 1.013 | 1.025 | 1.036 |
| 10 | 0.990 | 0.074 | 1.003 | 0.979 | 0.960 | 1.034 | 0.975 |
| 11 | 1.025 | 0.067 | 1.019 | 1.053 | 1.031 | 1.037 | 0.986 |
| 12 | 1.008 | 0.028 | 1.001 | 1.007 | 1.015 | 0.993 | 1.022 |
| 13 | 1.010 | 0.075 | 0.972 | 1.047 | 1.030 | 0.978 | 1.021 |
| 14 | 0.989 | 0.039 | 0.994 | 1.007 | 0.975 | 1.002 | 0.968 |
| 15 | 1.021 | 0.071 | 1.059 | 1.036 | 1.025 | 0.995 | 0.988 |
| 16 | 0.960 | 0.029 | 0.971 | 0.966 | 0.942 | 0.962 | 0.958 |
| 17 | 1.003 | 0.072 | 0.975 | 0.982 | 1.014 | 1.047 | 0.995 |
| 18 | 0.989 | 0.073 | 0.941 | 1.011 | 1.014 | 0.982 | 0.997 |
| 19 | 0.996 | 0.048 | 0.983 | 1.000 | 0.970 | 1.018 | 1.009 |
| 20 | 0.983 | 0.071 | 0.974 | 1.014 | 0.943 | 0.975 | 1.009 |

$\bar{\bar{x}} = 1.004$  $\bar{R} = 0.057$

**TABLE 9-3. Data and Statistics for $\bar{x}$ and R Charts Based on High-Density Polyethylene Process**

the sample range trial values (column 3 of Table 9-3) on the control chart as shown in Fig. 9-3.

Centerline:

$$\bar{R} = 0.057$$

Control Limits: (From Table 9-1, for n = 5, $D_3$ = 0.000 and $D_4$ = 2.115)

$$UCL_R = D_4\bar{R}$$

$$= (2.115)(0.057)$$

$$= 0.121$$

$$LCL_R = D_3\bar{R}$$

$$= (0.000)(0.057)$$

$$= 0.000$$

4. After the individual R values, centerline, and control limits have been plotted, the R chart is examined for out-of-control tendencies. The sample 7 R value (i.e., $R_7$ = 0.124) is above the upper control limit (i.e., $UCL_R$ = 0.121). Suppose further study reveals that one of the sample 7 melt index

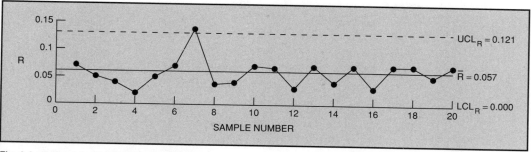

**Fig. 9-3. R Chart for Original Melt Index Data**

values had been recorded incorrectly, causing the appearance of an out-of-control condition. The $x_2$ value in sample 7 should have been recorded as 1.037 rather than as 1.073.

The value was corrected and the sample 7 $\bar{x}$ and R values recomputed (Table 9-4). The new overall mean $\bar{\bar{x}}$ and overall average range $\bar{R}$ are $\bar{\bar{x}} = 1.004$ and $\bar{R} = 0.056$, so that the updated centerline and control limits are

Centerline:

$$\bar{R} = 0.056$$

| Sample Number | $\bar{x}$ | R | $x_1$ | $x_2$ | $x_3$ | $x_4$ | $x_5$ |
|---|---|---|---|---|---|---|---|
| 1 | 0.995 | 0.074 | 1.033 | 0.988 | 1.007 | 0.990 | 0.959 |
| 2 | 1.022 | 0.049 | 1.039 | 0.999 | 1.048 | 1.004 | 1.020 |
| 3 | 1.000 | 0.038 | 1.010 | 0.998 | 1.017 | 0.979 | 0.998 |
| 4 | 1.013 | 0.020 | 1.015 | 1.026 | 1.007 | 1.006 | 1.013 |
| 5 | 1.006 | 0.047 | 0.995 | 1.004 | 0.998 | 1.039 | 0.992 |
| 6 | 1.003 | 0.075 | 0.967 | 1.002 | 0.975 | 1.042 | 1.031 |
| 7 | 1.011 | 0.090 | 1.033 | 1.037 | 0.998 | 0.949 | 1.039 |
| 8 | 1.016 | 0.135 | 1.014 | 1.001 | 1.013 | 1.015 | 1.036 |
| 9 | 1.032 | 0.038 | 1.051 | 1.035 | 1.013 | 1.025 | 1.034 |
| 10 | 0.990 | 0.074 | 1.003 | 0.979 | 0.960 | 1.034 | 0.975 |
| 11 | 1.025 | 0.067 | 1.019 | 1.053 | 1.031 | 1.037 | 0.986 |
| 12 | 1.008 | 0.029 | 1.001 | 1.007 | 1.015 | 0.993 | 1.022 |
| 13 | 1.010 | 0.075 | 0.972 | 1.047 | 1.030 | 0.978 | 1.021 |
| 14 | 0.989 | 0.039 | 0.994 | 1.007 | 0.975 | 1.002 | 0.968 |
| 15 | 1.021 | 0.071 | 1.059 | 1.036 | 1.025 | 0.995 | 0.988 |
| 16 | 0.960 | 0.029 | 0.971 | 0.966 | 0.942 | 0.962 | 0.958 |
| 17 | 1.003 | 0.073 | 0.941 | 1.011 | 1.014 | 1.047 | 0.995 |
| 18 | 0.989 | 0.073 | 0.941 | 1.011 | 1.014 | 0.982 | 0.997 |
| 19 | 0.996 | 0.048 | 0.983 | 1.000 | 0.970 | 1.018 | 1.009 |
| 20 | 0.983 | 0.071 | 0.974 | 1.014 | 0.943 | 0.975 | 1.009 |

$\bar{\bar{x}} = 1.004$, $\bar{R} = 0.056$

**TABLE 9-4. Data and Statistics for $\bar{x}$ and R Charts (Sample 7 $x_2$ value changed from 1.073 to 1.037)**

Control Limits:

$$\text{UCL}_\text{R} = (2.115)(0.056)$$

$$= 0.118$$

$$\text{LCL}_\text{R} = 0.000$$

Fig. 9-4 shows the updated R values plotted along with the new centerline and updated control limits.

5. Again, the R chart (Fig. 9-4) is examined for out-of-control tendencies. This time, however, there are none, implying that the process variation is in control.

6. Since the process variability is in control, the process standard deviation can be estimated from the data and used to develop the control limits for the $\bar{x}$ chart. The centerline and control limits are computed and plotted along with the $\bar{x}$ values in Fig. 9-5. (Note: The R chart portion of Fig. 9-5 is unchanged from Fig. 9-4.)

Centerline:

$$\bar{\bar{x}} = 1.004$$

Control Limits: (From Table 9-1, for n = 5, $A_2$ = 0.577)

$$\text{UCL}_{\bar{x}} = \bar{\bar{x}} + A_2\bar{R}$$

$$= 1.004 + (0.577)(0.056)$$

$$= 1.036$$

$$\text{LCL}_{\bar{x}} = \bar{\bar{x}} - A_2\bar{R}$$

$$= 1.004 - (0.577)(0.056)$$

$$= 0.971$$

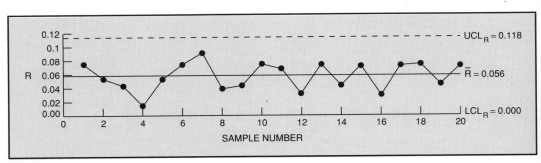

**Fig. 9-4. R Chart for Updated Melt Index Data (x₂ Value in Sample 7 Corrected)**

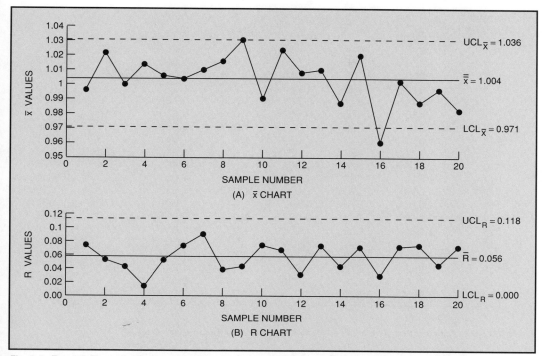

**Fig. 9-5.** $\bar{x}$ and R Charts for Updated (Revision 1) Melt Index Data ($x_2$ Value in Sample 7 Corrected)

7. The next step is to examine the $\bar{x}$ chart (Fig. 9-5) for out-of-control tendencies. The 0.960 $\bar{x}$ value of sample 16 is below the lower control limit. Suppose further study reveals that the sample 16 measurements were collected by a new employee. After discussion with the process engineers, the decision was made to omit the sample 16 measurements from the data (Table 9-5), to recompute the centerline and control limits for both the $\bar{x}$ and R charts based on the 19 sample results, and to replot the data (Fig. 9-6). The calculations based on the revised data are shown below.

Centerline for Revised R Chart:

$$\bar{R} = 0.057$$

Control Limits for Revised R Chart:

$$\text{UCL}_R = D_4\bar{R}$$
$$= (2.115)(0.057)$$
$$= 0.121$$
$$\text{LCL}_R = 0.000$$

| Sample Number | $\bar{x}$ | R | $x_1$ | $x_2$ | $x_3$ | $x_4$ | $x_5$ |
|---|---|---|---|---|---|---|---|
| 1 | 0.995 | 0.074 | 1.033 | 0.988 | 1.007 | 0.990 | 0.959 |
| 2 | 1.022 | 0.049 | 1.039 | 0.999 | 1.048 | 1.004 | 1.020 |
| 3 | 1.000 | 0.138 | 1.010 | 0.998 | 1.017 | 0.979 | 0.998 |
| 4 | 1.013 | 0.020 | 1.015 | 1.026 | 1.007 | 1.006 | 1.013 |
| 5 | 1.006 | 0.047 | 0.995 | 1.004 | 0.998 | 1.039 | 0.992 |
| 6 | 1.003 | 0.075 | 0.967 | 1.002 | 0.975 | 1.042 | 1.031 |
| 7 | 1.011 | 0.090 | 1.033 | 1.037 | 0.998 | 0.949 | 1.039 |
| 8 | 1.016 | 0.035 | 1.014 | 1.001 | 1.013 | 1.015 | 1.036 |
| 9 | 1.032 | 0.038 | 1.051 | 1.035 | 1.013 | 1.025 | 1.034 |
| 10 | 0.990 | 0.074 | 1.003 | 0.979 | 0.960 | 1.034 | 0.975 |
| 11 | 1.025 | 0.067 | 1.019 | 1.053 | 1.031 | 1.037 | 0.986 |
| 12 | 1.008 | 0.029 | 1.001 | 1.007 | 1.015 | 0.993 | 1.022 |
| 13 | 1.010 | 0.075 | 0.972 | 1.047 | 1.030 | 0.979 | 1.021 |
| 14 | 0.989 | 0.039 | 0.994 | 1.007 | 0.975 | 1.002 | 0.968 |
| 15 | 1.021 | 0.071 | 1.059 | 1.037 | 1.025 | 0.995 | 0.988 |
| 16 | | | | | | | |
| 17 | 1.003 | 0.072 | 0.975 | 0.982 | 1.014 | 1.046 | 0.995 |
| 18 | 0.989 | 0.073 | 0.941 | 1.011 | 1.014 | 0.982 | 0.997 |
| 19 | 0.996 | 0.048 | 0.983 | 1.000 | 0.970 | 1.018 | 1.009 |
| 20 | 0.983 | 0.071 | 0.974 | 1.014 | 0.943 | 0.975 | 1.009 |

$\bar{\bar{x}} = 1.006, \bar{R} = 0.057$

**TABLE 9-5. Data and Statistics for $\bar{x}$ and R Charts (Sample 16 Measurements Omitted)**

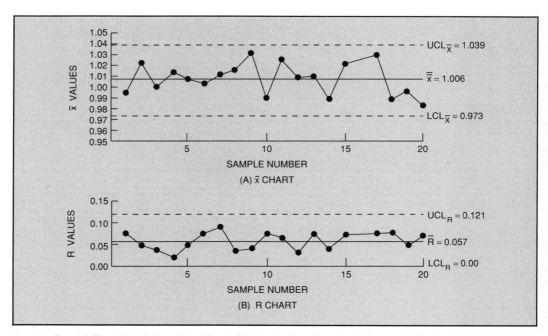

**Fig. 9-6. $\bar{x}$ and R Charts for Updated (Revision 2) Melt Index Data (Sample 16 Measurements Omitted)**

Centerline for Revised $\bar{x}$ Chart:

$$\bar{\bar{x}} = 1.006$$

Control Limits for Revised $\bar{x}$ Chart:

$$UCL_{\bar{x}} = \bar{\bar{x}} + A_2\bar{R}$$

$$= 1.006 + (0.577)(0.057)$$

$$= 1.039$$

$$LCL_{\bar{x}} = \bar{\bar{x}} - A_2\bar{R}$$

$$= 1.006 - (0.577)(0.057)$$

$$= 0.973$$

8. Examination of the $\bar{x}$ and R charts shown in Fig. 9-6 indicates that both the process mean and the process variation are now in control. At this point, the centerlines and control limits on both the $\bar{x}$ and R charts can be extended and used for process monitoring and controlling the melt index process characteristics.

9. Table 9-6 shows the sampling results from 20 additional production batches and the computed $\bar{x}$ and R values for

| Sample Number | Melt Index Values | | | | | | |
|---|---|---|---|---|---|---|---|
| | $\bar{x}$ | R | $x_1$ | $x_2$ | $x_3$ | $x_4$ | $x_5$ |
| 21 | 1.011 | 0.036 | 1.033 | 0.997 | 1.016 | 1.012 | 0.997 |
| 22 | 0.991 | 0.046 | 1.017 | 0.971 | 0.989 | 0.996 | 0.982 |
| 23 | 0.988 | 0.106 | 0.981 | 0.971 | 0.941 | 1.047 | 1.001 |
| 24 | 1.003 | 0.066 | 1.019 | 1.020 | 0.965 | 0.980 | 1.031 |
| 25 | 1.006 | 0.046 | 0.990 | 1.003 | 1.005 | 0.994 | 1.036 |
| 26 | 1.003 | 0.064 | 0.980 | 1.021 | 1.036 | 1.008 | 0.972 |
| 27 | 1.008 | 0.070 | 1.007 | 1.017 | 1.000 | 0.973 | 1.043 |
| 28 | 0.995 | 0.060 | 0.966 | 1.026 | 1.004 | 0.997 | 0.984 |
| 29 | 0.996 | 0.081 | 0.961 | 0.972 | 1.025 | 1.042 | 0.979 |
| 30 | 0.995 | 0.091 | 1.045 | 0.972 | 0.954 | 1.015 | 0.990 |
| 31 | 1.020 | 0.061 | 1.017 | 1.026 | 1.053 | 1.011 | 0.992 |
| 32 | 1.031 | 0.095 | 0.979 | 1.025 | 1.048 | 1.028 | 1.074 |
| 33 | 0.987 | 0.045 | 0.996 | 1.005 | 0.960 | 1.005 | 0.969 |
| 34 | 1.009 | 0.045 | 0.980 | 1.011 | 1.023 | 1.025 | 1.007 |
| 35 | 1.018 | 0.024 | 1.004 | 1.023 | 1.024 | 1.012 | 1.028 |
| 36 | 0.999 | 0.086 | 0.958 | 1.035 | 1.044 | 0.971 | 0.986 |
| 37 | 1.002 | 0.121 | 0.947 | 1.068 | 1.004 | 0.989 | 1.001 |
| 38 | 1.016 | 0.042 | 1.007 | 1.012 | 1.025 | 0.997 | 1.039 |
| 39 | 0.987 | 0.073 | 0.984 | 0.983 | 0.943 | 1.011 | 1.016 |
| 40 | 0.985 | 0.062 | 1.020 | 0.958 | 0.975 | 1.011 | 0.961 |

TABLE 9-6. Melt Index Measurements for 20 Additional Shipments of Polyethylene

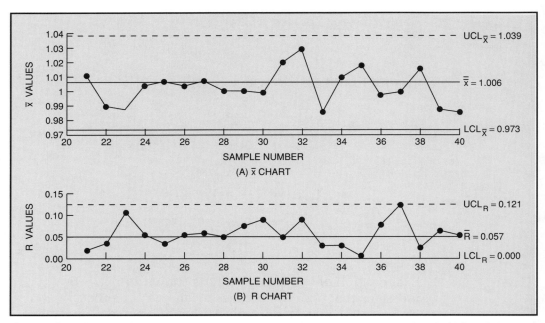

**Fig. 9-7. Extended x̄ and R Charts for Melt Index Data (Charts Include the Results of 20 Additional Samples)**

each sample. Fig. 9-7 shows these sample statistics plotted along with the original sample values. While no points fall outside the control limits on either chart, the range value for sample number 37 falls on the R chart's upper limit. As such, further study is warranted for the measurements found in that sample.

## 9-4. Standardized x̄ Chart

Standardization is a process that allows variables having different measurement scales to be more easily compared. Recall from Unit 6 (on the normal distribution) that variables are standardized by subtracting an estimate of the variable's mean from each value and dividing by an estimate of the variable's standard deviation.

In a similar manner, x̄ values can also be standardized. This is often done to avoid disclosure of proprietary data. For the x̄ chart, if each x̄ value is coded by subtracting the overall mean x̄̄ and dividing by the best estimate of the standard deviation of the mean $\sigma_{\bar{x}}$, standardized values are obtained. The standard deviation of the sample averages is estimated by $\bar{R}/(d_2 \sqrt{n})$. Table 9-7 shows the standardized measurements (and the associated sample statistics) that correspond to the melt index

| Sample Number | $\bar{x}$ | Std. $\bar{x}$ Values | R | $x_1$ | $x_2$ | $x_3$ | $x_4$ | $x_5$ |
|---|---|---|---|---|---|---|---|---|
| 1 | 0.995 | −1.004 | 0.074 | 1.033 | 0.988 | 1.007 | 0.990 | 0.959 |
| 2 | 1.022 | 1.460 | 0.049 | 1.039 | 0.999 | 1.048 | 1.004 | 1.020 |
| 3 | 1.000 | −0.547 | 0.138 | 1.010 | 0.998 | 1.017 | 0.979 | 0.998 |
| 4 | 1.013 | 0.639 | 0.020 | 1.015 | 1.026 | 1.007 | 1.006 | 1.013 |
| 5 | 1.006 | 0.000 | 0.047 | 0.995 | 1.004 | 0.998 | 1.039 | 0.992 |
| 6 | 1.003 | −0.274 | 0.075 | 0.967 | 1.002 | 0.975 | 1.042 | 1.031 |
| 7 | 1.011 | 0.458 | 0.090 | 1.033 | 1.037 | 0.998 | 0.949 | 1.039 |
| 8 | 1.016 | 0.912 | 0.035 | 1.014 | 1.001 | 1.013 | 1.015 | 1.036 |
| 9 | 1.032 | 2.372 | 0.038 | 1.051 | 1.035 | 1.013 | 1.025 | 1.034 |
| 10 | 0.990 | −1.460 | 0.074 | 1.003 | 0.979 | 0.960 | 1.034 | 0.975 |
| 11 | 1.025 | 1.734 | 0.067 | 1.019 | 1.053 | 1.031 | 1.037 | 0.986 |
| 12 | 1.008 | 0.182 | 0.029 | 1.001 | 1.007 | 1.015 | 0.993 | 1.022 |
| 13 | 1.010 | 0.365 | 0.075 | 0.972 | 1.047 | 1.030 | 0.979 | 1.021 |
| 14 | 0.989 | −1.551 | 0.039 | 0.994 | 1.007 | 0.975 | 1.002 | 0.968 |
| 15 | 1.021 | 1.369 | 0.071 | 1.059 | 1.037 | 1.025 | 0.995 | 0.988 |
| 16 | | | | | | | | |
| 17 | 1.003 | −0.274 | 0.072 | 0.975 | 0.982 | 1.014 | 1.046 | 0.995 |
| 18 | 0.989 | −1.551 | 0.073 | 0.941 | 1.011 | 1.014 | 0.982 | 0.997 |
| 19 | 0.996 | −0.912 | 0.048 | 0.983 | 1.000 | 0.970 | 1.018 | 1.009 |
| 20 | 0.983 | −2.099 | 0.071 | 0.974 | 1.014 | 0.943 | 0.975 | 1.009 |

Original Measurements: $\bar{\bar{x}} = 1.006$     $\bar{R} = 0.057$

$$\hat{\sigma}_{\bar{x}} = \bar{R}/(d_2\sqrt{n}) = 0.057/(2.326\sqrt{5}) = 0.011$$

Standardized Measurements $= (\bar{x}_i - \bar{\bar{x}})/\hat{\sigma}_{\bar{x}} = (\bar{x}_i - 1.006)/0.011$

**TABLE 9-7. Standardized Values and Statistics for $\bar{x}$ and R Charts (Sample 16 Measurements Omitted)**

data shown in Table 9-5. Fig. 9-8 shows the standardized data plotted on an $\bar{x}$ chart.

One obvious advantage of the standardization process for $\bar{x}$ control charts is that the centerline is always 0.00 and the three-sigma control limits are always ±3.00. One disadvantage

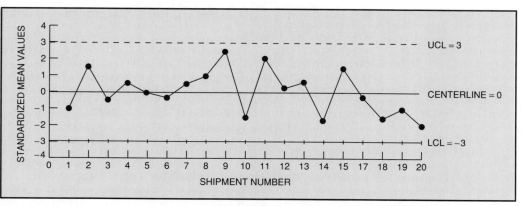

**Fig. 9-8. $\bar{x}$ Chart Based on Standardized Values of Melt Index Data (Sample 16 Value Omitted)**

of the standardization process is that all values plotted on control charts must first be standardized, an inconvenient step if the charts are developed manually. Of course, since standardized values lose their original identity, standardization is more appropriate in some situations than in others. Note that the pattern of points in Fig. 9-8 is identical to the pattern of points in the Fig. 9-6 $\bar{x}$ chart.

## Exercises

9-1. During a production process, five individual products were taken from each of 40 batches and an appropriate quality characteristic measured. The overall sample statistics were found to be $\bar{\bar{x}}$ = 1.432 and $\bar{R}$ = 0.004. Within what limits would you expect all 40 averages to fall if the process is in statistical control?

9-2. Suppose a process is in statistical control with $\bar{\bar{x}}$ = 50, $\bar{R}$ = 4.0, and n = 6. Compute three-sigma control limits for both an $\bar{x}$ chart and an R chart.

9-3. Both an $\bar{x}$ chart and an R chart were prepared for an operation based on 20 samples having five units in each sample. The overall mean $\bar{\bar{x}}$ was found to be 33.6 and the average range $\bar{R}$ = 6.20. The process was found to be in control. Later, a single sample of five units was taken. The quality characteristic measured 36, 43, 37, 35, and 38, respectively. What would you conclude regarding the process mean and process variation?

9-4. In a manufacturing process, 20 samples of six units each were found to have an overall average of 1.001 inches. The average of the 20 ranges was found to be 0.002 inch. What are the R chart control limits? What are the 3-sigma $\bar{x}$ chart control limits?

9-5. Control charts for averages (i.e., $\bar{x}$ charts) are primarily intended to satisfy which one of the following objectives? (a) Reduce the sample size used to develop the $\bar{x}$ chart. (b) Fix the risk of accepting a poor product. (c) Indicate when nonrandom causes of variation exist in the process. (d) Establish an acceptable quality level.

9-6. A process is checked at random by inspecting samples of size n = 4 and maintaining both $\bar{x}$ and R charts. Because of a production time constraint, the process foreman forced the quality analyst to rush his analysis. The analyst was able to develop measurements for only two units instead of the usual four. The sample range is just greater than the R chart's upper control limit. The analyst advises the department foreman to adjust the process. This decision indicates which one of the following? (a) The mean process level is out of control. (b) The mean process level is out of control, but the dispersion is in control. (c) The analyst is misusing the chart, since only two measurements were taken. (d) The process dispersion is out of control.

9-7. A process is routinely monitored by taking random samples of size n = 4 and maintaining $\bar{x}$ and R charts. An analyst making a spot check picks out two units, measures them accurately, and plots the value of each one on the $\bar{x}$ chart. Both points fall outside the control limits, one just above the UCL and one just below the LCL. The analyst advises the process foreman to adjust the process. This decision indicates which one of the following? (a) The process mean level is out of control. (b) Both the mean level and process dispersion are out of control. (c) The process mean level is out of control, but not the process dispersion. (d) The analyst is not using the chart correctly.

9-8. A probability value of 0.9973 refers to which one of the following? (a) Probability that the process is in control. (b) Probability that a correct decision will be made as to control or lack of control of the process. (c) Probability that a point will fall inside the three-sigma control limits on an $\bar{x}$ chart. (d) Probability that a point will fall inside the three-sigma limits for an $\bar{x}$ chart, if the process is in statistical control.

9-9. Eight melt index samples of size n = 4 each were taken from a polyethylene production process. The results are shown in the table below. (a) Calculate the $\bar{x}$ and R values for each of the eight samples. (b) Calculate $\bar{\bar{x}}$ and $\bar{R}$. (c) Calculate preliminary control limits for both the $\bar{x}$ and R charts. (d) Plot the centerlines, control limits, and sample statistics on both charts.

| Sample Number | 1 | 2 | 3 | 4 | 5 | 6 | 7 | 8 |
|---|---|---|---|---|---|---|---|---|
| $x_1$ | 1.04 | 1.01 | 0.95 | 1.04 | 1.03 | 1.03 | 0.97 | 1.04 |
| $x_2$ | 0.97 | 1.02 | 0.97 | 1.04 | 0.98 | 0.99 | 1.00 | 0.99 |
| $x_3$ | 1.00 | 1.04 | 0.97 | 0.95 | 1.03 | 1.00 | 0.95 | 0.97 |
| $x_4$ | 0.98 | 1.01 | 1.02 | 0.97 | 1.02 | 1.00 | 0.97 | 0.97 |
| $\bar{x}$ = | | | | | | | | |
| R = | | | | | | | | |

**Melt Index Measurements**

9-10.  Sample data from six recent shipments of plastic bottles are shown below. The inside diameter of the bottle neck is measured on four randomly selected bottles. When the process is in control, the process average is 0.650 inch and the four-sample process range is 0.010 inch. (a) Develop R chart control limits and plot the six range values on the chart. Is the process in control? (b) Develop $\bar{x}$ chart control limits and plot the sample $\bar{x}$ values. Is the process in control?

| Shipment | Bottle 1 | Bottle 2 | Bottle 3 | Bottle 4 |
|---|---|---|---|---|
| 1 | 0.651 | 0.653 | 0.642 | 0.655 |
| 2 | 0.657 | 0.641 | 0.646 | 0.653 |
| 3 | 0.640 | 0.642 | 0.656 | 0.659 |
| 4 | 0.653 | 0.640 | 0.648 | 0.660 |
| 5 | 0.668 | 0.652 | 0.643 | 0.646 |
| 6 | 0.643 | 0.653 | 0.658 | 0.660 |

**Inside Diameter of Bottle Neck Measurements**

9-11.  One key performance characteristic in polymer production is the modulus of elasticity. This property measures how rubber-like or plastic-like a polymer is (i.e., the lower the value, the more rubber-like). Since the modulus of elasticity is heavily dependent on sample preparation and since samples are regularly prepared by three different lab technicians, an experiment to determine if there are any real differences between the skills of the lab technicians is to be conducted.

Five random samples were taken from a single bag of polymer by each of the three lab technicians and prepared as "polymer blankets." From each blanket, three test samples were cut and modulus of elasticity measurements taken. The results are shown below.

Since the polymer was randomly selected from process output, the data including all three operators should be combined to estimate the overall process mean and average range values. Measurement results for each lab technician are then to be plotted on $\bar{x}$ and R charts. Is the process in control (i.e., are there significant differences between the modulus of elasticity estimates prepared by the three lab technicians?)?

| Sample | Measurement | | |
|---|---|---|---|
| | 1 | 2 | 3 |
| Lab Tech 1 | | | |
| 1 | 178 | 177 | 178 |
| 2 | 179 | 179 | 180 |
| 3 | 179 | 182 | 178 |
| 4 | 174 | 174 | 182 |
| 5 | 181 | 181 | 180 |
| Lab Tech 2 | | | |
| 1 | 176 | 175 | 177 |
| 2 | 176 | 179 | 181 |
| 3 | 174 | 178 | 180 |
| 4 | 180 | 167 | 171 |
| 5 | 178 | 173 | 169 |
| Lab Tech 3 | | | |
| 1 | 184 | 189 | 181 |
| 2 | 183 | 182 | 184 |
| 3 | 196 | 194 | 183 |
| 4 | 189 | 183 | 184 |
| 5 | 184 | 190 | 187 |

**Modulus of Elasticity Measurements**

9-12. Data from 20 shipments of carbon black are sampled for the iodine $(I_2)$ levels present, shown below. From each shipment, four measurements are taken. (a) Prepare an R chart and plot the 20 R values. (b) Assuming the process variation is in control, prepare an $\bar{x}$ chart and plot the 20 $\bar{x}$ values.

| Sample Number | $x_1$ | $x_2$ | $x_3$ | $x_4$ | $\bar{x}$ | R |
|---|---|---|---|---|---|---|
| 1 | 40.9 | 40.5 | 40.1 | 41.0 | 40.63 | 0.90 |
| 2 | 40.8 | 40.3 | 39.2 | 41.5 | 40.45 | 2.30 |
| 3 | 39.6 | 39.4 | 40.3 | 39.3 | 39.65 | 1.00 |
| 4 | 40.6 | 40.2 | 40.6 | 39.2 | 40.15 | 1.40 |
| 5 | 40.4 | 40.4 | 39.4 | 40.0 | 40.05 | 1.00 |
| 6 | 39.2 | 40.4 | 39.8 | 39.7 | 39.78 | 1.20 |
| 7 | 39.9 | 39.0 | 39.5 | 39.7 | 39.53 | 0.90 |

| Sample Number | $x_1$ | $x_2$ | $x_3$ | $x_4$ | $\bar{x}$ | R |
|---|---|---|---|---|---|---|
| 8 | 40.2 | 40.2 | 41.4 | 40.4 | 40.55 | 1.20 |
| 9 | 39.9 | 39.9 | 39.2 | 39.4 | 39.60 | 0.70 |
| 10 | 40.5 | 40.1 | 40.6 | 38.6 | 39.95 | 2.00 |
| 11 | 39.9 | 39.2 | 40.2 | 40.2 | 39.88 | 1.00 |
| 12 | 41.1 | 38.8 | 39.9 | 40.6 | 40.10 | 2.30 |
| 13 | 40.1 | 40.3 | 39.1 | 39.7 | 39.80 | 1.20 |
| 14 | 39.6 | 41.0 | 40.6 | 40.2 | 40.35 | 1.40 |
| 15 | 40.0 | 38.6 | 41.5 | 40.0 | 40.03 | 2.90 |
| 16 | 40.5 | 40.0 | 40.2 | 40.2 | 40.23 | 0.50 |
| 17 | 40.7 | 40.2 | 39.6 | 40.2 | 40.17 | 1.10 |
| 18 | 38.8 | 40.2 | 40.3 | 39.9 | 39.80 | 1.50 |
| 19 | 40.6 | 39.2 | 40.4 | 39.3 | 39.88 | 1.40 |
| 20 | 39.7 | 39.0 | 39.9 | 39.4 | 39.50 | 0.90 |

$\bar{\bar{x}} = 40.00$, $\bar{R} = 1.34$

**Iodine in Carbon Black**

# Unit 10:
# Evaluation of Control Charts

# UNIT 10

# Evaluation of Control Charts

Control chart limits are typically set three standard deviations above and below the centerline. This allows space for considerable random variation since nearly 100% of the plotted points will fall within these limits when the process is in control. In other words, three-sigma limits are very effective in avoiding the problem of overcontrol. But what about the problem of undercontrol—the failure to recognize that the process has somehow changed? Clearly, the setting of control limits involves a tradeoff with regard to the problems of undercontrol and overcontrol. This unit examines these issues and presents additional ways to avoid the problems associated with them.

**Learning Objectives** — When you have completed this unit, you should:

A. Understand the concepts of overcontrolling and undercontrolling a process and be able to compute some probabilities related to the possible occurrence of both problem types.

B. Understand the meaning of average run length and be able to estimate its value for different scenarios.

C. Understand and be able to apply additional control chart rules (zone rules) in order to avoid the problems associated with undercontrol.

## 10-1. Overcontrol and Undercontrol

A process is said to be out of statistical control if, in addition to common cause variation, variation is present in the process due to some special cause. Control charts are used to signal this nonrandom variation. Unfortunately, the signals provided by control charts are something less than perfect.

Overcontrol, adjusting a process when only common cause variation is present, is often referred to as a Type I error. The probability of committing a Type I error is referred to as the $\alpha$ risk. For three-sigma limits and a normally distributed product characteristic, the probability of overcontrolling the process (the probability of the chart indicating an out-of-control condition when none actually exists) is approximately 0.0027. Putting this in perspective, if a process is in control and sampled every two hours (i.e., 12 times per day), only about one time per month (i.e., once out of every 370 samples) would a false alarm be given.

Undercontrol refers to the problem of the control chart not indicating an out-of-control condition when one really does exist (i.e., when a special cause of variation is present). This problem is known as a Type II error; the probability of committing a Type II error is known as the $\beta$ risk. With the typical control chart and using three-sigma limits as the sole criterion for determining an out-of-control condition, undercontrol is generally more likely than overcontrol.

The probabilities related to making both types of errors are partially dependent on the sample size. The probability of undercontrol also depends on the severity of the trouble. For example, the process mean may shift a little or a lot. If the process mean shifts dramatically, the control chart may detect the shift in one sample. If the process mean shifts only slightly, the control chart will eventually detect the shift but may not do so for many samples.

A similar situation exists regarding overcontrol, but with three-sigma limits the $\alpha$ risk is small. For example, suppose that the process is centered at 1.00 and the process standard deviation is 0.03. If the process mean and standard deviation remain unchanged and individual values $(x_i)$ are plotted on an x chart, the probability of the control chart signaling an out-of-control condition by having a point fall outside the control limits (resulting in the possibility of overcontrol) is

$$\text{Pr(overcontrol)} = \text{Pr}(x_i \leq \text{LCL}) + \text{Pr}(x_i \geq \text{UCL})$$

$$= \text{Pr}(x_i \leq 0.91) + \text{Pr}(x_i \geq 1.09)$$

If the $x_i$ values are normally distributed, this probability is 0.0027 or 0.27%. (If the $x_i$ values are not normally distributed, the probability of overcontrol will probably be greater than

0.0027 but by how much will differ from case to case.) The situation is shown in Fig. 10-1.

To compute the probability of undercontrol, it is necessary to begin with a specific out-of-control situation. Of course, the more drastic the change, the easier it is to detect. Suppose the process mean shifts from 1.00 to 1.03 (i.e., a one standard deviation shift), while the process standard deviation remains at 0.03. The probability that undercontrol will occur, i.e., the probability of not detecting this shift in one sample, is the probability that an individual $x_i$ value falls within the control limits even though a shift has occurred.

Pr (undercontrol)

= Probability of not detecting a change in the process in one sample

= Probability of a single plotted point falling within the control limits even though the process mean has changed; in this example, the shift is one standard deviation, from 1.00 to 1.03.

$= \Pr(x_i \geq \text{LCL and } x_i \leq \text{UCL})$

$= \Pr(\text{LCL} \leq x_i \leq \text{UCL})$

$= \Pr(x_i \leq \text{UCL}) - \Pr(x_i \leq \text{LCL})$

$= \Pr(x_i \leq \text{UCL when } \mu_x = 1.03) - \Pr(x_i \leq \text{LCL when } \mu_x = 1.03)$

$= \Pr(z \leq (\text{UCL} - \mu_x)/\sigma_x) - \Pr(z \leq (\text{LCL} - \mu_x)/\sigma_x)$

$= \Pr(z \leq (1.09 - 1.03)/0.03) - \Pr(z \leq (0.91 - 1.03)/0.03)$

$= \Pr(z \leq 2) - \Pr(z \leq -4)$

$= 0.9772 - 0.0000$

$= 0.9772$

The situation is shown in Fig. 10-2.

The above computation indicates that the probability that undercontrol will occur on the basis of one sample's results when the process mean shifts by one standard deviation is 0.9772. That is, the chance of not detecting this shift in a single sample is extremely high. In Table 10-1, the probability of

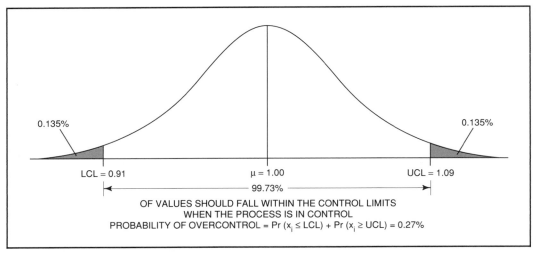

OF VALUES SHOULD FALL WITHIN THE CONTROL LIMITS
WHEN THE PROCESS IS IN CONTROL
PROBABILITY OF OVERCONTROL = $Pr(x_i \leq LCL) + Pr(x_i \geq UCL) = 0.27\%$

**Fig. 10-1. Probability of Possible Overcontrol**

undercontrol for various sizes of shifts in the process mean is shown.

Even casual inspection of Table 10-1 (as well as common sense) reveals that the larger the shift, the more likely it is that the shift will be detected in just one sample. For example, there is

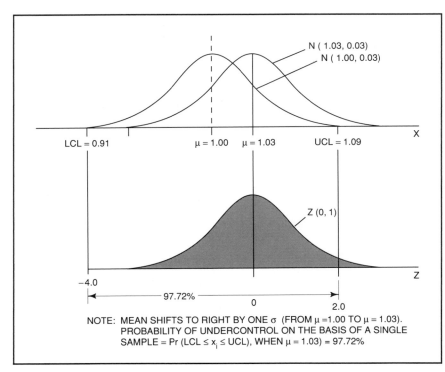

NOTE: MEAN SHIFTS TO RIGHT BY ONE $\sigma$ (FROM $\mu = 1.00$ TO $\mu = 1.03$).
PROBABILITY OF UNDERCONTROL ON THE BASIS OF A SINGLE
SAMPLE = $Pr(LCL \leq x_i \leq UCL)$, WHEN $\mu = 1.03) = 97.72\%$

**Fig. 10-2. Probability of Undercontrol**

| M, Size of Process Mean Shift (in Standard Deviations) | Probability of Not Detecting the Shift in One Sample | Probability of Detecting the Shift in One Sample |
|---|---|---|
| 1 | 0.9772 | 0.0228 |
| 2 | 0.8413 | 0.1587 |
| 3 | 0.5000 | 0.5000 |
| 4 | 0.1587 | 0.8413 |
| 5 | 0.0227 | 0.9973 |

Note: The probability of undercontrol is defined here as the probability of not detecting a shift of size M in a single sample. Calculations are based on samples of size n = 1 plotted on an x chart.

**TABLE 10-1. Probability of Undercontrol**

a 0.9973 probability of detecting a shift of five standard deviations on the basis of a single observation but only a 0.5000 probability of detecting a three-standard-deviation shift.

## 10-2. Average Run Length (ARL)

As shown in Table 10-1, the probability of undercontrol is often quite high. The shift will eventually be detected, however. The average number of samples required to detect an out-of-control condition for a shift in the process mean of a particular magnitude is called the average run length (ARL). The average run length may be estimated by using the formula shown below (mean of a geometric distribution):

$$ARL = 1/[1 - Pr(undercontrol\ in\ one\ sample)]$$

For example, for a process mean shift of one standard deviation, the ARL is 44 [i.e., ARL = 1/(1 − 0.9772)]. Both Table 10-2 and Fig. 10-3 show the ARLs for various sizes of shifts in the process mean. For instance, both show that on the

| Size of Process Mean Shift (in Standard Deviations) | Probability of Not Detecting the Shift in One Sample | Probability of Detecting the Shift in One Sample | Average Run Length |
|---|---|---|---|
| 1 | 0.9772 | 0.0228 | 44.0 |
| 2 | 0.8413 | 0.1587 | 6.3 |
| 3 | 0.5000 | 0.5000 | 2.0 |
| 4 | 0.1587 | 0.8413 | 1.2 |
| 5 | 0.0227 | 0.9972 | 1.0 |

**TABLE 10-2. Probability of Undercontrol and Average Run Length**

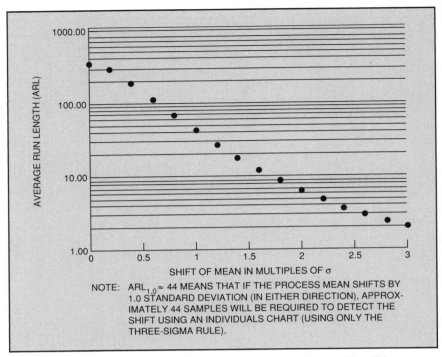

**Fig. 10-3. Average Run Lengths for Various Sizes of Shifts in the Process Mean Using an Individuals Chart**

average it takes approximately 44 samples to detect a shift of one standard deviation in the process mean using an individuals chart, while a three-sigma shift in the process mean will be detected in two samples on the average.

## 10-3. Analysis of Control Chart Patterns: Zone Rules

When a point on a control chart falls outside the control limits, a signal that indicates an out-of-control condition is given. A search for the cause is then carried out and, if a reason for the condition is found, corrective action is taken. An obvious disadvantage of this "point outside the control limits" approach is that control charts quickly detect only relatively large changes in the process. Of course, from the beginning of these control chart discussions, other means of identifying the presence of special causes, repeatedly searching for nonrandom patterns, have been alluded to. In this section, formal recognition is given to several such patterns along with rules of thumb for recognizing them.

A typical control chart may be divided into three zones, as shown in Fig. 10-4. Zone C (i.e., close) represents the area

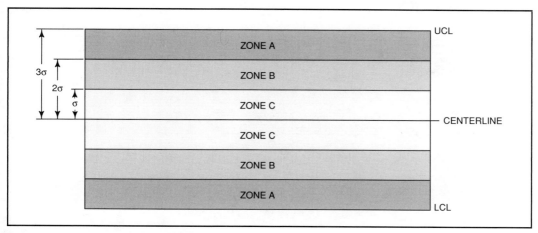

**Fig. 10-4. Zones for Detecting Unnatural Patterns**

within one standard deviation of the chart's centerline. Zone B represents the area between one and two standard deviations of the chart's centerline. Zone A represents the area between two and three standard deviations of the centerline. In general, most points can be expected to fall in zone C, the next most points in zone B, and the fewest points in zone A. Using these guidelines as a starting point, several zone rules may be stated.

An out-of-control signal is given if one point falls beyond zone A (Fig. 10-5). This is known as the "three-sigma rule." It is the rule on which most of the previous control chart decisions have been based.

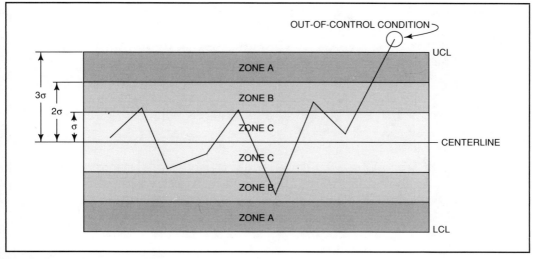

**Fig. 10-5. Three-Sigma Rule Example**

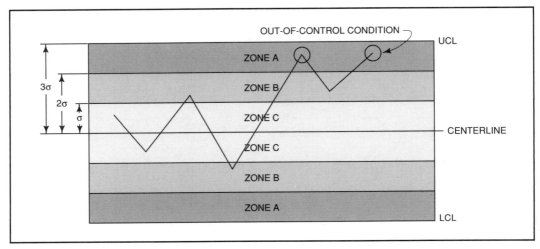

**Fig. 10-6. Three-Successive-Points Rule Example**

An out-of-control signal is given if any two out of three successive points fall on the same side of the centerline in zone A or beyond (i.e., beyond two sigma) (Fig. 10-6). This is sometimes called the "three-successive-points rule" and is symptomatic of a sudden process shift.

An out-of-control signal is given if any four out of five successive points fall on the same side of the centerline in zone B or beyond (i.e., beyond one sigma) (Fig. 10-7). This is sometimes called the "five-successive-points rule." It is also indicative of a shift in the process.

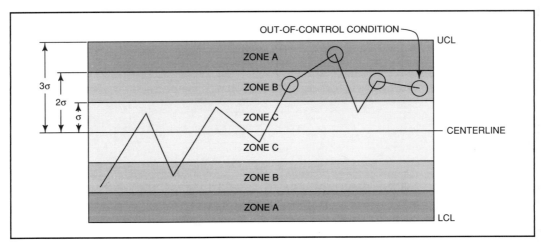

**Fig. 10-7. Five-Successive-Points Rule Example**

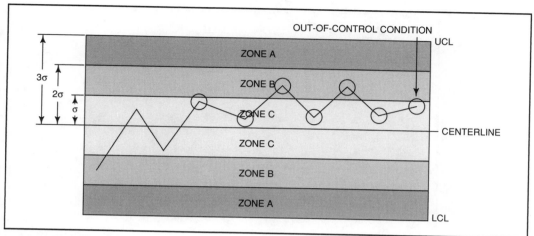

**Fig. 10-8.  Run Rule Example**

An out-of-control signal is given if seven successive points fall anywhere above the centerline or seven successive points fall anywhere below the centerline (Fig. 10-8). This is referred to as the "run rule" and is indicative of a sustained process shift.

Fig. 10-9 demonstrates three other nonrandom variation rules of thumb: (1) a trend is signaled when seven consecutive points increase or seven consecutive points decrease, both patterns indicative of a gradual process shift; (2) "a zig-zag" pattern is signaled when 14 consecutive points alternate in an up-down sequence, often symptomatic of overcontrol; and, (3) a "hugging" pattern is signaled when 15 consecutive points fall in zone C, symptomatic of an inappropriate standard deviation estimate. Such a pattern is often the result of taking samples of multiple measurements at approximately the same point in time from a homogeneous process (see Mixing, Unit 11).

Other nonrandom patterns might also signal the presence of a special cause of variation. Fig. 10-10 shows three such patterns: (1) systematic, though not necessarily alternating, patterns often symptomatic of nonrational subgroups (e.g., shift change, material change, product change); (2) cycling patterns, clearly indicative of a high degree of autocorrelation present in the process and possibly the presence of a special cause of variation, even if no "rules" are violated; and, (3) unexpectedly wide groupings, often indicative of sampling from two or more process streams having dramatically different

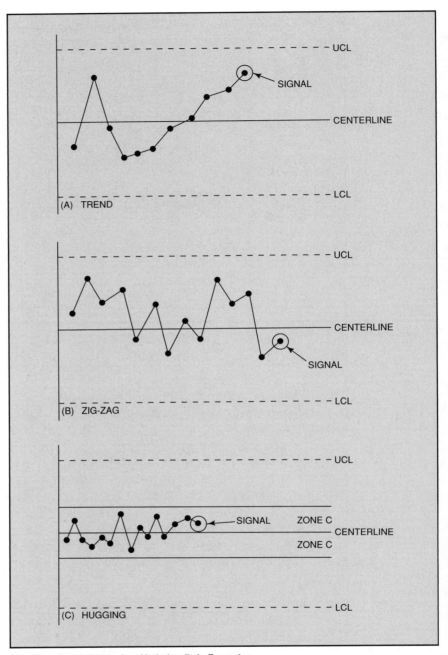

**Fig. 10-9. Other Nonrandom Variation Rule Examples**

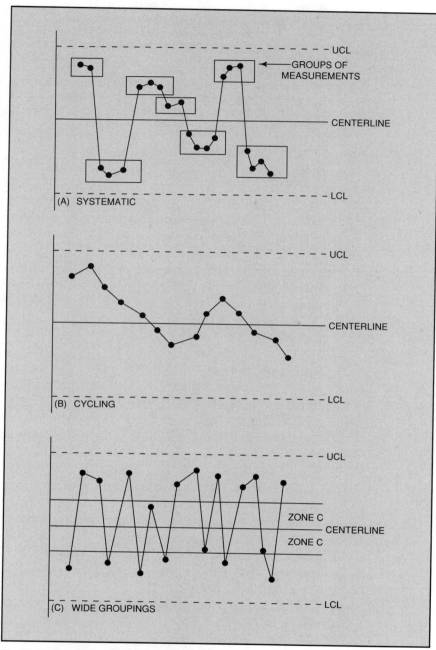

Fig. 10-10.  **Other Out-of-Control Patterns**

1. Three-Sigma Rule: one point falls beyond zone A.
2. Three-Successive-Points Rule: two out of three points fall on the same side of the centerline in zone A or beyond.
3. Five-Successive-Points Rule: four out of five points fall on the same side of the centerline in zone B or beyond.
4. Run Rule: seven consecutive points fall on one side of the centerline.
5. Trend Rule: seven consecutive points either increase or decrease.
6. Zig-Zag Rule: fourteen successive points alternate in an up-down pattern.
7. Hugging Rule: fifteen successive points fall in zone C.
8. Other Nonrandom Patterns: (a) systematic pattern, (b) cycling pattern, and (c) wide grouping pattern.

**TABLE 10-3. Rules of Thumb for Identifying Nonrandom Variation**

variability. This situation can be recognized when significantly more than $\frac{1}{3}$ of the points fall outside zone C.

The point of all these rules and patterns is that an out-of-control process is one that exhibits something other than random variation. They are summarized in Table 10-3.

## 10-4. Variable Sampling Intervals

Another way to more quickly identify the presence of a special cause of variation is by varying the sampling interval. For instance, suppose that a four-hour sampling interval is being used to monitor a certain process. If an out-of-control condition is suspected, the sampling interval might be reduced to two hours.

The following rule of thumb is sometimes applied: If a single point falls in zone A (i.e., between 2 and 3 standard deviations from the mean) or beyond, the sampling interval is halved, i.e., reduced to half the original sampling interval. If the next point falls in zones B or C (i.e., between 0 and 2 standard deviations from the process mean), the sampling interval is returned to its original length; if it falls in the 2 to 3 standard deviation range or beyond, the reduced sampling interval is continued. This sampling interval decision process can be continued indefinitely. Fig. 10-11 shows a flowchart for this sequence.

An example that demonstrates a slight variation of the Fig. 10-11 sequence is shown in Fig. 10-12 for a process with a two-hour sampling interval. At 4:00 p.m., a plotting point falls in zone A. As such, the two-hour sampling interval is halved, to one hour. The next sample is then taken at 5:00 p.m. It falls above zone A, thus violating the three-sigma rule. Assume that

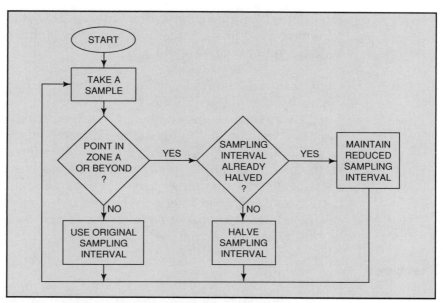

**Fig. 10-11.  Flowchart of Variable Sampling Interval Process**

the special cause of variation is quickly found and that the process is adjusted. However, because of the nature of the process, time is required for the process to move back to target. The sampling frequency remains at the reduced interval length until it is apparent that the process target has been reestablished. After plotting the quality characteristic once an hour for several hours, it seems that the process target has been reestablished. At 10:00 p.m., the sampling interval is returned to its original two-hour length. The danger of switching back to

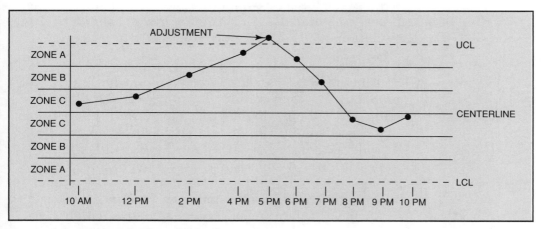

**Fig. 10-12.  Variable Sampling Interval Example**

the original sampling frequency too soon is that the process may have been either underadjusted or overadjusted and may soon go out of control again.

Of course, the amount by which the sampling interval is decreased when a warning is given is more art than science. The "twice the original frequency" rule is strictly a rule of thumb. It may be that the sampling interval should be reduced to $\frac{1}{2}$, $\frac{1}{4}$, or $\frac{1}{8}$ the original interval. Such a decision depends on many factors, including how fast the process is expected to change. By choosing an appropriate variable sampling interval, particularly a smaller interval when an out-of-control process is suspected, the response time to an out-of-control condition can be significantly reduced.

## Exercises

10-1.  What are some of the problems associated with overcontrol?

10-2.  What are some of the problems associated with undercontrol?

10-3.  Table 10-1 gives the probability of detecting a process shift in one sample for various sizes of shifts in the process mean. (a) What are the corresponding probabilities of detecting a process shift of one standard deviation in two samples? (b) In five samples? (c) In 10 samples? (d) In 25 samples?

10-4.  Table 10-2 gives the average run length for shifts in the process mean of 1, 2, 3, 4, and 5 standard deviations. Expand the table by computing the ARL for shifts in the process mean of 0.5, 1.5, 2.5, 3.5, and 4.5 standard deviations.

10-5.  If a process is in control (assuming a normally distributed performance characteristic), what is the probability of each of the following: (a) that a single point will fall outside the three-sigma control limits? (b) that a single point will fall above the upper control limit? (c) that two consecutive points will fall in either the upper or lower A zones? (d) that two out of three successive points will fall in the upper A zone? (e) that four out of five successive points will fall in the lower A or B zones? (f) that seven successive points will fall in the upper A, B, or C zones?

10-6. Suppose that a process has been running in control for several weeks with a process mean of 10, but that an upward trend has become evident. All points are within the three-sigma control limits and none of the zone rules have been violated. Is there reason for concern (i.e., is the process out of control?)?

10-7. A process engineer noticed a distinct up or down movement in a process control point at the beginning of each shift. While the engineer was discussing the issue with a process operator, the operator made the following statement: "I've been working with those guys on the A shift for years—and they always run the process too hot." Discuss the situation briefly. Be sure to comment on how you suggest the problem be remedied.

10-8. A variable sampling interval procedure is used to help monitor a volatile production process. The rule of thumb discussed earlier in the unit to set the sampling interval is employed, with the standard sampling interval set at one hour. (a) Suppose that a single point falls in zone A. When should the next sample be taken? (b) Suppose that the sampling interval has returned to one time per hour, but that for the next 12 samples every fourth point falls in zone A. At the time of the thirteenth sample, how much time has passed since the first sample was taken? Is there reason to believe that the process is out of control?

# Unit 11:
# Issues in Control Charting

# Unit 11

# Issues in Control Charting

This unit describes several important issues that are related to control charting in the process industries, including those related to deciding what, when, and where to measure, underestimation of process variation, overcontrol, stratification, mixing, and autocorrelation.

**Learning Objectives** — When you have completed this unit, you should:

A. Know the problems related to what, when, and where to take performance measurements.

B. Know the problems associated with underestimating the process variance or standard deviation.

C. Know the problems associated with overestimating the process variance or standard deviation, in particular those problems associated with stratification and improper sample mixing.

D. Know the problems related to process autocorrelation.

## 11-1. Introduction

In a typical production process, variation due only to common causes is thought to result in products with normally distributed performance measures. When special causes are present, the performance measures follow some nonnormal pattern and are therefore recognizable. Several such situations were described in Unit 10. Unfortunately, this straightforward approach of identifying special cause variation is often inappropriate for the continuous processing industry because many of the performance measures are not normally distributed, even when no special causes of variation are present.

In component manufacturing industries, where control charts have been most widely applied, processes are generally well understood and, since output is in discrete units having clear specifications, the problems of what, when, and where to measure are less likely to arise. This simplifies the solution approach, so that although quality problems may be difficult to solve, the procedures for solving them tend to be clear.

The situation in the process industries is distinctly different, however. Processes are often multi-staged, feedback- or feedforward-controlled around some process set point. Each process has numerous input variables, dozens of control variables (such as temperature and pressure), and a variety of product variations. The effects and relationships between all of these variables and controls are not usually known without error, so that when problems do occur, it is not clear what action should be taken to correct it. Multiple processes are usually interconnected, sometimes with feedback loops for recycling, so that a highly complex input-output system exists. There are also timing considerations and delays in reaction time so that the process effects of system-changing actions may take hours to occur.

Products are often mixtures of components that combine in a homogeneous fluid. They may be either gas or liquid depending on the temperature and pressure in which they are stored. They are typically kept in large storage tanks, so that several days of production may be incompletely mixed before being shipped off to the customer. In addition, samples of in-process characteristics are often difficult—possibly even dangerous—to obtain. Further, measurements of process components are generally less precise than measurements of component parts, so much so that in some cases correlated variables must be used. As a result of the above factors and others, obtaining meaningful measurements of product quality can be a challenge both during and after production and often result in data that is autocorrelated, nonnormal, and not well understood.

Several components of variation are typically present in process measurements: (1) short-term random variation, (2) long-term process variation, (3) measurement error, and (4) sampling variation. Short-term process variation is observed when products having the same nominal inputs, the same process conditions, and taking place at nearly the same time on the same unit show different results. Its causes can be anything from slight variation in raw materials to changes in environmental conditions, such as an ambient temperature change. Long-term process variation can be the result of subtle changes in the process, such as a buildup of waste products in the unit or catalyst aging, as well as operator induced change. Measurement errors are caused by the limited precision and accuracy of measuring devices. Sampling variation is due to the error inherent in estimating population parameters. All of these components of variation can be significant, so that the effective use of control charts in continuous processing environments is a continuous challenge.

## 11-2. What to Measure

The answer to the question of what to measure is often given by the product's specifications (e.g., a gasoline's octane rating). However, the characteristics described may be difficult to measure or may only be measurable near the end of the sequence of production equipment, too late for timely process adjustments. As such, it is sometimes necessary to measure other more readily measurable or more timely characteristics. In these cases, it is important that the characteristic measured is closely correlated with the quality characteristic described in the specifications. A generalized five-step procedure may help determine what characteristic to monitor.

1. Determine what the finished product is supposed to do, what makes the finished product valuable to the consumer.

2. Determine how the product's success at accomplishing its intended purpose can be determined.

3. Identify the characteristics, particularly any key performance characteristics, that contribute to the product's success.

4. Determine how to measure the key characteristic or some other correlated characteristic that contributes to the product's success.

5. Determine a way to control the quality characteristic being measured during production.

**Example 11-1:** Consider a simplified version of the production process for aspirin tablets. Using the five-step procedure, determine what characteristic should be monitored.

1. What is the aspirin supposed to accomplish? The consumer is interested in the aspirin's ability to get rid of pain quickly without side effects.

2. How can one determine how successful the aspirin's performance will be without consuming it? By determining what it is about the aspirin that makes it more or less effective. (In fact, laboratory experiments are necessary to make this determination.)

3. On what characteristics do the aspirin's successful performance depend? Analysis showed that the aspirin's performance is primarily a function of the amount of chemical x present in the aspirin. Unfortunately, it is only after the aspirin has been produced that the amount of chemical x present can be determined.

4. If it can't be measured during production, how can one determine how much chemical x is present in individual aspirin? Further study showed that the weight of individual aspirin tablets is highly correlated with the amount of chemical x present in the tablet. Therefore, control charts were set up on the aspirin's weight.

5. How is aspirin weight best controlled during production? Through a correlation study, the producer learned that the weight of individual aspirin tablets is closely related to molding pressure. As a result, control methods were developed to monitor molding pressure online.

## 11-3. When and Where to Measure

While the approach presented above can be applied to any production process, there is an important accompanying issue. As a general rule, the characteristic monitored should be one that can be modified early in the sequence of production equipment and operating steps. For instance, molding pressure is a controllable characteristic positioned early in the aspirin production process rather than being an after-the-fact product characteristic. Another example concerns the production of polyethylene resins. The melt index is a key performance measure. Unfortunately, when the melt index is found to be out of control, it may take several hours to bring the process back to target. Clearly, earlier detection, perhaps via a correlated variable, could be extremely valuable.

**Example 11-2:** DBP is a key carbon black quality characteristic. As such, DBP values for the finished product are measured and plotted on a control chart. Unfortunately, if problems are found with the finished product's DBP measurement, the quality of the carbon black cannot be changed.

In an attempt to obtain a more timely indication of carbon black quality, DBP levels at some earlier point in the process were monitored. The process involves a smoke header well prior to completion. Therefore, DBP measurements were also taken at the smoke header. However, since the relationship between DBP measurements at the smoke header and finished product DBP measurements was unknown, a correlation study was performed. DBP measurements were made on the carbon black at two-hour intervals at both the smoke header and for finished products. The results are shown in Table 11-1.

The first question addressed was whether or not DBP measurements taken at the smoke header are correlated with the finished product DBP readings and, if so, at what lag times they are most closely related. (Note: A lag time of 2 means that DBP measurements at the smoke header and for finished products are offset by two hours before the correlation analysis is performed. For example, the smoke header reading at 7 a.m. is paired with the finished product reading at 9 a.m., the smoke header reading at 9 a.m. is paired with the finished product

| Time | Smoke Header | Finished Product |
|------|--------------|------------------|
| 7 a.m. | 94.8 | 90.5 |
| 9 a.m. | 94.8 | 91.1 |
| 11 a.m. | 94.2 | 89.1 |
| 1 p.m. | 94.4 | 89.2 |
| 3 p.m. | 93.4 | 89.3 |
| 5 p.m. | 94.2 | 89.2 |
| 7 p.m. | 94.6 | 87.3 |
| 9 p.m. | 96.6 | 88.2 |
| 11 p.m. | 96.3 | 89.7 |
| 1 a.m. | 96.6 | 91.1 |
| 3 a.m. | 96.7 | 90.6 |

**TABLE 11-1. Sample DBP Measurements**

| Lag Time (hours) | Correlation Coefficient |
|---|---|
| 0 | 0.28 (based on 11 measurement pairs) |
| 2 | 0.58 (based on 10 measurement pairs) |
| 4 | 0.82 (based on 9 measurement pairs) |
| 6 | 0.42 (based on 8 measurement pairs) |

**TABLE 11-2. Correlation between DBP Measurements at Smoke Header and for Finished Products**

reading at 11 a.m., and so forth.) The results of the correlation study are shown in Table 11-2 with accompanying scatterplots shown in Fig. 11-1. (Note: The process of correlation analysis is described in detail in Unit 5.)

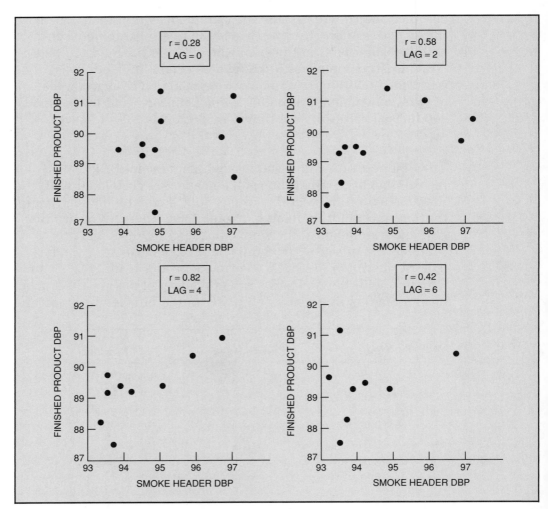

**Fig. 11-1. Scatterplots of DBP Measurements for Finished Products and at the Smoke Header for Lag Times of 0, 2, 4, and 6 Hours**

Based on the results shown, DBP readings at the smoke header are most closely correlated with finished product DBP measurements taken four hours later. This does not indicate that smoke header DBP measurements remain unchanged during the following four hours or that the smoke header DBP readings cause the finished product DBP reading. It does suggest, however, that there is a predictable relationship between DBP readings taken at the smoke header and finished product DBP readings that occur four hours later. The implication is that since this relationship exists, the quality of the carbon black produced (as indicated by finished product DBP measurements) can to some extent be controlled by controlling DBP levels at the smoke header.

## 11-4. Underestimation of Process Variation

If there is significant variation between subgroups, control limits based primarily on within-sample variation may underestimate the true process variation, resulting in inappropriately narrow control limits. This is illustrated with an example.

**Example 11-3:**  A producer of fireproof artificial stones used control charts to help control the stones' breaking strength. Because of the destructiveness of the test and the small production batches, samples were taken from single stones. Two cylindrical pieces were cut from each stone selected for testing. Each piece was then stressed until it broke, and the breaking strength was recorded. Using this sample size of two, the stones' producer set up a range chart to track process variation and an $\bar{x}$ chart to monitor the process mean.

Table 11-3 shows the values of the breaking strength measurements for 12 sample pairs. Also shown in Table 11-3 are the calculations to develop the centerlines and control limits for both the $\bar{x}$ and R charts.

Fig. 11-2 shows the $\bar{x}$ and R charts for the situation. The range chart indicates a well-controlled process dispersion. However, the $\bar{x}$ chart shows several points outside the control limits. As such, the implication is that the process is out of control.

| Sample | Measurements | | | |
|--------|------|------|------|------|
| Number | #1 | #2 | x̄ | R |
| 1 | 374 | 326 | 350 | 48 |
| 2 | 410 | 446 | 428 | 36 |
| 3 | 327 | 333 | 330 | 6 |
| 4 | 442 | 418 | 430 | 24 |
| 5 | 381 | 359 | 370 | 22 |
| 6 | 425 | 475 | 450 | 50 |
| 7 | 452 | 498 | 475 | 46 |
| 8 | 512 | 488 | 500 | 24 |
| 9 | 475 | 445 | 460 | 30 |
| 10 | 593 | 527 | 560 | 66 |
| 11 | 463 | 497 | 485 | 24 |
| 12 | 354 | 336 | 345 | 18 |

$\bar{\bar{x}} = 431.9$,  $\bar{R} = 32.8$

**TABLE 11-3. Breaking Strength of Artificial Stones**

R Chart:

Centerline:

$$\bar{R} = 32.8$$

Control Limits:

$$UCL_R = D_4\bar{R} = (3.268)(32.8) = 107.3$$
$$LCL_R = D_3\bar{R} = (0)(32.8) = \quad\quad 0.0$$

x̄ Chart:

Centerline:

$$\bar{\bar{x}} = 431.9$$

Control Limits:

$$UCL_{\bar{x}} = \bar{\bar{x}} + A_2\bar{R} = 431.9 + (1.88)(32.8) = 493.6$$
$$LCL_{\bar{x}} = \bar{\bar{x}} - A_2\bar{R} = 431.9 - (1.88)(32.8) = 370.2$$

It is more likely, however, that the process variation has been underestimated. The two samples taken from each stone produce relatively similar results (i.e., within-sample variation), while the differences between stones are relatively large (i.e., between-sample variation).

A more appropriate approach would be to average the two samples from each stone, treat the average value as an individual value, and then develop a two-period moving range chart to monitor the variation between stones. Once the variation between stones is in control, an x chart can be set up. Table 11-4 shows these calculations and Fig. 11-3 shows the two charts. Both charts indicate that the process is in control.

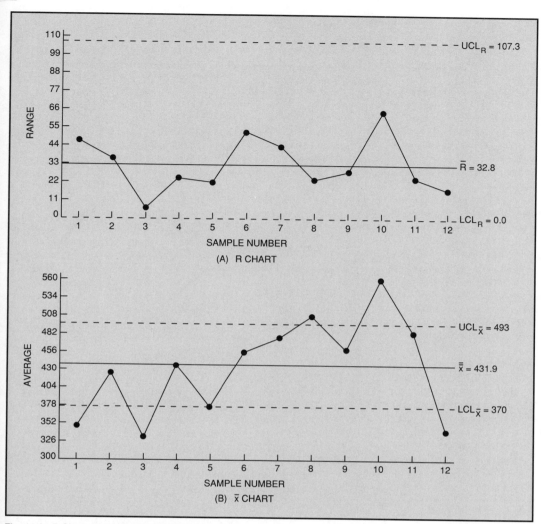

Fig. 11-2. R Chart and x̄ Chart for Artificial Stones

| Sample | Individual x | Two-Per. Moving Range $R_m$ |
|---|---|---|
| 1 | 350 | — |
| 2 | 428 | 78 |
| 3 | 330 | 98 |
| 4 | 430 | 100 |
| 5 | 370 | 60 |
| 6 | 450 | 80 |
| 7 | 475 | 25 |
| 8 | 500 | 25 |
| 9 | 460 | 40 |
| 10 | 560 | 100 |
| 11 | 485 | 75 |
| 12 | 345 | 140 |

$\bar{x} = 431.9, \quad \bar{R}_m = 74.6$

TABLE 11-4. Average Breaking Strength of Artificial Stones Treated as Individual Values

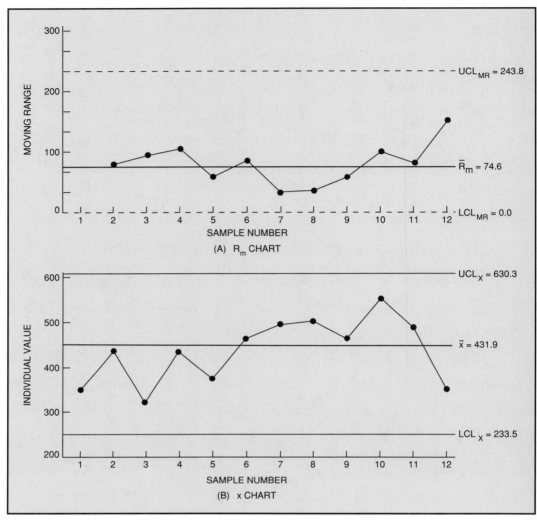

Fig. 11-3. $R_m$ Chart and x Chart for Artificial Stones

$R_m$ Chart:

Centerline:

$$\overline{R}_m = 74.6$$

Control Limits:

$$UCL_{MR} = D_4\overline{R}_m = 3.268\overline{R}_m = (3.268)(74.6) = 243.8$$
$$LCL_{MR} = D_3\overline{R}_m = 0.000\overline{R}_m = (0)(74.6) \quad\quad = \quad 0.0$$

x Chart:

Centerline:

$$\overline{x} = 431.9$$

Control Limits:

$$UCL_x = \bar{x} + E_2\bar{R}_m = \bar{x} + 2.66\bar{R}_m$$
$$= 431.9 + 2.66(74.6) = 630.3$$
$$LCL_x = \bar{x} - E_2\bar{R}_m = \bar{x} - 2.66\bar{R}_m$$
$$= 431.9 - 2.66(74.6) = 233.5$$

Note: $D_4$, $D_3$, and $E_2$ are based on a two-period moving range.

**Example 11-4:** In order to calibrate a scale used to weigh hopper cars loaded with finished product, three separate weighings of a standard test car thought to weigh about 266,000 pounds were performed each morning before the scale was used to weigh finished products. The sequence, performed three times, is as follows: the car is moved onto the scale, weighed, then moved off.

The results of 20 days of weighings are shown in Table 11-5, along with the calculations necessary to develop the control limits and centerlines for $\bar{x}$ and R charts. Averages and ranges based on the three readings were plotted on the charts as shown in Fig. 11-4. While the R chart seems to indicate that the process variation is well-behaved, 11 of the 20 points plotted on the $\bar{x}$ chart fall outside the control limits, a seemingly clear signal of an out-of-control process.

| Day | First Weighing | Second Weighing | Third Weighing | $\bar{x}$ | R |
|-----|----------------|-----------------|----------------|-----------|-----|
| 1 | 265,952 | 265,944 | 266,004 | 265,967 | 60 |
| 2 | 265,930 | 265,873 | 265,895 | 265,899 | 57 |
| 3 | 266,105 | 266,113 | 266,101 | 266,107 | 12 |
| 4 | 265,943 | 265,878 | 265,931 | 265,917 | 65 |
| 5 | 266,031 | 266,009 | 266,000 | 266,013 | 30 |
| 6 | 266,064 | 266,030 | 266,070 | 266,055 | 40 |
| 7 | 266,093 | 266,129 | 266,154 | 266,125 | 61 |
| 8 | 265,963 | 265,978 | 265,966 | 265,969 | 15 |
| 9 | 265,982 | 266,005 | 265,970 | 265,986 | 36 |
| 10 | 266,052 | 266,046 | 266,029 | 266,042 | 23 |
| 11 | 265,986 | 265,920 | 265,944 | 265,950 | 66 |
| 12 | 266,036 | 266,084 | 266,054 | 266,058 | 49 |
| 13 | 266,035 | 266,136 | 266,128 | 266,100 | 101 |
| 14 | 266,070 | 266,016 | 266,111 | 266,066 | 95 |
| 15 | 266,015 | 265,990 | 265,950 | 265,985 | 65 |
| 16 | 266,049 | 265,988 | 266,000 | 266,012 | 60 |
| 17 | 266,139 | 266,153 | 266,151 | 266,148 | 14 |
| 18 | 266,077 | 266,012 | 266,005 | 266,031 | 72 |
| 19 | 265,932 | 265,899 | 265,944 | 265,925 | 46 |
| 20 | 266,115 | 266,087 | 266,078 | 266,093 | 37 |

$\bar{\bar{x}} = 266,022$,  $\bar{R} = 50$

**TABLE 11-5. Weighings of Standard Hopper Car**

R Chart:

Centerline:

$$\overline{R} = 50$$

Control Limits:

$$UCL_R = D_4\overline{R} = (2.574)(50) = 129$$
$$LCL_R = D_3\overline{R} = (0)(50)\qquad = \quad 0$$

$\overline{x}$ Chart:

Centerline:

$$\overline{\overline{x}} = 266{,}022$$

Control Limits:

$$UCL_{\overline{x}} = \overline{\overline{x}} + A_2\overline{R} = 266{,}022 - (1.023)(50) = 266{,}073$$
$$LCL_{\overline{x}} = \overline{\overline{x}} - A_2\overline{R} = 266{,}022 - (1.023)(50) = 265{,}971$$

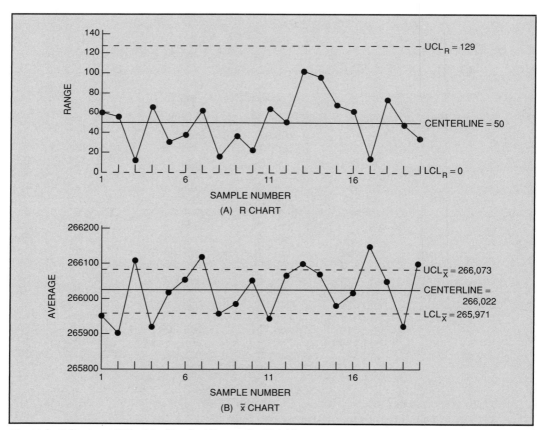

Fig. 11-4. R Chart and $\overline{x}$ Chart for Standard Hopper Car Weighings

| n | $A_2$ | $E_2$ | $d_2$ | $D_3$ | $D_4$ |
|---|-------|-------|-------|-------|-------|
| 2 | 1.880 | 2.659 | 1.128 | 0.000 | 3.268 |
| 3 | 1.023 | 1.772 | 1.693 | 0.000 | 2.574 |
| 4 | 0.729 | 1.458 | 2.059 | 0.000 | 2.282 |
| 5 | 0.577 | 1.290 | 2.326 | 0.000 | 2.114 |
| 6 | 0.483 | 1.180 | 2.534 | 0.000 | 2.004 |

TABLE 11-6. Factors for Control Charts

This situation is similar to the one described in the previous example. Again, two types of variation are present: one based on repeated measurements made on the same day and one based on measurements made on separate days. The average range of the three daily measurements is 50 pounds. This means that the estimated standard deviation of the $\bar{x}$ values is roughly 17.1 pounds (i.e., $\bar{R}/(d_2\sqrt{3}) = 50/[(1.693)(1.732)]$). (For convenience, the factor values for $A_2$, $E_2$, $d_2$, $D_3$, and $D_4$ are repeated in Table 11-6.) However, an estimate of the standard deviation of x (i.e., averages as individuals) based on a two-period moving range (Table 11-7) of the means is approximately 84.2 pounds (i.e., $\bar{R}_m/d_2 = 95/1.128$).

| Days | Average of Three Weighings as Individual Values | Two-Period Moving Range Values, $R_m$ |
|------|------------------------------------------------|---------------------------------------|
| 1 | 265,967 | — |
| 2 | 265,899 | 68 |
| 3 | 266,107 | 208 |
| 4 | 265,917 | 190 |
| 5 | 266,013 | 96 |
| 6 | 266,055 | 42 |
| 7 | 266,125 | 70 |
| 8 | 265,969 | 156 |
| 9 | 265,986 | 14 |
| 10 | 266,042 | 56 |
| 11 | 265,950 | 92 |
| 12 | 266,058 | 108 |
| 13 | 266,100 | 42 |
| 14 | 266,066 | 34 |
| 15 | 265,985 | 81 |
| 16 | 266,012 | 27 |
| 17 | 266,148 | 136 |
| 18 | 266,031 | 117 |
| 19 | 265,925 | 106 |
| 20 | 266,093 | 168 |

$\bar{x} = 266,022$        $\bar{R}_m = 95$

TABLE 11-7. Average Hopper Car Weights Treated as Individual Values

The moving range-based estimate is considerably larger than the range-based estimate. This means that the weight variation between days is significantly larger than the weight variation within days. The $\bar{x}$ chart's control limits based on within-days variation are therefore inappropriate.

Table 11-7 shows the average daily readings from Table 11-5 as individual values and shows the accompanying two-period moving range calculations. Fig. 11-5 shows the moving range and individual charts for the weighing process. Both charts indicate an in-control process. In other words, while there is clearly variation present, the process is performing at a consistent level within the constraints of the system. Changes to the system, such as purchasing a new scale, are necessary to reduce the variation further.

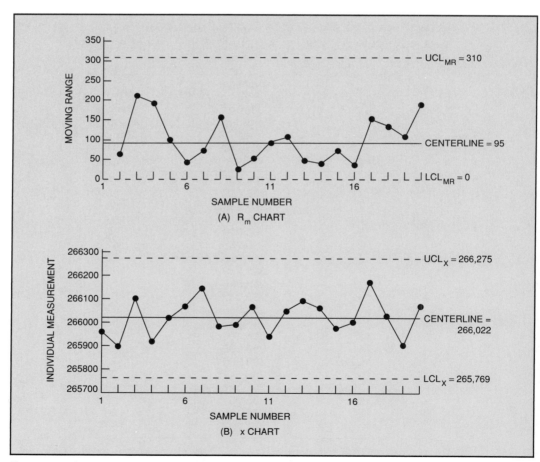

Fig. 11-5. $R_m$ Chart and x Chart for Standard Hopper Car Weighings

$R_m$ Chart:

Centerline:

$$\overline{R}_m = 95$$

Control Limits:

$$UCL_{MR} = D_4\overline{R}_m = 3.268\overline{R}_m = (3.268)(95) = 310$$
$$LCL_{MR} = D_4\overline{R}_m = 0.000\ \overline{R}_m = (0)(95)\quad = \quad 0$$

x Chart:

Centerline:

$$\overline{x} = 266{,}022$$

Control Limits:

$$UCL_x = \overline{x} + E_2\overline{R}_m$$
$$= \overline{x} + 2.66\overline{R}_m = 266{,}022 + 2.66(95) = 266{,}275$$
$$LCL_x = \overline{x} - E_2\overline{R}_m$$
$$= \overline{x} - 2.66\overline{R}_m = 266{,}022 - 2.66(95) = 265{,}769$$

## 11-5. Overcontrol

Fig. 11-6 shows a control chart pattern in which the control variable alternates between the lower and upper regions of the chart with all points within the control limits, a pattern frequently observed on x charts in the process industries. This pattern is a sign of process overcontrol. The implication is that each time a point falls below the set point or mean, the process is adjusted upward, often overcompensating. And, periodically, when a point falls above the set point or mean, the process is adjusted downward, again, often overcompensating. Ironically,

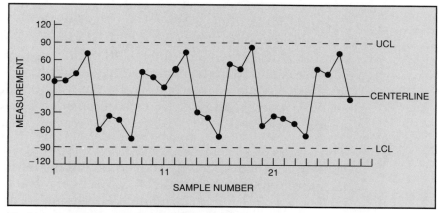

**Fig. 11-6. Control Chart Indicating Process Overcontrol**

such overcontrol actually increases rather than decreases the process variation.

It is sometimes argued that such actions are not really a problem in the process industries, that blending will take care of the resulting variation. This philosophy violates one of the most important principles of total quality management—do it right the first time—and obviously takes additional time and money. Therefore, overcontrolling situations should be avoided or remedied, since such patterned variation is likely to cause further variation later in the production process.

## 11-6. Stratification and Mixing

It is sometimes tempting to combine the output of several parallel and seemingly identical machines or production units into a single sample for monitoring on a single control chart (e.g., concurrent filling of paint containers using multiple nozzles). This practice can lead to two troublesome situations. One is referred to as stratification and the other as mixing.

### Stratification of Processes

The problem referred to as stratification is actually inappropriate stratification. When the results from parallel processes are combined and monitored with a single control chart, the implication is that the results from all of the separate process streams are identical (i.e., that they are from one stratum) and that they can be logically combined for decision making purposes. In fact, the separate process streams are invariably different from each other (i.e., they are from multiple strata), so that combining their results for monitoring purposes inappropriately masks their individualities.

**Example 11-5:** Control charts are to be used to monitor the production of injection molded bottles. Experience has shown that the outside diameter of the bottle is an appropriate measure of process performance. Suppose that an injection molding machine that molds four bottles at a time is used. Samples of size n = 4 are taken, with one measurement taken from each molding head.

The results of 20 samples are shown in Table 11-8. The columns headed $x_1$, $x_2$, $x_3$, and $x_4$ contain the measurements taken from heads 1, 2, 3, and 4, respectively. Note that the table's last two columns contain each sample's $\bar{x}$ and R values. Control limit and centerline calculations are also shown. Fig.

| Sample Number | $x_1$ | $x_2$ | $x_3$ | $x_4$ | $\bar{x}$ | R |
|---|---|---|---|---|---|---|
| 1 | 2.01 | 2.08 | 2.08 | 2.04 | 2.05 | 0.07 |
| 2 | 1.97 | 2.03 | 2.09 | 2.10 | 2.05 | 0.13 |
| 3 | 2.03 | 2.09 | 2.08 | 2.07 | 2.07 | 0.06 |
| 4 | 1.96 | 2.06 | 2.07 | 2.11 | 2.05 | 0.15 |
| 5 | 1.94 | 2.02 | 2.06 | 2.11 | 2.03 | 0.17 |
| 6 | 2.01 | 2.03 | 2.07 | 2.11 | 2.06 | 0.10 |
| 7 | 2.00 | 2.04 | 2.09 | 2.06 | 2.05 | 0.09 |
| 8 | 2.01 | 2.08 | 2.09 | 2.09 | 2.07 | 0.08 |
| 9 | 2.01 | 2.00 | 2.02 | 2.07 | 2.03 | 0.07 |
| 10 | 2.01 | 1.96 | 2.08 | 2.11 | 2.04 | 0.15 |
| 11 | 1.99 | 1.99 | 2.09 | 2.10 | 2.04 | 0.11 |
| 12 | 1.98 | 2.02 | 2.03 | 2.08 | 2.03 | 0.10 |
| 13 | 1.99 | 1.98 | 2.05 | 2.04 | 2.02 | 0.07 |
| 14 | 2.01 | 2.05 | 2.07 | 2.08 | 2.05 | 0.07 |
| 15 | 2.00 | 2.05 | 2.06 | 2.06 | 2.04 | 0.06 |
| 16 | 2.00 | 2.00 | 2.08 | 2.14 | 2.06 | 0.14 |
| 17 | 2.01 | 2.00 | 2.05 | 2.15 | 2.05 | 0.15 |
| 18 | 2.01 | 2.01 | 2.01 | 2.11 | 2.04 | 0.10 |
| 19 | 1.99 | 2.10 | 2.09 | 2.09 | 2.07 | 0.11 |
| 20 | 2.03 | 2.09 | 2.11 | 2.12 | 2.09 | 0.09 |
| $\bar{x}_i =$ | 1.998 | 2.034 | 2.068 | 2.092 | $\bar{\bar{x}} = 2.048$ | $\bar{R} = 0.104$ |
| $s_i =$ | 0.022 | 0.040 | 0.026 | 0.030 | | |

TABLE 11-8. Sample Measurements for Injection Molded Bottles

11-7 shows the sample statistics plotted on the resulting R and $\bar{x}$ charts.

R Chart:

Centerline:

$$\bar{R} = 0.104$$

Control Limits:

$$UCL_R = D_4\bar{R} = (2.28)(0.104) = 0.236$$
$$LCL_R = D_3\bar{R} = (0)(0.104) \quad = 0.000$$

$\bar{x}$ Chart:

Centerline:

$$\bar{\bar{x}} = 2.048$$

Control Limits:

$$UCL_{\bar{x}} = \bar{\bar{x}} + A_2\bar{R} = 2.048 + (0.729)(0.104) = 2.124$$
$$LCL_{\bar{x}} = \bar{\bar{x}} - A_2\bar{R} = 2.048 - (0.729)(0.104) = 1.972$$

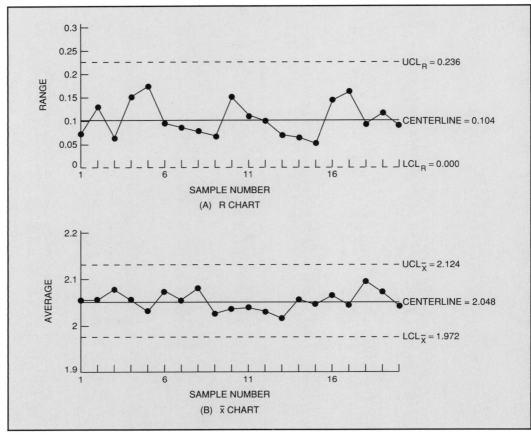

**Fig. 11-7. R Chart and x̄ Chart for Injection Molded Bottles**

Since the R chart indicates that the process variability is in control, the x̄ chart is examined. At first glance, the x̄ chart seems to indicate an extremely well-behaved process. In fact, the x̄ values closely follow the centerline. While this situation seems almost too good to be true, in actuality there is a problem. The variation in bottle diameter measurements for the process as a whole is significantly larger than the charts imply. The problem is that the data have been inappropriately stratified. That is, while the four molding heads actually represent four individual processes (i.e., four strata), they have been combined into one category (i.e., one stratum). As a result, characteristics of the individual processes are obscured.

Fig. 11-8 shows a run chart of the four individual molding head measurements. Taken individually, the molding measurements from each of the four heads seem to be well behaved, with similar standard deviations of 0.022, 0.040, 0.026, and 0.030, respectively. However, unknown to the individual examining

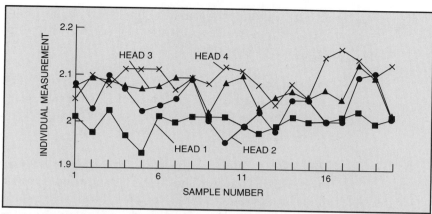

**Fig. 11-8. Plot of Individual Measurements for the Four Molding Heads**

only the Fig. 11-7 control charts, the mean levels of the
measurements taken from the four molding heads are quite
different, 1.998, 2.034, 2.068, and 2.092, respectively. The
difference between the largest mean and the smallest mean is
0.094 (i.e., 2.092 − 1.998), considerably more than the 0.076
three standard deviation spread of the $\bar{x}$ chart.

The standard deviation used in the $\bar{x}$ chart of Fig. 11-7 was
estimated using the range method, the result is 0.0253. That is,

$$3\hat{\sigma}_{\bar{x}} = A_2 \bar{R}$$

$$\hat{\sigma}_{\bar{x}} = (0.729)(0.104)/3$$

$$= 0.0253$$

If the standard deviation of the sample mean $\bar{x}$ is estimated by
taking the square root of the sum of the variances divided by 4,
the result is 0.151. That is,

$$s_{\bar{x}} = \sqrt{(s_{x1}^2 + s_{x2}^2 + s_{x3}^2 + s_{x4}^2)/n}$$

$$= \sqrt{(0.022^2 + 0.040^2 + 0.026^2 + 0.030^2)/4}$$

$$= 0.0151$$

The two estimates of the standard deviation of the mean differ
significantly because of the differences between the four
process means. The range-based estimate (0.0253) is
approximately 1.7 times larger than the variance-based estimate
(0.0151) because it includes both the process variation and the
differences between the means of the four heads as part of the

standard deviation estimate. Therefore, the range-based $\bar{x}$ chart control limits are inappropriately wide and may provide a false sense of process control.

Two related problems typically result. First, the control chart is insensitive to changes in the overall process mean. Second, the control chart is insensitive to changes in individual process means.

Table 11-9 shows 10 additional samples taken from each of the four molding heads. The first five samples (samples 21–25) reflect an average increase of one standard deviation for each of the four molding heads. This might occur, for instance, if there is a common problem with raw materials. The next five samples (samples 26–30) reflect normal variation in the results taken from molding heads 1, 3, and 4 (i.e., similar readings to those in samples 1–20), but show a two standard deviation increase in the results taken from molding head number 2 (i.e., from $\bar{x}_2 = 2.034$ to $\bar{x}_2 = 2.112$; note $s_2 = 0.040$).

Fig. 11-9 shows the extended results plotted on an R chart and an $\bar{x}$ chart. Notice that while there is an increase in the level of the plotted points from sample number 21 on (i.e., $\bar{x}$ chart), no points fall outside the three-sigma limits as the result of either problem. Of course, as the result of both process changes, there are runs of points above the centerline.

To avoid the stratification problem, individual control charts should be maintained on each of the four heads. For example, an x chart for head number 2 is shown in Fig. 11-10. It is apparent that the two-standard deviation shift in the mean of

| Sample Number | $x_1$ | $x_2$ | $x_3$ | $x_4$ | $\bar{x}$ | R |
|---|---|---|---|---|---|---|
| 21 | 2.01 | 1.97 | 2.08 | 2.07 | 2.03 | 0.11 |
| 22 | 1.97 | 1.97 | 2.03 | 2.08 | 2.01 | 0.11 |
| 23 | 1.99 | 2.05 | 2.05 | 2.05 | 2.03 | 0.06 |
| 24 | 2.01 | 2.09 | 1.98 | 2.07 | 2.04 | 0.11 |
| 25 | 2.04 | 2.03 | 2.05 | 2.09 | 2.05 | 0.06 |
| 26 | 1.97 | 2.11 | 2.07 | 2.11 | 2.07 | 0.14 |
| 27 | 1.98 | 2.13 | 2.07 | 2.02 | 2.05 | 0.09 |
| 28 | 1.94 | 2.10 | 2.04 | 2.11 | 2.05 | 0.17 |
| 29 | 1.97 | 2.11 | 2.06 | 2.12 | 2.07 | 0.15 |
| 30 | 2.02 | 2.10 | 2.02 | 2.03 | 2.04 | 0.02 |

TABLE 11-9. Additional Measurements for the Four Molding Heads

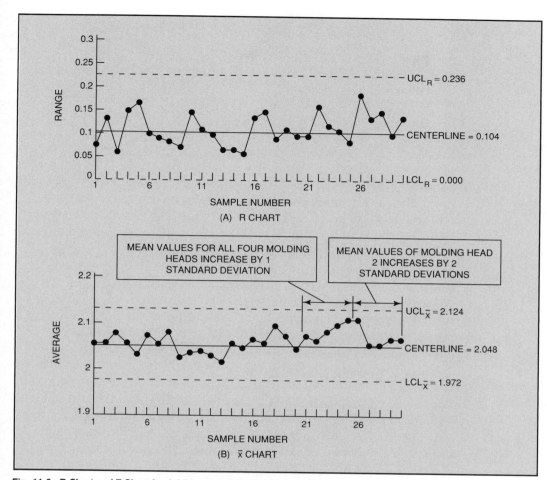

Fig. 11-9.  R Chart and $\bar{x}$ Chart for Additional Molding Measurements

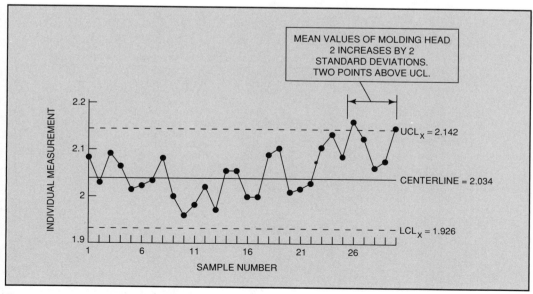

Fig. 11-10.  x Chart for Molding Head #2

head number 2 that took place just before sample 26 would have been detected quickly.

## Mixture of Processes

A related but slightly different problem, referred to as mixing, sometimes occurs when the data from multiple processes are combined to create a single control chart but observations from single processes are plotted on the chart. Fig. 11-11 shows an unusual pattern in which the plotted points tend to be well above or well below the centerline, but not outside either control limit. This pattern often occurs when multiple processes having different means are monitored with a single chart, with samples taken from individual processes plotted on the chart. For example, in the bottle production example discussed earlier, the pattern might occur as the result of plotting sample values from only one molding head at a time (e.g., observations from head number 3 at 1 p.m., observations from head number 1 at 2 p.m., and so forth) on a control chart whose centerline and control limits were created by combining the results from all four molding heads. The individual processes may or may not be in statistical control, but since the control limits are based on a mixture of all four processes, the limits tend to be wider than they would be for individual processes. In summary, each process stream should have a separate control chart.

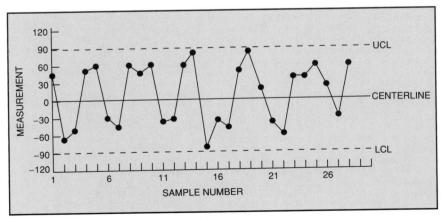

Fig. 11-11. Single Control Chart from a Mixture of Processes

## 11-7.  Autocorrelation

Autocorrelation, first described in Unit 5, is a measure of the degree to which individual observations from a single process are related to each other. If autocorrelation exists to a significant degree in a process, usually two types of variation are present: short-term variation (that results in dependencies between successive observations) and long-term variation (that results in cycles or trends). Short-term variation can be estimated using the moving range chart, while both short- and long-term variation can be estimated using a procedure that utilizes the sample estimate of the standard deviation.

In statistical process control applications, the process standard deviation (i.e., the standard deviation of individual measurements) is typically estimated based on the average range (i.e., $s = \overline{R}/d_2$). The range-based estimate is generally used for two reasons: (1) because of the awkward formula for computing the sample standard deviation and (2) because the moving range frequently results in a better estimate of the standard deviation, especially if a special cause of variation is present. Of course, since electronic calculators are readily available, the first reason is now less compelling.

One of the major differences between the process industries and the component parts industries is the frequency of applications that involve autocorrelation. In the process industries, successive measurements are often autocorrelated. Statistically, because autocorrelated processes tend to have closely bunched values in individual subgroups, the result is that the range-based estimate of the process standard deviation tends to be smaller than the true process standard deviation. As a consequence, when process results are autocorrelated, x or $\overline{x}$ chart control limits based on the moving range are typically too narrow.

**Example 11-6:**  A process results in the production of carbon black pellets. The measurements used to monitor the process are made on a performance variable known as DBP. Seventy-two individual values were recorded and used to compute the centerline and the accompanying control limits. These sample values were taken at four-hour intervals over a 12-day period and are shown in Table 11-10.

| | | | | | **Days** | | | | | | | |
|---|---|---|---|---|---|---|---|---|---|---|---|---|
| **Times** | **Sample No.** | **1–2** | **Sample No.** | **3–4** | **Sample No.** | **5–6** | **Sample No.** | **7–8** | **Sample No.** | **9–10** | **Sample No.** | **11–12** |
| 3 p.m. | 1 | 95 | 13 | 109 | 25 | 103 | 37 | 78 | 49 | 97 | 61 | 97 |
| 7 p.m. | 2 | 100 | 14 | 110 | 26 | 103 | 38 | 102 | 50 | 97 | 62 | 98 |
| 11 p.m. | 3 | 104 | 15 | 100 | 27 | 98 | 39 | 112 | 51 | 93 | 63 | 99 |
| 3 a.m. | 4 | 105 | 16 | 104 | 28 | 103 | 40 | 95 | 52 | 98 | 64 | 101 |
| 7 a.m. | 5 | 111 | 17 | 97 | 29 | 102 | 41 | 96 | 53 | 101 | 65 | 99 |
| 11 a.m. | 6 | 99 | 18 | 127 | 30 | 106 | 42 | 90 | 54 | 98 | 66 | 102 |
| 3 p.m. | 7 | 100 | 19 | 112 | 31 | 93 | 43 | 91 | 55 | 94 | 67 | 105 |
| 7 p.m. | 8 | 108 | 20 | 106 | 32 | 98 | 44 | 97 | 56 | 98 | 68 | 106 |
| 11 p.m. | 9 | 101 | 21 | 103 | 33 | 108 | 45 | 90 | 57 | 100 | 69 | 107 |
| 3 a.m. | 10 | 105 | 22 | 100 | 34 | 111 | 46 | 90 | 58 | 94 | 70 | 105 |
| 7 a.m. | 11 | 113 | 23 | 98 | 35 | 107 | 47 | 90 | 59 | 97 | 71 | 103 |
| 11 a.m. | 12 | 114 | 24 | 102 | 36 | 104 | 48 | 100 | 60 | 103 | 72 | 116 |

**TABLE 11-10. Sample DBP Values from a Carbon Black Production Process**

The first step is to establish that the process variability is in control. As such, a two-period moving range chart is developed (Fig. 11-12).

$R_m$ Chart:

Centerline:

$$\overline{R}_m = 5.5$$

Control Limits:

$$UCL_{MR} = 3.268\,\overline{R}_m = (3.268)(5.48) = 17.9$$

$$LCL_{MR} = 0.000\,\overline{R}_m = 0.0$$

Sample numbers 18, 36, and 37 have $R_m$ values well above the upper control limit. The event log indicated that the process was running with "low tint" when sample number 18 was taken. This problem was corrected. The low value of sample number 37 was the result of a "ligno problem." This problem was corrected as well.

Since the control limits were artificially inflated by the two outliers, they were revised by replacing the outliers with the average of the preceding and succeeding points. The original sample number 18 value of 127 was replaced with $(112 + 97)/2 = 104.5$, rounded off to 105, and the sample number 37 value of 78 was replaced with $(104 + 102)/2 = 103$.

The revised moving range chart had the following characteristics: $UCL_{MR} = 14.3$, $LCL_{MR} = 0.0$, centerline = 4.4.

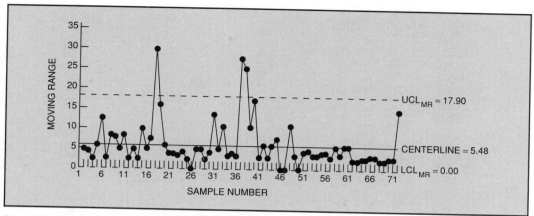

Fig. 11-12. Two-Period $R_m$ Chart for Carbon Black Process

Moving range number 39 fell above the new upper control limit, a problem also attributable to low tint for sample number 39. The 112 value was replaced by the average of samples 38 and 40 and the control limits recomputed (i.e., $UCL_{MR} = 13.4$, $LCL_{MR} = 0.0$, centerline $= 4.1$). No moving ranges fell outside these limits indicating an in-control process variation. The revised set of data is shown in Table 11-11 and the revised $R_m$ chart shown in Fig. 11-13. Table 11-11 also includes several other statistical results, one an estimate of the autocorrelation (for lag $= 1$) present in the process.

| Times | \multicolumn{12}{c}{Days} |
|---|---|---|---|---|---|---|---|---|---|---|---|---|
| | \multicolumn{2}{c}{1–2} | \multicolumn{2}{c}{3–4} | \multicolumn{2}{c}{5–6} | \multicolumn{2}{c}{7–8} | \multicolumn{2}{c}{9–10} | \multicolumn{2}{c}{11–12} |
| | $x_i$ | $x_i - \bar{x}$ | $x_i$ | $x_i - \bar{x}$ | $x_i$ | $x_i - \bar{x}$ | $x_i$ | $x_i - \bar{x}$ | $x_i$ | $x_i - \bar{x}$ | $x_i$ | $x_i - \bar{x}$ |
| 3 p.m. | 95 | −6.2 | 109 | 7.8 | 103 | 1.8 | 103 | 1.8 | 97 | −4.2 | 97 | −4.2 |
| 7 p.m. | 100 | −1.2 | 110 | 8.8 | 103 | 1.8 | 102 | 0.8 | 97 | −4.2 | 98 | −3.2 |
| 11 p.m. | 104 | 2.8 | 100 | −1.2 | 98 | −3.2 | 99 | −2.2 | 93 | −8.2 | 99 | −2.2 |
| 3 a.m. | 105 | 3.8 | 104 | 2.8 | 103 | 1.8 | 95 | −6.2 | 98 | −3.2 | 101 | −0.2 |
| 7 a.m. | 111 | 9.8 | 97 | −4.2 | 102 | 0.8 | 96 | −5.2 | 101 | −0.2 | 99 | −2.2 |
| 11 a.m. | 99 | −2.2 | 105 | 3.8 | 106 | 4.8 | 90 | −11.2 | 98 | −3.2 | 102 | 0.8 |
| 3 p.m. | 100 | −1.2 | 112 | 10.8 | 93 | −8.2 | 91 | −10.2 | 94 | −7.2 | 105 | 3.8 |
| 7 p.m. | 108 | 6.8 | 106 | 4.8 | 98 | −3.2 | 97 | −4.2 | 98 | −3.2 | 106 | 4.8 |
| 11 p.m. | 101 | −0.2 | 103 | 1.8 | 108 | 6.8 | 90 | −11.2 | 100 | −1.2 | 107 | 5.8 |
| 3 a.m. | 105 | 3.8 | 100 | −1.2 | 111 | 9.8 | 90 | −11.2 | 94 | −7.2 | 105 | 3.8 |
| 7 a.m. | 113 | 11.8 | 98 | −3.2 | 107 | 5.8 | 90 | −11.2 | 97 | −4.2 | 103 | 1.8 |
| 11 a.m. | 114 | 12.8 | 102 | 0.8 | 104 | 2.8 | 100 | −1.2 | 103 | 1.8 | 116 | 14.8 |

Average DBP Value $= \bar{x} = 101.2$
Average Moving Range $= \bar{R}_m = 4.1$
Estimated Standard Deviation (based on $\bar{R}_m$) $= \bar{R}_m / 1.128 = 3.6$
Estimated Standard Deviation (based on $s_x$) $= s_x = 5.8$
$\Sigma(x_i - \bar{x})(x_{i+1} - \bar{x}) = 1409.4$
Estimated Autocorrelation (lag $= 1$) $= r = 0.59$
TABLE 11-11. Revised DBP Values for Carbon Black Production Process

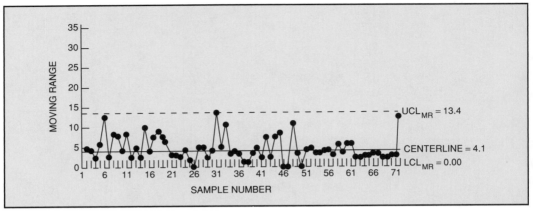

**Fig. 11-13. Revised Two-Period R$_m$ Chart for Carbon Black Process**

The next step is to develop the x chart's control limits based on an estimate of the process standard deviation. This is usually accomplished in one of two ways: (1) by using a direct estimate of the process standard deviation or (2) by using a moving range-based estimate. The lag = 1 autocorrelation estimate of r = 0.59 indicates considerable autocorrelation present in the process. (As a rule of thumb, autocorrelation is significant when it is more than $\pm 2/\sqrt{n}$, where n is the total number of data points used to calculate the autocorrelation coefficient.) In such cases, the moving range tends to underestimate the true process variation by considering only short-term variation, so that a direct calculation of the process standard deviation is more effective. The direct estimate of the standard deviation is $s_x = 5.8$ (from Table 11-11). The resulting x chart is shown in Fig. 11-14 and the control limit calculations are shown below. An examination of Fig. 11-14 indicates that the process is in control. (Note: The presence of a significant degree of autocorrelation in the process in effect negates the usefulness of the run rules. As such, violations of these rules in Fig. 11-14 are ignored.)

x Chart:

Centerline:

$$\bar{x} = 101.2$$

Control Limits:

$$UCL_x = \bar{x} + 3s_x = 101.2 + 3(5.8) = 118.6$$

$$LCL_x = \bar{x} - 3s_x = 101.2 - 3(5.8) = \phantom{0}83.8$$

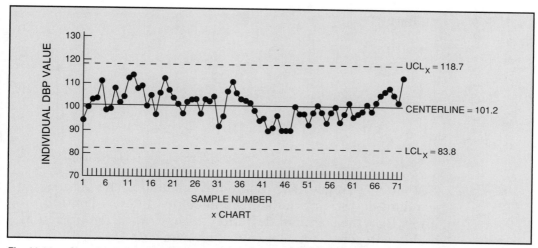

Fig. 11-14. x Chart for Carbon Black Process (Standard Deviation Estimate Based on Standard Deviation Method)

To demonstrate the problem with using the range-based method of estimating the process standard deviation when autocorrelation is present, x chart control limits using this approach are developed for the same process. The revised set of 72 data points shown in Table 11-11 were used. The x chart computations, based on the two-period average moving range estimate of 4.1, are shown below, while a plot of the individual measurements is shown in Fig. 11-15. Note that the control limits are significantly narrower than those developed for the Fig. 11-14 x chart. Seven points fall outside the control limits, even though no special cause could be identified.

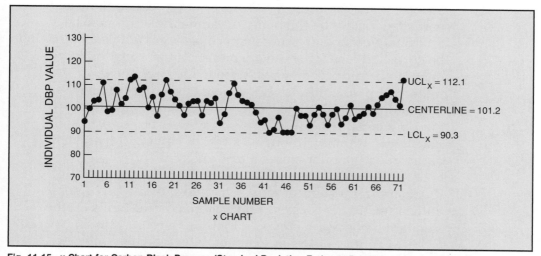

Fig. 11-15. x Chart for Carbon Black Process (Standard Deviation Estimate Based on Average Moving Range)

x Chart:

Centerline:

$$\overline{x} = 101.2$$

Control Limits:

$$UCL_x = \overline{x} + A_2\overline{R}_m = 101.2 + 2.66(4.1) = 112.1$$

$$LCL_x = \overline{x} - A_2\overline{R}_m = 101.2 - 2.66(4.1) = \phantom{0}90.3$$

The moving range-based method of calculating the process standard deviation results in significantly different control limits than the standard deviation method when the process is highly autocorrelated. The moving range-based method treats the variation due to process autocorrelation as special cause variation (note out-of-control points in Fig. 11-13), while the standard deviation method treats this variation as common cause variation (note no out-of-control points in Fig. 11-12).

The logical question then is, which method should be used to compute control limits, the standard deviation method or the range-based method? Unfortunately, the answer often is not a simple one. A more basic question is, what is the purpose of control charting? The purpose of control charting is to distinguish between variation due to common causes and special causes. If common cause variation is statistically described by a random variable that is independent and normally distributed, variation due to autocorrelation is not common cause variation (since the values are neither independent nor normally distributed). On the other hand, if special cause variation is defined as any problem that can be corrected locally by the operator, autocorrelation may be accurately described as common cause variation (since it cannot be corrected locally by the operator). Autocorrelation in a continuous process may result from a variety of causes, including poor control rules, process overcontrol, process undercontrol, variation in raw materials, and variation in environmental conditions. These can only be corrected by management intervention. As a result, solving the problem of autocorrelation often poses a real dilemma.

Two short-term solutions are sometimes used when significant autocorrelation is present: (1) base the control limits on the standard deviation method and ignore the run rules, and (2) use CUSUM control charts or exponentially weighted moving average (EWMA) control charts rather than one of the more traditional control charts. CUSUM charts (presented in Unit 13) and EWMA charts (presented in Unit 14) have been effectively employed to monitor processes having significant autocorrelation.

## Exercises

11-1. In typical production processes, variation due only to common causes results in products with normally distributed performance measures. Unfortunately, this is sometimes not the case in continuous processing plants. Why not?

11-2. What are the key issues in choosing appropriate performance measures for control charting?

11-3. What are the key issues in deciding when and where to collect process data for charting?

11-4. A gasoline processing plant recently instituted a control charting procedure on one of its units. The procedure is set up as follows: One time each hour, a small beaker of gasoline is sampled and immediately taken to the lab for analysis. The gasoline in the beaker is poured into five separate test tubes. The gasoline in each test tube is analyzed, resulting in five octane rating values. Using the measurement values obtained, $\bar{x}$ and R values are calculated for each sample and $\bar{x}$ and R charts developed and maintained. Do you see anything wrong with the control charting procedure? Discuss briefly.

11-5. A control charting procedure has been set up to monitor pump wear. Vibration measurements are taken daily on all four corners of the pump's base. Average and range values are then computed daily and plotted on $\bar{x}$ and R charts. Do you see any problems with the control charting procedure? Discuss briefly.

11-6. Three identically constructed production units continuously produce the same chemical compound. Because of the sampling and analysis time required, however, only one of the three units is sampled each hour (i.e., each unit is sampled once every three hours). Four measurements are taken at each sample point. Results from the 15-hour span are shown below. (a) Compute $\bar{x}$ and R chart control limits based on the data. Is the process in control? (b) Compute $\bar{x}$ and R chart control limits for each of the three individual units. Are all three units in control? (c) Comment on your findings in parts (a) and (b).

| Sample No. | Unit No. | Measurements | | | |
|---|---|---|---|---|---|
| | | 1 | 2 | 3 | 4 |
| 1 | 1 | 77 | 73 | 76 | 71 |
| 2 | 2 | 79 | 84 | 78 | 85 |
| 3 | 3 | 69 | 75 | 72 | 67 |
| 4 | 1 | 74 | 73 | 75 | 79 |
| 5 | 2 | 81 | 84 | 86 | 79 |
| 6 | 3 | 65 | 64 | 68 | 70 |
| 7 | 1 | 78 | 76 | 74 | 72 |
| 8 | 2 | 79 | 87 | 82 | 83 |
| 9 | 3 | 72 | 64 | 67 | 69 |
| 10 | 1 | 79 | 71 | 75 | 75 |
| 11 | 2 | 81 | 86 | 85 | 83 |
| 12 | 3 | 71 | 63 | 65 | 65 |
| 13 | 1 | 69 | 74 | 72 | 73 |
| 14 | 2 | 78 | 84 | 82 | 82 |
| 15 | 3 | 73 | 69 | 68 | 65 |

**Measurements**

11-7.  A polyethylene product in pellet form is shipped to customers in large rail cars. Before shipping, pellets are randomly selected from three positions in the rail car (one from one end, one from the middle, and one from the other end) before the car is shipped. A performance characteristic is measured on each set of pellets and $\bar{x}$ and R values calculated. The following table shows the results from 20 shipments. (a) Compute $\bar{x}$ and R chart control limits based on the data. Is the process in control? (b) If each $\bar{x}$ value is treated as if it were a single value, x and $R_m$ charts can be developed based on the 20 individual values. Is the process in control? (c) Discuss the difference between your findings in parts (a) and (b).

| Sample No. | Position | | |
|---|---|---|---|
| | 1 | 2 | 3 |
| 1 | 0.81 | 0.84 | 0.83 |
| 2 | 0.79 | 0.75 | 0.77 |
| 3 | 0.81 | 0.79 | 0.75 |
| 4 | 0.88 | 0.86 | 0.85 |
| 5 | 0.82 | 0.78 | 0.77 |
| 6 | 0.84 | 0.87 | 0.89 |
| 7 | 0.79 | 0.84 | 0.86 |
| 8 | 0.74 | 0.77 | 0.74 |
| 9 | 0.74 | 0.79 | 0.72 |

| Sample | Position | | |
| No. | 1 | 2 | 3 |
|---|---|---|---|
| 10 | 0.81 | 0.76 | 0.84 |
| 11 | 0.73 | 0.71 | 0.70 |
| 12 | 0.80 | 0.79 | 0.82 |
| 13 | 0.85 | 0.76 | 0.79 |
| 14 | 0.81 | 0.84 | 0.76 |
| 15 | 0.74 | 0.77 | 0.76 |
| 16 | 0.73 | 0.78 | 0.76 |
| 17 | 0.71 | 0.69 | 0.73 |
| 18 | 0.79 | 0.89 | 0.85 |
| 19 | 0.77 | 0.75 | 0.72 |
| 20 | 0.81 | 0.84 | 0.86 |

**Measurements from Polyethylene Process**

11-8. Upper and lower control limits for an individuals chart
are 610 and 590, respectively. The table below shows 10
individual values taken from the process. (a) After
constructing an x chart, plot the 10 values. (b) Estimate
the process standard deviation from the x chart's control
limits. (c) Estimate the process standard deviation from
the 10 data values shown in the table (use the two-period
moving range approach). (d) Comment on the difference
between the two standard deviation estimates,
particularly in terms of possible causes.

| Sample No. | Measurement |
|---|---|
| 1 | 605 |
| 2 | 592 |
| 3 | 608 |
| 4 | 593 |
| 5 | 606 |
| 6 | 597 |
| 7 | 604 |
| 8 | 593 |
| 9 | 607 |
| 10 | 591 |

11-9. A continuous production process is sampled on an
hourly basis. The table below shows the sampling results
for a 24-hour period in which the process appeared to be
well controlled. (a) Compute x chart control limits using
the moving range-based estimate of the standard
deviation and plot the 24 measurements. (b) Compute
the x chart control limits using a direct estimate of the
standard deviation based on the 24 measurements and

plot the measurements on the chart. (c) Comment on the
differences between the two control charts.

| Sample No. | Measurement | Sample No. | Measurement |
|---|---|---|---|
| 1 | 225 | 13 | 212 |
| 2 | 217 | 14 | 208 |
| 3 | 204 | 15 | 201 |
| 4 | 208 | 16 | 205 |
| 5 | 217 | 17 | 214 |
| 6 | 223 | 18 | 222 |
| 7 | 227 | 19 | 230 |
| 8 | 231 | 20 | 221 |
| 9 | 225 | 21 | 218 |
| 10 | 222 | 22 | 214 |
| 11 | 217 | 23 | 209 |
| 12 | 211 | 24 | 203 |

# Unit 12:
# Process Capability

# Unit 12

# Process Capability

Since product specifications are typically externally imposed customer requirements, even an in-control process may not produce a high proportion of products within specifications. This unit describes widely used methods for measuring the capability of a process to meet specifications in both the short run and the long run.

**Learning Objectives** — When you have completed this unit, you should:

A. Be able to compute and interpret both process-centered ($C_p$) and one-sided ($C_{pk}$) process capability indexes.

B. Be able to compute and interpret the process performance index ($P_p$) and the performance index adjusted for the process average ($P_{pk}$).

C. Be able to recognize different types of process capability and process performance problems and suggest alternatives for their solution.

## 12-1. Basic Principles

Recall that a process is said to be in statistical control when only common cause variation is present. While being in statistical control implies that the process is stable (i.e., predictable output), it does not guarantee that a high percentage of the process output will be produced within customer specification limits (i.e., a process can be consistently "bad"). Specifications are determined by the needs of customers and are not necessarily dependent on the capability of the production process. As such, the fact that a production process is in control is not necessarily indicative of its ability to produce within specification limits.

Process capability (sometimes called process potential) refers to the ability of a process to produce products that meet customer specifications. The process capability index, discussed later in this unit, is a numeric measure of the potential of a process to produce within specification limits. Process capability

245

calculations should be reserved for in-control processes. That is, when a process is not in statistical control, it is unstable. Process capability calculations made on an unstable process are simply numbers; they are not able to meaningfully describe the quality level achieved by the process.

Process performance calculations are distinguished from process capability calculations in two rather subtle ways: (1) by the period of time over which process data is collected and (2) by the fact that the data collected may include one or more time periods when the process is not in statistical control. Process performance calculations are intended to describe process performance over a long period of time, such as several weeks or months, while process capability calculations are intended to describe the capability of a process to meet customer specifications over a short period of time, such as minutes or hours. In fact, if process capability values are sent to customers along with the product, the data on which the calculations are based should be representative of the production run shipped.

An in-control process will produce nearly 100% of its product within $\pm 3\sigma$ of the process mean. If the process average is consistently maintained halfway between the upper and lower specification limits (i.e., USL and LSL) and the difference between the upper and lower specifications is greater than $\pm 3\sigma$, almost all of the process output will be within specifications. On the other hand, if the process mean is centered between the upper and lower specification limits and the difference between the upper and lower specifications is less than $\pm 3\sigma$, a significant proportion of the product will not be within specifications. If the process is not centered between the specification limits, the limit closest to the process mean becomes the more crucial one in determining the capability of the process to meet customer specifications. Of course, some processes may only have one specification limit, in which case that limit becomes the crucial one. The next few sections describe the mechanics of making process capability and process performance calculations.

**Example 12-1:** Fig. 12-1 shows a centered, in-control, normally distributed process with a mean of 20 and a process standard deviation of 3. Customer specification limits are $20 \pm 9$.

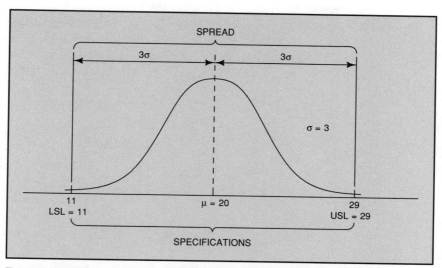

**Fig. 12-1. Centered, In-Control, Normally Distributed Process (Specifications Equal Spread)**

Since the process mean is centered between the specification limits and since these specification limits have an allowable spread exactly equal to the $6\sigma$ process spread, as long as process control is tightly maintained, the process is capable of producing almost all (99.73%) of its products within specification limits. Any shift in the process mean or increase in the process variation, however, will result in out-of-spec production. As a result, the process is marginally capable.

**Example 12-2:** Fig. 12-2 shows a centered, in-control, normally distributed process with a mean of 20 and a process standard deviation of 3. Customer specification limits are 20 $\pm$ 10.

This is a more favorable situation than the one described in Example 12-1 since the specifications are larger than the spread. The $6\sigma$ process spread is 18 and customer specification limits have a range of 20. As long as control of the process is tightly maintained, the process is capable of producing virtually all (>99.73%) of its products within specification limits. In fact, a small shift in the process mean ($\pm1$) or slight increase in process variation can be tolerated without producing less than 99.73% within specifications. As a result, the process is said to be capable.

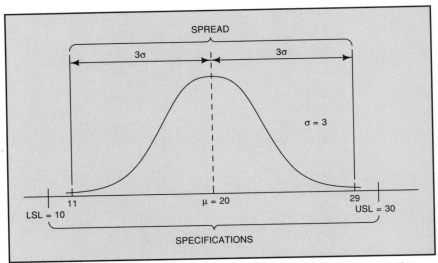

**Fig. 12-2. Centered, In-Control, Normally Distributed Process (Specifications Greater than Spread)**

**Example 12-3:** Fig. 12-3 shows a centered, in-control, normally distributed process with a mean of 20 and a process standard deviation of 3. Customer specification limits are 20 ± 7.

This situation is clearly an unsatisfactory one. The $6\sigma$ process spread is 18 and customer specification limits have a range of 14. Even when the process is centered and control is

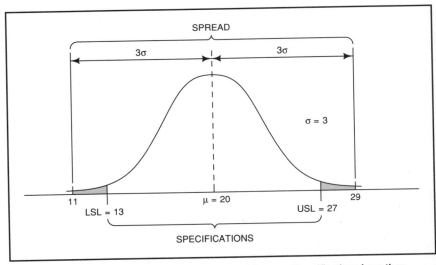

**Fig. 12-3. Centered, In-Control, Normally Distributed Process (Specifications Less than Spread)**

maintained, a significant proportion of its products will be produced outside specification limits. As a result, the process is not capable.

**Example 12-4:** Fig. 12-4 shows an in-control, normally distributed process with a mean of 25 and a process standard deviation of 3. Customer specification limits are 20 $\pm$ 14.

Since the $6\sigma$ process spread is 18 and customer specification limits have a range of 28, at first glance the process would seem to have little difficulty producing within specifications. However, since the process is not centered between the two specification limits, the upper specification limit becomes much more critical than the lower one.

Even with the process centered at 25, the process is capable of producing almost all of its product within specification limits. If the process mean were to exceed 25 by even a small amount, however, an increasing amount of product above the upper specification limit would be the inevitable result. On the other hand, the process mean would have to slip drastically (below 15) before products would consistently fall below the lower specification limit; that is, the potential of the process to produce within-specification product is great, but close attention must still be given to the process mean.

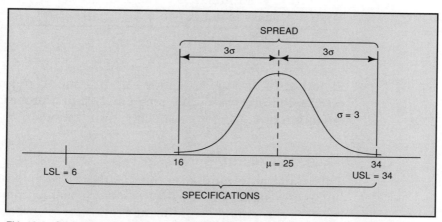

Fig. 12-4. Off-Center, In-Control, Normally Distributed Process (Specifications Greater than Spread)

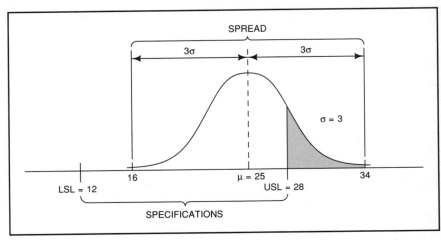

**Fig. 12-5. Off-Center, In-Control, Normally Distributed Process (Specifications Less than Spread & Problem with USL)**

**Example 12-5:** Fig. 12-5 shows an in-control, normally distributed process with a mean of 25 and a process standard deviation of 3. Customer specification limits are 20 ± 8.

Because the process is not centered between the specification limits, a large proportion of products is certain to be produced above the upper specification limit. However, even if the process were to be centered, since the process spread is larger than the range of the specification limits, a significant proportion of products is certain to be outside specifications. Such a process is not capable.

**Example 12-6:** Fig. 12-6 shows an in-control, normally distributed process with a mean of 17 and a process standard deviation of 3. Customer specification limits are 20 ± 8.

This situation is similar to the one described in Example 12-5 but exhibits a problem with the lower specification limit. The result is the same: a significant proportion of products is certain to be outside specification limits.

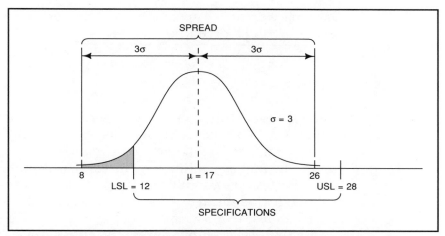

**Fig. 12-6. Off-Center, In-Control, Normally Distributed Process (Specifications Less than Spread and Problem with LSL)**

**Example 12-7:** Fig. 12-7 shows an in-control, normally distributed process with a mean of 19 and a reduced process standard deviation of 2. Customer specification limits are 20 ± 8.

In this situation, the process is not centered between the specification limits, but since the customer's specification range is greater than the process spread and since the process is not

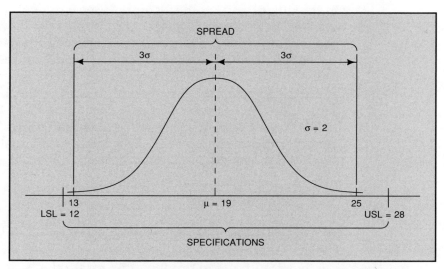

**Fig. 12-7. Off-Center, In-Control, Normally Distributed Process (Specifications More than Spread and Process Center Nearer LSL)**

alarmingly close to a specification limit, very few out-of-spec products will be produced.

## 12-2. Capability Indexes

A process capability index is a numeric indicator of the ability or potential of a process to produce products within specification limits. Intended to be representative of the short-run production capability of a process, a capability index value $<1$ indicates that a significant proportion of process output for the time period during which data was collected will be outside specifications, while a capability index $\geq 1$ indicates that almost all process output during the critical time span will be within specifications. Of course, capability index values significantly greater than 1 are preferred. In fact, process capability index values between 1.00 and 1.33 are generally considered only marginally acceptable values.

If an in-control process is centered, a measure of the capability of the process to meet customer specifications may be determined by comparing the actual process spread (i.e., $6\sigma$) with the customer specifications. Examples 12-1, 12-2, and 12-3 dealt with this situation. The capability index known as $C_p$ is intended for the process-centered situation.

On the other hand, if an in-control process is not centered between the customer's specification limits (or if only one specification limit is involved), a measure of the capability of the process to meet specifications may be determined by comparing half the actual process spread (i.e., $3\sigma$) with the difference between the process mean and the specification limit that is closer to the process mean. Examples 12-4, 12-5, 12-6, and 12-7 dealt with off-centered process situations. The capability index known as $C_{pk}$ is intended for situations in which the process is not centered between specifications.

### The $C_p$ Capability Index

Process capability index $C_p$ provides a numeric indication of the capability of a process that is centered between its specification limits to produce in-spec products. It is calculated as follows (i.e., specs over spread):

$$C_p = \frac{\text{Upper Specification Limit} - \text{Lower Specification Limit}}{\text{Process Spread}}$$

$$= \frac{\text{USL} - \text{LSL}}{6\sigma}$$

For the "marginally capable" situation shown in Fig. 12-1, the process capability index is

$$C_p = \frac{29 - 11}{29 - 11} = \frac{18}{18} = 1.00$$

For the "more capable" situation shown in Fig. 12-2, the process capability index is

$$C_p = \frac{30 - 10}{29 - 11} = \frac{20}{18} = 1.11$$

For the "not capable" situation shown in Fig. 12-3, the process capability index is

$$C_p = \frac{27 - 13}{29 - 11} = \frac{14}{18} = 0.78$$

The three capability index values provide indicators for three clearly different situations, although all three processes are centered between the specification limits. The first two $C_p$ values are $\geq 1$, representing potentially few cases of out-of-spec products, while the third $C_p$ value is $<1$, indicating a significant proportion of out-of-spec production.

Some companies use the inverse of the capability index, $1/C_p$, referred to as the process ratio, to describe process capability. Of course, using this ratio, values less than one indicate capable processes and values greater than or equal to one indicate incapable processes.

### The $C_{pk}$ Capability Index

Process capability index $C_{pk}$ provides a numeric indication of the capability of a process that is not centered between its specification limits to produce in-spec products. When this situation exists, the result is that one specification, the one closer to the process mean, becomes the process capability focal point. As a result, $C_{pk}$ provides a worst-case capability index, a process capability index value based on the specification most likely to be exceeded.

$C_{pk}$ is defined as the minimum of two one-sided capability indexes, $C_{pu}$ (based on the upper specification limit) and $C_{pl}$ (based on the lower specification limit), where $C_{pu}$ and $C_{pl}$ are calculated as follows:

$$C_{pu} = \frac{USL - \mu}{3\sigma}$$

$$C_{pl} = \frac{\mu - LSL}{3\sigma}$$

where, during the period of production in question, $\mu$ is the process mean and $\sigma$ is the process standard deviation.
For the situation shown in Fig. 12-4, the process capability index $C_{pk} = 1.00$, since

$$C_{pu} = \frac{34 - 25}{3 \times 3} = \frac{9}{9} = 1.00$$

$$C_{pl} = \frac{25 - 6}{3 \times 3} = \frac{19}{9} = 2.11$$

For the situation shown in Fig. 12-5, the process capability index $C_{pk} = 0.33$, since

$$C_{pu} = \frac{28 - 25}{3 \times 3} = \frac{3}{9} = 0.33$$

$$C_{pl} = \frac{25 - 12}{3 \times 3} = \frac{13}{9} = 1.44$$

For the situation shown in Fig. 12-6, the process capability index $C_{pk} = 0.55$, since

$$C_{pu} = \frac{28 - 17}{3 \times 3} = \frac{11}{9} = 1.22$$

$$C_{pl} = \frac{17 - 12}{3 \times 3} = \frac{5}{9} = 0.55$$

For the situation shown in Fig. 12-7, the process capability index $C_{pk} = 1.17$, since

$$C_{pu} = \frac{28 - 19}{3 \times 2} = \frac{9}{6} = 1.50$$

$$C_{pl} = \frac{19 - 12}{3 \times 2} = \frac{7}{6} = 1.17$$

The four capability index values provide indicators for four distinctly different situations. None of the processes are centered between the specification limits, but the first and last $C_{pk}$ values (Fig. 12-4 and Fig. 12-7) indicate processes that are at least marginally capable of meeting specifications.

Regardless of whether or not a process is centered between the specification limits, however, there are only three ways to improve the capability index for a process: (1) by moving the process mean, (2) by reducing the process spread, and (3) by increasing the range between the upper and lower specifications. Since customer specification limits are more likely to be reduced than expanded over time, most process improvement efforts tend to be focused on productive changes in the process mean or on process improvements leading to reductions in the process standard deviation (i.e., overall process spread).

Since process capability calculations are intended to be representative of a process over a relatively brief time period (e.g., minutes or hours or days), the question of how much data is required to meaningfully estimate the process mean and standard deviation is an important one. Assuming that the process is monitored using conventional control charts and that the process is in statistical control, the process standard deviation can be calculated using the standard formula of $6\sigma = 6\bar{R}/d_2$ and the process mean can be calculated using $\bar{x}$, provided that 10 or more samples (i.e., 10 subgroups) have been taken. Too few sample results provide only a marginally meaningful $C_p$ or $C_{pk}$ value.

## 12-3.  Process Capability Index and Fraction Nonconforming

Estimates of the fraction nonconforming represent the expected proportion of product that will be produced outside specifications. If the in-control characteristic being measured is approximately normally distributed, the properties of the normal distribution may be used to estimate the nonconforming proportions.

**Example 12-8:**  Fig. 12-8 shows an in-control, normally distributed process whose mean and standard deviation are 20 and 5, respectively, and whose specification limits are 10 and 30. Since the process mean is centered between the specification limits, the $C_p$ value is

$$C_p = \frac{30 - 10}{6(5)} = \frac{20}{30} = 0.67$$

Clearly, the process is not capable, but what fraction of the process output will not meet specifications?

If X is a random variable that represents the measurement of the product characteristic, the product is said to be out of specifications when the value of X for an individual product is either smaller than 10 or larger than 30. To estimate the fraction of nonconforming products, it is necessary to calculate the expected probability of an individual product that has a measurement value less than 10 or greater than 30.

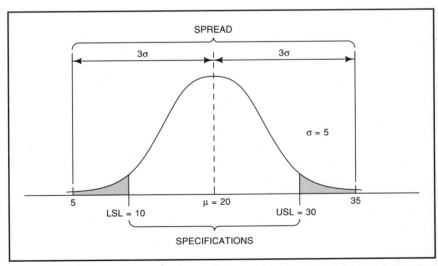

**Fig. 12-8. Estimating the Fraction Nonconforming (Process Centered between Specification Limits)**

Pr(out-of-specification product)

$$= Pr(X > 30) + Pr(X < 10),$$

when $\mu_x = 20$ and $\sigma_x = 5$

$$= Pr\left(Z > \frac{X - \mu_x}{\sigma_x}\right) + Pr\left(Z < \frac{X - \mu_x}{\sigma_x}\right)$$

$$= Pr\left(Z > \frac{30 - 20}{5}\right) + Pr\left(Z < \frac{10 - 20}{5}\right)$$

$$= Pr(Z > 2.0) + Pr(Z < -2.0)$$

$$= 1 - Pr(Z \leq 2) + 1 - Pr(Z \leq 2.0)$$

(then using Table B-1)

$$= (1 - 0.977) + (1 - 0.977)$$

$$= 0.046$$

The calculations show that, for this situation, approximately 4.6% of the products produced by the process during the period of time in question will be outside customer specification limits.

**Example 12-9:** Fig. 12-9 shows an in-control, normally distributed process having a process mean of 24, a process standard deviation of 3, and specification limits of 10 and 30.

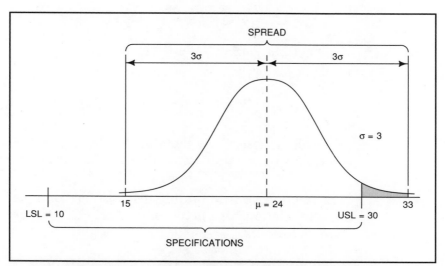

**Fig. 12-9. Estimating the Fraction Nonconforming (Process Not Centered between Specification Limits)**

Since the process is not centered between the specification limits, $C_{pk} = 0.67$, since

$$C_{pu} = \frac{30 - 24}{3(3)} = \frac{6}{9} = 0.67$$

$$C_{pl} = \frac{24 - 10}{3(3)} = \frac{14}{9} = 1.56$$

Once again, the process is not capable, but what is the fraction nonconforming?

When the measurement of the quality characteristic for an individual product is either smaller than 10 or larger than 30, the characteristic is outside specifications and the product is nonconforming.

Pr(out-of-specification product)

$$= Pr(X > 30) + Pr(X < 10),$$

when $\mu_x = 24$ and $\sigma_x = 3$

$$= Pr\left(Z > \frac{X - \mu_x}{\sigma_x}\right) + Pr\left(Z < \frac{X - \mu_x}{\sigma_x}\right)$$

$$= Pr\left(Z > \frac{30 - 24}{3}\right) + Pr\left(Z < \frac{10 - 24}{3}\right)$$

$$= Pr(Z > 2) + Pr(Z < -4.67)$$

$$= 1 - Pr(Z \leq 2) + 1 - Pr(Z \leq 4.67)$$

(then using Table B-1)

$$= (1 - 0.977) + (1 - 1)$$

$$= 0.023$$

The calculations show that about 2.3% of the products produced by the process will be outside specification limits.

The fraction nonconforming may also be computed using the simple relationships between $C_p$, $C_{pu}$, $C_{pl}$, and the fraction nonconforming.

For a centered process:

$$p_{nc} = 2Pr(Z \leq -3C_p)$$

For a noncentered process:

$$p_{nc} = \Pr(Z \leq -3C_{pu}) + \Pr(Z \leq -3C_{pl})$$

(Note: If only $C_{pk}$ is known, then $2\Pr(Z \leq -3C_{pk})$ provides an upper bound for the process fraction nonconforming.)

For the situations in Examples 12-8 and 12-9, the fraction nonconforming estimates may be computed as follows:

For Example 12-8:

$$C_p = 0.67$$
$$p_{nc} = 2\Pr[Z \leq -3(0.67)]$$
$$= 2\Pr(Z \leq -2.0)$$
$$= 2[1 - \Pr(Z \leq 2.0)]$$
$$= 2(1 - 0.977)$$
$$= 2(0.023)$$
$$= 0.046$$

For Example 12-9:

$$C_{pu} = 0.67$$
$$C_{pl} = 1.56$$
$$p_{nc} = \Pr(Z \leq -3C_{pu}) + \Pr(Z \leq -3C_{pl})$$
$$= \Pr(Z \leq -3(0.67) + \Pr[Z \leq -3(1.56)]$$
$$= \Pr(Z \leq -2.0) + \Pr(Z \leq -4.67)$$
$$= [1 - \Pr(Z \leq 2.0)] + [1 - \Pr(Z \leq 4.67)]$$
$$= (1 - 0.977) + (1 - 1)$$
$$= 0.023$$

These estimates are identical to those originally computed in Examples 12-8 and 12-9.

If process data are normally distributed, they can be plotted as a straight line on normal probability paper. Estimates of the expected percent of nonconforming product (as well as estimates of the process mean and standard deviation) can then be read directly from the chart. Fig. 12-10 shows the situation

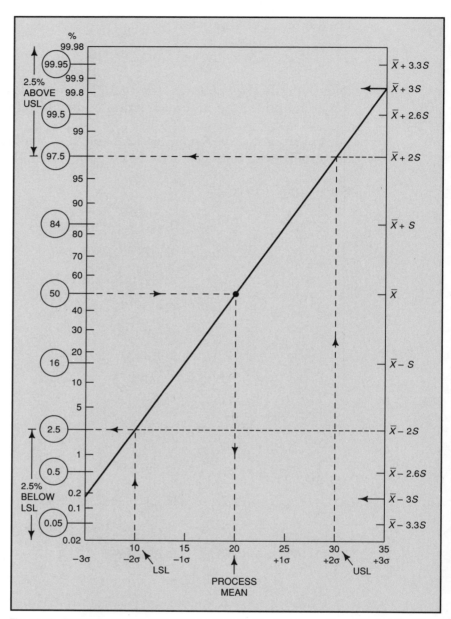

**Fig. 12-10. Estimating the Fraction of Nonconforming Product from a Normal Probability Plot**

for the case in which the process mean is 20, the process standard deviation is 5, and the specification limits are 10 and 30. The percent nonconforming is approximately 5%, 2.5% above the upper specification limit and 2.5% below the lower specification limit.

Table 12-1 shows the expected percent of nonconforming products for various $C_p$ values. Notice that when the $C_p$ value is

| $C_p$ | 0.4 | 0.6 | 0.8 | 1.0 | 1.2 | 1.4 | 1.6 |
|---|---|---|---|---|---|---|---|
| Percent Nonconforming | 23% | 7.2% | 1.6% | 0.27% | 0.03% | 0.003% | 0.0002% |

TABLE 12-1. Approximate Percent Nonconforming for Various $C_p$ Values

greater than 1, changes in $C_p$ seem to have little impact on the expected percent of nonconforming material. On the other hand, when the $C_p$ value is less than 1, $C_p$ value changes seem to have a much greater impact on the expected percent of nonconforming material.

The Table 12-1 results can be misleading. They, of course, are based on the assumption that the production process remains unchanged (i.e., the process mean and process standard deviation do not change). While it is statistically accurate to say that production processes whose $C_p$ values are 1.2 and 1.4 both produce nearly 100% of product within specification limits, it is also true that even small changes in the mean or standard deviation of the "1.2 process" are likely to have a much more drastic effect on product quality than small changes in the "1.4 process." In fact, a process having a $C_p$ value of 1.4 produces 10 times fewer out-of-spec products than a process whose $C_p$ is 1.2! In addition, the larger the $C_p$ value, the smaller the effect a shifting mean or slightly increasing standard deviation will have on the process output.

## 12-4. Process Performance Indexes

The process performance index $P_p$ is a measure of process capability over a long period of time (e.g., weeks or months). Over long periods, processes tend to exhibit greater variation. In fact, even a generally well-controlled process may have periods of lack of control over a period of several months. The process performance index is defined as follows:

$$P_p = \frac{USL - LSL}{6s}$$

where s is the long-term calculated standard deviation for the included population.

The performance index adjusted for the process average $P_{pk}$ is similar to $C_{pk}$, but uses the calculated process average for the entire included population rather than $\mu$ in its formulation. It is intended as an estimate of the process performance capability over an extended period of time rather than over a short period (such as a single customer's production run). $P_{pk}$ is the minimum of two one-sided indexes.

$$P_{pu} = \frac{USL - PA}{3s}$$

$$P_{pl} = \frac{PA - LSL}{3s}$$

where PA is the estimated process average over the entire period of time in question and s is an estimate of the process standard over the same period of time.

**Example 12-10:** For the last two months, a single supplier has provided all incoming materials for a production process. The upper and lower specification limits are 85 and 50. The process mean and process standard deviation based on data collected during this time period are PA = 66 and s = 5. Both a performance index ($P_p$) and a performance index adjusted for the process average ($P_{pk}$) are to be calculated.

Performance Index:

$$P_p = \frac{USL - LSL}{6s} = \frac{85 - 50}{6(5)} = 1.17$$

Performance Index Adjusted for the Process Average:

$$P_{pu} = \frac{85 - 66}{3(5)} = \frac{19}{15} = 1.27$$

$$P_{pl} = \frac{66 - 50}{3(5)} = \frac{16}{15} = 1.07$$

Since $P_{pu}$ is the minimum of the two, $P_{pk} = 1.07$.

## 12-5. Summary

When $C_p$ and $C_{pk}$ (or $P_p$ and $P_{pk}$) are calculated for a process that is centered, the two calculation methods yield the same index number. $C_{pk}$ is generally more widely used than $C_p$ since it is applicable whether or not the process is centered. However, the disadvantage of using only the $C_{pk}$ value is that it does not reveal whether a poor process capability is the result of a large process dispersion or is the result of a poorly centered process. If both $C_p$ and $C_{pk}$ are calculated and found to be significantly different, the difference is a clear sign that the process is off-center.

Both process capability indexes and process performance indexes depend on the customer specification limits and on the process itself. In reality, the specification limits may have been established somewhat arbitrarily. If specifications are narrower than actual process spread, the result will be small $C_{pk}$ values with correspondingly large percentages of nonconforming material.

Frequent changes in the specification limits may create confusion regarding the true process capability and true process performance. While a producer may have several customers for a single product, each with slightly different specifications, if the producer maintains one representative set of specifications, a representative $P_{pk}$ value may also be calculated.

Sorting conforming from nonconforming product allows only those products that meet specifications to be shipped but is, in effect, an open admission that the process is not capable (Fig. 12-11). In fact, sorting and poor process capability index values go hand in hand. For example, if the process mean and standard deviation are 20 and 5, respectively, and the customer specification limits are 10 and 28, the process performance index value $P_{pk} = 0.53$ [i.e., $(28 - 20)/(3 \times 5)$], even if every item shipped is within specifications. Sorting is time-consuming and costly, clearly does not improve the process, and can lead to embarrassing questions from customers who are expecting products from a capable process.

Three assumptions are implicit in the calculation of a meaningful process capability index value. Assumption 1 is that the process is in statistical control. If the process is not in control, capability index computations are meaningless. This assumption has been discussed at several points in the unit.

Assumption 2 is that estimates of the process mean and process standard deviation used in the capability index calculations are representative of the process. Ideally, these estimates should be based on a representative number of samples (more than 20) taken throughout the process.

Often these estimates are taken directly from the control chart. If autocorrelation is present in the process, the range-based estimate will significantly underestimate the true process standard deviation. This is because measurement values from autocorrelated processes tend to vary less within samples than

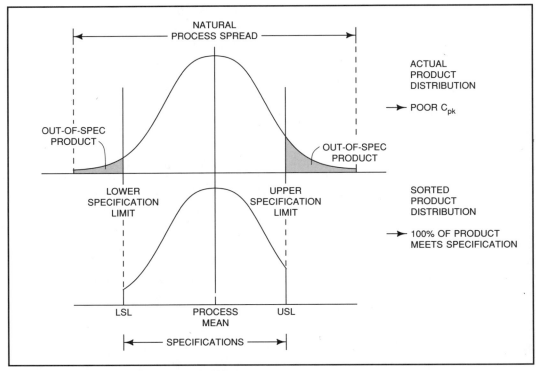

**Fig. 12-11.  Relationship between Sorting and Process Capability**

between samples. If the standard deviation is underestimated, capability index values will be unwittingly inflated since the process spread (which appears in the denominator of the various capability formulas) is underestimated. (See Autocorrelation, Unit 11.)

Assumption 3 is that the quality characteristic in question is approximately normally distributed. If the process is not normally distributed, the relationships presented earlier between $C_p$, $C_{pk}$, and percent nonconforming material are not valid.

Skewed product characteristic distributions are common in the processing industry. They often occur when the process is approaching some natural limit (e.g., 100% purity) or the detection limit of the measuring device (e.g., device does not record below 100 parts per million). Of course, it may be that the process is capable of meeting customer specifications even though the distribution of the process characteristic is skewed. One approach that is sometimes used in estimating the process capability index for a skewed process is to collect sufficient data to estimate the process spread even though it may be greater than $6\sigma$. The $C_{pk}$ formula may then be used with the estimate of the actual spread above and below the process mean replacing $3\sigma$.

Understanding the capability of a process can be helpful in a number of ways. For example, a process whose performance index is less than 1 even after considerable effort has been made to improve it may or may not warrant additional resources, depending on the potential economic benefits and the potential degree of process improvement. In fact, if the expense of correcting the problem cannot be recovered, one alternative is to get out of the business entirely rather than incur the costs associated with inspection and recycling or be known as a poor quality supplier.

On the other hand, a process with a very high process capability index gives management an opportunity to improve the product's competitive position in the market place. For example, if a process has a performance index of 3 or higher, it may be possible to distinguish the product by agreeing to tighter specifications that will eliminate some of the competition; or it may be possible to distinguish the product by the increased consistency (i.e., smaller variation) that the process offers.

A high process performance index may provide other positive options. For example, it may be appropriate to reduce the inspection frequency of a process or shift the process mean closer to the specification limit in order to reduce energy consumption. Both scenarios allow potentially increased profits.

Another reason that $C_{pk}$ values significantly greater than 1 are desirable is that each individual product is often only one part of a system having many components. For example, suppose a product (e.g., an automobile) is composed of 1,000 parts, each part having come from a process with $C_{pk} = 1$. The probability that any one individual part is defective is 0.0027. However, the probability that at least one of the 1,000 parts is defective is $1 - 0.9973^{1000} = 0.933$. That is, even when all 1,000 components have a $C_{pk} = 1$, there is more than a 93% chance of having at least one defective component in the product!

The primary criticism of these indexes is that they tend to oversimplify process characteristics by providing a single number for judging a process. While all processes have a variety of important measures, capability and performance indexes tend to reduce the focus to only one. Clearly, one single measure cannot substitute for plotting and thoughtfully analyzing a variety of process measures over time.

## Exercises

*Note: Since $C_p$ and $C_{pk}$ are much more widely used than $P_p$ and $P_{pk}$, these exercises have been set up for $C_p$ and $C_{pk}$. However, they are equally applicable for $P_p$ and $P_{pk}$ depending on the span of time over which the data has been collected.*

12-1. *Suppose that specification limits for a process are 500 ± 100 and that the process is in statistical control. What are the $C_p$ values for the process under each of the following conditions?*
(a) mean = 500 and standard deviation = 30
(b) mean = 500 and standard deviation = 40
(c) mean = 500 and standard deviation = 70
(d) mean = 500 and standard deviation = 20

12-2. *Suppose that specification limits for a process are 700 ± 100 and that the process is in statistical control. What are the $C_{pk}$ values for the process under each of the following conditions?*
(a) mean = 650 and standard deviation = 30
(b) mean = 680 and standard deviation = 30
(c) mean = 650 and standard deviation = 70
(d) mean = 650 and standard deviation = 20
(e) mean = 720 and standard deviation = 25
(f) mean = 720 and standard deviation = 40

12-3. *To monitor a process, samples of size n = 5 are taken from each of five batches of product. The overall average and accompanying average range are $\bar{\bar{x}}$ = 1.432 and $\bar{R}$ = 0.004, respectively.*
(a) *If the process specification limits are 1.430 ± 0.010, what is the $C_{pk}$ value for the process?*
(b) *If the process specification limits are 1.430 ± 0.015, what is the $C_{pk}$ value for the process?*
(c) *Assuming that the process performance characteristic is normally distributed and centered at 1.430, what specification limits should be set so that 95% of the individual items will fall within these limits?*
(d) *Assuming that the process performance characteristic is normally distributed and centered at 1.430, what specification limits should be set so that $C_p$ is approximately 1.5?*

(e) Assuming that the process performance characteristic is normally distributed, must be centered at 1.430, and must exhibit a $C_p$ value of 2.0, what must the process standard deviation be if the specification limits are $1.430 \pm 0.012$?

12-4. A normally distributed process measurement has an overall mean of 758 and a standard deviation of 19.4.
    (a) If the specification limits are 700 and 800, what percent of product can be expected to fall outside the specification limits if the process characteristic measured follows a normal distribution?
    (b) What is the $C_{pk}$ value for the process?
    (c) If the process can be centered at 750, what specification limits are necessary for $C_p$ to be 1.6?

12-5. Suppose that a process performance characteristic follows a normal distributed pattern with a mean of $\mu = 100$ and a standard deviation of $\sigma = 5.0$.
    (a) What proportion of production will fall outside the specification limits if the customer's specifications are $95 \pm 5$?
    (b) What is the $C_{pk}$ value for the process?
    (c) If the process mean is 100 and the $C_p$ goal is 1.5, what is the company's dilemma?

12-6. Four parallel processes are used to produce the same standard product whose specification limits are $1.500 \pm 0.005$ inch. A study of the processes carried out over several weeks yielded the following information:

| Machine | Average ($\bar{x}$) | $6\sigma$ |
|---|---|---|
| 1 | 1.495 in. | 0.004 in. |
| 2 | 1.502 in. | 0.006 in. |
| 3 | 1.500 in. | 0.012 in. |
| 4 | 1.498 in. | 0.002 in. |

    (a) Compute $C_{pk}$ values for each process.
    (b) If the average value can be readily shifted by adjusting the process, based on the data available, which is the best process (based on $C_p$)?

12-7. Calculate an upper limit for the proportion nonconforming (i.e., proportion of product outside specification limits) when:
    (a) $C_p = 0.9$
    (b) $C_p = 0.75$
    (c) $C_p = 1.00$

# Unit 13:
# CUSUM Control Charts

# Unit 13

# CUSUM Control Charts

In the processing industry, the use of control charts based on individual measurements is often necessary, because taking multiple measurements at a single point in time is often impractical. Typically, in such situations, the x chart is used. Unfortunately, the x chart is often slow to recognize small but consistent shifts in the process mean. In this unit, an alternative control chart, the cumulative sum chart, is presented.

Cumulative sum charts, better known as CUSUM charts, are not as widely used as the more traditional Shewhart x charts. One reason is the belief that modified x chart control rules (i.e., three-sigma control limits enhanced with zone rules and run rules) are sufficiently sensitive to process shifts. A second reason is that CUSUM charts are less quick to detect large, short-term changes in the process average. A third reason is the belief that CUSUM charts are overly complicated.

CUSUM charts have several advantages over more traditional control charts, however. They are usually able to detect small, sustained shifts in the process mean in fewer samples than x charts; they can be designed to detect specific sizes of process shifts; they tend to magnify the situation, making the process shift more obvious; they give fewer false signals than x charts; and, once set up, they are nearly as easy to apply as x charts.

**Learning Objectives** — When you have completed this unit, you should:

A. Know the basis for using a CUSUM chart.

B. Be able to construct and interpret a decision interval CUSUM chart.

C. Be able to use the average run length concept in constructing a CUSUM chart.

D. Understand the concept of the V-mask CUSUM chart.

## 13-1. Introduction

The CUSUM chart is created from the accumulation of (hence cumulative sum or CUSUM) a performance measure taken from successive samples. The cumulative sum plotted may be based on virtually any performance measure. These include counts (e.g., number of defectives, number of defects), measures (e.g., weight, volume), and sample statistics (e.g., sample means, sample standard deviations, sample ranges).

For a continuous process, the cumulative sum of any of these characteristics would approach infinity if it were not adjusted in some way. This can be accomplished by subtracting the process mean or target value from each measurement and then forming the cumulative sum. For instance, instead of summing the individual $x_i$ values, the deviations of these individual values from the process mean might be summed. As such, if the process is in control at some $\bar{x}$, the CUSUM value plotted (i.e., $\Sigma(x_i - \bar{x})$) will vary around zero.

Unit 8 showed that x charts are most effective in identifying sudden, dramatic changes in the process mean (i.e., spikes), but that they are often slow in detecting smaller, less dramatic, more consistent shifts. Unit 10 showed that modified control charts (i.e., control charts enhanced with zone rules and run rules) are considerably more effective than traditional control charts using only the three-sigma rule. CUSUM charts, however, are generally more effective than either x charts or modified x charts at identifying and portraying small, sustained shifts in the process mean.

The CUSUM chart (like the x chart) should be accompanied by a moving range chart. This is done for two reasons: (1) CUSUM charts may not identify a sudden process shift (i.e., spike). If, however, the CUSUM chart is accompanied by a moving range chart, the sudden shift is more likely to be detected. (2) The moving range chart is able to indicate when the process variation is in control. The average moving range of the in-control process can then be used to estimate the process standard deviation, which is needed to set up the control limits for the CUSUM chart.

**Example 13-1:** Table 13-1 shows the results of 10 sample measurements taken from a process having a target value of 10. Differences between the individual values and the target, the cumulative sums of those differences, and two-period moving ranges are also shown. Fig. 13-1 shows a plot of the cumulative sums plus preliminary $R_m$ and x charts based on the 10 points.

Each of the charts indicates a well-behaved process. (Note: $UCL_{MR} = 7.6$, $LCL_{MR} = 0.0$, and centerline = 2.3 for $R_m$ chart; $UCL_x = 5.5$, $LCL_x = -5.5$, and centerline = 0.0 for x chart.) For illustration purposes, the control limits developed for the x and $R_m$ charts are extended. Table 13-2 shows the results of five additional samples and the associated differences, cumulative sums, and moving ranges.

Fig. 13-2 shows a plot of the cumulative sums, the $R_m$ chart, and the x chart for all 15 values. While neither the $R_m$ chart nor the x chart shows any out-of-control indication (even if the zone rules and run rules are applied), the cumulative sum plot shows a distinct change in the process. What really happened regarding the process is another question.

Suppose that just after sample 10 was taken, but unknown to anyone, the process mean shifted upward by two units (i.e., increased to 12). Fig. 13-3 describes the situation. By observing the x chart and $R_m$ chart for samples 11-15, however, nothing particularly noteworthy can be seen [Fig. 13-2, (b) and (c)]. On

| Sample Number | Target Value $x_T$ | Individual values $x_i$ | Diff. $(x_i - x_T)$ | Cumulative Sums of $(x_i - x_T)$ | Moving Ranges, $R_m$ $|x_i - x_{i-1}|$ |
|---|---|---|---|---|---|
| 1 | 10 | 9 | −1 | −1 | — |
| 2 | 10 | 11 | 1 | 0 | 2 |
| 3 | 10 | 9 | −1 | −1 | 2 |
| 4 | 10 | 11 | 1 | 0 | 2 |
| 5 | 10 | 9 | −1 | −1 | 2 |
| 6 | 10 | 10 | 0 | −1 | 1 |
| 7 | 10 | 12 | 2 | 1 | 2 |
| 8 | 10 | 10 | 0 | 1 | 2 |
| 9 | 10 | 7 | −3 | −2 | 3 |
| 10 | 10 | 12 | 2 | 0 | 5 |

**TABLE 13-1. CUSUM Example (10 Values)**

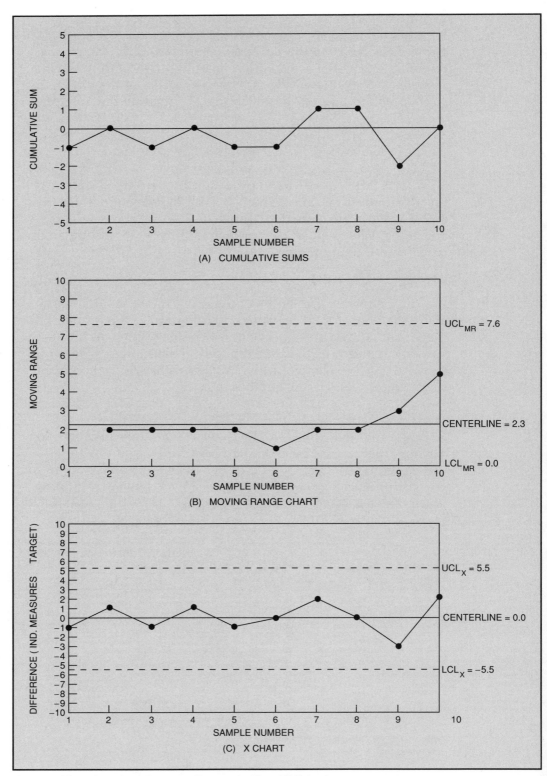

**Fig. 13-1. Plot of Cumulative Sums, $R_m$ Chart, and x Chart (10 Values)**

| Sample Number | Target Value $x_T$ | Individual values $x_i$ | Diff. $(x_i - x_T)$ | Cumulative Sums of $(x_i - x_T)$ | Moving Ranges, $R_m$ $\lvert x_i - x_{i-1} \rvert$ |
|---|---|---|---|---|---|
| 11 | 10 | 14 | 4 | 4 | 2 |
| 12 | 10 | 11 | 1 | 5 | 3 |
| 13 | 10 | 9 | −1 | 4 | 2 |
| 14 | 10 | 14 | 4 | 8 | 5 |
| 15 | 10 | 12 | 2 | 10 | 2 |

TABLE 13-2. CUSUM Example (Next 5 Values)

the other hand, the cumulative sum plot [Fig. 13-2 (a)] seems to be moving upward rather sharply for samples 11-15.

In fact, during the five additional samples, the cumulative sum of the differences between the individual measurements and the target value increased by 10 units. That is, the cumulative sum increased on the average by two units per sample during this period of time after having increased (on the average) none at all during the first 10 samples. Because of the obvious change in the cumulative sum, it might be concluded that there has been a shift in the process mean. In simple terms, this is how the cumulative sum chart works.

Traditionally, CUSUM charts have been applied in two equivalent forms. These two forms are known as the CUSUM decision interval chart and the CUSUM V-mask chart. The decision interval chart has the advantage of being easier to apply, however.

## 13-2. The Decision Interval Chart

The decision interval chart is a CUSUM chart that looks much like a typical Shewhart control chart. It has a centerline and two parallel control limits, $UCL_{CUSUM}$ and $LCL_{CUSUM}$. It is different, however, in that two sets of points are plotted on the chart: cumulative sum points for positive deviations and cumulative sum points for negative deviations. When a point from either set of points exceeds its control limit, an out-of-control signal is given.

Step 1. Compute and plot the decision interval chart's control limits and centerline. To do this, an estimate of the process standard deviation is required. Assuming that a moving range chart has been maintained on the process and that the process variation is in control, an estimate of the process standard

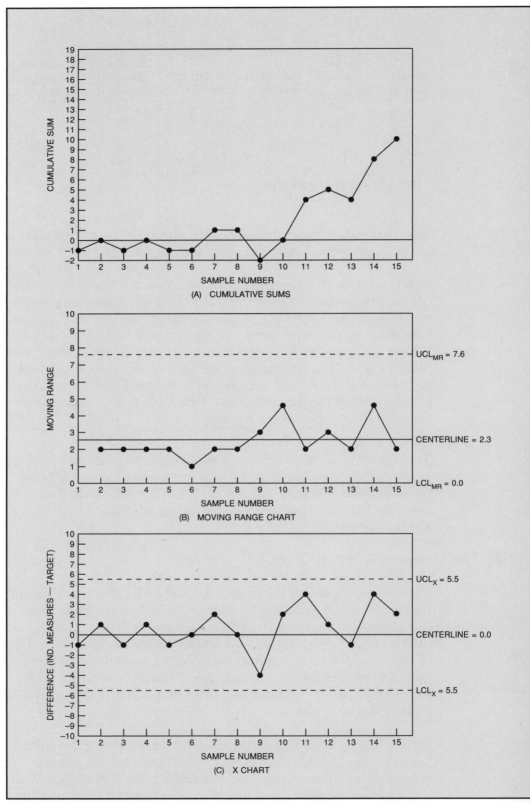

**Fig. 13-2. Plot of Cumulative Sums, R$_m$ Chart, and x Chart (15 Values)**

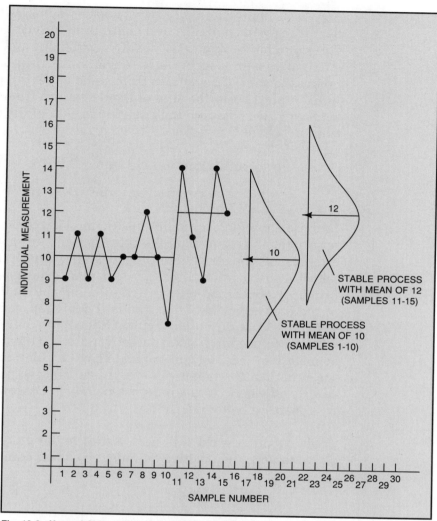

**Fig. 13-3. Upward Shift of Two Units in Process Mean**

deviation can be computed based on the average moving range, $\overline{R}_m$ (i.e., $\sigma_x = \overline{R}_m/d_2$), so that three-sigma control limits can then be set as follows:

$$UCL_{CUSUM} = +3\overline{R}_m/d_2$$

$$LCL_{CUSUM} = -3\overline{R}_m/d_2$$

Recall that the value of factor $d_2$ is dependent on the number of individual measurements used in each calculation of the moving range—usually two. The centerline of the decision interval chart is always set at zero.

Step 2. Compute and plot two truncated cumulative sums beginning with sample 1 and continuing through sample n. One cumulative sum is for positive deviations and the other cumulative sum is for negative deviations. Also, instead of taking the sum of deviations from some target $x_T$ as was done in Example 13-1 or the sum of the deviations from the process average $\bar{x}$, we compute the cumulative sum of the deviations from D, where D is defined in two ways:

For positive cumulative sums, $D^+ = x_T + q\hat{\sigma}_x/2$.

For negative cumulative sums, $D^- = x_T - q\hat{\sigma}_x/2$.

In these equations, $x_T$ represents the process target value and $\hat{\sigma}_x$ represents the estimate of the process standard deviation, while q represents the size of the process shift we wish to be able to detect. For example, if the CUSUM chart's designers are primarily concerned with the chart being able to detect a shift in the process mean of one standard deviation, q is set equal to 1. (Note: As in the case of typical Shewhart control charts, whether to use the process target value $x_T$ or the process average $\bar{x}$ in the decision interval chart calculations depends on the situation. If a target value is known and the process can be readily adjusted, $x_T$ is a reasonable choice. Otherwise, using $\bar{x}$ is probably a better decision.)

To detect an upward shift (i.e., a shift in the process mean above target), the positive cumulative sum is computed:

$$CUSUM_n^+ = CUSUM_{n-1}^+ + x_n - D^+$$

If this cumulative sum becomes negative, it is immediately reset to zero. As such, it is a truncated cumulative sum. This is done so that an upward shift will not first have to overcome a negative sum; in other words, the sum is truncated so that the positive cumulative sum is able to detect upward shifts more quickly.

To detect a downward shift (i.e., a shift in the process mean below target), the negative cumulative sum is computed:

$$CUSUM_n^- = CUSUM_{n-1}^- + x_n - D^-$$

If this sum becomes positive, it is immediately reset to zero. As was also true with the positive cumulative sum, this is done so that downward shifts are detected more quickly.

An obvious question regarding both cumulative sums is, "Why should these particular D values be used?" Somewhat amazingly, it has been shown that to detect a shift in the mean of q standard deviations as fast as possible, the cumulative sum should be composed of individual values equal to the mean (or target) plus half the shift size subtracted from the individual measurements. In the above discussion, the D values are simply the target values plus half the size of the shift to be detected.

After they are computed, both cumulative sums can be plotted on the decision interval chart. To begin the plotting process, set the initial CUSUM values equal to zero (i.e., $CUSUM_0^+ = CUSUM_0^- = 0$). Recall that the centerline of the decision interval chart is always zero.

Of course, if an out-of-control situation occurs, the cause of variation must be found and corrective action taken. Once the original process mean or target value has been reestablished, both the positive and negative CUSUM values should be reset to zero before continuing. That is, the next pair of CUSUM calculations should begin with the current CUSUM values set equal to zero.

Step 3. Once the control limits and cumulative sums have been plotted on the chart, out-of-control conditions can be identified and corrective action begun. (Note: Since the points plotted on CUSUM charts are by design autocorrelated, the modified control chart rules presented in Unit 10 are not applicable.)

**Example 13-2:** Individual carbon monoxide measurements (CO, in parts per million) are made on 40 shipments of ethylene (Table 13-3). A decision interval chart capable of detecting a

| Shipment No. | CO | Shipment No. | CO | Shipment No. | CO | Shipment No. | CO |
|---|---|---|---|---|---|---|---|
| 1 | 3.0 | 11 | 5.1 | 21 | 0.3 | 31 | 7.6 |
| 2 | 1.6 | 12 | 8.0 | 22 | 7.7 | 32 | 10.7 |
| 3 | 3.6 | 13 | 4.4 | 23 | 1.7 | 33 | 3.7 |
| 4 | 5.6 | 14 | 6.0 | 24 | 1.9 | 34 | 6.9 |
| 5 | 7.1 | 15 | 5.8 | 25 | 10.7 | 35 | 9.9 |
| 6 | 5.9 | 16 | 0.4 | 26 | 1.9 | 36 | 3.2 |
| 7 | 3.0 | 17 | 6.4 | 27 | 8.6 | 37 | 10.6 |
| 8 | 5.9 | 18 | 7.3 | 28 | 3.2 | 38 | 3.2 |
| 9 | 6.0 | 19 | 0.4 | 29 | 8.5 | 39 | 1.0 |
| 10 | 0.0 | 20 | 0.0 | 30 | 5.6 | 40 | 1.2 |

**TABLE 13-3. CO Measurements from Ethylene Production Process**

shift of one standard deviation in the process mean is to be used to monitor the ethylene production process.

Before constructing the decision interval chart on the individual CO measurements, a two-period moving range chart is set up to establish that the process dispersion is in control and to develop an estimate of $\sigma_x$.
Centerline:

$$\overline{R}_m = 3.77$$

Control Limits:

$$UCL_{MR} = D_4\overline{R}_m = (3.268)(3.77) = 12.3$$

$$LCL_{MR} = D_3\overline{R}_m = 0.0$$

The moving range chart's centerline, control limits, and individual moving ranges are plotted (Fig. 13-4). Since all points fall within the control limits, the process variation is in control.

The next step is to calculate and plot the chart's centerline and control limits (Fig. 13-5). Since $\overline{R}_m = 3.77$, the three-sigma control limits are:

$$UCL_{CUSUM} = +3\overline{R}_m/d_2 = +3(3.77/1.128) = 10.03$$

$$LCL_{CUSUM} = -3\overline{R}_m/d_2 = -3(3.77/1.128) = -10.03$$

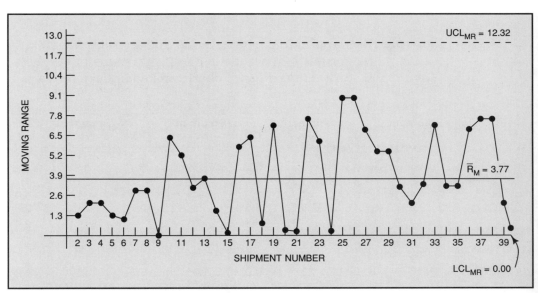

**Fig. 13-4. Two-Period Moving Range Chart for CO Measurements**

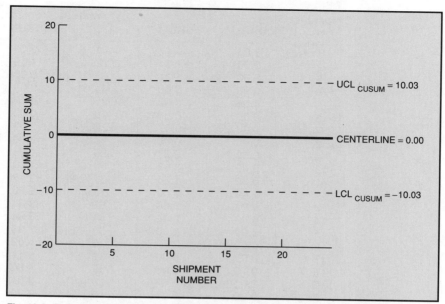

**Fig. 13-5. Decision Interval Chart Control Limits and Centerline for CO Measurements**

As mentioned above, the centerline for the decision interval chart is always zero.

Once the limits are in place, the positive and negative cumulative sums $CUSUM_i^+$ and $CUSUM_i^-$ can be calculated and plotted. The first step in this process is to estimate the process mean and standard deviation based on the 40 CO measurements. The overall mean is $\bar{x} = 4.84$ and, since $\bar{R}_m = 3.77$, the estimate of the process standard deviation is:

$$\hat{\sigma}_x = \frac{\bar{R}_m}{d_2} = \frac{3.77}{1.128} = 3.34$$

$D^+$ and $D^-$ are then computed as follows:

$$D^+ = \bar{x} + \frac{q\hat{\sigma}_x}{2} = 4.84 + \frac{(1)(3.34)}{2} = 6.51$$

$$D^- = \bar{x} - \frac{q\hat{\sigma}_x}{2} = 4.84 - \frac{(1)(3.34)}{2} = 3.17$$

where q, the size of the shift we wish to detect, is 1.0 standard deviations.

Calculations for the first two cumulative sum pairs are shown below, while all 40 pairs of CUSUM values are shown in Table

| Shipment No. | CUSUM$^+$ | CUSUM$^-$ | Shipment No. | CUSUM$^+$ | CUSUM$^-$ |
|---|---|---|---|---|---|
| 1 | 0.00 | −0.17 | 21 | 0.00 | −8.81 |
| 2 | 0.00 | −1.74 | 22 | 1.19 | −4.28 |
| 3 | 0.00 | −1.31 | 23 | 0.00 | −5.75 |
| 4 | 0.00 | 0.00 | 24 | 0.00 | −7.02 |
| 5 | 0.59 | 0.00 | 25 | 4.19 | 0.00 |
| 6 | 0.00 | 0.00 | 26 | 0.00 | −1.27 |
| 7 | 0.00 | −0.17 | 27 | 2.09 | 0.00 |
| 8 | 0.00 | 0.00 | 28 | 0.00 | 0.00 |
| 9 | 0.00 | 0.00 | 29 | 1.99 | 0.00 |
| 10 | 0.00 | −3.17 | 30 | 1.08 | 0.00 |
| 11 | 0.00 | −1.24 | 31 | 2.17 | 0.00 |
| 12 | 1.49 | 0.00 | 32 | 6.36 | 0.00 |
| 13 | 0.00 | 0.00 | 33 | 3.55 | 0.00 |
| 14 | 0.00 | 0.00 | 34 | 3.94 | 0.00 |
| 15 | 0.00 | 0.00 | 35 | 7.33 | 0.00 |
| 16 | 0.00 | −2.77 | 36 | 4.02 | 0.00 |
| 17 | 0.00 | 0.00 | 37 | 8.11 | 0.00 |
| 18 | 0.79 | 0.00 | 38 | 4.80 | 0.00 |
| 19 | 0.00 | −2.77 | 39 | 0.00 | −2.17 |
| 20 | 0.00 | −5.94 | 40 | 0.00 | −4.14 |

**TABLE 13-4. Decision Interval Chart Cumulative Sum Results for 40 CO Measurements**

13-4. The cumulative sums are then plotted on the decision interval chart (Fig. 13-6).

For n = 1:

$$CUSUM_1^+ = CUSUM_0^+ + (x_1 - D^+)$$

$$= 0 + (3 - 6.51)$$

$$= -3.51$$

$$= 0.0$$

(CUSUM$^+$ is reset to zero since the calculated CUSUM$^+$ < 0.)

$$CUSUM_1^- = CUSUM_0^- + (x_1 - D^-)$$

$$= 0 + (3 - 3.17)$$

$$= -0.17$$

For n = 2:

$$CUSUM_2^+ = CUSUM_1^+ + (x_2 - D^+)$$

$$= 0 + (1.6 - 6.51)$$

$$= -4.91$$

$$= 0.0 \text{ (because CUSUM}^+ < 0)$$

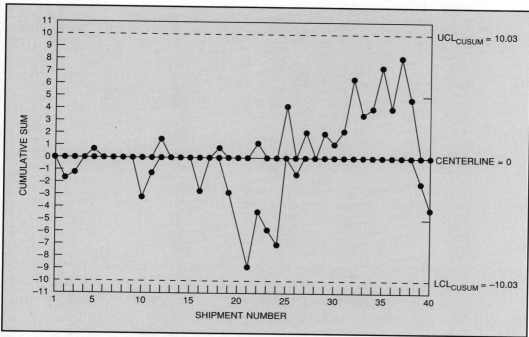

**Fig. 13-6. Decision Interval Chart for 40 CO Measurements**

$$CUSUM_2^- = CUSUM_1^- + (x_2 - D^-)$$

$$= -0.17 + (1.6 - 3.17)$$

$$= -1.74$$

Inspection of the decision interval chart (Fig. 13-6) indicates that the process is in control. Note that in shipment number 22 both $CUSUM^+$ and $CUSUM^-$ have nonzero values. While this is clearly not typical, it is certainly acceptable—and not an error.

In Table 13-5, CO measurements for shipments 41 through 60 are shown along with the two-period moving range calculations. Fig. 13-7 shows the two-period moving range chart for all 60 shipments. The moving range chart indicates that the process variation remains in control.

Table 13-6 shows the 20 positive and negative cumulative sums for shipments 41–60, and Fig. 13-8 shows the sums plotted on the extended decision interval chart. The chart first gives an out-of-control signal at shipment 52 and, except for shipment 54, remains out of control through shipment 60.

| Shipment Number | CO | 2-Period Mov. Range | Shipment Number | CO | 2-Period Mov. Range |
|---|---|---|---|---|---|
| 41 | 10.9 | 9.7 | 51 | 11.0 | 3.5 |
| 42 | 6.2 | 4.7 | 52 | 11.7 | 0.7 |
| 43 | 4.6 | 1.6 | 53 | 2.7 | 9.0 |
| 44 | 6.3 | 1.7 | 54 | 10.0 | 7.3 |
| 45 | 2.6 | 3.7 | 55 | 9.5 | 0.5 |
| 46 | 7.5 | 4.9 | 56 | 10.0 | 0.5 |
| 47 | 2.8 | 4.7 | 57 | 12.0 | 2.0 |
| 48 | 3.3 | 0.5 | 58 | 4.5 | 7.5 |
| 49 | 6.7 | 4.4 | 59 | 10.0 | 5.5 |
| 50 | 7.5 | 0.8 | 60 | 8.5 | 1.5 |

Note: The CO measurement for shipment number 40 is 1.2 (from Table 13-3).

**Table 13-5. CO Measurements for Shipments 41–60**

Recall that once the cause of variation is found and corrective action is taken to reestablish the target value (or original process mean), both the positive and negative CUSUM values should be reset to zero before continuing. In this case, assuming that the cause of variation is found and corrected after shipment 60, the CUSUM values for shipment 61 will be

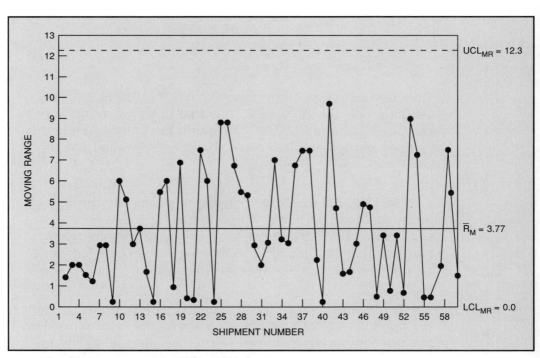

**Fig. 13-7. Two-Period Moving Range Chart for 60 CO Measurements**

| Shipment No. | CUSUM⁺ | CUSUM⁻ | Shipment No. | CUSUM⁺ | CUSUM⁻ |
|:---:|:---:|:---:|:---:|:---:|:---:|
| 41 | 4.39 | 0.00 | 51 | 5.67 | 0.00 |
| 42 | 4.08 | 0.00 | 52 | 10.86 | 0.00 |
| 43 | 2.17 | 0.00 | 53 | 7.05 | −0.47 |
| 44 | 1.96 | 0.00 | 54 | 10.54 | 0.00 |
| 45 | 0.00 | −0.57 | 55 | 13.53 | 0.00 |
| 46 | 0.99 | 0.00 | 56 | 17.02 | 0.00 |
| 47 | 0.00 | −0.37 | 57 | 22.51 | 0.00 |
| 48 | 0.00 | −0.24 | 58 | 20.50 | 0.00 |
| 49 | 0.19 | 0.00 | 59 | 23.99 | 0.00 |
| 50 | 1.18 | 0.00 | 60 | 25.98 | 0.00 |

**TABLE 13-6. Decision Interval Chart Cumulative Sum Results for Shipment 41-60 CO Measurements**

calculated as follows:

$$CUSUM_{61}^+ = CUSUM_{60}^+ + (x_{61} - D^+)$$

$$= 0 + (x_{61} - 6.51)$$

$$CUSUM_{61}^- = CUSUM_{60}^- + (x_{61} - D^-)$$

$$= 0 + (x_{61} - 3.17)$$

For comparison with the CUSUM chart, an x chart is shown for the same 60 shipments (Fig. 13-9). As in the case of the

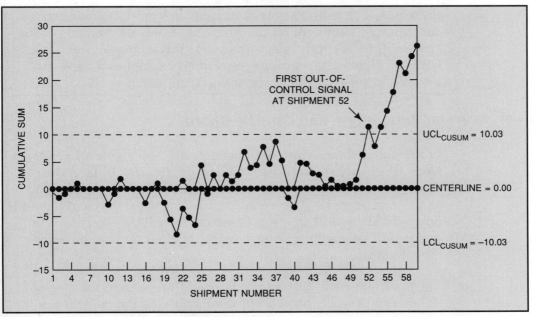

**Fig. 13-8. Decision Interval Chart for 60 CO Measurements**

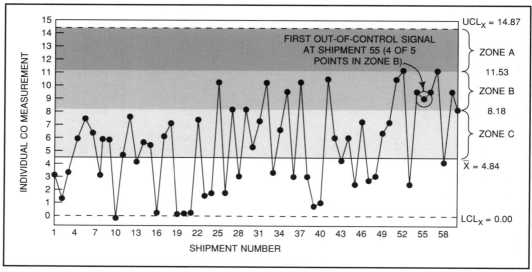

**Fig. 13-9. x Chart for 60 CO Measurements**

decision interval chart, the x chart's control limits and centerline are based on the first 40 samples (i.e., $UCL_x = 4.84 + (2.66)(3.77) = 14.87$, $LCL_x = 4.84 - (2.66)(3.77) = -5.19 = 0.00$, since LCL calculated value is negative and CO measurements cannot be negative, centerline = 4.84).

Since no points are outside the control limits, the traditional Shewhart x chart gives no out-of-control signal. The modified Shewhart x chart, however, first indicates an out-of-control condition at shipment 55 on the basis of four out of five points in zone B or beyond. In summary, for this example, the CUSUM chart outperformed the x chart by first detecting the out-of-control situation three samples sooner.

## 13-3. Average Run Length and CUSUM Charts

In the above discussion, the decision interval's control limits were arbitrarily set at three standard deviations. In fact, the decision has more impact than is apparent at first glance. The choice influences both how often false signals will be given and how quickly a shift in the process mean will be detected. The concept of average run length (ARL) is often used to describe the situation.

The acronym $ARL_0$ is commonly used to represent the average number of samples until a point falls outside the control limits when there has been no change in the process mean. In other words, even if the process mean remains unchanged (i.e., no shift at all, q = 0), the control limits on the CUSUM decision interval chart will give a false alarm on the average once every $ARL_0$ samples. Of course, this characteristic is not unique to the CUSUM decision interval chart; all control charts are vulnerable to false alarms.

$ARL_q$ represents the average number of samples until a process shift of q standard deviations (i.e., process shift = $q\sigma_x$) is recognized. In other words, if the process mean shifts either upward or downward by $q\sigma_x$, $ARL_q$ samples will be required on the average before a point will fall outside the decision interval chart's control limits.

Three factors influence the values of $ARL_0$ and $ARL_q$: the process standard deviation $(\sigma_x)$, the size of the shift in standard deviations we wish to be able to recognize (q), and the number of standard deviations from the chart's centerline that the control limits are set (h; typically, h = 3).

Table 13-7 shows both $ARL_0$ and $ARL_q$ values for various combinations of $\sigma_x$, q, and h. (Note: Table 13-7 assumes that the process variation is in control.) For instance, for q = 1 (i.e., detect a one standard deviation shift) and $h/\sigma_x$ = 3.0 (i.e., three-sigma control limits), $ARL_0$ = 120 and $ARL_1$ = 6.4. That is, even if the process mean remains unchanged, a false alarm will occur on the average once every 120 samples. In addition, if the process mean either increases or decreases by one standard deviation, the shift will be detected on the average in 6.4 samples.

The equations defining the decision interval chart's control limits are as follows:

$$UCL_{CUSUM} = +h$$

$$= +\frac{h}{\sigma_x}(\sigma_x)$$

$$= \left(\frac{h}{\sigma_x}\right)\left(\frac{\overline{R}_m}{d_2}\right)$$

$$LCL_{CUSUM} = -h$$

$$= \frac{-h}{\sigma_x}(\sigma_x)$$

$$= -\left(\frac{h}{\sigma_x}\right)\left(\frac{\overline{R}_m}{d_2}\right)$$

where $h/\sigma_x$ values form the leftmost column in Table 13-7. Therefore, to set the chart's control limits, it is only necessary to know the $h/\sigma_x$ value chosen from Table 13-7 and the $\bar{R}_m/d_2$ ratio. (Recall that for a two-period moving average $d_2 = 1.128$.)

Table 13-7 may be used to custom design a CUSUM chart. Suppose a decision interval chart is to be designed that is capable of detecting a one-standard deviation shift in the process mean (i.e., $q = 1$), but one that on the average gives a false alarm no more frequently than once every 300 samples. From Table 13-7 under $q = 1$, $ARL_0 = 340$, and an accompanying $ARL_1 = 8.4$ for $h/\sigma_x = 4.0$. If this setting is chosen, the decision interval's control limits will be set at four sigma (i.e., four standard deviations from the centerline), a false alarm will occur on the average once every 340 samples, and shifts in the process mean of one standard deviation will be detected on the average in 8.4 samples. If the two-period average moving range calculated from the data is 5.0, the custom-designed decision interval chart's control limits are as follows:

$$UCL_{CUSUM} = (4.0)(5.0/1.128)$$

$$= 17.73$$

$$LCL_{CUSUM} = -(4.0)(5.0/1.128)$$

$$= -17.73$$

As a second example, suppose a decision interval chart capable of detecting a shift in the process mean of 0.6 standard deviations is to be designed. False alarms are on the average to occur no more frequently than once every 75 samples. From Table 13-7 under $q = 0.6$, when $ARL_0 = 75$, $ARL_1 = 10.7$ and $h/\sigma_x = 3.6$. If the two-period average moving range calculated from the data is $\bar{R}_m = 5.0$, the decision interval chart's control limits are as follows:

$$UCL_{CUSUM} = (3.6)(5.0/1.128)$$

$$= 15.96$$

$$LCL_{CUSUM} = -(3.6)(5.0/1.128)$$

$$= -15.96$$

Fig. 13-10 presents four curves showing the relationship between the average run length (ARL) and various sized shifts

| $h/\sigma_x$ | q = 0.6 | | q = 0.8 | | q = 1 | | q = 1.2 | | q = 1.4 | | q = 1.6 | | q = 1.8 | | q = 2 | |
|---|---|---|---|---|---|---|---|---|---|---|---|---|---|---|---|---|
| | $ARL_0$ | $ARL_q$ | $ARL_0$ | $ARL_q$ | $ARL_0$ | $ARL_q$ | $ARL_0$ | $ARL_q$ | $ARL_0$ | $ARL_q$ | $ARL_0$ | $ARL_q$ | $ARL_0$ | $ARL_q$ | $ARL_0$ | $ARL_q$ |
| 2.0 | | | | | 39 | 4.4 | 54 | 4.0 | 78 | 3.6 | 120 | 3.2 | 170 | 3.0 | 260 | 2.7 |
| 2.2 | | | | | 49 | 4.8 | 71 | 4.3 | 110 | 3.8 | 160 | 3.5 | 250 | 3.2 | 390 | 2.9 |
| 2.4 | | | | | 61 | 5.2 | 92 | 4.6 | 140 | 4.1 | 220 | 3.7 | 360 | 3.4 | 590 | 3.1 |
| 2.6 | | | | | 76 | 5.6 | 120 | 5.0 | 190 | 4.4 | 310 | 4.0 | 520 | 3.6 | 880 | 3.3 |
| 2.8 | | | | | 95 | 6.0 | 150 | 5.3 | 250 | 4.7 | 430 | 4.2 | 750 | 3.9 | 1300 | 3.5 |
| 3.0 | 48 | 8.8 | 74 | 7.4 | 120 | 6.4 | 200 | 5.6 | 340 | 5.0 | 590 | 4.5 | 1100 | 4.1 | | |
| 3.2 | 56 | 9.4 | 88 | 7.9 | 150 | 6.8 | 250 | 5.9 | 450 | 5.3 | 816 | 4.7 | | | | |
| 3.4 | 65 | 10.0 | 110 | 8.4 | 180 | 7.2 | 320 | 6.3 | 600 | 5.6 | 1100 | 5.0 | | | | |
| 3.6 | 75 | 10.7 | 130 | 8.9 | 220 | 7.6 | 410 | 6.6 | 780 | 5.8 | | | | | | |
| 3.8 | 87 | 11.3 | 150 | 9.4 | 270 | 8.0 | 530 | 6.9 | 1000 | 6.1 | | | | | | |
| 4.0 | 100 | 11.9 | 180 | 9.9 | 340 | 8.4 | 670 | 7.3 | | | | | | | | |
| 4.2 | 120 | 12.6 | 210 | 10.4 | 420 | 8.8 | 850 | 7.6 | | | | | | | | |
| 4.4 | 130 | 13.2 | 250 | 10.9 | 510 | 9.2 | 1100 | 7.9 | | | | | | | | |
| 4.6 | 150 | 13.9 | 300 | 11.4 | 620 | 9.6 | | | | | | | | | | |
| 4.8 | 170 | 14.5 | 350 | 11.8 | 760 | 10.0 | | | | | | | | | | |

TABLE 13-7. Average Run Length Chart (for a Decision Interval CUSUM Chart)

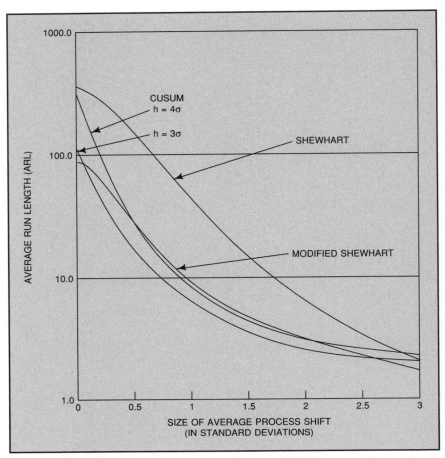

**Fig. 13-10. Average Run Length vs. Size of Process Shift CUSUM Charts and x Charts with q = 1**

in the process mean. Fig. 13-10 shows these curves for a decision interval chart designed to detect a q = 1 standard deviation shift in the process mean. The curves represent four different control charting situations: (1) a Shewhart x chart using only the three-sigma rule (Shewhart); (2) a Shewhart x chart enhanced with zone rules (modified Shewhart); (3) a CUSUM chart whose control limits are set at $\pm 3\sigma_x$ ($h = 3\sigma_x$); and (4) a CUSUM chart whose control limits are set at $\pm 4\sigma_x$ ($h = 4\sigma_x$).

If the process mean remains unchanged (i.e., no shift occurs), the four charts react as follows: (1) the three-sigma Shewhart x chart will give a false signal on the average every 370 samples; (2) the modified Shewhart x chart will give a false signal on the average every 92 samples; (3) the $3\sigma_x$ CUSUM chart will give a false signal on the average every 118 samples; and, (4) the $4\sigma_x$ CUSUM chart will give a false signal, on the average, every 337 samples. That is, the modified Shewhart x chart tends to give more false signals than either CUSUM chart and considerably more than the three-sigma Shewhart chart.

If the process mean shifts either up or down by one standard deviation, the four charts react as follows: (1) the three-sigma Shewhart x chart will recognize the shift in about 44 samples; (2) the modified Shewhart x chart will recognize the shift in about 9 samples; (3) the $3\sigma_x$ CUSUM chart will detect the shift in about 6.5 samples; and, (4) the $4\sigma_x$ CUSUM chart will detect the shift in about 8.5 samples. That is, both the $3\sigma_x$ and $4\sigma_x$ CUSUM charts are slightly more efficient than the modified Shewhart x chart when the process mean shifts by one standard deviation and all are considerably more efficient than the three-sigma Shewhart x chart.

Of course, the simplest case occurs when the process mean shifts dramatically. While the modified Shewhart chart is slightly more efficient at recognizing such shifts than either the $3\sigma_x$ or $4\sigma_x$ CUSUM charts (1.7 samples to 1.8 and 2.2 samples, respectively), the differences are minimal. Of course, the ideal is to be able to recognize the process shift in a single sample. To reduce the average recognition time, both CUSUM and Shewhart x charts should always be accompanied by a moving range chart.

Although it is clearly possible to design any number of CUSUM charts, it is reasonable in practice to set the control limits at three or four standard deviations and apply the decision interval chart in conjunction with a moving range chart.

## 13-4. V-Mask Version of the CUSUM Chart

Another form of the CUSUM chart is known as the V-mask. It is so named because of the V-like shape of its control limits (Fig. 13-11). It is applied by placing the chart's center point (P) on each plotted cumulative sum, one at a time, while keeping the centerline of the V-mask horizontal and examining each of the previously plotted points relative to the control limits. As long as all previous cumulative sums fall within the V-shaped control limits, the process is assumed to be in control. When one or more points fall outside the V-mask control limits, an out-of-control signal is given (Fig. 13-12). In terms of results,

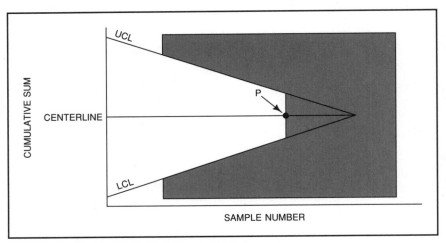

**Fig. 13-11. General Form of V-Mask CUSUM Chart**

the CUSUM decision interval chart and the CUSUM V-mask chart are equivalent.

The idea of the V-mask is that each new cumulative sum should be viewed in light of previous cumulative sums. That is, each cumulative sum is evaluated from the perspective, "Assuming that the current cumulative sum is reasonable, are previous cumulative sums in line with this one?"

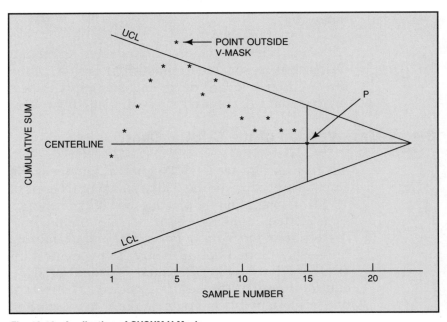

**Fig. 13-12. Application of CUSUM V-Mask**

The advantage of the V-mask version of the CUSUM chart over the decision interval version is that the cumulative sum calculation is more straightforward. The cumulative sums represent the deviations of individual measurements $x_i$ from their mean $\bar{x}$ (or target $x_T$); that is,

$$\text{CUSUM}_n = \sum_{i=1}^{n} (x_i - \bar{x}) = \text{CUSUM}_{n-1} + (x_n - \bar{x})$$

For instance, the first cumulative sum is $(x_1 - \bar{x})$, the second $(x_1 - \bar{x}) + (x_2 - \bar{x})$, the third $(x_1 - \bar{x}) + (x_2 - \bar{x}) + (x_3 - \bar{x})$, etc. The disadvantage of the V-mask approach is that the V-shaped control limits are awkward to construct and apply. Since the two forms are equivalent—and the V-mask version more awkward—there is really no reason to use the V-mask approach.

## Exercises

13-1. To monitor the accuracy and precision of an instrument used to measure the melt index (MI) for a high-density polyethylene production process, a standard batch of the material is measured each shift. The table below shows 15 melt index measurements taken using a single instrument over 5 shifts. (a) Using the 15 measurements, set up a moving range chart and, once the process variation is in control, a $3\sigma_x$ decision interval chart. Let $q = 1$. Plot appropriate points on both charts. Are all points within the control limits?

| No. | MI | No. | MI | No. | MI |
|-----|-------|-----|-------|-----|-------|
| 1 | 0.788 | 6 | 0.777 | 11 | 0.785 |
| 2 | 0.793 | 7 | 0.780 | 12 | 0.778 |
| 3 | 0.770 | 8 | 0.797 | 13 | 0.782 |
| 4 | 0.775 | 9 | 0.797 | 14 | 0.778 |
| 5 | 0.797 | 10 | 0.795 | 15 | 0.790 |

**Melt Index Measurements on Standard Material**

(b) The following table shows 10 additional measurements taken after the charts have been developed. Continue plotting the cumulative sums and the moving range. Are there any out-of-control signals?

| No. | MI | No. | MI |
|-----|-------|-----|-------|
| 16 | 0.793 | 21 | 0.763 |
| 17 | 0.798 | 22 | 0.758 |
| 18 | 0.770 | 23 | 0.770 |
| 19 | 0.767 | 24 | 0.782 |
| 20 | 0.792 | 25 | 0.792 |

**Additional Melt Index Measurements**

13-2. (a) Using the first 15 measurements of Exercise 13-1, set up a moving range chart and, once the process variation is in control, an x chart. Is the process in control? (b) Extend both charts and consider the next 10 measurement values. Are any out-of-control signals given?

13-3. The table below shows 30 individual measurements of an additive for a high-density polyethylene resin and the corresponding two-period moving ranges. The measurement x is in parts per million (ppm). Using the 30 measurements, set up a moving range chart and, once the process variation is in control, a $3\sigma_x$ decision interval chart. Let q = 2. Is the process in control?

| No. | x | $R_m$ | No. | x | $R_m$ | No. | x | $R_m$ |
|-----|------|-----|-----|------|-----|-----|------|-----|
| 1 | 950 | — | 11 | 915 | 64 | 21 | 971 | 47 |
| 2 | 947 | 3 | 12 | 906 | 9 | 22 | 936 | 35 |
| 3 | 949 | 3 | 13 | 948 | 42 | 23 | 916 | 20 |
| 4 | 878 | 71 | 14 | 972 | 24 | 24 | 945 | 29 |
| 5 | 953 | 75 | 15 | 975 | 3 | 25 | 969 | 24 |
| 6 | 956 | 3 | 16 | 978 | 3 | 25 | 985 | 16 |
| 7 | 977 | 21 | 17 | 929 | 49 | 27 | 896 | 89 |
| 8 | 956 | 21 | 18 | 950 | 21 | 28 | 932 | 35 |
| 9 | 922 | 34 | 19 | 941 | 9 | 29 | 939 | 7 |
| 10 | 979 | 57 | 20 | 924 | 17 | 30 | 937 | 2 |
| SUM | 9467 | 287 | | 9438 | 241 | | 9426 | 305 |

**Additive Measurements**

13-4. The data shown in the following table represent the chlorine content in a polymer (in percent). Construct a two-period moving range chart to monitor chlorine content and, once the variation is in control, a $3\sigma_x$ decision interval chart (with q = 1) as well. Use the chlorine target value of 36.5 (as $x_T$) to calculate cumulative sums. Plot CUSUM values until the first out-of-control point, then reset the offending CUSUM value *to zero (0.0) and plot until the second out-of-control point. Then stop. Comment on your findings.*

| Sample No. | Chlorine Content | Sample No. | Chlorine Content | Sample No. | Chlorine Content |
|---|---|---|---|---|---|
| 1 | 36.4 | 16 | 36.6 | 31 | 36.6 |
| 2 | 36.6 | 17 | 36.0 | 32 | 36.8 |
| 3 | 36.3 | 18 | 37.1 | 33 | 36.4 |
| 4 | 35.6 | 19 | 36.6 | 34 | 36.9 |
| 5 | 35.1 | 20 | 36.5 | 35 | 35.8 |
| 6 | 35.1 | 21 | 36.8 | 36 | 37.0 |
| 7 | 35.3 | 22 | 37.1 | 37 | 34.8 |
| 8 | 36.0 | 23 | 37.0 | 38 | 35.5 |
| 9 | 36.1 | 24 | 36.7 | 39 | 36.5 |
| 10 | 34.5 | 25 | 36.1 | 40 | 36.5 |
| 11 | 36.4 | 26 | 36.1 | 41 | 36.2 |
| 12 | 36.1 | 27 | 36.6 | 42 | 35.1 |
| 13 | 36.6 | 28 | 36.1 | 43 | 35.5 |
| 14 | 36.5 | 29 | 36.5 | 44 | 35.0 |
| 15 | 36.7 | 30 | 36.5 | 45 | 35.3 |

**Chlorine Content of a Polymer**

# Unit 14:
# Moving Average and Exponentially Weighted Moving Average Control Charts

# UNIT 14

# Moving Average and Exponentially Weighted Moving Average Control Charts

In the processing industry, the use of individual measurement charts is common (primarily because there are many instances in which taking multiple observations at a single point in time is impractical). One problem with using an individual measurement chart (x chart) is that even with the modified control chart rules numerous samples are commonly required to recognize a small or gradual process shift. In addition, x chart control limits are based on two assumptions: (1) that the individual measurements are independent and (2) that they are approximately normally distributed. These assumptions are frequently incorrect in the processing industry. Individual measurements are more often autocorrelated and follow some type of nonnormal distribution. The CUSUM chart, described in Unit 13, was presented as one alternative to the x chart. This unit presents two additional, closely related, alternatives: (1) the moving average (MA) chart and (2) the exponentially weighted moving average (EWMA) chart.

Learning Objectives — When you have completed this unit, you should:

A. Understand the principles behind a moving average chart and know when and how to use one.

B. Understand the principles behind an exponentially weighted moving average chart and know when and how to use one.

## 14-1. Introduction

While both MA charts and EWMA charts use current individual measurements, they also include past measurements in developing plotting points. The effect of including multiple values in the calculations is that process noise (i.e., common cause variation) tends to be smoothed out, so trends and shifts are more easily recognized. A second advantage of averaging multiple individual measurements is that the resulting plotting points tend to be normally distributed, because of the central limit theorem, even though the individual measurements are not independent. In addition, since successive moving averages are by design autocorrelated, the fact that the individual measurements are autocorrelated is of little impact. On the other hand, both MA charts and EWMA charts tend to be less sensitive than an x chart to sudden process changes (i.e., spikes).

Both the MA and EWMA charts should be used in combination with a moving range chart. This is important for two reasons: (1) because while MA and EWMA charts are less sensitive than x charts to process spikes, the accompanying moving range chart is often able to recognize such situations; and, (2) like the x and CUSUM charts, the application of both charts depends first on the process variation being in control. Once the process is stable, a meaningful estimate of the process standard deviation may be calculated.

Before either an MA or EWMA chart can be set up, a decision regarding the relative importance that will be given to current measurements must be made. For the MA chart, the question is how many periods should be used in computing the moving average; for the EWMA chart, the question is what weighting factor ($\lambda$) should be chosen. In general, the more successive periods included in the MA calculation and the smaller the $\lambda$ in the EWMA calculation, the greater the smoothing effect and the more the chart will emphasize trends rather than point-to-point fluctuations. As rules of thumb, for the MA chart, between three and eight periods are often used; for the EWMA chart, weighting factors between 0.50 and 0.20 are common, while values of $\lambda$ less than 0.20 are not uncommon.

Before getting into the details of both chart types, one other issue deserves mention. Only the three-sigma rule is employed to identify an out-of-control condition when using MA or EWMA charts. The zone rules and run rules presented in Unit 10 are not appropriate since they are based on the assumption of independent observations and the points plotted on both MA and EWMA charts are not independent. Rather, since every plotted point is a function of both the most recent measurement and one or more past measurements, they are by design autocorrelated.

## 14-2.  Moving Average (MA) Chart

The moving average chart is similar in its looks and development to the individuals chart, except that the values plotted include data from the past as well as the present. The practical result of using both old and new data is that the moving average chart tends to be more sensitive to small process shifts (i.e., drifts, trends, etc.) than an individuals chart.

A moving average is simple to compute. Suppose that n individual measurements have been collected. The n-period moving average at time t is defined as

$$MA_t = (x_t + x_{t-1} + x_{t-2} + \cdots + x_{t-(n-2)} + x_{t-(n-1)})/n$$

For example, suppose that three individual measurements 10, 14, and 12 have been collected, with 10 the oldest and 12 the most recent. The three-period average is 12.

$$MA_3 = \frac{(x_3 + x_2 + x_1)}{3}$$

$$= \frac{(12 + 14 + 10)}{3}$$

$$= 12$$

When a value of 16 is collected one period later, the 10 is dropped and the new three-period moving average becomes 14.

$$MA_4 = \frac{(x_4 + x_3 + x_2)}{3}$$

$$= \frac{(16 + 12 + 14)}{3}$$

$$= 14$$

One period later, a value of 20 is collected, the 14 is dropped, and the new three-period moving average becomes 16. In general, if n represents the number of periods included in the moving average at time period t, the oldest measurement $x_{t-n}$ is discarded and the newest one, $x_t$, is included. The general updating equation is shown below.

$$MA_t = MA_{t-1} - \frac{x_{t-n}}{n} + \frac{x_t}{n}$$

$$= \frac{x_t + x_{t-1} + x_{t-2} + \cdots + x_{t-(n-1)}}{n}$$

The centerline of the moving average control chart is usually the overall mean $\bar{x}$, the average of all the individual measurements available when the control chart is set up, but a process target value $x_T$ may also be used if it is more appropriate. The standard deviation of the moving average is $\sigma_{\bar{x}} = \sigma_x/\sqrt{n}$, where $\sigma_x$ is the true standard deviation of the individual measurements and n is the number of measurements used to calculate each moving average. The control limits are familiar.

$$\mathrm{UCL_{MA}} = \bar{x} + 3\sigma_{\bar{x}}$$
$$= \bar{x} + 3\sigma_x/\sqrt{n}$$
$$\mathrm{LCL_{MA}} = \bar{x} - 3\sigma_{\bar{x}}$$
$$= \bar{x} - 3\sigma_x/\sqrt{n}$$

If the process standard deviation $\sigma_x$ is unknown (which is typical), it must be estimated. It is usually estimated based on an estimate of the average moving range $\bar{R}_m$, typically a two-period average moving range. Note, however, that it is not appropriate to use the average range-based control limits formula $\bar{x} \pm A_2\bar{R}$ developed for the $\bar{x}$ chart since the standard deviation of the moving average distribution is not the same as the standard deviation of the $\bar{x}$ distribution. For the moving average chart, the standard deviation of the moving averages is approximated by $\bar{R}_m/(d_2\sqrt{n})$, where n is the number of periods in the moving average and $d_2$ is based on the number of periods used to calculate the moving range. Since a two-period moving range is commonly used, $d_2$ typically equals 1.128. The moving average control limits are usually set as follows:

$$\mathrm{UCL_{MA}} = \bar{x} + 3\sigma_{\bar{x}}$$
$$= \bar{x} + 3\sigma_x/\sqrt{n}$$
$$= \bar{x} + 3(\bar{R}_m/d_2)/\sqrt{n}$$
$$= \bar{x} + \frac{3\bar{R}_m}{d_2\sqrt{n}}$$
$$\mathrm{LCL_{MA}} = \bar{x} - 3\sigma_{\bar{x}}$$
$$= \bar{x} - 3\sigma_x/\sqrt{n}$$
$$= \bar{x} - 3(\bar{R}_m/d_2)/\sqrt{n}$$
$$= \bar{x} - \frac{3\bar{R}_m}{d_2\sqrt{n}}$$

**Example 14-1:** An important characteristic monitored in the process of blending gasoline is the RVP (Reid vapor pressure) value. Producers are required to maintain RVP levels within certain limits by performing laboratory tests on the gasoline they produce or face stiff fines for exceeding those limits. Unfortunately, because of the length of time required to run such tests, process control decisions are usually based on the RVP results from an online analyzer.

One danger associated with using an online analyzer for process control is that it can, over time, gradually move out of calibration. To prevent this from occurring and to meet federal regulations, laboratory RVP tests are carried out on gasoline samples every four hours. Moving range and moving average charts are then maintained on the differences between timewise-comparable online and laboratory RVP readings.

Table 14-1 shows the RVP specification (in ppm) plus concurrent RVP lab and online analyzer measurements taken over a period of several days.

Before the moving average chart can be developed, it is necessary to first be sure that the process variation is in control. Once the process variation is stable, a moving range-based estimate of the standard deviation of the moving average can be computed. The following steps describe the development of a two-period moving range chart.

Step 1. Accurately record the RVP values for both the laboratory and the online analyzer.

Step 2. Next, two-period moving ranges based on the absolute values of differences between concurrent lab and online measurements are computed (as shown in Table 14-1). The first four two-period moving range computations are shown below.

$$R_{m1} = |-0.4 - 0.4| = 0.8$$

$$R_{m2} = |\ 0.4 + 0.8| = 1.2$$

$$R_{m3} = |-0.8 - 0.4| = 1.2$$

$$R_{m4} = |\ 0.4 - 0.4| = 0.0$$

Step 3. Set the two-period moving range chart's centerline and control limits, include them on the $R_m$ chart, and plot the 29

| Sample No. | RVP Spec | RVP Values | | Difference Lab-Online | 2-Period Moving Range |
|---|---|---|---|---|---|
| | | Lab | Online | | |
| 1 | 13.5 | 12.4 | 12.8 | −0.4 | — |
| 2 | 13.5 | 12.5 | 12.1 | 0.4 | 0.8 |
| 3 | 13.5 | 11.4 | 12.2 | −0.8 | 1.2 |
| 4 | 13.5 | 13.2 | 12.8 | 0.4 | 1.2 |
| 5 | 13.5 | 12.6 | 12.2 | 0.4 | 0.0 |
| 6 | 13.5 | 11.4 | 11.1 | 0.3 | 0.1 |
| 7 | 13.5 | 12.3 | 12.2 | 0.1 | 0.2 |
| 8 | 13.5 | 13.2 | 13.0 | 0.2 | 0.1 |
| 9 | 13.5 | 11.4 | 12.0 | −0.6 | 0.8 |
| 10 | 13.5 | 11.1 | 11.9 | −0.8 | 0.2 |
| 11 | 13.5 | 11.7 | 12.2 | −0.5 | 0.3 |
| 12 | 13.5 | 11.8 | 12.4 | −0.6 | 0.1 |
| 13 | 13.5 | 11.7 | 12.2 | −0.5 | 0.1 |
| 14 | 13.5 | 12.4 | 12.1 | 0.3 | 0.8 |
| 15 | 13.5 | 12.4 | 12.1 | 0.3 | 0.0 |
| 16 | 13.5 | 12.0 | 12.2 | −0.2 | 0.5 |
| 17 | 13.5 | 13.2 | 8.3 | 4.9 | 5.1 |
| 18 | 13.5 | 11.8 | 11.5 | 0.3 | 4.6 |
| 19 | 13.5 | 9.8 | 8.6 | 1.2 | 0.9 |
| 20 | 13.5 | 9.2 | 9.7 | −0.5 | 1.7 |
| 21 | 13.5 | 13.1 | 13.3 | −0.2 | 0.3 |
| 22 | 13.5 | 11.9 | 11.9 | 0 | 0.2 |
| 23 | 13.5 | 10.7 | 10.7 | 0 | 0.0 |
| 24 | 13.5 | 12.8 | 12.9 | −0.1 | 0.1 |
| 25 | 13.5 | 12.3 | 12.2 | 0.1 | 0.2 |
| 26 | 13.5 | 12.2 | 11.7 | 0.5 | 0.4 |
| 27 | 13.5 | 11.1 | 11.3 | −0.2 | 0.7 |
| 28 | 13.5 | 10.6 | 11.6 | −1 | 0.8 |
| 29 | 13.5 | 11.6 | 11.6 | 0 | 1.0 |
| 30 | 13.5 | 11.9 | 11.5 | 0.4 | 0.4 |
| Totals | | 355.7 | 352.3 | 3.4 | 22.8 |

**TABLE 14-1.  RVP Measurements from Gasoline Blending Process**

moving ranges. The calculations shown below are based on the totals from Table 14-1.

Centerline:

$$\overline{R}_m = 22.8/29 = 0.79$$

Control Limits:

$$UCL_{MR} = D_4\overline{R}_m = 3.268(0.79) = 2.57$$

$$LCL_{MR} = D_3\overline{R}_m = 0.000(0.79) = 0.00$$

(Note: The $D_3$ and $D_4$ values are based on a two-period moving range.)

Step 4. After the centerline and control limits have been drawn, the individual two-period moving ranges are plotted on the same chart (Fig. 14-1).

The moving ranges based on sample numbers 17 and 18 are well above the upper control limit, indicating an out-of-control condition. A check of the event log and discussion with the process' engineers revealed that the sample number 17 online RVP value was incorrectly recorded. The single incorrect reading, however, caused two erroneous moving range calculations (both 17 and 18), a common result when there is a spike in the individual data. Since the correct value could not be determined, sample 17 was deleted and the centerline and control limits recomputed.

Centerline:

$$\overline{R}_m = 13.6/28 = 0.49$$

Control Limits:

$$UCL_{MR} = D_4\overline{R}_m = 3.268(0.49) = 1.59$$
$$LCL_{MR} = D_3\overline{R}_m = 0.000(0.49) = 0.00$$

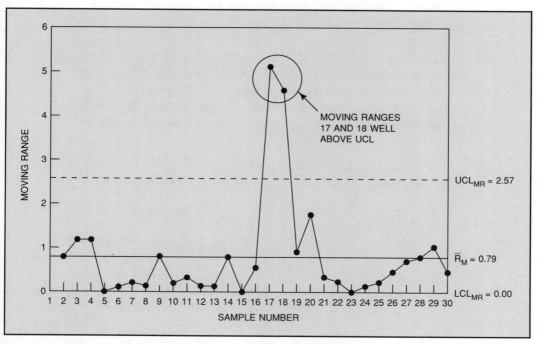

Fig. 14-1. Two-Period Moving Range Chart for RVP Differences (30 samples)

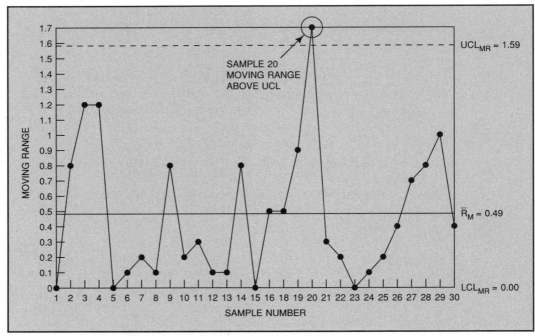

**Fig. 14-2. Two-Period Moving Range Chart for RVP Differences (29 samples)**

Again, the centerline, control limits, and two-period moving ranges were plotted (Fig. 14-2).

This time the sample number 20 moving range fell above the new upper control limit. Further checking of the event log revealed that online sample number 19 was probably contaminated because of trash in the sample line. As such, sample number 19 was also removed from the data set.

A centerline value and control limits for the $R_m$ chart were calculated a third time, this time using only 28 data points.

Centerline:

$$\overline{R}_m = 11.8/27 = 0.44$$

Control Limits:

$$UCL_{MR} = D_4\overline{R}_m = 3.268(0.44) = 1.43$$

$$LCL_{MR} = D_3\overline{R}_m = 0.000(0.44) = 0.00$$

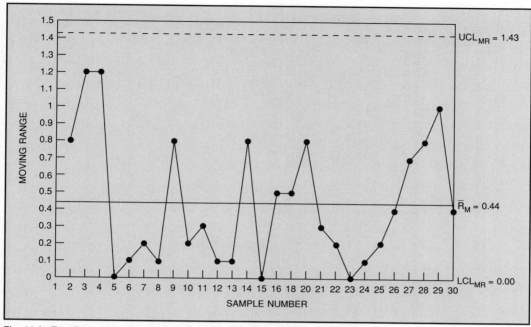

Fig. 14-3. Two-Period Moving Range Chart for RVP Differences (28 samples)

The new centerline, control limits, and two-period moving ranges were plotted (Fig. 14-3). This time the process variation seemed to be in control. As such, attention turned to the construction of a moving average chart.

Step 5. Typically, the first step in developing a moving average chart is to compute an estimate of the process mean based on the (remaining) k measurements. In this case, however, it is more appropriate to use the target difference of 0.00 (i.e., $x_T$ = 0.00) between the lab values and the online analyzer as the centerline.

In addition, before computing the control limits a decision must be made regarding the number of periods to use in the moving average computation. A three-period moving average was chosen as a starting point and three-period moving averages based on the remaining 28 RVP differences were computed (Table 14-2). Table 14-3 shows the 3-period moving average computation for the first six data points.

Based on the totals in Table 14-2 and the earlier computation of the moving range, the centerline and control limits for the

| Sample No. | RVP Spec | RVP Values | | Difference Lab-Online | 2-Period Moving Range | 3-Period Moving Average |
|---|---|---|---|---|---|---|
| | | Lab | Online | | | |
| 1 | 13.5 | 12.4 | 12.8 | −0.4 | — | — |
| 2 | 13.5 | 12.5 | 12.1 | 0.4 | 0.8 | 0.00 |
| 3 | 13.5 | 11.4 | 12.2 | −0.8 | 1.2 | −0.27 |
| 4 | 13.5 | 13.2 | 12.8 | 0.4 | 1.2 | 0.00 |
| 5 | 13.5 | 12.6 | 12.2 | 0.4 | 0.0 | 0.00 |
| 6 | 13.5 | 11.4 | 11.1 | 0.3 | 0.1 | 0.37 |
| 7 | 13.5 | 12.3 | 12.2 | 0.1 | 0.2 | 0.27 |
| 8 | 13.5 | 13.2 | 13.0 | 0.2 | 0.1 | 0.20 |
| 9 | 13.5 | 11.4 | 12.0 | −0.6 | 0.8 | −0.10 |
| 10 | 13.5 | 11.1 | 11.9 | −0.8 | 0.2 | −0.40 |
| 11 | 13.5 | 11.7 | 12.2 | −0.5 | 0.3 | −0.63 |
| 12 | 13.5 | 11.8 | 12.4 | −0.6 | 0.1 | −0.63 |
| 13 | 13.5 | 11.7 | 12.2 | −0.5 | 0.1 | −0.53 |
| 14 | 13.5 | 12.4 | 12.1 | 0.3 | 0.8 | −0.27 |
| 15 | 13.5 | 12.4 | 12.1 | 0.3 | 0.0 | 0.03 |
| 16 | 13.5 | 12.0 | 12.2 | −0.2 | 0.5 | 0.13 |
| 18 | 13.5 | 11.8 | 11.5 | 0.3 | 0.5 | 0.13 |
| 20 | 13.5 | 9.2 | 9.7 | −0.5 | 0.8 | −0.13 |
| 21 | 13.5 | 13.1 | 13.3 | −0.2 | 0.3 | −0.13 |
| 22 | 13.5 | 11.9 | 11.9 | 0 | 0.2 | −0.23 |
| 23 | 13.5 | 10.7 | 10.7 | 0 | 0.0 | −0.07 |
| 24 | 13.5 | 12.8 | 12.9 | −0.1 | 0.1 | −0.03 |
| 25 | 13.5 | 12.3 | 12.2 | 0.1 | 0.2 | 0.00 |
| 26 | 13.5 | 12.2 | 11.7 | 0.5 | 0.4 | 0.17 |
| 27 | 13.5 | 11.1 | 11.3 | −0.2 | 0.7 | 0.13 |
| 28 | 13.5 | 10.6 | 11.6 | −1 | 0.8 | −0.23 |
| 29 | 13.5 | 11.6 | 11.6 | 0 | 1.0 | −0.40 |
| 30 | 13.5 | 11.9 | 11.5 | 0.4 | 0.4 | −0.20 |
| Totals | | | | | 11.8 | −2.83 |

**TABLE 14-2. Revised RVP Measurements (samples 17 and 19 omitted)**

moving average chart are set as follows:

Centerline:

$$x_T = 0.00 \text{ (target value)}$$

Control Limits:

$$UCL_{MA} = x_T + 3\bar{R}_m/(d_2\sqrt{n})$$

$$= 0.00 + 3(0.44)\,/(1.128\sqrt{3})$$

$$= 0.00 + 0.67$$

$$= 0.67$$

$$LCL_{MA} = x_T - 3\bar{R}_m/(d_2\sqrt{n})$$

$$= 0.00 - 3(0.44)/(1.128\sqrt{3})$$

$$= 0.00 - 0.67$$

$$= -0.67$$

| Sample No. | RVP Spec | RVP Values | | Difference Lab-Online | 3-Period Moving Average | 3-Period Moving Average Calculations |
|---|---|---|---|---|---|---|
| | | Lab | Online | | | |
| 1 | 13.5 | 12.4 | 12.8 | −0.4 | — | — |
| 2 | 13.5 | 12.5 | 12.1 | 0.4 | — | — |
| 3 | 13.5 | 11.4 | 12.2 | −0.8 | −0.27 | (−0.4 + 0.4 − 0.8)/3 |
| 4 | 13.5 | 13.2 | 12.8 | 0.4 | 0.00 | (0.4 − 0.8 + 0.4)/3 |
| 5 | 13.5 | 12.6 | 12.2 | 0.4 | 0.00 | (−0.8 + 0.4 + 0.4)/3 |
| 6 | 13.5 | 11.4 | 11.1 | 0.3 | 0.37 | (0.4 + 0.4 + 0.3)/3 |

**TABLE 14-3. Three-Period Moving Average Computations (first 6 data points)**

Recall that the $d_2$ factor is based on the number of periods used to calculate the moving range (which in this case is, as usual, two periods).

Step 6. After plotting the moving average chart's centerline and control limits (Fig. 14-4), the individual moving averages are plotted and the chart examined. Although some cycling is present because of the autocorrelated moving averages, the process' moving average appears to be well behaved and in control. As such, the centerlines and control limits for both the moving range and moving average charts are extended.

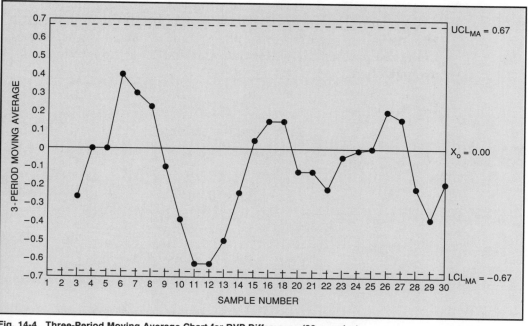

**Fig. 14-4. Three-Period Moving Average Chart for RVP Differences (28 samples)**

| Sample No. | RVP Spec | RVP Values | | Difference Lab-Online | 2-Period Moving Range | 3-Period Moving Average |
|---|---|---|---|---|---|---|
| | | Lab | Online | | | |
| 1 | 13.5 | 12.4 | 12.8 | −0.4 | — | — |
| 2 | 13.5 | 12.5 | 12.1 | 0.4 | 0.8 | — |
| 3 | 13.5 | 11.4 | 12.2 | −0.8 | 1.2 | −0.27 |
| . . . | . . . | . . . | . . . | . . . | . . . | . . . |
| 28 | 13.5 | 10.6 | 11.6 | −1 | 0.8 | −0.23 |
| 29 | 13.5 | 11.6 | 11.6 | 0 | 1.0 | −0.40 |
| 30 | 13.5 | 11.9 | 11.5 | 0.4 | 0.4 | −0.20 |
| 31 | 13.5 | 12.1 | 11.4 | 0.7 | 0.3 | 0.37 |
| 32 | 13.5 | 12.4 | 11.5 | 0.9 | 0.2 | 0.67 |
| 33 | 13.5 | 12.3 | 11.6 | 0.7 | 0.2 | 0.77 |

TABLE 14-4.  Extended RVP Measurements (samples 31, 32, and 33 added)

It is at this point that the true value of the moving average chart becomes apparent. Table 14-4 shows an extension of Table 14-2. Three additional RVP measurement pairs are included, along with the associated two-period moving range and three-period moving average computations. Fig. 14-5 shows the previously computed moving range and moving average charts with the new values included. While the moving range seems to be in control, the moving average chart shows a definite increase in the differences in RVP measurements. In fact, the online analyzer has gone out of calibration.

For comparison with the moving average chart, an individuals chart is developed for the same situation. Starting from the point where the process variation is in control, the remaining 28 data values are used to set the x chart's control limits. These limits are predictably wider than the limits for the moving average chart.

Centerline:

$$x_T = 0.00 \text{ (target value)}$$

Control Limits:

$$\bar{R}_m = 0.44$$

$$UCL_x = x_T + 2.66\bar{R}_m$$

$$= 0.00 + 2.66(0.44)$$

$$= 0.00 + 1.17$$

$$= 1.17$$

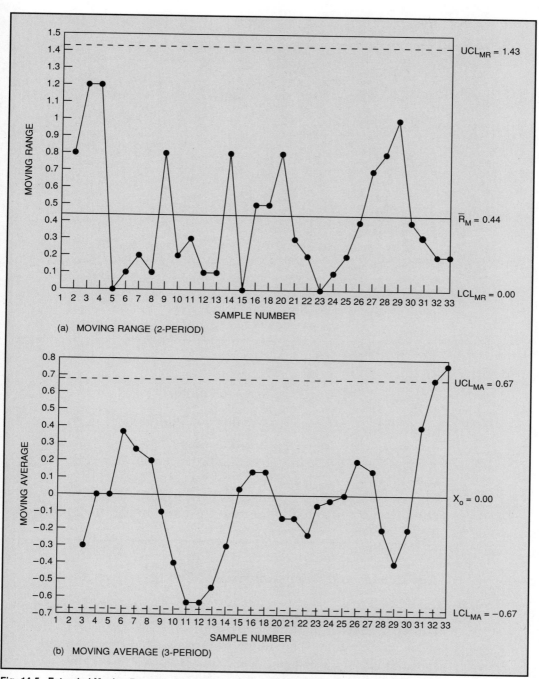

Fig. 14-5. Extended Moving Range and Moving Average Charts for RVP Differences

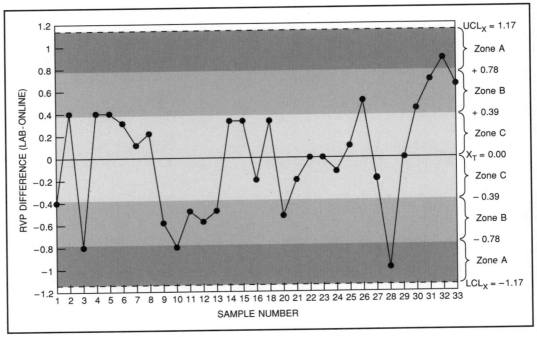

**Fig. 14-6. Extended x Chart for RVP Differences**

$$LCL_x = x_T - 2.66\overline{R}_m$$

$$= 0.00 - 2.66(0.44)$$

$$= 0.00 - 1.17$$

$$= -1.17$$

Fig. 14-6 shows the extended x chart. No out-of-control condition is indicated (although it is close using the 2-of-3 and 4-of-5 rules).

## Advantages and Disadvantages of Moving Average Charts

The primary advantage of the moving average chart lies in its ability to detect small but consistent shifts in the process mean more quickly than the x chart. One associated disadvantage is that the moving average chart requires both storing and working with a changing set of n data values. Another disadvantage is that present and past values are given equal weights, a policy that may or may not be appropriate.

An appropriate choice of n, the number of data points used to compute the moving average, is critical for the effective performance of the moving average chart. If n is too small, the moving average tends to be sensitive to noise. If n is too large, the moving average tends to be insensitive to changes in the process mean, i.e., the chart tends to require a large number of samples before the moving average chart indicates a process change. The rule of thumb that n be between three and eight provides a reasonable starting point, but experimentation with different values of n on past sets of process measurements may be required to find the most appropriate choice for a particular process.

Since the moving average chart will not usually detect large, momentary changes in a process (unless they are enormous), the MA chart should always be accompanied by a moving range chart, and possibly even by an x chart.

## 14-3. Exponentially Weighted Moving Average (EWMA) Chart

Another control chart with many of the same characteristics as the moving average chart, but one that is somewhat easier to administer, is the exponentially weighted moving average (EWMA) chart. Like the MA chart, the EWMA chart is often able to detect small process shifts more quickly than an individuals chart, but with two advantages over the MA chart: (1) smaller data storage requirements and (2) variable weights for current and past data values.

The EWMA method has several variations. The simplest version (and the only one presented in this ILM) uses a combination of two values to develop the next plotting point: the most recent exponentially weighted moving average value and a single new individual measurement. This means that only two data values need to be stored.

A weighting factor $\lambda$, whose values range from 0 to 1, is used to indicate the relative importance (or weight) given to the most recent individual value. For example, if the weighting factor $\lambda$ is 0.60, the most recent individual value is 30, the most recent EWMA value is 20, and the next EWMA value is $(0.60)(30) + (1 - 0.60)(20) = 26$. In other words, in deciding the state of the process, the most recent individual value is given 60% weight and the last EWMA the other 40% (i.e., $1 - 0.60$).

In general, if $x_t$ denotes the individual observation value at time t, a new EWMA value, $EWMA_t$, is then computed by a weighted combination of the most recent past average $EWMA_{t-1}$ and a single new individual observation $x_t$, using the following formula:

$$EWMA_t = \lambda x_t + (1 - \lambda)EWMA_{t-1}$$

Three-standard deviation control limits are given by the equations shown below: (Note: An explanation of the development of the control limits is beyond the scope of this text.)

$$UCL_{EWMA} = \bar{x} + 3\sqrt{\lambda/(2 - \lambda)}\,\sigma_x$$

$$= \bar{x} + 3\sqrt{[\lambda/(2 - \lambda)]}\,\frac{\bar{R}_m}{d_2}$$

$$LCL_{EWMA} = \bar{x} - 3\sqrt{\lambda/(2 - \lambda)}\,\sigma_x$$

$$= \bar{x} - 3\sqrt{[\lambda/(2 - \lambda)]}\,\frac{\bar{R}_m}{d_2}$$

The centerline is typically set using the overall mean $\bar{x}$. As usual, $\sigma_x$ represents the process standard deviation (i.e., the standard deviation of the individual measurements). When the moving range $R_m$ is used to estimate the process standard deviation $\sigma_x$ (i.e., $\hat{\sigma}_x = \bar{R}_m/d_2$), the factor $A_3 = 3\sqrt{[\lambda/(2 - \lambda)]}/d_2$ may be used for simplification. That is,

$$UCL_{EWMA} = \bar{x} + A_3\bar{R}_m$$

$$LCL_{EWMA} = \bar{x} - A_3\bar{R}_m$$

As in the case of the moving average choice of n, the EWMA choice of $\lambda$ is process dependent. If the primary goal is to detect sudden process variations, a relatively large $\lambda$ should be used. On the other hand, if the goal is primarily to quickly detect gradual process changes (which is more typical), a relatively small $\lambda$ should be selected. Evaluation of past process data sequences using EWMA charts and a variety of $\lambda$ values (to see

| $\lambda$ | 0.1 | 0.2 | 0.3 | 0.4 | 0.5 | 0.6 | 0.7 | 0.8 | 0.9 |
|-----------|-----|-----|-----|-----|-----|-----|-----|-----|-----|
| $A_3$ | 0.610 | 0.887 | 1.117 | 1.330 | 1.536 | 1.741 | 1.952 | 2.172 | 2.175 |

Note: If a value of $\lambda$ that does not appear in Table 14-5 is used or if other than a two-period moving range is used, $A_3$ must be calculated using the formula shown above.

TABLE 14-5. $A_3$ Factor Values for Various $\lambda$ Values (Assuming $\bar{R}_m$ Based on Two-Period Moving Range)

which $\lambda$ value is most effective) is a pragmatic way of determining an appropriate $\lambda$ level. A $\lambda$ value between 0.2 and 0.5 is often a good starting point. If $\lambda = 0.2$, $A_3 = 0.887$, and the EWMA chart's control limits are:

$$UCL_{EWMA} = \bar{x} + 0.887\bar{R}_m$$

$$LCL_{EWMA} = \bar{x} - 0.887\bar{R}_m$$

The EWMA chart should be accompanied by a moving range chart, and possibly by an x chart, to help detect sudden shifts in the process mean.

**Example 14-2:** In the production of carbon black, DBP is a major quality characteristic. Table 14-6 shows a series of DBP measurements taken from a carbon black production process over a period of 12 days.

A two-period moving range chart is used to monitor the process variation.

Centerline:

$$\bar{R}_m = 234/71 = 3.30$$

Control Limits:

$$UCL_{MR} = 3.268\bar{R}_m = 3.268(3.30) = 10.8$$

$$LCL_{MR} = 0.000\bar{R}_m = 0.0$$

| | Day | | | | | |
|---|---|---|---|---|---|---|
| **Time** | **1–2** | **3–4** | **5–6** | **7–8** | **9–10** | **11–12** |
| 3 p.m. | 95 | 105 | 103 | 103 | 102 | 97 |
| 7 p.m. | 100 | 107 | 103 | 102 | 100 | 98 |
| 11 p.m. | 104 | 100 | 98 | 99 | 99 | 99 |
| 3 a.m. | 105 | 104 | 103 | 100 | 98 | 101 |
| 7 a.m. | 108 | 97 | 102 | 96 | 101 | 99 |
| 11 a.m. | 99 | 105 | 106 | 95 | 98 | 102 |
| 3 p.m. | 100 | 107 | 96 | 93 | 94 | 105 |
| 7 p.m. | 104 | 105 | 98 | 93 | 98 | 108 |
| 11 p.m. | 101 | 103 | 108 | 94 | 100 | 102 |
| 3 a.m. | 105 | 100 | 106 | 95 | 94 | 105 |
| 7 a.m. | 102 | 98 | 102 | 103 | 97 | 98 |
| 11 a.m. | 101 | 102 | 104 | 100 | 103 | 101 |

TABLE 14-6. Sample DBP Values from a Carbon Black Production Process

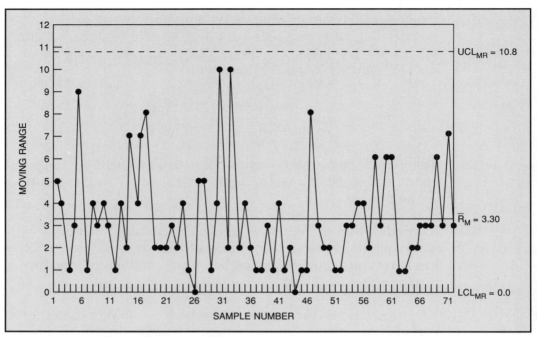

**Fig. 14-7. Two-Period Moving Range Chart for Carbon Black Process**

Fig. 14-7 shows no points outside the control limits, indicating that the process variation is in control. As such, the exponentially weighted moving average chart is constructed.

Step 1. Set the centerline and control limits. In this situation, the centerline must be calculated.

Centerline:

$$\bar{x} = \Sigma x_i / k = 7301/72 = 101.4$$

Based on an evaluation of similar process data (not included in this example) previous data, $\lambda$ is set at 0.4, so that $A_3 = 1.330$ (Table 14-5) and the control limits are as follows:

Control Limits:

$$UCL_{EWMA} = \bar{x} + A_3\bar{R}_m = 101.4 + (1.330)(3.30) = 105.2$$

$$LCL_{EWMA} = \bar{x} - A_3\bar{R}_m = 101.4 - (1.330)(3.30) = \phantom{0}96.4$$

Step 2. After plotting the control limits and centerline, the exponentially weighted moving averages are calculated. Table 14-7 shows the EWMA calculations for the first few DBP measurements.

| Time | DBP | EWMA | Computation |
|---|---|---|---|
| 3 p.m. | 95 | 98.8 | (0.4)(95) + (0.6)(101.29) |
| 7 p.m. | 100 | 99.3 | (0.4)(100) + (0.6)(98.8) |
| 11 p.m. | 104 | 101.2 | (0.4)(104) + (0.6)(99.3) |
| 3 a.m. | 105 | 102.7 | (0.4)(105) + (0.6)(101.2) |
| 7 a.m. | 108 | 104.8 | (0.4)(108) + (0.6)(102.7) |
| 11 a.m. | 99 | 102.5 | (0.4)(99) + (0.6)(104.8) |
| 3 p.m. | 100 | 101.5 | (0.4)(100) + (0.6)(102.5) |

Note: In this case, the first EWMA value was calculated as $EWMA_1 = \lambda x_1 + (1 - \lambda)\bar{x}$. Other schemes are also used to obtain the first EWMA value. One of the most common is to set $EWMA_1 = \lambda x_1 + (1 - \lambda)x_1$.

**TABLE 14-7. First Few EWMA Values (using $\lambda$ = 0.4 and $EWMA_t = \lambda x_t + (1 - \lambda) EWMA_{t-1}$)**

Step 3. Once the exponentially weighted moving averages are calculated, they are plotted along with the centerline and control limits (Fig. 14-8). The EWMA values for samples 43 through 46 are below the lower control limit, indicating a process shift. In fact, the EWMA values for sample numbers 41 through 66 are all below the chart's centerline. Further investigation revealed that two problems existed during the sample number 41 to sample number 66 time frame: (1) new control equipment that had not been properly calibrated was both installed and used (EWMA values corresponding to samples 41–46) and (2) raw materials obtained from a new

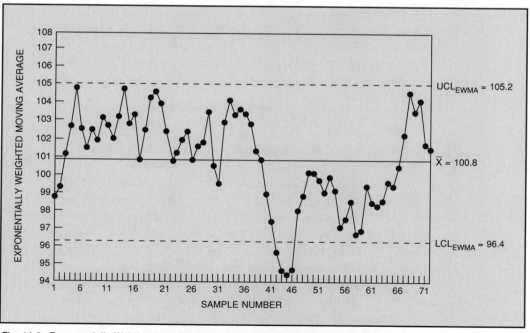

**Fig. 14-8. Exponentially Weighted Moving Average Chart for Carbon Black Process**

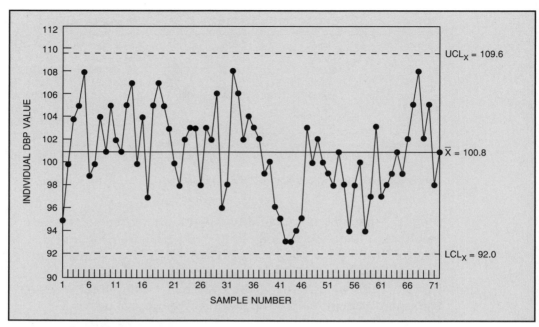

**Fig. 14-9.  x Chart for Carbon Black Process**

supplier were used (EWMA values corresponding to samples 47–65).

Fig. 14-9 shows an x chart for the same carbon black production process. If only the three-sigma rule is applied, no out-of-control signal is given. However, if the zone rules are employed, an out-of-control indication is given on sample number 44 on the basis of the two of three successive points falling in zone A.

## Advantages and Disadvantages of the EWMA Chart

In general, the EWMA chart has the same advantages and disadvantages as the moving average chart presented earlier in this unit with two exceptions: (1) To compute the next EWMA value requires only that the last EWMA value and the most recent individual measurement be retained, rather than having to keep the last n individual measurements. As such, updating the EWMA chart is computationally simpler than updating the MA chart. (2) More recent values are given more weight. As is apparent from inspection of the equations shown below, an

EWMA value can be written as an infinite sum of past EWMA values.

$$\text{EWMA}_t = \lambda X_t + (1 - \lambda)\text{EWMA}_{t-1}$$

$$= \lambda X_t + (1 - \lambda)[\lambda X_{t-1} + (1 - \lambda)\text{EWMA}_{t-2}]$$

$$= \lambda X_t + (1 - \lambda)\lambda X_{t-1} + (1 - \lambda)^2\text{EWMA}_{t-2}$$

$$= \lambda X_t + (1 - \lambda)\lambda X_{t-1} + (1 - \lambda)^2[\lambda X_{t-2} + (1 - \lambda)\text{EWMA}_{t-3}]$$

$$= \lambda X_t + \lambda(1 - \lambda)X_{t-1} + \lambda(1 - \lambda)^2 X_{t-2} + (1 - \lambda)^3\text{EWMA}_{t-3}$$

$$= \lambda\Sigma(1 - \lambda)^i X_{t-i}$$

In other words, the EWMA method weights past values in an exponentially decreasing manner. Since "older" values are less likely to reflect the present process mean, the EWMA approach is conceptually preferable to the moving average approach (as well as computationally preferable).

Table 14-8 shows the effective weighting factors for both current and past periods for various values of $\lambda$. That is, the current EWMA value is actually a weighted moving average of all past measurements, with the current measurement having the greatest weight and past measurements having progressively less weight. For example, if $\lambda = 0.1$, the current measurement is given a weight of 0.1000, while the measurement taken one period earlier has a weight of 0.0900, the measurement taken two periods earlier has a weight of 0.0810, and so forth. (Note: These coefficient weights can easily be verified by the following sequence: for current period, $\lambda =$

| Periods Past | $\lambda$ | | | | |
|---|---|---|---|---|---|
| | 0.1 | 0.2 | 0.3 | 0.4 | 0.5 |
| Current | 0.1000 | 0.2000 | 0.3000 | 0.4000 | 0.5000 |
| 1 | 0.0900 | 0.1600 | 0.2100 | 0.2400 | 0.2500 |
| 2 | 0.0810 | 0.1280 | 0.1470 | 0.1440 | 0.1250 |
| 3 | 0.0729 | 0.1024 | 0.1029 | 0.0864 | 0.0625 |
| 4 | 0.0656 | 0.0819 | 0.0720 | 0.0518 | 0.0313 |
| 5 | 0.0590 | 0.0655 | 0.0504 | 0.0311 | 0.0156 |
| 6 | 0.0531 | 0.0524 | 0.0353 | 0.0187 | 0.0078 |
| 7 | 0.0478 | 0.0419 | 0.0247 | 0.0112 | 0.0039 |

TABLE 14-8. Effective Weights of Past Individual Measurements for Various $\lambda$ Values

| n | 3 | 4 | 5 | 6 | 7 | 8 |
|---|---|---|---|---|---|---|
| λ | 0.50 | 0.40 | 0.33 | 0.29 | 0.25 | 0.22 |

(Note: $\lambda = 2/(n + 1)$)

**TABLE 14-9. Equivalent λ and n Values for EWMA and MA Charts**

0.10; past period 1, $(0.1)(1 - 0.1) = (0.1)(0.9) = 0.09$; past period 2, $(0.1)(1 - 0.1)^2 = (0.1)(0.9)^2 = (0.1)(0.81) = 0.081$; past period 3, $(0.1)(1 - 0.1)^3 = (0.1)(0.9)^3 = (0.1)(0.729) = 0.0729$; etc.)

## 14-4. Relationship Between n and λ

While an appropriate choice of n is important to assure the effectiveness of the moving average chart, an appropriate choice of λ is critical for the meaningful performance of the EWMA chart. In fact, the two charts can be used (almost) interchangeably. If λ is chosen as $2/(n + 1)$, similar results can be achieved using either the MA or EWMA charts. The smoothing effect on the values plotted on both charts will be similar and the control limits will be identical. For example, for a MA chart with n = 4 and a EWMA chart with λ = 0.4, the control limits for both charts will be $\bar{x} + 1.5\bar{R}_m/d_2$. Table 14-9 shows corresponding n and λ values.

## Exercises:

14-1. *The table below shows the results of 30 individual measurements taken over a period of several days (including two-period moving range values). The chemical is an additive to a plastic production process.*

| No. | x | $R_m$ | No. | x | $R_m$ | No. | x | $R_m$ |
|---|---|---|---|---|---|---|---|---|
| 1 | 950 | — | 11 | 915 | 64 | 21 | 971 | 47 |
| 2 | 947 | 3 | 12 | 906 | 9 | 22 | 936 | 35 |
| 3 | 949 | 2 | 13 | 948 | 42 | 23 | 916 | 20 |
| 4 | 878 | 71 | 14 | 972 | 24 | 24 | 945 | 29 |
| 5 | 953 | 75 | 15 | 975 | 3 | 25 | 969 | 24 |
| 6 | 956 | 3 | 16 | 978 | 3 | 26 | 985 | 16 |
| 7 | 977 | 21 | 17 | 929 | 49 | 27 | 896 | 89 |
| 8 | 956 | 21 | 18 | 950 | 21 | 28 | 932 | 36 |
| 9 | 922 | 34 | 19 | 941 | 9 | 29 | 939 | 7 |
| 10 | 979 | 57 | 20 | 924 | 17 | 30 | 937 | 2 |
| SUM | 9467 | 287 | | 9438 | 241 | | 9426 | 305 |

**Chemical Additive**

(a) Construct a two-period moving range chart to establish that the process variation is in control. Note: If any point is out of control for any of the charts developed, assume that there is an assignable cause, omit the point, and recompute. (b) Set up a 3-period MA chart, plot the control limits and MA values, and interpret the results. (c) Choose an appropriate λ corresponding to $n = 3$, set up an EWMA chart, plot the centerline, the control limits, and the EWMA values, and interpret the results.

14-2. In order to monitor the calibration of a laboratory instrument, samples collected over the last 20 days are used to set up a control chart. The measurement values are shown in the following table. Each day three samples are taken from a standard product batch, one during each shift, and an instrument reading made on each one. As long as the instrument remains calibrated, the readings should be similar.

(a) Construct a two-period moving range chart to establish that the process variation is in control. (b) Set up a 4-period MA chart, plot the control limits and MA values, and interpret the results. (c) Choose an appropriate λ corresponding to $n = 4$, set up an EWMA chart, plot the centerline, the control limits, and the EWMA values, and interpret the results.

| Day | $x_1$ | $R_m$ | $x_2$ | $R_m$ | $x_3$ | $R_m$ |
|-----|-------|-------|-------|-------|-------|-------|
| 1 | 0.98 | — | 0.96 | 0.02 | 0.96 | 0.00 |
| 2 | 1.02 | 0.06 | 0.92 | 0.10 | 0.92 | 0.00 |
| 3 | 1.00 | 0.08 | 1.05 | 0.05 | 1.04 | 0.01 |
| 4 | 1.03 | 0.01 | 1.04 | 0.01 | 0.98 | 0.06 |
| 5 | 0.92 | 0.06 | 1.09 | 0.17 | 0.96 | 0.13 |
| 6 | 1.06 | 0.10 | 0.98 | 0.08 | 1.05 | 0.07 |
| 7 | 0.97 | 0.08 | 0.99 | 0.02 | 0.99 | 0.00 |
| 8 | 0.99 | 0.00 | 1.02 | 0.03 | 1.01 | 0.01 |
| 9 | 1.04 | 0.03 | 0.95 | 0.09 | 0.90 | 0.05 |
| 10 | 0.86 | 0.04 | 0.85 | 0.01 | 0.83 | 0.03 |

Instrument Readings

14-3. The table below shows 20 individual values taken from the process. (a) Construct a two-period moving range chart to establish control of the process variation. (b) Set up a two-period moving average chart, plot the control limits and the moving average values, and interpret the results. (c) Set up an EWMA control chart λ = 0.8, plot the EWMA values, and interpret the results.

| Sample No. | Measurement |
|------------|-------------|
| 1 | 605 |
| 2 | 592 |
| 3 | 608 |
| 4 | 593 |
| 5 | 606 |
| 6 | 597 |
| 7 | 604 |
| 8 | 593 |
| 9 | 607 |
| 10 | 591 |
| 11 | 612 |
| 12 | 598 |
| 13 | 611 |
| 14 | 600 |
| 15 | 613 |
| 16 | 602 |
| 17 | 612 |
| 18 | 605 |
| 19 | 609 |
| 20 | 603 |

14-4. A continuous production process is sampled on an hourly basis. The following table shows the sampling results for a 24-hour period in which the process appeared to be well controlled. (a) Construct a two-period moving range chart to establish control of the process variation. (b) Set up a three-period moving average chart, plot the control limits and the moving average values, and interpret the results. (c) Set up an EWMA control chart corresponding to $n = 3$, plot the EWMA values, and interpret the results.

| Sample No. | Measurement | Sample No. | Measurement |
|------------|-------------|------------|-------------|
| 1 | 225 | 13 | 212 |
| 2 | 217 | 14 | 208 |
| 3 | 204 | 15 | 201 |
| 4 | 208 | 16 | 205 |
| 5 | 217 | 17 | 214 |
| 6 | 223 | 18 | 222 |
| 7 | 227 | 19 | 230 |
| 8 | 231 | 20 | 221 |
| 9 | 225 | 21 | 218 |
| 10 | 222 | 22 | 214 |
| 11 | 217 | 23 | 209 |
| 12 | 211 | 24 | 203 |

# Unit 15:
# Control Charts for Attributes

# UNIT 15

## Control Charts for Attributes

An attribute is an inherent quality characteristic (e.g., a smooth surface or a blemish, an on time or late shipment, an acceptable or defective item). Attribute data is based on counts or proportions of such characteristics for individual items. For example, the number of blemishes on a sheet of glass, the number of late shipments, and the proportion of defective ballpoint pens are examples of attribute data. Control charts set up to monitor attributes on the basis of counts or proportions are called control charts for attributes. This unit describes several important control charts for attributes.

**Learning Objectives** — When you have completed this unit, you should:

    A. Know the characteristics of attribute data.

    B. Know when and how to set up and use four specific control charts for attributes, the c, u, p, and np charts.

## 15-1. Introduction

Attributes are quality characteristics that can be observed, classified, and counted. This often means classifying entire items as either good or bad (i.e., it either conforms or does not conform to specifications), but can also mean determining whether or not an item possesses particular characteristics, such as cracks, dents, tears, etc.

One important distinction regarding an item's attributes is the difference between a defect and a defective. A defect is a single nonconformity. Individual items may have multiple defects (multiple nonconformities). For example, a single shirt may have multiple tears and multiple missed stitches. A defective is an individual item that in one or more ways fails to conform to specifications and is rejected. For example, a shirt with one small tear or two missed stitches might be considered defective. As a result, there are two categories of control charts for attribute data: (1) control charts for nonconforming items (i.e., defectives) and (2) control charts for nonconformities (i.e., defects).

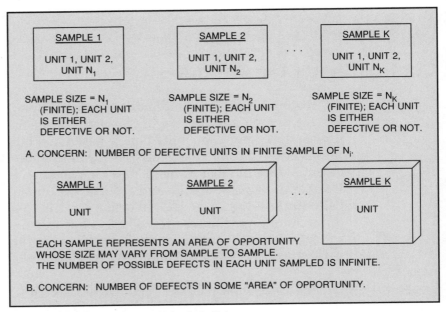

**Fig. 15-1. Clarifying Differences in Attribute Data**

A second distinction regarding attribute data concerns the subgroup or sample. In some cases, the sample is finite in size. For example, 10 computer screens or 50 ballpoint pens might be examined with the objective of determining how many are defective. At most 10 computer screens and 50 ballpoint pens might be so classified (regardless of the number of defects each individual unit possesses). In other cases, each sample represents a span of opportunity in which the number of defects possible is theoretically infinite. For example, in one year the number of possible lost-time accidents in a plant is infinite, the number of possible blemishes on a piece of glass of a certain size is infinite, and the number of possible defects on a single computer screen is infinite. Fig. 15-1 is presented to further clarify distinctions in attribute data.

Before beginning the examination of specific control charts in each category of attribute data, however, a brief discussion of the important difference between variation due to sampling fluctuation and variation due to process changes is presented.

## 15-2. Variation Due to Process Changes and Sampling Fluctuation

Suppose a large production plant has a "population" of 200 pumps in inventory and that, unknown to those at the plant, 4% of the pumps (a total of eight) are defective. Suppose that several randomly chosen samples of 10 pumps each are drawn from inventory. Simple math shows that on the average a sample of 10 pumps will contain $(10)(0.04) = 0.4$ defective pumps. However, no samples will contain exactly 0.4 defective pumps, some samples will have no defective pumps, others will have one defective pump, and a few samples will have even more. In other words, even when the population is unchanged, there will inevitably be variation in the number of defective items found in individual samples. This variation (i.e., the variation in the number of defective pumps found in individual samples when the population is unchanged) is referred to as sampling fluctuation.

If the number of defective pumps in the plant were 10% instead of 4%, however, then the expected number of defective pumps in a sample of size 10 increases to 1.0. Still, some of the samples will have no defective pumps, some will have one defective pump, and some more than one defective pump. Of course, since the number of defective pumps in the population has increased, more defective pumps are likely to be found in individual samples. The increased average number of defectives is due to a change in the population (i.e., a process change).

The difficulty lies in being able to distinguish between variation due to sampling fluctuation and variation due to process changes. For example, even for the situation in which 10% of the pumps are defective, a high percentage (35%) of the samples of size 10 will contain no defective pumps.

The goal, of course, is to quickly distinguish between variation due to process changes and variation due to sampling fluctuation. Using the most appropriate control chart provides a starting point.

## 15-3. Control Charts for Defectives (Nonconforming Items)

### np Chart

It is frequently important to monitor the number of defective (nonconforming items). When the sample size is finite and constant, an np chart is an appropriate control chart choice. The number of defective items found in each sample is plotted on an np chart. For example, if ball bearings are produced in batches of size 50 and each one is inspected using a go-nogo gauge, an np chart can be used to monitor the number of defective ball bearings.

The np chart is based on the binomial distribution, whose mean is n times p, where n is the size of each individual sample and p is the true proportion defective in the population or process. For example, if there are 200 pumps in inventory and 8 pumps are defective, the true proportion of defective pumps is 8/200 = 0.04. Since p is typically unknown, it is estimated by $\bar{p}$, the average proportion defective of the items found. Therefore, $n\bar{p}$ is an estimate of the expected number of defective items in a sample of size n. The standard deviation of the binomial distribution is usually estimated by $\sqrt{np(1 - \bar{p})}$.

The np chart's centerline and three-sigma control limits are usually shown as follows:

Centerline:

$$n\bar{p}$$

Control Limits:

$$UCL_{np} = n\bar{p} + 3\sqrt{n\bar{p}(1 - \bar{p})}$$

$$LCL_{np} = n\bar{p} - 3\sqrt{n\bar{p}(1 - \bar{p})}$$

When the proportion defective is based on data outside the process or on a target value, $\bar{p}$ is replaced by $p_T$ in the above equations. For example, suppose a new ball bearing production process has been set up but has not yet begun to produce, so no data is available from the process. Since an "identical" ball bearing production process at a sister plant produces on the average one defective per 500 ball bearings, $\bar{p}$ is replaced by $p_T$ = 1/500 = 0.002.

**Example 15-1:** Shipments of goods are accompanied by standard papers listing the buyer's name, address, account number, the number and type of goods desired, and so forth. If any of this information is in error, confusion is added to the process and some type of backtracking is required. As such, a shipping paper is said to be defective if it contains one or more errors. For instance, if the part number or the dollar amount (or both) is listed incorrectly, the shipping paper is said to be defective (i.e., nonconforming). Table 15-1 shows the number

| Day | No. of Defective Papers ($D_i$) | Day | No. of Defective Papers ($D_i$) | Day | No. of Defective Papers ($D_i$) |
|---|---|---|---|---|---|
| 1 | 3 | 11 | 2 | 21 | 4 |
| 2 | 3 | 12 | 1 | 22 | 6 |
| 3 | 1 | 13 | 2 | 23 . | 0 |
| 4 | 5 | 14 | 1 | 24 | 1 |
| 5 | 2 | 15 | 4 | 25 | 3 |
| 6 | 1 | 16 | 1 | 26 | 2 |
| 7 | 3 | 17 | 1 | 27 | 2 |
| 8 | 3 | 18 | 0 | 28 | 4 |
| 9 | 3 | 19 | 3 | 29 | 2 |
| 10 | 0 | 20 | 2 | 30 | 1 |

TABLE 15-1. Number of Defective Shipping Papers (Samples of Size 50)

of defective shipping papers found in daily samples of 50 shipments over a period of 30 days. (Note: In each daily sample of shipping papers, at most 50 can be defective. Hence, n = 50.)

Fig. 15-2 shows a run chart of the number of defectives by day. Clearly, variation is present. The question is whether the variation is due primarily to sampling fluctuation (in which case there is no special cause present) or is the result of a

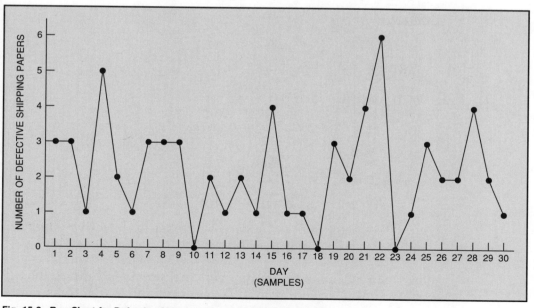

Fig. 15-2. Run Chart for Defective Shipping Papers (Samples of Size 50)

change in the process (in which case a search should be undertaken to find the special cause and to correct it).

The first step in developing an np chart for the process is to estimate the average number of defectives per sample and the average proportion defective.

$$\overline{np} = \text{average number of defective shipping papers}$$

$$\text{per sample}$$

$$= \text{total number of defectives observed/total number}$$

$$\text{of samples}$$

$$= \Sigma D_i / N$$

$$= 66/30$$

$$= 2.2$$

$$\overline{p} = \text{average proportion of defective shipping papers}$$

$$= \overline{np}/n$$

$$= 2.2/50$$

$$= 0.044$$

The np chart's centerline and control limits are then set as follows:

Centerline:

$$\overline{np} = 2.2$$

Control Limits:

$$UCL_{np} = \overline{np} + 3\sqrt{\overline{np}(1 - \overline{p})}$$

$$= 2.2 + 3\sqrt{2.2(1 - 0.044)}$$

$$= 6.55$$

$$LCL_{np} = \overline{np} - 3\sqrt{\overline{np}(1 - \overline{p})}$$

$$= 2.2 - 3\sqrt{2.2(1 - 0.044)}$$

$$= 0.00 \text{ (since a negative number of defective papers}$$
$$\text{is not possible)}$$

Fig. 15-3 shows the initial np chart. All points fall inside the control limits, an indication that the variation is due to sampling fluctuation. (Note: Neither the zone rules nor the run

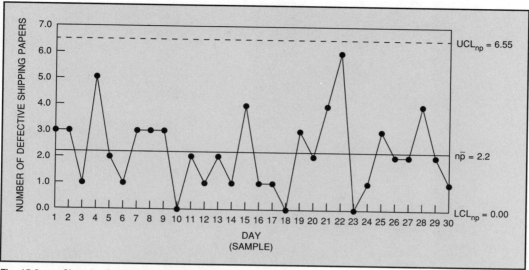

Fig. 15-3. np Chart for Defective Shipping Papers (Samples 1–30)

rules are applicable since np values are typically nonnormal. This issue is discussed in more detail in the Summary.) Since the process seems to be in control, the control limits are extended. (Note: None of the attribute charts require an accompanying dispersion chart, such as an R or $R_m$ chart, since the mean and standard deviation for attribute data are functionally related. This issue is also discussed in the unit's Summary.) Table 15-2 shows the number of defective shipping papers in daily samples of 50 for 10 subsequent days.

Fig. 15-4 shows the sampling results for the entire 40-day period plotted on an extended np chart. Two points fall above the upper control limit. A check with the supplier revealed that a new hire had begun handling the shipping papers on day 36. The supplier gave assurances that the employee would be properly trained.

In practice, the number of defectives is sometimes monitored using x or $\bar{x}$ charts (and accompanying $R_m$ or R charts). Since

| Day | 31 | 32 | 33 | 34 | 35 | 36 | 37 | 38 | 39 | 40 |
|---|---|---|---|---|---|---|---|---|---|---|
| No. of Defective Papers | 2 | 4 | 5 | 2 | 4 | 8 | 4 | 4 | 8 | 5 |

TABLE 15-2. Number of Defective Shipping Papers for 10 Subsequent Days

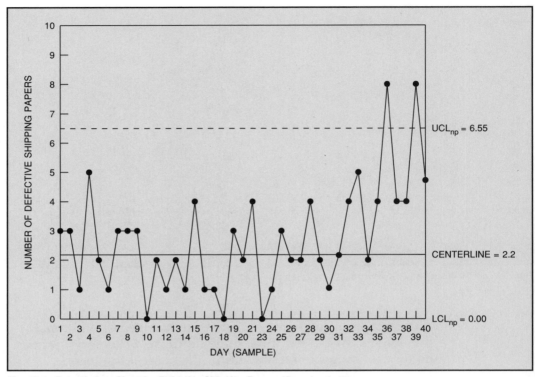

**Fig. 15-4. Extended np Chart for Defective Shipping Papers (Samples 1–40)**

the number of defectives is a count rather than a measurement and since the binomial distribution is skewed for combinations of small n and small p values (Fig. 15-5), x and $\bar{x}$ charts, which are based on the assumption of a normally distributed control variable, are not usually as effective as the np chart at identifying out-of-control points. When n and p are simultaneously large (say, $n \geq 20$ and $p \geq 0.20$), however, the binomial distribution becomes nearly symmetrical and follows a near-normal pattern (Fig. 15-6).

The practical implication is that x and $\bar{x}$ charts, along with accompanying $R_m$ and R charts, can be effectively used in place of the np chart when n and p are simultaneously large. Fig. 15-7 shows an x chart and an accompanying $R_m$ chart for the defective shipping data of Tables 15-1 and 15-2. (Note: The centerline and control limits are based on the first 30 data values. The day 22 value of 6 defectives was omitted when it caused an out-of-control signal on the initial $R_m$ chart.) In this situation, n is relatively large (i.e., 50) but p is small (i.e.,

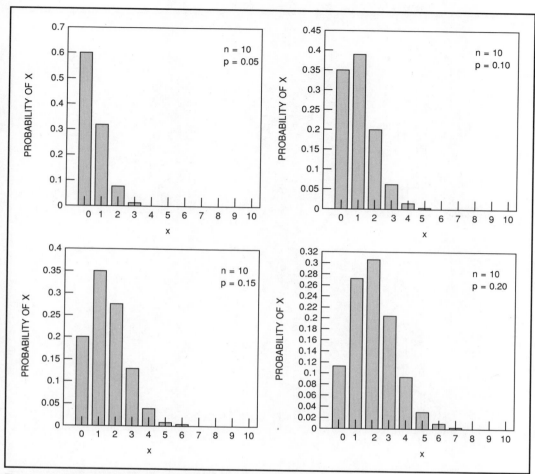

**Fig. 15-5. Binomial Distribution (Small n and p Values)**

0.044), so the np chart is not clearly a better choice. In fact, as in the case of the np chart, both day 36 and day 39 values give out-of-control signals on the x chart.

## p Chart

A p chart (p stands for proportion) is useful in situations similar to those described for the np chart but is considerably more versatile. The proportion defective or proportion nonconforming is plotted on a p chart. As such, the p chart is the better choice when the sample size is variable or when the goal is to compare two or more processes. For example, suppose that instead of examining samples of exactly 50

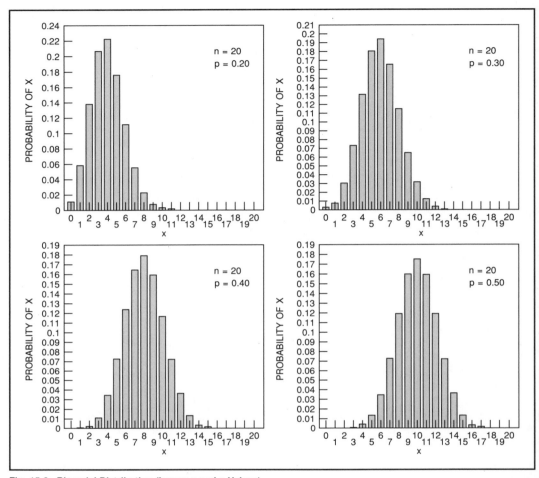

**Fig. 15-6. Binomial Distribution (Larger n and p Values)**

shipping papers per day, every shipping paper is examined and classified as defective or not. Since different numbers of shipments are made daily, the result is a variety of daily sample sizes (i.e., n changes from sample to sample). Even if the fraction defective does not change, each different sample size means a different centerline and different control limits for the np chart. In this case, the p chart is clearly a better choice.

The p chart's centerline and three-sigma control limits are usually set as shown below. Of course, when the average proportion defective is based on information outside the process (e.g., on data from a similar process) or on a target value, $\bar{p}$ is replaced by $p_T$.

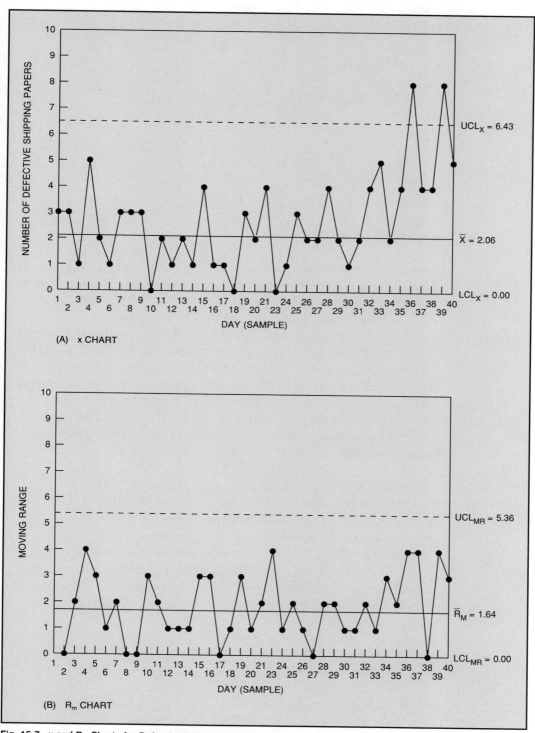

Fig. 15-7. x and $R_m$ Charts for Defective Shipping Papers

Centerline:

$$\overline{p}$$

Control Limits:

$$UCL_p = \overline{p} + 3\sqrt{\frac{\overline{p}(1 - \overline{p})}{n}}$$

$$LCL_p = \overline{p} - 3\sqrt{\frac{\overline{p}(1 - \overline{p})}{n}}$$

(Note: To use percentages rather than proportions in the control limits, replace the proportional $\overline{p}$ values with percentages and change the 1 to 100.)

By inspecting the formulas, it is apparent that if the sample size n changes from sample to sample, it is theoretically necessary to compute one set of control limits for each different sample size. For example, samples of size n = 100 would have narrower control limits than samples of size n = 50 (since n is in the denominator). An effective alternative for handling the changing sample size issue is to develop one set of control limits for the maximum sample size, develop one set of control limits for the minimum sample size, and make evaluations based on these two sets of limits—developing individual control limits only when the decision is in doubt. Application details regarding this procedure are presented in Example 15-2.

**Example 15-2:** Consider a blow molding plastic bottle production process. To control the number of defective bottles produced, all bottles are inspected. A bottle is said to be defective (i.e., nonconforming) if it contains one or more defects. The number of bottles produced varies from day to day. Table 15-3 shows the number of defective bottles, the number of bottles produced daily, and the daily proportion defective over a 30-day period.

A total of 2820 ($\times$ 100) bottles were produced, 254 of them defective. The p chart's centerline is then $\overline{p} = 0.090$ (i.e., 254/2820).

Since the number of bottles produced varies from day to day, either the individual control limits for each day must be computed or some alternative approach must be used. In this case, the max–min procedure mentioned earlier is employed. Two sets of control limits, one set of inner limits (based on the

| Day | No. of Defectives | No. of Bottles Produced (× 100) | Prop. Defect. p | Day | No. of Defectives | No. of Bottles Produced (× 100) | Prop. Defect. p |
|---|---|---|---|---|---|---|---|
| 1 | 7 | 90 | 0.078 | 16 | 8 | 100 | 0.080 |
| 2 | 3 | 60 | 0.050 | 17 | 20 | 110 | 0.182 |
| 3 | 5 | 90 | 0.056 | 18 | 12 | 110 | 0.109 |
| 4 | 8 | 80 | 0.100 | 19 | 7 | 80 | 0.088 |
| 5 | 2 | 80 | 0.025 | 20 | 11 | 80 | 0.138 |
| 6 | 3 | 90 | 0.033 | 21 | 7 | 90 | 0.078 |
| 7 | 8 | 80 | 0.100 | 22 | 5 | 90 | 0.056 |
| 8 | 3 | 70 | 0.043 | 23 | 8 | 90 | 0.089 |
| 9 | 7 | 100 | 0.070 | 24 | 14 | 110 | 0.127 |
| 10 | 9 | 100 | 0.090 | 25 | 16 | 110 | 0.145 |
| 11 | 10 | 100 | 0.100 | 26 | 4 | 80 | 0.050 |
| 12 | 14 | 110 | 0.127 | 27 | 3 | 80 | 0.038 |
| 13 | 13 | 110 | 0.118 | 28 | 7 | 90 | 0.078 |
| 14 | 17 | 120 | 0.142 | 29 | 11 | 100 | 0.110 |
| 15 | 5 | 110 | 0.045 | 30 | 7 | 110 | 0.064 |

**TABLE 15-3. 30-Day Summary of Blow Molding Operation**

maximum sample size) and one set of outer limits (based on the minimum sample size), are developed and plotted. The sampling results can then be interpreted based on three criteria: (1) If all the plotted p values fall inside the inner control limits, the process is in control and no individual control limits need be calculated; (2) if one or more of the plotted p values fall outside the outer limits, the process is out of control and special causes should be investigated; and, (3) if one or more p values fall between the inner and outer control limits, it is necessary to compute individual control limits for those particular samples before making a judgment.

Inner control limits (for daily production maximum of 120):

$$UCL_p = \bar{p} + 3\sqrt{\frac{\bar{p}(1 - \bar{p})}{n}}$$

$$= 0.090 + 3\sqrt{\frac{(0.090)(0.910)}{120}}$$

$$= 0.090 + 0.078$$

$$= 0.168$$

$$LCL_p = \bar{p} - 3\sqrt{\frac{\bar{p}(1 - \bar{p})}{n}}$$

$$= 0.090 - 0.078$$

$$= 0.012$$

Outer control limits (for daily production minimum of 60):

$$UCL_p = \bar{p} + 3\sqrt{\frac{\bar{p}(1 - \bar{p})}{n}}$$

$$= 0.090 + 3\sqrt{\frac{(0.090)(0.910)}{60}}$$

$$= 0.090 + 0.111$$

$$= 0.201$$

$$LCL_p = \bar{p} - 3\sqrt{\frac{\bar{p}(1 - \bar{p})}{n}}$$

$$= 0.090 - 0.111$$

$$= 0.000 \text{ (since a negative proportion defective is impossible)}$$

Fig. 15-8 shows the proportion of defective bottles produced for the 30-day period, as well as both sets of control limits.

One point, the proportion defective for day 17, falls between the inner and outer upper control limits. As such, it is necessary to compute the upper control limit for day 17. On day 17, 110 ($\times$ 100) bottles were produced.

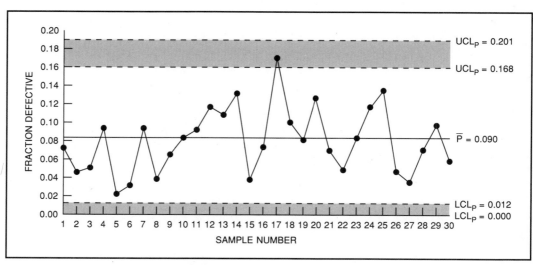

**Fig. 15-8. p Chart for Blow Molding Bottle Process**

$$UCL_p = 0.090 + 3\sqrt{\frac{(0.090)(0.910)}{110}}$$

$$= 0.090 + 0.082$$

$$= 0.172$$

Since the day 17 proportion defective of 0.182 is greater than 0.172, an out-of-control signal is given. The problem was identified and subsequently corrected. Then, omitting the day 17 results, a new centerline plus new inner and outer control limits were computed. Since the p values for the other 29 days were all between the revised inner control limits, both sets of control limits were extended and used to monitor the blow molding process.

## 15-4. Control Charts for Defects (Nonconformities)

### c Chart

It is often appropriate to monitor the number of nonconformities or defects. (Note: Recall the difference between defects and defectives presented in the Introduction.) When the area of opportunity for the occurrence of a defect is constant, a c chart (c is for count) may be appropriately used. The c chart is based on the Poisson distribution, named after the eighteenth-century mathematician Simeon Poisson. The Poisson distribution describes probabilities related to the occurrence of "rare" events—events that may occur in relation to time, area, volume, or length.

For example, a c chart is appropriate for monitoring the following: (1) the number of lost-time accidents per week, (2) the number of blemishes in the enamel paint on a refrigerator door (constant size refrigerator door), (3) the number of impurities in quart containers of drinking water, (4) the number of off-color resins per batch (constant batch size), and (5) the number of breakdowns in a given length of insulated wire subjected to a constant voltage.

Control limits for the c chart are quite simple to develop because the Poisson distribution has the unusual characteristic of having the square of its standard deviation (i.e., its variance) equal to its mean (in magnitude). That is, if an estimate of the process mean is computed by dividing the total number of nonconformities observed in a number of samples by the total number of items inspected, the centerline and three-sigma control limits are usually shown as follows:

Centerline:

$$\bar{c}$$

Control Limits:

$$UCL_c = \bar{c} + 3\sqrt{\bar{c}}$$

$$LCL_c = \bar{c} - 3\sqrt{\bar{c}}$$

If the process mean is based on other information (such as the mean of a similar process) or on a target value, $\bar{c}$ is typically shown as $c_T$ in the above equations.

Two assumptions accompany the application of a c chart: (1) independent data and (2) constant expected values. For example, for the Poisson distribution to apply, individual lost-time accidents should be independent of each other (i.e., the occurrence of one lost-time accident does not change the probability of the occurrence of a second lost-time accident) and the probability of a lost-time accident should be constant from period to period (i.e., the probability of a lost-time accident is the same in week 1, week 2, etc.).

**Example 15-3:** Table 15-4 lists the number of surface imperfections observed in 30 constant-sized rolls of coated paper. (Note: You might think of this as "defects per constant area.") Preliminary control limits are developed on the results

| Roll Number | Number Flaws in Roll | Roll Number | Number Flaws in Roll | Roll Number | Number Flaws in Roll |
|---|---|---|---|---|---|
| 1 | 24 | 11 | 20 | 21 | 18 |
| 2 | 21 | 12 | 24 | 22 | 11 |
| 3 | 16 | 13 | 25 | 23 | 24 |
| 4 | 19 | 14 | 16 | 24 | 30 |
| 5 | 15 | 15 | 20 | 25 | 41 |
| 6 | 31 | 16 | 19 | 26 | 10 |
| 7 | 20 | 17 | 12 | 27 | 17 |
| 8 | 28 | 18 | 17 | 28 | 16 |
| 9 | 3 | 19 | 13 | 29 | 18 |
| 10 | 16 | 20 | 22 | 30 | 12 |

**TABLE 15-4. Count of Imperfections in Individual Paper Rolls**

found to date. Since 578 imperfections were observed in the 30 rolls, the initial centerline and three-sigma control limits are

Centerline:

$$\overline{c} = 578/30 = 19.27$$

Control Limits:

$$UCL_c = \overline{c} + 3\sqrt{\overline{c}}$$
$$= 19.27 + 3\sqrt{19.27}$$
$$= 32.44$$
$$LCL_c = \overline{c} - 3\sqrt{\overline{c}}$$
$$= 19.27 - 3\sqrt{19.27}$$
$$= 6.10$$

The c chart in Fig. 15-9 includes results from each of the 30 rolls. The number of imperfections found in rolls 9 and 25 resulted in points outside the control limits. Investigation of the roll 9 results revealed an inspector error. The unusually large number of imperfections in roll 25 resulted from an equipment problem, which was repaired.

Since assignable (special) causes were found for both out-of-control points, the sample 9 and 25 values were omitted from the set of data and a revised centerline and revised control limits were calculated.

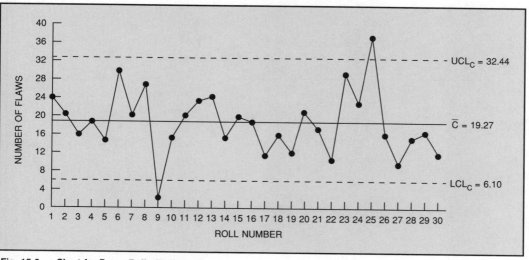

**Fig. 15-9. c Chart for Paper Rolls (Rolls 1–30)**

Centerline:

$$\bar{c} = 534/28 = 19.07$$

Control Limits:

$$UCL_c = 19.07 + 3\sqrt{19.07}$$

$$= 32.17$$

$$LCL_c = 19.07 - 3\sqrt{19.07}$$

$$= 5.97$$

None of the remaining 28 values plotted on the revised c chart fell outside the control limits, indicating an in-control process (Fig. 15-10). As such, these control limits were extended and used for the subsequent plotting of additional imperfection counts. Table 15-5 shows the number of imperfections found in 10 subsequent paper rolls.

Fig. 15-11 shows a plot that includes the 10 additional imperfection counts on the revised c chart. Inspection of the figure indicates that the process is still in control.

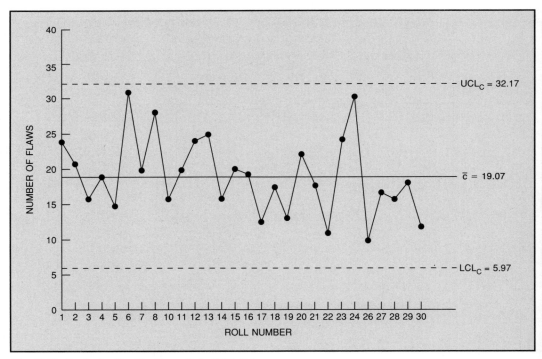

**Fig. 15-10. Revised c Chart for Paper Rolls (28 Rolls)**

| Roll Number | Number Flaws in Roll | Roll Number | Number Flaws in Roll |
|---|---|---|---|
| 31 | 16 | 36 | 27 |
| 32 | 18 | 37 | 20 |
| 33 | 12 | 38 | 25 |
| 34 | 11 | 39 | 19 |
| 35 | 23 | 40 | 18 |

TABLE 15-5. Count of Imperfections in Individual Paper Rolls (Rolls 31–40)

In practice, x charts are often used in place of c charts to monitor processes where the number of defects is counted. While there are occasions in which the x chart (and accompanying $R_m$ chart) is nearly as appropriate, the c chart is a better choice if the average number of defects is small (say less than 25). There are two closely related reasons for preferring a c chart to a normal-distribution-based x chart: (1) counts are discrete and usually follow a Poisson distribution (so that a normal distribution is inappropriate), and (2) Poisson distributions are skewed when the mean is small (so that a normal distribution, which is symmetric, is inappropriate).

Fig. 15-12 shows Poisson distributions for four different means. Clearly, for small mean values, the Poisson distribution is

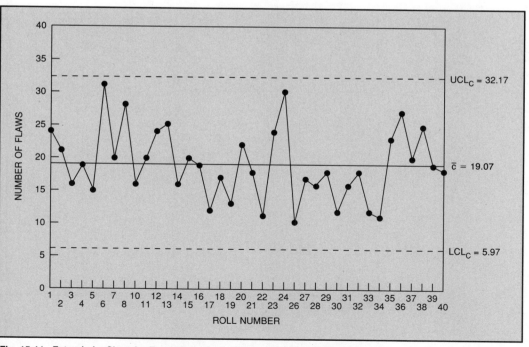

Fig. 15-11. Extended c Chart for Paper Rolls (Including Results from Rolls 31–40)

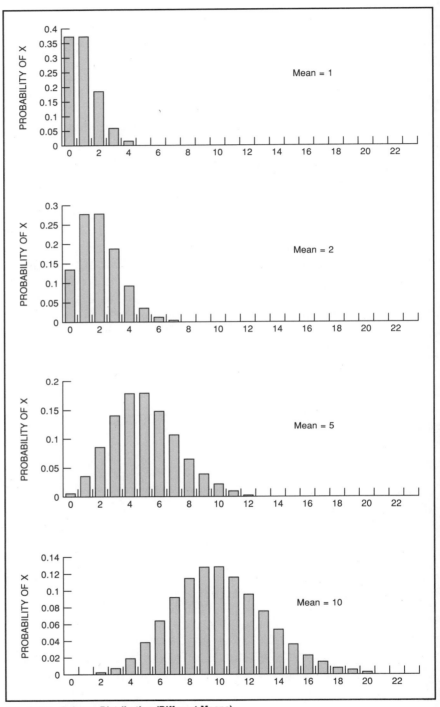

**Fig. 15-12.  Poisson Distribution (Different Means)**

skewed right. Since x charts are based on the assumption that
the characteristic plotted is approximately normally distributed,
incorrect judgments regarding the process are more likely. For
distributions with large means, the Poisson tends to closely
approximate the normal. In fact, the Poisson follows the normal
closely when the mean is approximately 25 or more. In such
cases, although the c chart is theoretically preferable (since
counts are discrete and cannot theoretically be normally
distributed), the x chart (and accompanying $R_m$ chart) will
likely be equally effective.

---

**Example 15-4: (Continuation of 15-3)**  Fig. 15-13 shows both an
x chart and a $R_m$ chart based on the initial paper roll data
(Table 15-4). Since $\bar{c} = 19.27$ (near 25), the x chart and $R_m$
chart pair can be expected to be nearly as effective as the c
chart in identifying out-of-control conditions. In fact, both the x
chart and the $R_m$ chart show an out-of-control condition
resulting from the high sample 25 value. After omitting point
25 (as was done in Example 15-3) and revising the control
limits, the moving range based on roll 8 and roll 9 (i.e., $R_m$ =
25) also indicated an out-of-control condition. In other words,
the x chart/$R_m$ chart combination identified the same two out-
of-control points as the c chart.

---

## u Chart

If the probability of a defect or a nonconformity changes from
unit to unit (e.g., different numbers of days per month, various
batch sizes, a variety of paper roll sizes), a u chart (a variation
of the c chart) is a more appropriate control charting choice.
The number of defects per unit is plotted on a u chart (e.g.,
maintenance calls per day, impurities per 10,000 gallons,
imperfections per square foot).

Obviously, for a changing unit size, a c chart could provide
misleading results since only a count is plotted. For example,
"40 impurities" has a different meaning in a 50,000 gallon
batch than in a 10,000 gallon batch. However, if the unit size is
based on a constant batch size, say 10,000 gallons, results from
different batch sizes can easily be compared. For example, 40
impurities in a batch of 50,000 gallons and 4 impurities in a
batch of 5,000 gallons both imply 8 impurities per 10,000
gallons.

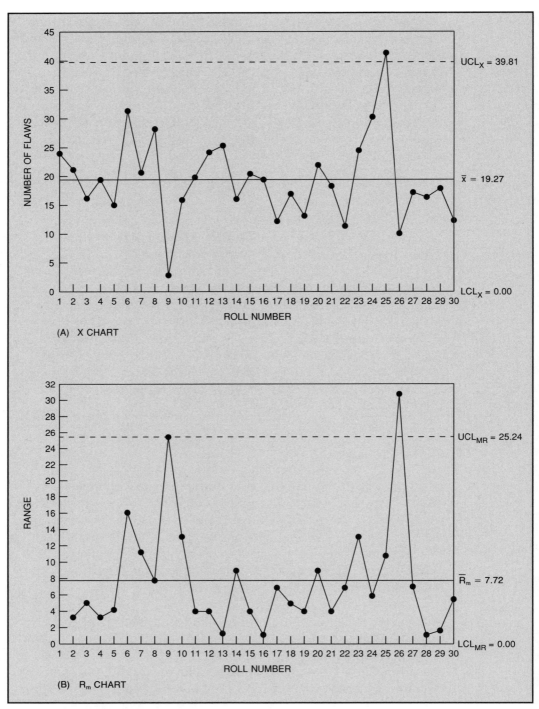

**Fig. 15-13.** x and $R_m$ Charts (Rolls 1–30)

The symbol u (u stands for count per unit) is used to represent the number of nonconformities per unit, where $u = c/k$, c is the count of nonconformities, and k is the standard unit of measure chosen. For example, if the number of impurities per 10,000 gallons is charted, $k = 5$ for a batch of 50,000 gallons and $k = 0.5$ for a batch of 5,000 gallons. The centerline is set equal to the average number of nonconformities per unit, and control limits are set three standard deviations above and below the centerline.

Centerline:

$$\bar{u} = \frac{\sum\limits_{i=1}^{m} c_i}{\sum\limits_{i=1}^{m} k_i}$$

where $i$ = sample number; $m$ = number of samples.

Control Limits:

$$UCL_u = \bar{u} + \sqrt{\frac{\bar{u}}{k_i}}$$

$$LCL_u = \bar{u} - 3\sqrt{\frac{\bar{u}}{k_i}}$$

As in the case of the c chart, when the expected number of occurrences per unit is known from other similar processes or when a target value has been established, $u_T$ is used in place of $\bar{u}$ in the above formulas.

Note that the equations call for individual control limits for each different unit size (e.g., each different $k_i$). For example, although they would have the same centerline, batches of 50,000 gallons have narrower control limits than batches of 25,000 gallons. Because of the tedium involved in setting and explaining individual control limits, an alternative approach (discussed originally in Example 15-2) that is based on maximum and minimum unit sizes is usually employed.

**Example 15-5:** A window production company wants to monitor the quality of the windows it produces and has identified the number of blemishes (defects) as an appropriate quality measure. Several different window sizes are manufactured. Table 15-6 summarizes the inspection results of 20 recently produced windows. Since the quality characteristic monitored is the number of blemishes and since the windows produced are of several different sizes, a u chart is selected. The standard unit of measure chosen is one square meter. Individual u values are then found by dividing the number of blemishes by that particular window's surface area in square meters.

The total surface area examined is 63.3 m$^2$, and the total number of blemishes observed is 147. The average number of blemishes per square meter is then

$$\bar{u} = \text{total number of blemishes/total surface area}$$

$$= 147/63.3$$

$$= 2.32$$

As mentioned above, each different surface area size should (theoretically) have a different set of control limits (i.e., one set for 2 m$^2$, one set for 2.5 m$^2$, one set for 2.8 m$^2$, etc.). However, to reduce the amount of work involved and to simplify the analysis process, we initially develop only two sets of control limits—one set for the maximum surface area and one set for the minimum surface area—and use these for all samples. In this example, one set of control limits is based on the

| Window No. | Surface Area, m$^2$ | Number of Blemishes | u | Window No. | Surface Area, m$^2$ | Number of Blemishes | u |
|---|---|---|---|---|---|---|---|
| 1 | 2.0 | 4 | 2.0 | 11 | 2.8 | 4 | 1.4 |
| 2 | 2.0 | 5 | 2.5 | 12 | 2.8 | 8 | 2.9 |
| 3 | 2.0 | 1 | 0.5 | 13 | 3.2 | 8 | 2.5 |
| 4 | 4.0 | 9 | 2.3 | 14 | 3.4 | 16 | 4.7 |
| 5 | 5.0 | 14 | 2.8 | 15 | 3.2 | 8 | 2.5 |
| 6 | 2.5 | 3 | 1.2 | 16 | 3.2 | 8 | 2.5 |
| 7 | 3.0 | 6 | 2.0 | 17 | 4.2 | 8 | 1.9 |
| 8 | 3.0 | 6 | 2.0 | 18 | 4.2 | 12 | 2.9 |
| 9 | 3.0 | 3 | 1.0 | 19 | 2.8 | 6 | 2.1 |
| 10 | 4.2 | 10 | 2.4 | 20 | 2.8 | 8 | 2.9 |

**TABLE 15-6. Summary of Blemishes per Window**

maximum window area size (i.e., k = 5 square meters) and the other set of control limits is based on the minimum window area size (i.e., k = 2 square meters). Since the centerline is the expected number of defects per unit, both sets of control limits use the same centerline, $\bar{u} = 2.32$.

Inner control limits (for a maximum window surface area of 5 m²):

$$UCL_u = 2.32 + 3\sqrt{(2.32/5)}$$

$$= 4.36$$

$$LCL_u = 2.32 - 3\sqrt{(2.32/5)}$$

$$= 0.28$$

Outer control limits (for a minimum window surface area of 2 m²):

$$UCL_u = 2.32 + 3\sqrt{(2.32/2)}$$

$$= 5.55$$

$$LCL_u = 2.32 - 3\sqrt{(2.32/2)}$$

$$= 0.00 \text{ (since a negative number of nonconformities is not possible)}$$

Fig. 15-14 shows the initial u chart. The u value sampling results are interpreted as follows: (1) If all the plotted u values

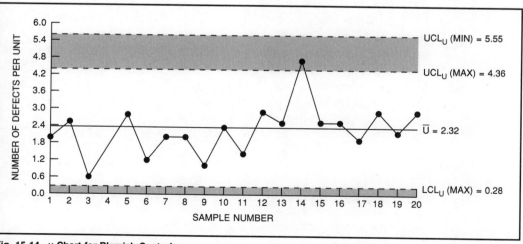

**Fig. 15-14. u Chart for Blemish Control**

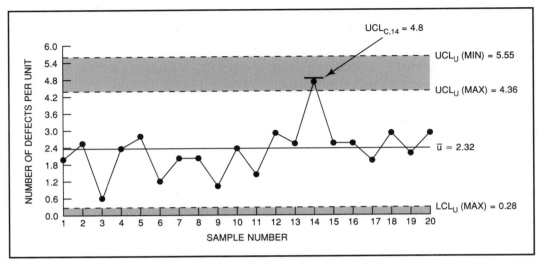

**Fig. 15-15. u Chart for Blemish Control with Individual Upper Control Limit for Window 14**

fall inside the inner limits, the process is in control and no individual control limits need be computed. (2) If one or more of the plotted u values fall outside the outer limits, then the process is out of control. (3) If one or more u values fall between the inner and outer limits, it is necessary to compute individual control limits for those particular sampling units before making a judgment.

All u values, except the sample number 14 u value, are within the inner limits. The sample 14 u value falls between the inner and outer upper limits. This means that only sample 14 needs to have its individual upper control limit calculated. The upper limit for sample 14 is $UCL_u = 2.32 + 3\sqrt{(2.32/3.4)} = 4.8$ (Fig. 15-15). Since the observed u value is 4.7, no out-of-control signal is given. The two sets of control limits based on the original 20 windows can be extended and additional sample results plotted. Of course, if one or more out-of-control u values had been identified and the root cause or causes found, those sample results would be omitted and new inner and outer control limits calculated.

## 15-5. Summary

Several questions are often asked regarding control charts for attributes. Many of the questions revolve around the fact that attribute control charts are not based on the normal distribution. Several such questions are addressed in this section.

Why are no dispersion charts mentioned with regard to control charts for attributes (i.e., why no R or $R_m$ charts?)? The answer is that because of the underlying distributions for all the attribute control charts presented, the mean and standard deviation are functionally related, so one chart is able to monitor changes in both the process mean and process standard deviation. That is, for each control chart for attributes, if the mean changes (e.g., c moves from 6 to 9), the standard deviation must also change (e.g., $\sqrt{c}$ moves from $\sqrt{6}$ to $\sqrt{9}$). No such relationships exist between the mean and standard deviation for variables control charts.

Do the run rules presented in Unit 10 apply for the control charts for attributes? In general, the answer is no. The reason is that since both the Poisson and binomial distributions are skewed for small mean values, well over half the values tend to fall below the mean. For example, for a c chart with a centerline of 3 (i.e., process mean = 3), the probability of an individual c value falling below the centerline is approximately 65%, not 50% as is expected in the normally distributed case. As a result, if the normal-distribution-based run rules are applied on an attributes chart, false signals are a likely consequence, particularly for runs below the centerline. In fact, run rules having probabilities similar to the normal-distribution-based run rules could be developed for attributes charts. Unfortunately, unlike the normal-distribution-based run rules that apply for all normally distributed situations, a different set of rules would be necessary—if the same probabilities were to apply—for each different parameter value and each different distribution!

Do the zone rules presented in Unit 10 apply for control charts for attributes? In general, since the values plotted on attribute charts are not normally distributed, the normal-based zone rules should not be used. While the probability of finding a value more than three standard deviations from the mean is 0.27% for all normally distributed values, the probability of finding a Poisson distributed value more than three standard deviations from the mean varies significantly depending on the mean value.

Table 15-7 shows probabilities associated with zones A, B, and C for the standard normal distribution and for several mean values of the Poisson distribution. As expected, the Poisson probabilities within each zone approach the normal probabilities as the Poisson mean increases. For small Poisson means, the probabilities within each zone are considerably different from the normally distributed probabilities (because of the skewed nature of Poisson distributions with small means).

One rule of thumb is to use the normal-distribution-based zone rules as decision guidelines on control charts for attributes when the mean is approximately 10 or more, realizing that the associated probabilities are somewhat different from those for the normal-based rules and disregard the zone rules completely for mean values less than 10, looking only for unnatural patterns in the data, such as zig-zag sequences, clusters of points, or long sequences of increasing or decreasing points.

Are the c chart and u chart really different? In some situations, it may at first appear that there is no difference. For example, suppose that the number of lost-time accidents per 100,000 manhours worked is to be monitored. Since lost-time accidents are typically rare in a safe plant, each occurrence might be recorded on a checksheet in increments of 100,000 manhours, then plotted on a c chart. Suppose that the mean number of lost-time accidents per 100,000 manhours is 9. The control limits are computed as follows:

Control Limits:

$$UCL_c = \bar{c} + 3\sqrt{\bar{c}}$$
$$= 9 + 3\sqrt{9}$$
$$= 9 + 9$$
$$= 18$$
$$LCL_c = \bar{c} - 3\sqrt{\bar{c}}$$
$$= 9 - 3\sqrt{9}$$
$$= 9 - 9$$
$$= 0$$

Similarly, using the same checksheet information based on increments of 100,000 manhours, k = 1 (i.e., data collected and recorded in same increments used in control chart, 100,000

| Distribution | Mean | Zone* | | | |
|---|---|---|---|---|---|
| | | C | B | A | >A |
| Normal | any | 68.3% | 27.2% | 4.3% | 0.3% |
| Poisson | 1 | 92.0% | 6.1% | 1.5% | 0.4% |
| Poisson | 4 | 79.7% | 18.2% | 1.8% | 0.3% |
| Poisson | 9 | 76.0% | 21.2% | 2.6% | 0.2% |
| Poisson | 16 | 74.1% | 22.7% | 3.0% | 0.2% |
| Poisson | 25 | 72.9% | 23.7% | 3.2% | 0.2% |

*Zone C represents the area within ±1 standard deviation of the mean; zone B, the area between 1 and 2 standard deviations from the mean; zone A, the area between 2 and 3 standard deviations from the mean; and >A, the area greater than 3 standard deviations from the mean. The percentages shown represent both C zones, both B zones, and both A zones.

**TABLE 15-7. Probabilities Associated with Zones for the Standard Normal and Several Poisson Distributions**

manhours) and the u chart control limits are identical to the c chart control limits.

$$UCL_u = \bar{u} + 3\sqrt{(\bar{u}/k)}$$
$$= 9 + 3\sqrt{(9/1)}$$
$$= 9 + 3(3)$$
$$= 9 + 9$$
$$= 18$$
$$LCL_u = \bar{u} - 3\sqrt{(\bar{u}/k)}$$
$$= 9 - 3\sqrt{(9/1)}$$
$$= 9 - 9$$
$$= 0$$

On the other hand, if the same data are used but the number of occurrences are recorded in increments of 25,000 hours, with four consecutive values summed before plotting a single value on a u chart, k = 0.25 (i.e., 25,000/100,000) and the u chart control limits are as follows:

$$UCL_u = \bar{u} + 3\sqrt{(\bar{u}/k)}$$
$$= 9 + 3\sqrt{9/(0.25)}$$
$$= 9 + 3\sqrt{36}$$
$$= 9 + 3(6)$$
$$= 9 + 18$$
$$= 27$$

$$LCL_u = \bar{u} - 3\sqrt{(\bar{u}/k)}$$
$$= 9 - 3\sqrt{9/(0.25)}$$
$$= 9 - 3(6)$$
$$= 9 - 18$$
$$= 0 \text{ (since a negative number of lost-time accidents}$$
$$\text{is not possible)}$$

The control limits for the second u chart are obviously different from those of the first u chart as well as those of the c chart. The reason, of course, is that the standard deviation for the c and u values are the same only if the k value in the denominator of the u variable's standard deviation formula is 1 (i.e., only if the "area of opportunity" is the same in all cases). In this case, since k = 0.25, the standard deviation for the second u variable is twice as large as the standard deviation for the first u variable or the c variable (i.e., 6 to 3). The second u chart is different (and correct) because of the manner in which the data was collected and recorded. While either a c chart or a u chart can be used to monitor lost-time accidents, the control limits depend on the manner in which the data is collected.

Is it always apparent which type of control chart should be used? Unfortunately, the best control chart choice is sometimes unclear. For example, suppose the number of hours of overtime is to be monitored. Since the number of hours is counted, not measured, an attribute control chart seems at first to be the more appropriate choice. However, since the distribution of the number of overtime hours is more likely to be normal-like than Poisson-like because of the potentially high mean value, an x chart/$R_m$ chart combination may be the better choice. Fortunately, in most situations, the best choice is apparent.

## Exercises:

15-1. (a) Name two control charts used to monitor the number of defects.
(b) Name a control chart used to monitor the number of defectives per sample.
(c) Name a control chart used to monitor the proportion of defectives per sample.
(d) When the fraction defective is small (say 0.05 or less) in comparison to the sample size, the number

of defectives (or the proportion defective) tends to follow which probability distribution?

(e) When the number of defects is small relative to the area of opportunity, the quality characteristic tends to follow what probability distribution?

15-2. Suppose that a process is in control with an average proportion defective of 0.10 and n = 100. Compute the centerlines and three-sigma control limits for both (a) a p chart and (b) an np chart.

15-3. Suppose that a paper production process is in control and producing on the average four blemishes per roll.
(a) Compute the centerline and three-sigma control limits for a c chart to monitor the process.
(b) If the largest roll produced is 10,000 square feet, the smallest roll is 5,000 square feet, and the average number of defects per roll is 4, compute the maximum and minimum control limits for a u chart to monitor the process. (Note: Let k = 10 and k = 5.)

15-4. The table below shows the number of defects found in a daily sample of five assemblies over a five-day period.

|  | Assembly | | | | |
|---|---|---|---|---|---|
| Day | 1 | 2 | 3 | 4 | 5 |
| 1 | 77 | 61 | 59 | 22 | 54 |
| 2 | 64 | 49 | 54 | 92 | 22 |
| 3 | 75 | 65 | 41 | 89 | 49 |
| 4 | 93 | 45 | 87 | 55 | 33 |
| 5 | 45 | 77 | 40 | 25 | 20 |

Defects Found in Assembly Samples

Assume that a c chart is to be used to monitor future production.
(a) Compute a centerline and three-sigma control limits based on the above data.
(b) If any points fall outside the preliminary control limits, discard them and revise the control limits. Repeat this procedure until an acceptable set of control limits has been found.

15-5. A supplier of rubber seals maintains a p chart on his production process. At the last audit, the process seemed to be in control at a level of 5% nonconforming

seals. Recently thirty successive samples of 50 seals
each were taken from the production line. They
contained (in order) 3, 2, 3, 0, 5, 6, 3, 3, 5, 6, 2, 3, 3, 2,
6, 10, 5, 4, 6, 5, 8, 9, 3, 4, 2, 6, 8, 5, 7, and 6
nonconforming seals. Plot the corresponding p values
on a p chart and determine whether or not the process
is still in statistical control.

15-6. The following table shows the amount of chlorine
present (in parts per million) in 40 shipments of
bromine.
  (a) Using a c chart, determine whether or not the
      process is in statistical control.
  (b) Assuming that each shipment is 50,000 gallons,
      how would a u chart be different?

| Shipment No. | Chlorine Count | Shipment No. | Chlorine Count | Shipment No. | Chlorine Count | Shipment No. | Chlorine Count |
|---|---|---|---|---|---|---|---|
| 1 | 19 | 11 | 17 | 21 | 9 | 31 | 21 |
| 2 | 16 | 12 | 15 | 22 | 14 | 32 | 10 |
| 3 | 11 | 13 | 10 | 23 | 24 | 33 | 9 |
| 4 | 14 | 14 | 16 | 24 | 9 | 34 | 13 |
| 5 | 12 | 15 | 19 | 25 | 13 | 35 | 11 |
| 6 | 17 | 16 | 18 | 26 | 9 | 36 | 13 |
| 7 | 23 | 17 | 10 | 27 | 10 | 37 | 13 |
| 8 | 11 | 18 | 12 | 28 | 12 | 38 | 14 |
| 9 | 13 | 19 | 14 | 29 | 11 | 39 | 10 |
| 10 | 15 | 20 | 16 | 30 | 14 | 40 | 17 |

Amount of Chlorine Present in Bromine Shipments

15-7. The maintenance department of a large chemical plant
maintains repair records on all major equipment units.
The number of monthly repairs made during the last 12
months are shown below. (a) What type of control chart
should be used to monitor the process? (b) Compute an
appropriate centerline and control limits, plot the data
on the control chart chosen, and make appropriate
comments on your findings.

| Month | No. of Repairs | Month | No. of Repairs |
|---|---|---|---|
| 1 | 17 | 7 | 11 |
| 2 | 14 | 8 | 18 |
| 3 | 11 | 9 | 13 |
| 4 | 25 | 10 | 13 |
| 5 | 10 | 11 | 22 |
| 6 | 7 | 12 | 23 |

Number of Maintenance Actions (By Month)

15-8. A textile mill produces bolts of cloth. A control chart is maintained for the number of imperfections found in individual bolts. Develop appropriate centerline and control limit values, create a control chart, and determine whether or not the process is in statistical control. The following table contains production and quality data for 20 bolts of cloth.

| Bolt No. | Bolts Produced | No. of Imperfections | Bolt No. | Bolts Produced | No. of Imperfections |
|---|---|---|---|---|---|
| 1 | 23 | 27 | 11 | 27 | 26 |
| 2 | 25 | 23 | 12 | 20 | 22 |
| 3 | 24 | 30 | 13 | 24 | 33 |
| 4 | 23 | 12 | 14 | 24 | 8 |
| 5 | 21 | 25 | 15 | 22 | 25 |
| 6 | 26 | 19 | 16 | 22 | 15 |
| 7 | 23 | 31 | 17 | 25 | 27 |
| 8 | 20 | 37 | 18 | 21 | 41 |
| 9 | 25 | 23 | 19 | 22 | 27 |
| 10 | 27 | 19 | 20 | 27 | 20 |

**Cloth Imperfections**

15-9. The table below shows daily results from an aluminum can production process. During the prior three months, the process was in statistical control at 5% defective. Plot the data on an appropriate control chart. Is the process still in statistical control?

| Day | No. Inspected | No. Defective | Day | No. Inspected | No. Defective | Day | No. Inspected | No. Defective |
|---|---|---|---|---|---|---|---|---|
| 1 | 1092 | 54 | 11 | 1236 | 61 | 21 | 1134 | 79 |
| 2 | 1159 | 57 | 12 | 1266 | 63 | 22 | 1444 | 101 |
| 3 | 1389 | 69 | 13 | 1102 | 55 | 23 | 1421 | 99 |
| 4 | 1485 | 74 | 14 | 1364 | 68 | 24 | 1306 | 91 |
| 5 | 1169 | 58 | 15 | 1026 | 51 | 25 | 1220 | 85 |
| 6 | 1361 | 68 | 16 | 1176 | 58 | 26 | 1406 | 98 |
| 7 | 1042 | 52 | 17 | 1362 | 68 | 27 | 1421 | 99 |
| 8 | 1110 | 55 | 18 | 1205 | 60 | 28 | 1081 | 75 |
| 9 | 1095 | 54 | 19 | 1376 | 68 | 29 | 1003 | 70 |
| 10 | 1220 | 61 | 20 | 1140 | 57 | 30 | 1217 | 85 |

**Defectives in Aluminum Can Production Process**

15-10. Each day a plant's maintenance department inspects 25 machines and judges each one as needing immediate maintenance attention or not. On the average, two per day are marked for immediate attention. (a) Develop an appropriate centerline and control limits to monitor the number of machines needing immediate maintenance *action. (b) If during a two-day span eight and nine machines, respectively, were judged in need of immediate attention, is there evidence that the plant's machinery has begun to show significant signs of wear?*

15-11. *List the name of the most appropriate control chart (or charts) to use to monitor each of the following industry-related situations:*
   *(a) Defects in a weld*
   *(b) Errors in an engineering design drawing*
   *(c) Nonconformances in a shipment of material*
   *(d) Rejected batches of materials*
   *(e) Finished product nonconformities*
   *(f) Painting errors*
   *(g) Errors on a shipping document*

15-12. *List the name of the most appropriate control chart (or charts) to use to monitor each of the following health-care-related situations:*
   *(a) Readmissions to hospital*
   *(b) Returns to surgery*
   *(c) Delinquent patient care charts*
   *(d) Deaths occurring in hospital*
   *(e) Length of stay*
   *(f) Cardiac arrests occurring in hospital*
   *(g) Transfers from regular care to intensive care*

15-13. *Some situations do not lend themselves to easy categorization regarding chart type. For example, a process engineer in a paper mill wanted to monitor the amount of off-spec (nonconforming) paper produced during each shift. He considered using an x chart (i.e., weight measure), a p chart (i.e., fraction defective), and a u chart (i.e., number of defects per production shift). Discuss each choice.*

## Epilogue

This book describes the essential statistical process control tools—with emphasis on their use in the process industries. Beginning with an introduction to SPC (Unit 2), the book progresses through graphical tools (Units 3 and 4), descriptive statistics (Unit 5), the normal distribution (Unit 6), the principles of developing and evaluating control charts (Units 7 and 10), and process capability (Unit 12). Special emphasis is given to control charting issues in the process industries (Unit 11) and separate units are devoted to control charts for individual measurements (Unit 8), control charts for averages and ranges (Unit 9), CUSUM control charts (Unit 13), moving average and exponentially weighted moving averages (Unit 14), and control charts for attributes (Unit 15). Figure E-1 is intended as an aid to the selection of the most appropriate control chart for a variety of situations.

The book's theme is that SPC is widely applicable—and that the tools are appropriate in the process industries as well as in discrete part manufacturing and in the service industries. The book also focuses on the important differences between the use of SPC in discrete part manufacturing and service environments and the use of SPC in the process industries.

The book does not answer all of the questions regarding SPC or SPC in the process industries. In fact, although SPC as a field is well over half a century old, there are many unanswered questions. For example, how does one identify special causes in situations where there are dozens of process inputs and control variables? How does the matter of economics fit into the SPC process? How does one effectively blend automatic process control techniques with statistical process control techniques?

A variety of approaches, particularly in the area of experimental design, have been developed and applied in the process industries to help answer some of the unanswered questions for particular situations. Classical experimental designs, factorial designs, fractional factorial designs, time series analysis, and Taguchi methods are a few approaches that have been successfully used.

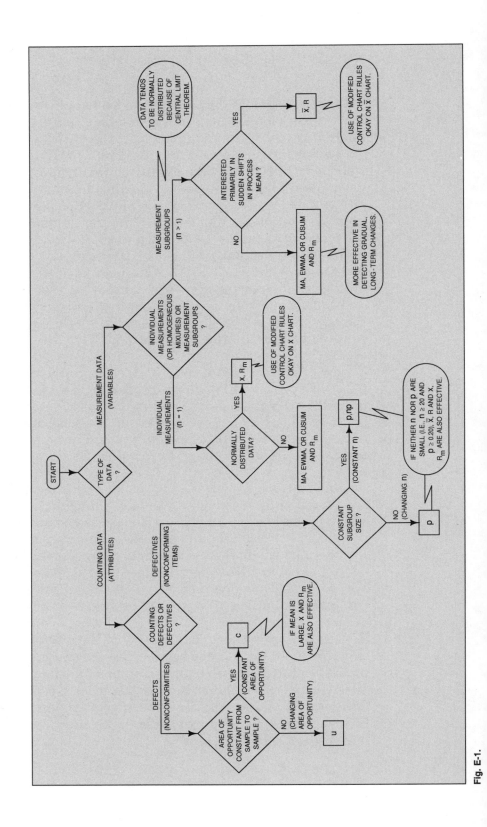

**Fig. E-1.**

360

# Appendix A:
# Suggested Readings

# APPENDIX A

# Suggested Readings

## Textbooks (Selected Titles)

Box, G., and G. M. Jenkins, *Time Series Analysis* (Holden-Day, 1980).

Deming, W. E., *Out of the Crisis* (Massachusetts Institute of Technology, Center for Advanced Engineering Study, 1982).

Grant, E. L., and R. S. Leavenworth, *Statistical Quality Control*, 6th ed. (McGraw-Hill, 1988).

Ishikawa, K., *Guide to Quality Control* (Asian Productivity Organization, Nordica International Limited, 1976).

Johnson, N. L., and F. C. Leone, *Statistics and Experimental Design: Volume 1* (John Wiley & Sons, 1977).

Juran, J. M., and F. M. Gryna, *Quality Planning and Analysis* (McGraw-Hill, 1980).

Neter, J.; W. Wasserman; and G. A. Whitmore, *Applied Statistics*, 3rd ed. (Allyn and Bacon, 1988).

Neter, J.; W. Wasserman; and M. H. Kutner, *Applied Linear Statistical Models*, 2nd ed. (Richard D. Irwin, 1985).

Scherkenbach, W. W., *Deming's Road to Continual Improvement* (SPC Press, 1991).

Taguchi, G., E. A. Elsayed, and T. Hsiang, *Quality Engineering in Production Systems* (McGraw-Hill, 1989).

Wadsworth, H. M., K. S. Stephens, and A. B. Godfrey, *Modern Methods for Quality Control and Improvement* (John Wiley & Sons, 1986).

Wheeler, D. J., and D. S. Chambers, *Understanding Statistical Process Control* (SPC Press, 1986).

# Appendix B:
# Tables, Factors, Formulas, and Forms

# APPENDIX B
## Tables, Factors, Formulas, and Forms

## TABLE B-1
## Normal Distribution Tables

| Z | .00 | .01 | .02 | .03 | .04 | .05 | .06 | .07 | .08 | .09 |
|---|---|---|---|---|---|---|---|---|---|---|
| 0.0 | .50000 | .49603 | .49204 | .48805 | .48407 | .48008 | .47610 | .47212 | .46814 | .46416 |
| -0.1 | .46019 | .45622 | .45226 | .44830 | .44435 | .44040 | .43646 | .43252 | .42859 | .42467 |
| -0.2 | .42076 | .41685 | .41295 | .40906 | .40518 | .40131 | .39745 | .39360 | .38975 | .38592 |
| -0.3 | .38210 | .37829 | .37450 | .37071 | .36694 | .36318 | .35944 | .35570 | .35199 | .34828 |
| -0.4 | .34459 | .34092 | .33725 | .33361 | .32998 | .32637 | .32277 | .31919 | .31562 | .31208 |
| -0.5 | .30855 | .30504 | .30154 | .29807 | .29461 | .29117 | .28775 | .28435 | .28097 | .27760 |
| -0.6 | .27426 | .27094 | .26764 | .26436 | .26109 | .25785 | .25464 | .25144 | .24826 | .24510 |
| -0.7 | .24197 | .23886 | .23577 | .23270 | .22966 | .22663 | .22363 | .22066 | .21770 | .21477 |
| -0.8 | .21186 | .20898 | .20611 | .20328 | .20046 | .19767 | .19490 | .19216 | .18944 | .18674 |
| -0.9 | .18407 | .18142 | .17879 | .17619 | .17361 | .17106 | .16853 | .16603 | .16355 | .16109 |
| -1.0 | .15866 | .15625 | .15387 | .15151 | .14917 | .14686 | .14458 | .14231 | .14007 | .13786 |
| -1.1 | .13567 | .13350 | .13136 | .12924 | .12715 | .12508 | .12303 | .12100 | .11900 | .11703 |
| -1.2 | .11507 | .11314 | .11124 | .10935 | .10749 | .10565 | .10384 | .10204 | .10028 | .09583 |
| -1.3 | .09680 | .09510 | .09342 | .09176 | .09012 | .08851 | .08692 | .08535 | .08380 | .08227 |
| -1.4 | .08076 | .07927 | .07781 | .07636 | .07494 | .07353 | .07215 | .07078 | .06944 | .06811 |
| -1.5 | .06681 | .06552 | .06426 | .06301 | .06178 | .06057 | .05938 | .05821 | .05705 | .05592 |
| -1.6 | .05480 | .05370 | .05262 | .05155 | .05050 | .04947 | .04846 | .04746 | .04648 | .04551 |
| -1.7 | .04457 | .04363 | .04272 | .04182 | .04093 | .04006 | .03920 | .03836 | .03754 | .03673 |
| -1.8 | .03593 | .03515 | .03438 | .03363 | .03288 | .03216 | .03144 | .03074 | .03005 | .02938 |
| -1.9 | .02872 | .02807 | .02743 | .02680 | .02619 | .02559 | .02500 | .02442 | .02385 | .02330 |
| -2.0 | .02275 | .02222 | .02169 | .02118 | .02068 | .02018 | .01970 | .01923 | .01876 | .01831 |
| -2.1 | .01786 | .01743 | .01700 | .01659 | .01618 | .01578 | .01539 | .01500 | .01463 | .01426 |
| -2.2 | .01390 | .01355 | .01321 | .01287 | .01255 | .01222 | .01191 | .01160 | .01130 | .01101 |
| -2.3 | .01072 | .01044 | .01017 | .00990 | .00964 | .00939 | .00914 | .00889 | .00866 | .00842 |
| -2.4 | .00820 | .00798 | .00776 | .00755 | .00734 | .00714 | .00695 | .00676 | .00657 | .00639 |
| -2.5 | .00621 | .00604 | .00587 | .00570 | .00554 | .00539 | .00523 | .00509 | .00494 | .00480 |
| -2.6 | .00466 | .00453 | .00440 | .00427 | .00415 | .00402 | .00391 | .00379 | .00368 | .00357 |
| -2.7 | .00347 | .00336 | .00326 | .00317 | .00307 | .00298 | .00289 | .00280 | .00272 | .00264 |
| -2.8 | .00256 | .00248 | .00240 | .00233 | .00226 | .00219 | .00212 | .00205 | .00199 | .00193 |
| -2.9 | .00187 | .00181 | .00175 | .00169 | .00164 | .00159 | .00154 | .00149 | .00144 | .00139 |
| -3.0 | .001350 | .001306 | .001264 | .001223 | .001183 | .001144 | .001107 | .001070 | .001035 | .001001 |
| -3.5 | .000233 | .000224 | .000216 | .000208 | .000200 | .000193 | .000185 | .000179 | .000172 | .000165 |
| -4.0 | .000032 | .000030 | .000029 | .000028 | .000027 | .000026 | .000025 | .000024 | .000023 | .000022 |

**TABLE B-1 (a). Cumulative Standardized Normal Distribution $Pr(Z \leq z)$ for $z \leq 0$**

Examples: $Pr(Z \leq -2.57) = .00509$

$Pr(Z > -1.64) = 1 - Pr(Z \leq -1.64) = 1 - 0.05050 = 0.94950$

| Z | .00 | .01 | .02 | .03 | .04 | .05 | .06 | .07 | .08 | .09 |
|---|---|---|---|---|---|---|---|---|---|---|
| 0.0 | .50002 | .50397 | .50796 | .51195 | .51593 | .51992 | .52390 | .52788 | .53186 | .53584 |
| 0.1 | .53981 | .54378 | .54774 | .55170 | .55565 | .55960 | .56354 | .56748 | .57141 | .57533 |
| 0.2 | .57924 | .58315 | .58705 | .59094 | .59482 | .59869 | .60255 | .60640 | .61025 | .61408 |
| 0.3 | .61790 | .62171 | .62550 | .62929 | .63306 | .63682 | .64056 | .64430 | .64801 | .65172 |
| 0.4 | .65541 | .65908 | .66275 | .66639 | .67002 | .67363 | .67723 | .68081 | .68438 | .68792 |
| 0.5 | .69145 | .69496 | .69846 | .70193 | .70539 | .70883 | .71225 | .71565 | .71903 | .72240 |
| 0.6 | .72574 | .72906 | .73236 | .73564 | .73891 | .74215 | .74536 | .77934 | .78230 | .78523 |
| 0.7 | .75803 | .76114 | .76423 | .76730 | .77034 | .77337 | .77637 | .74856 | .75174 | .75490 |
| 0.8 | .78814 | .79102 | .79389 | .79672 | .79954 | .80233 | .80510 | .80784 | .81056 | .81326 |
| 0.9 | .81593 | .81858 | .82121 | .82381 | .82639 | .82894 | .83147 | .83397 | .83645 | .83891 |
| 1.0 | .84134 | .84375 | .84613 | .84849 | .85083 | .85314 | .85542 | .85769 | .85993 | .86214 |
| 1.1 | .86433 | .86650 | .86864 | .87076 | .87285 | .87492 | .87697 | .87900 | .88100 | .88297 |
| 1.2 | .88493 | .88686 | .88876 | .89065 | .89251 | .89435 | .89616 | .89796 | .89972 | .90147 |
| 1.3 | .90320 | .90490 | .90658 | .90824 | .90988 | .91149 | .91308 | .91465 | .91620 | .91773 |
| 1.4 | .91924 | .92073 | .92219 | .92364 | .92506 | .92647 | .92785 | .92922 | .93056 | .93189 |
| 1.5 | .93319 | .93448 | .93574 | .93699 | .93822 | .93943 | .94062 | .94179 | .94295 | .94408 |
| 1.6 | .94520 | .94630 | .94738 | .94845 | .94950 | .95053 | .95154 | .95254 | .95352 | .95449 |
| 1.7 | .95543 | .95637 | .95728 | .95818 | .95907 | .95994 | .96080 | .96164 | .96246 | .96327 |
| 1.8 | .96407 | .96485 | .96562 | .96637 | .96712 | .96784 | .96856 | .96926 | .96995 | .97062 |
| 1.9 | .97128 | .97193 | .97257 | .97320 | .97381 | .97441 | .97500 | .97558 | .97615 | .97670 |
| 2.0 | .97725 | .97778 | .97831 | .97882 | .97932 | .97982 | .98030 | .98077 | .98124 | .98169 |
| 2.1 | .98214 | .98257 | .98300 | .98341 | .98382 | .98422 | .98461 | .98500 | .98537 | .98574 |
| 2.2 | .98610 | .98645 | .98679 | .98713 | .98745 | .98778 | .98809 | .98840 | .98870 | .98899 |
| 2.3 | .98928 | .98956 | .98983 | .99010 | .99036 | .99061 | .99086 | .99111 | .99134 | .99158 |
| 2.4 | .99180 | .99202 | .99224 | .99245 | .99266 | .99286 | .99305 | .99324 | .99343 | .99361 |
| 2.5 | .99379 | .99396 | .99413 | .99430 | .99446 | .99461 | .99477 | .99491 | .99506 | .99520 |
| 2.6 | .99534 | .99547 | .99560 | .99573 | .99585 | .99598 | .99609 | .99621 | .99632 | .99643 |
| 2.7 | .99653 | .99664 | .99674 | .99683 | .99693 | .99702 | .99711 | .99720 | .99728 | .99736 |
| 2.8 | .99744 | .99752 | .99760 | .99767 | .99774 | .99781 | .99788 | .99795 | .99801 | .99807 |
| 2.9 | .99813 | .99819 | .99825 | .99831 | .99836 | .99841 | .99846 | .99851 | .99856 | .99861 |
| 3.0 | .998650 | .998694 | .998736 | .998777 | .998817 | .998856 | .998893 | .998930 | .998965 | .998999 |
| 3.5 | .999767 | .999776 | .999784 | .999792 | .999800 | .999807 | .999815 | .999822 | .999828 | .999835 |
| 4.0 | .999968 | .999970 | .999971 | .999972 | .999973 | .999974 | .999975 | .999976 | .999977 | .999978 |

**TABLE B-1 (b).  Cumulative Standardized Normal Distribution Pr(Z ≤ z) for z ≥ 0**

Examples: Pr(Z ≤ 2.57) = .99491

Pr(Z > 1.64) = 1 − Pr(Z ≤ 1.64)= 1 − 0.94950 = 0.05050

## TABLE B-2
## Factors for Normal Probability Plots

Note: These factors are used with the normal probability paper shown in Figure B-1. Their use is discussed in Unit 6.

### $F_i$ Values

#### No. of Points

| Rank | 5 | 6 | 7 | 8 | 9 | 10 | 11 | 12 |
|------|------|------|------|------|------|------|------|------|
| 1 | 11.9 | 10.0 | 8.6 | 7.6 | 6.8 | 6.1 | 5.6 | 5.1 |
| 2 | 31.0 | 26.0 | 22.4 | 19.7 | 17.6 | 15.9 | 14.4 | 13.3 |
| 3 | 50.0 | 42.0 | 36.2 | 31.8 | 28.4 | 25.6 | 23.3 | 21.4 |
| 4 | 69.0 | 58.0 | 50.0 | 43.9 | 39.2 | 35.4 | 32.2 | 29.6 |
| 5 | 88.1 | 74.0 | 63.8 | 56.1 | 50.0 | 45.1 | 41.1 | 37.8 |
| 6 |  | 90.0 | 77.6 | 68.2 | 60.8 | 54.9 | 50.0 | 45.9 |
| 7 |  |  | 91.4 | 80.3 | 71.6 | 64.6 | 58.9 | 54.1 |
| 8 |  |  |  | 92.4 | 82.4 | 74.4 | 67.8 | 62.2 |
| 9 |  |  |  |  | 93.2 | 84.1 | 76.7 | 70.4 |
| 10 |  |  |  |  |  | 93.9 | 85.6 | 78.6 |
| 11 |  |  |  |  |  |  | 94.4 | 86.7 |
| 12 |  |  |  |  |  |  |  | 94.9 |

### $F_i$ Values

#### No. of Points

| Rank | 13 | 14 | 15 | 16 | 17 | 18 | 19 | 20 |
|------|------|------|------|------|------|------|------|------|
| 1 | 4.7 | 4.4 | 4.1 | 3.8 | 3.6 | 3.4 | 3.2 | 3.1 |
| 2 | 12.3 | 11.4 | 10.7 | 10.0 | 9.4 | 8.9 | 8.4 | 8.0 |
| 3 | 19.8 | 18.4 | 17.2 | 16.2 | 15.2 | 14.4 | 13.6 | 13.0 |
| 4 | 27.4 | 25.4 | 23.8 | 22.3 | 21.0 | 19.9 | 18.8 | 17.9 |
| 5 | 34.9 | 32.5 | 30.3 | 28.5 | 26.8 | 25.3 | 24.0 | 22.8 |
| 6 | 42.5 | 39.5 | 36.9 | 34.6 | 32.6 | 30.8 | 29.2 | 27.8 |
| 7 | 50.0 | 46.5 | 43.4 | 40.8 | 38.4 | 36.3 | 34.4 | 32.7 |
| 8 | 57.5 | 53.5 | 50.0 | 46.9 | 44.2 | 41.8 | 39.6 | 37.7 |
| 9 | 65.1 | 60.5 | 56.6 | 53.1 | 50.0 | 47.3 | 44.8 | 42.6 |
| 10 | 72.6 | 67.5 | 63.1 | 59.2 | 55.8 | 52.7 | 50.0 | 47.5 |
| 11 | 80.2 | 74.6 | 69.7 | 65.4 | 61.6 | 58.2 | 55.2 | 52.5 |
| 12 | 87.7 | 81.6 | 76.2 | 71.5 | 67.4 | 63.7 | 60.4 | 57.4 |
| 13 | 95.3 | 88.6 | 82.8 | 77.7 | 73.2 | 69.2 | 65.6 | 62.3 |
| 14 |  | 95.6 | 89.3 | 83.8 | 79.0 | 74.7 | 70.8 | 67.3 |
| 15 |  |  | 95.9 | 90.0 | 84.8 | 80.1 | 76.0 | 72.2 |
| 16 |  |  |  | 96.2 | 90.6 | 85.6 | 81.2 | 77.2 |
| 17 |  |  |  |  | 96.4 | 91.1 | 86.4 | 82.1 |
| 18 |  |  |  |  |  | 96.6 | 91.6 | 87.0 |
| 19 |  |  |  |  |  |  | 96.8 | 92.0 |
| 20 |  |  |  |  |  |  |  | 96.9 |

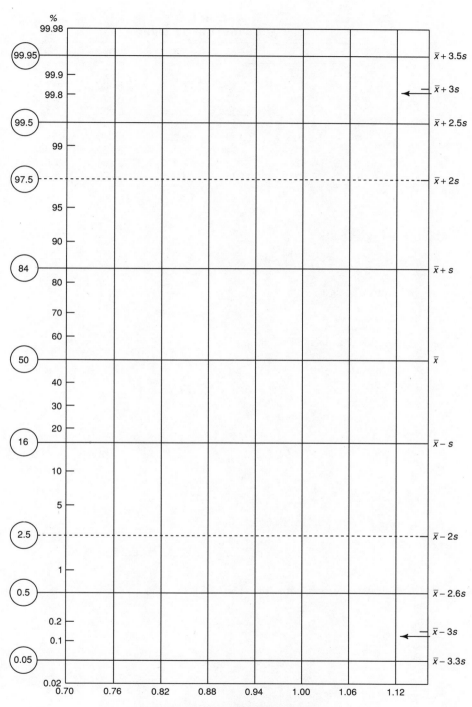

**Figure B-1  Normal Probability Paper**

**TABLE B-3**
**Control Chart Factors**

| n | $A_2$ | $E_2$ | $d_2$ | $D_3$ | $D_4$ |
|---|-------|-------|-------|-------|-------|
| 2 | 1.880 | 2.659 | 1.128 | 0.000 | 3.268 |
| 3 | 1.023 | 1.772 | 1.693 | 0.000 | 2.574 |
| 4 | 0.729 | 1.458 | 2.059 | 0.000 | 2.282 |
| 5 | 0.577 | 1.290 | 2.326 | 0.000 | 2.114 |
| 6 | 0.483 | 1.180 | 2.534 | 0.000 | 2.004 |
| 7 | 0.419 | 1.109 | 2.704 | 0.076 | 1.924 |
| 8 | 0.373 | 1.054 | 2.847 | 0.136 | 1.864 |
| 9 | 0.337 | 1.010 | 2.970 | 0.184 | 1.816 |
| 10 | 0.308 | 0.975 | 3.078 | 0.223 | 1.777 |

# Selected Formulas

## Unit 5:  Descriptive Statistics

Sample Range:

$$R = x_{max} - x_{min}$$

Sample Standard Deviation:

$$s = \sqrt{\frac{1}{n - 1}\left[\sum_{i=1}^{n} (x_i - \bar{x})^2\right]}$$

Correlation Coefficient:

$$r_{xy} = \frac{1}{n - 1}\sum_{i=1}^{n}\left[\frac{x_i - \bar{x}}{s_x}\right]\left[\frac{y_i - \bar{y}}{s_y}\right]$$

$$= \frac{1}{n - 1}\sum_{i=1}^{n}\frac{(x_i - \bar{x})(y_i - \bar{y})}{s_x s_y}$$

Autocorrelation Coefficient (Lag = 1):

$$r_1 = \frac{1}{n - 1}\sum_{t=1}^{n-1}\frac{(x_t - \bar{x})(x_{t+1} - \bar{x})}{s^2}$$

Autocorrelation Coefficient (Lag = k):

$$r_k = \frac{1}{n - 1}\sum_{t=1}^{n-k}\frac{(x_t - \bar{x})(x_{t+k} - \bar{x})}{s^2}$$

Standardization Formulas:

$$Z = (X - \mu_x)/\sigma_x$$
$$Z = (X - \bar{x})/s \text{ (when } \mu_x, \sigma_x \text{ unknown)}$$

Relationship Between $\sigma_x$ and $\sigma_{\bar{x}}$:

$$\sigma_{\bar{x}} = \sigma_x / \sqrt{n}$$
$$\sigma_{\bar{x}} = s_x / \sqrt{n}$$

## Unit 8:  Control Charts for Individual Measurements

Moving Range ($R_m$) Chart:

$$R_{mi} = |x_i - x_{i-1}|$$
$$\bar{R}_m = \sum_{i=1}^{k-1} \frac{R_{mi}}{(k-1)}$$

Centerline: $\bar{R}_m$

Control Limits:

$$UCL_{MR} = D_4 \, \bar{R}_m$$
$$LCL_{MR} = D_3 \, \bar{R}_m$$

Individuals (x) Chart:

Centerline: $\bar{x}$ or $x_r$

Control Limits:

$$
\begin{aligned}
UCL_x &= \mu_x + 3\sigma_x \\
&= \bar{x} + 3\,\bar{R}_m / d_2 \\
&= \bar{x} + (3/d_2)\bar{R}_m \\
&= \bar{x} + E_2 \bar{R}_m \\
LCL_x &= \mu_x - 3\sigma_x \\
&= \bar{x} - 3\bar{R}_m / d_2 \\
&= \bar{x} - (3/d_2)\bar{R}_m \\
&= \bar{x} - E_2 \bar{R}_m
\end{aligned}
$$

## Unit 9:  Control Charts for Averages and Ranges

Range (R) Chart:

Centerline: $\bar{R}$

Control Limits:

$$UCL_R = D_4 \bar{R}$$
$$UCL_R = D_3 \bar{R}$$

Average ($\bar{x}$) Chart:

Centerline: $\bar{\bar{x}}$ or $x_T$

Control Limits:

$$\begin{aligned}
\text{UCL}_{\bar{x}} &= \mu_{\bar{x}} + 3\sigma_{\bar{x}} \\
&= \bar{\bar{x}} + 3\hat{\sigma}_x/\sqrt{n} \\
&= \bar{\bar{x}} + 3\bar{R}/(d_2\sqrt{n}) \\
&= \bar{\bar{x}} + A_2\bar{R} \\
\text{LCL}_{\bar{x}} &= \mu_{\bar{x}} - 3\sigma_{\bar{x}} \\
&= \bar{\bar{x}} - 3\hat{\sigma}_x/\sqrt{n} \\
&= \bar{\bar{x}} - 3\bar{R}/(d_2\sqrt{n}) \\
&= \bar{\bar{x}} - A_2\bar{R}
\end{aligned}$$

## Unit 12: Process Capability

Process Capability Indexes:

$$C_p = \frac{\text{Upper Specification Limit} - \text{Lower Specification Limit}}{\text{Process Spread}}$$

$$= \frac{\text{USL} - \text{LSL}}{6\sigma}$$

$$C_{pu} = \frac{\text{USL} - \mu}{3\sigma}$$

$$C_{pl} = \frac{\mu - \text{LSL}}{3\sigma}$$

Performance Indexes:

$$P_p = \frac{\text{USL} - \text{LSL}}{6s}$$

$$P_{pu} = \frac{\text{USL} - \text{Process Average}}{3s}$$

$$P_{pl} = \frac{\text{Process Average} - \text{LSL}}{3s}$$

## Unit 13:  CUSUM Control Charts

Decision Interval Chart:

Centerline: 0.0

$$\text{UCL}_{\text{CUSUM}} = +3\bar{R}_m/d_2$$
$$\text{LCL}_{\text{CUSUM}} = -3\bar{R}_m/d_2$$

For positive cumulative sums, $D^+ = x_T + q\sigma_x/2$

For negative cumulative sums, $D^- = x_T - q\sigma_x/2$

$$CUSUM_n^+ = CUSUM_{n-1}^+ + x_n - D^+$$

$$CUSUM_n^- = CUSUM_{n-1}^- + x_n - D^-$$

## Unit 14: Moving Average and Exponentially Weighted Moving Average Control Charts

Moving Average Chart:

$$MA_t = MA_{t-1} - \frac{x_{t-n}}{n} + \frac{X_t}{n}$$

$$= \frac{x_t + x_{t-1} + x_{t-2} + \ldots + x_{t-(n-1)}}{n}$$

Centerline: $\bar{x}$ or $x_T$

Control Limits:

$$UCL_{MA} = \bar{x} + 3\sigma_{\bar{x}}$$

$$= \bar{x} + 3\sigma_x/\sqrt{n}$$

$$= \bar{x} + 3(\bar{R}_m/d_2)/\sqrt{n}$$

$$= \bar{x} + \frac{3\bar{R}_m}{d_2\sqrt{n}}$$

$$LCL_{MA} = \bar{x} + 3\sigma_{\bar{x}}$$

$$= \bar{x} - 3\sigma_x/\sqrt{n}$$

$$= \bar{x} - 3(\bar{R}_m/d_2)/\sqrt{n}$$

$$= \bar{x} - \frac{3\bar{R}_m}{d_2\sqrt{n}}$$

Exponentially Weighted Moving Average Chart:

$$EWMA_t = \lambda X_t + (1 - \lambda)EWMA_{t-1}.$$

Centerline: $\bar{x}$ or $x_T$

Control Limits:

$$UCL_{EWMA} = \bar{x} + 3\sqrt{\lambda/(2 - \lambda)}\,\sigma_x$$

$$= \bar{x} + 3\sqrt{[\lambda/(2 - \lambda)]}\,\frac{\bar{R}_m}{d_2}$$

$$= \bar{x} + A_3\bar{R}$$

$$LCL_{EWMA} = \bar{x} - 3\sqrt{\lambda/(2 - \lambda)}\,\sigma_x$$

$$= \bar{x} - 3\sqrt{[\lambda/(2 - \lambda)]}\,\frac{\bar{R}_m}{d_2}$$

$$= \bar{x} - A_3\bar{R}$$

## Unit 15:  Control Charts for Attributes

np Chart:

Centerline: $n\bar{p}$

Control Limits:

$$UCL_{np} = n\bar{p} + 3\sqrt{n\bar{p}(1 - \bar{p})}$$
$$LCL_{np} = n\bar{p} - 3\sqrt{n\bar{p}(1 - \bar{p})}$$

p Chart:

Centerline: $\bar{p}$

Control Limits:

$$UCL_p = \bar{p} + 3\sqrt{\frac{\bar{p}(1 - \bar{p})}{n}}$$

$$LCL_p = \bar{p} - 3\sqrt{\frac{\bar{p}(1 - \bar{p})}{n}}$$

c Chart:

Centerline: $\bar{c}$

Control Limits:

$$UCL_c = \bar{c} + 3\sqrt{(\bar{c})}$$
$$LCL_c = \bar{c} - 3\sqrt{(\bar{c})}$$

u Chart:

Centerline:

$$\bar{u} = \frac{\sum_{i=1}^{m} c_i}{\sum_{i=1}^{m} k_i}$$

where i = sample number; m = number of samples

Control Limits:

$$UCL_u = \bar{u} + 3\sqrt{\frac{\bar{u}}{k_i}}$$

$$LCL_u = \bar{u} - 3\sqrt{\frac{\bar{u}}{k_i}}$$

# Appendix C
# Solutions to All Exercises

# APPENDIX C

## Solutions to All Exercises

### Unit 2

Exercise 2-1.

Traditional SQC focuses on inspection and on final product; SPC focuses on process, on doing those things correctly that will result in defect free final product. Idea of SPC is (after listening to customer) control process well and products meeting customer requirements will result.

Exercise 2-2.

Two key questions in SPC: (1) Is process well behaved (in control)? (2) Is process capable of meeting specifications?

Exercise 2-3.

Dr. Deming views the customer as the most important part of the process. His chain of quality begins with focus on customer satisfaction. His systems view also begins (at the end!) with focus on customer satisfaction, so that all those processes leading to the customer are viewed in light of their ultimate impact on the customer.

Exercise 2-4.

Both customers and processes exhibit variation. Customer variation occurs in two primary ways: (1) customer needs are different and (2) customer requirements change. Process variation occurs in a variety of ways, but there are contributing factors in five categories: (1) people variation, (2) equipment variation, (3) material variation, (4) variation in procedures, and (5) variation in environment.

Exercise 2-5.

Quality is conformance to specifications; quality is fitness for use; quality is customer determined and always changing (i.e., it is whatever the customer says it is).

Exercise 2-6.

The four quality cost categories and an example of each: (1) prevention costs (vendor auditing); (2) appraisal costs (process monitoring with control charts); (3) internal failure costs (scrap and rework costs); (4) external failure costs (returned products or warranty costs).

Exercise 2-7.

(1) Automatic process control (APC) depends on the reaction of the computer; statistical process control (SPC) depends on the reaction of the operator/engineer. (2) APC views an in-control process as one whose target is within acceptable engineering tolerances; SPC views an in-control pro-

cess as one in which only random variation (noise) is present. (3) APC focuses on the immediate regulation of the process to keep it within tolerances; SPC focuses on identifying root causes of variation and eliminating them. (4) APC views the production system as one that is both known and understood; SPC views the process as one that cannot be completely understood and whose variation cannot be completely eliminated. (5) APC reacts to second-to-second variation, viewing the process as dynamic; SPC views the process as static by taking periodic "snapshots" of the process.

## Unit 3
Exercise 3-1.

Histogram/Polygon Development Worksheet; Process: Project Budget Performance; Variable: Percent of Budget Expended; No. of data points (N): 30; Maximum data value (M): 129; Minimum data value (m): 88; Difference (M − m): 41; Approximate No. Intervals ($\sqrt{N}$): $\sqrt{30}$ = 5 or 6; Approximate Interval Size ((M − m)/$\sqrt{N}$): 41/6 = 7; Convenient Interval Size (D): 10.

| Interval Boundaries | Interval Midpoints | Interval Frequencies | Count | Summary Cum. Count | Cum. Percent |
|---|---|---|---|---|---|
| 80–89 | 85 | II | 2 | 2 | 6.7% |
| 90–99 | 95 | IIIII IIIII IIIII | 15 | 17 | 56.7% |
| 100–109 | 105 | IIIII IIII | 9 | 26 | 86.7% |
| 110–119 | 115 | III | 3 | 29 | 96.7% |
| 120–129 | 125 | I | 1 | 30 | 100.0% |
| | | | 30 | | |

(a, b)

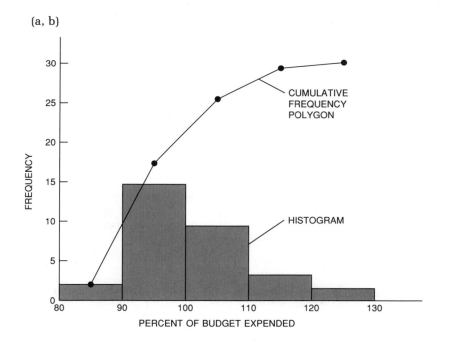

(c) Run Chart

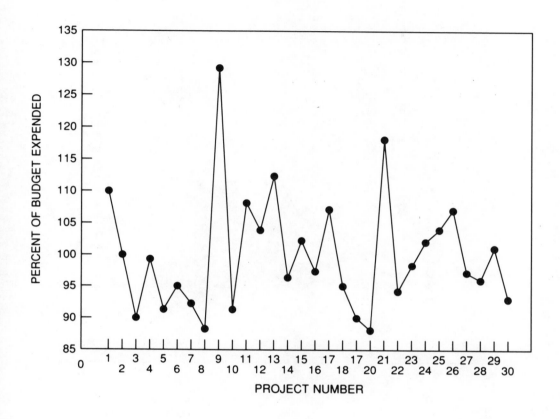

Exercise 3-2.

Histogram/Polygon Development Worksheet; Process: Chlorine Content of Polymer; Variable: Chlorine Content (%); N: 45; M: 37.1; m: 34.5; M − m: 2.6; $\sqrt{N}$: 7 (or 6); (M − m)/$\sqrt{N}$): 2.6/7 = 0.37; D: 0.50 (or 0.40).

| Interval Boundaries | Interval Midpoints | Interval Frequencies | Count | Summary Cum. Count | Cum. Percent |
|---|---|---|---|---|---|
| 34.5–34.9 | 34.75 | ‖ | 2 | 2 | 4.4% |
| 35.0–35.4 | 35.25 | ‖‖‖ ‖ | 6 | 8 | 17.8% |
| 35.5–35.9 | 35.75 | ‖‖‖ | 4 | 12 | 26.7% |
| 36.0–36.4 | 36.25 | ‖‖‖ ‖‖‖ ‖ | 12 | 24 | 53.3% |
| 36.5–36.9 | 36.75 | ‖‖‖ ‖‖‖ ‖‖‖ ‖ | 17 | 41 | 91.1% |
| 37.0–37.4 | 37.25 | ‖‖‖ | 4 | 45 | 100.0% |

## (a, b) Histogram, Cumulative Frequency Polygon

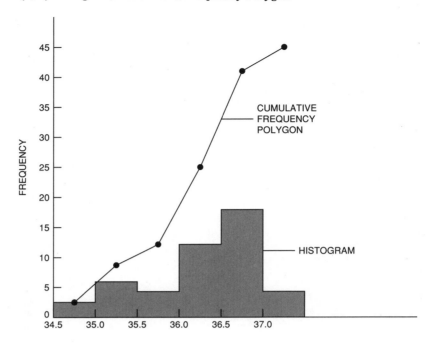

## (c) Run Chart

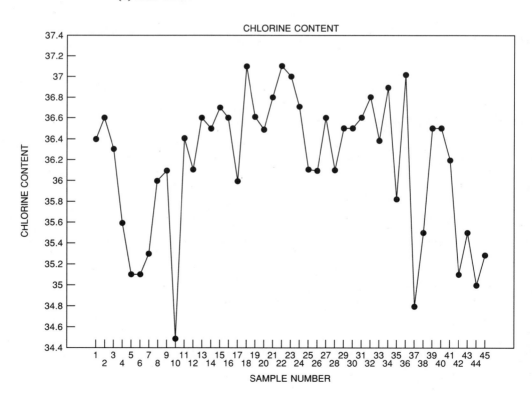

Exercise 3-3.

Histogram/Polygon Development Worksheet; Process: High Density Polyethylene; Variable: Melt Index; N: 150; M: 1.166; m: 0.908; M − m: 0.258; $\sqrt{N}$: 12; (M − m)/$\sqrt{N}$): 0.021; D: 0.02; Rounded Lower Interval-Limit: 0.901; Rounded Upper Interval-Limit: 1.180.

| Interval Boundaries | Interval Midpoints | Interval Frequencies | Count | Summary Cum. Count | Cum. Percent |
|---|---|---|---|---|---|
| 0.901–0.920 | 0.91 | III | 3 | 3 | 2.0% |
| 0.921–0.940 | 0.93 | IIIII I | 6 | 9 | 6.0% |
| 0.941–0.960 | 0.95 | IIIII II | 7 | 16 | 10.7% |
| 0.961–0.980 | 0.97 | IIIII IIIII II | 12 | 28 | 18.7% |
| 0.981–1.000 | 0.99 | IIIII IIIII IIIII I | 16 | 44 | 29.3% |
| 1.001–1.020 | 1.01 | IIIII IIIII IIIII IIIII | 20 | 64 | 42.7% |
| 1.021–1.040 | 1.03 | IIIII IIIII IIIII IIIII IIIII | 25 | 89 | 59.3% |
| 1.041–1.060 | 1.05 | IIIII IIIII IIIII III | 18 | 107 | 71.3% |
| 1.061–1.080 | 1.07 | IIIII IIIII IIIII | 15 | 122 | 81.3% |
| 1.081–1.100 | 1.09 | IIIII IIIII | 10 | 132 | 88.0% |
| 1.101–1.120 | 1.11 | IIIII I | 6 | 138 | 92.0% |
| 1.121–1.140 | 1.13 | IIIII | 5 | 143 | 95.3% |
| 1.141–1.160 | 1.15 | IIIII | 5 | 148 | 98.7% |
| 1.161–1.180 | 1.17 | II | 2 | 150 | 100.0% |
| | | | 150 | | |

(a) Histogram

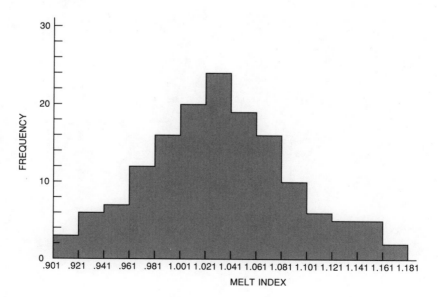

(b) Cumulative Frequency Polygon

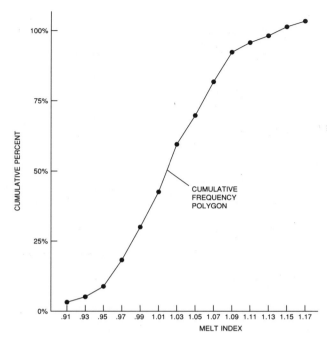

(c) (1) 0.98, (2) 1.02, (3) 1.10, (4) 0.98, 1.06, (5) Generally symmetric; slightly skewed right.

Exercise 3-4.

Melt Index Values and Temperature Measurements; (a) Run Charts

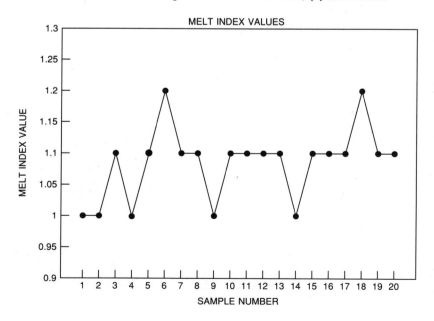

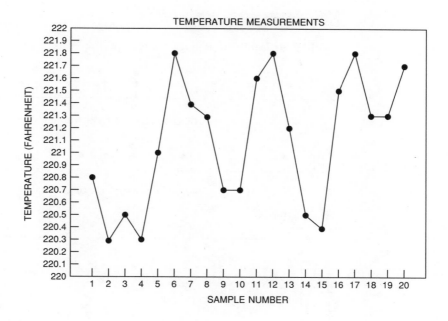

(b) Scatterplot

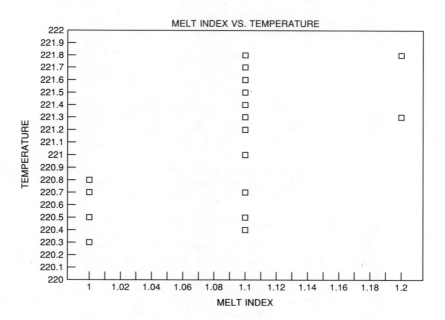

(c) Both melt index values and temperature measurements are trending slightly upward over time (from run charts); melt index values tend to increase as temperatures increase, although the relationship is far from exact.

Exercise 3-5.

Drill Hole Depth vs. Pollution Level; (a) Dot Plots

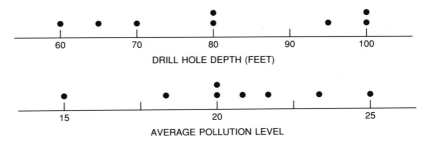

(b) Scatterplot

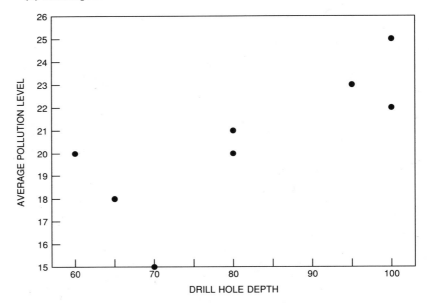

(c) Relationship between drill hole depth and average pollution levels (i.e., according to data, deeper holes generally mean more pollution), but it is far from exact.

Exercise 3-6.

(a) Histograms; Variable: Flow Index Values (Lab 1); N: 25; M: 3.85; m: 2.45; M − m: 1.40; $\sqrt{N}$: 5; (M − m)/$\sqrt{N}$): 0.28; D: 0.30.

| Interval Boundaries | Interval Midpoints | Interval Frequencies | Count | Summary Cum. Count | Cum. Percent |
|---|---|---|---|---|---|
| 2.41–2.70 | 2.55 | III | 3 | 3 | 12% |
| 2.71–3.00 | 2.85 | IIIII IIII | 9 | 12 | 48% |
| 3.01–3.30 | 3.15 | IIIII II | 7 | 19 | 76% |
| 3.31–3.60 | 3.45 | III | 3 | 22 | 88% |
| 3.61–3.90 | 3.75 | III | 3 | 25 | 100% |

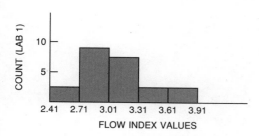

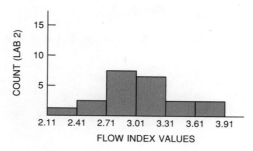

(a) (continued) Variable: Flow Index Values (Lab 2); N: 25; M: 3.90; m: 2.26; M − m: 1.64; $\sqrt{N}$: 5; (M − m)/$\sqrt{N}$): 0.328; D: 0.30.

| Interval Boundaries | Interval Midpoints | Interval Frequencies | Count | Summary Cum. count | Cum. Percent |
|---|---|---|---|---|---|
| 2.11–2.40 | 2.25 | I | 1 | 1 | 4% |
| 2.41–2.70 | 2.55 | III | 3 | 4 | 16% |
| 2.71–3.00 | 2.85 | IIIII III | 8 | 12 | 48% |
| 3.01–3.30 | 3.15 | IIIII II | 7 | 19 | 76% |
| 3.31–3.60 | 3.45 | III | 3 | 22 | 88% |
| 3.61–3.90 | 3.75 | III | 3 | 25 | 100% |

(b) Scatterplot

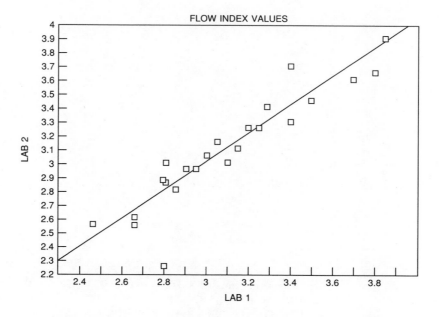

(c) Strong relationship between flow index values in the two labs. A few pairs of values violate the strong relationship (e.g., #13, Lab 1 = 2.80, Lab 2 = 2.26).

Exercise 3-7.

Seal Failure Times (Hours); Dot Plots

**COMPANY A:**

SEAL FAILURES

**COMPANY B:**

SEAL FAILURES

Company A's seals seem on the average to last longer, but company B's seals seem to be more consistent. Which company's seals are 'better' is not clear.

Exercise 3-8.

Flow Rate vs. Flow Height; Scatterplot

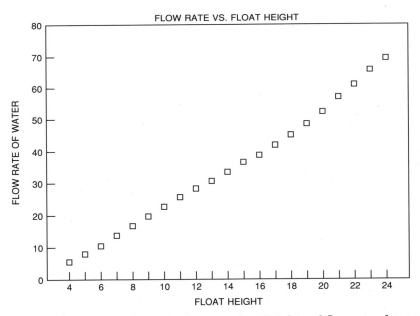

Near linear relationship exists between float height and flow rate of water. As flow rates get higher, however, float height seems to increase at a faster rate (i.e., possible quadratic relationship).

Exercise 3-9.

Brine Feed Temperatures

| | | April | | | | May | |
|---|---|---|---|---|---|---|---|
| 153 | 1 | | | | 140 | | |
| 154 | 1 | 154 = lower whisker | | | 141 | | |
| 155 | 5 | 155 = lower box | | | 142 | 1 | |
| 156 | 3 | 156.5 = median | | | 143 | 1 | 143 = lower whisker |
| 157 | 4 | | | | 144 | 2 | |
| 158 | 3 | 158 = upper box | | | 145 | 1 | |
| 159 | 2 | 159 = upper whisker | | | 146 | 1 | 146.5 = lower box |
| 160 | 1 | | | | 147 | 3 | |
| | 20 | | | | 148 | 3 | 148 = median |
| | | | | | 149 | 3 | 149.5 = upper box |
| | | | | | 150 | 2 | |
| | | | | | 151 | 1 | |
| | | | | | 152 | 1 | 152 = upper whisker |
| | | | | | 153 | 1 | |
| | | | | | | 20 | |

Box Plot

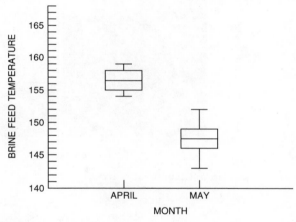

Exercise 3-10.

Residual Metal; (a) Run Chart

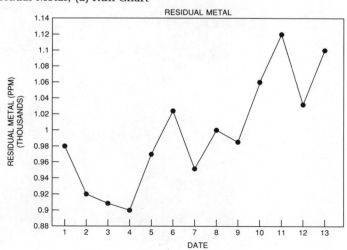

(b) Dot Plot

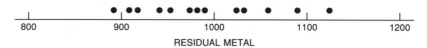

Unit 4

Exercise 4-1.

Nonconformities in Bottle Production
(a) Pareto Diagram (totals)

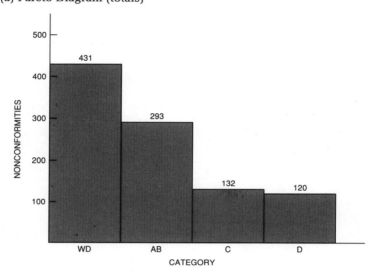

(b) Pareto Diagrams (by week)

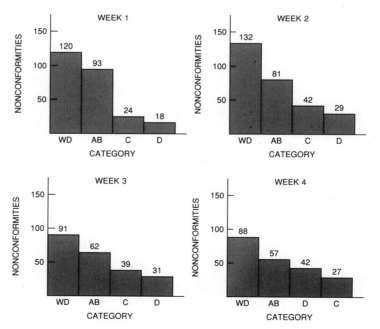

Exercise 4-2.

Injuries in Chemical Plant
(a) Pareto Diagram (month)

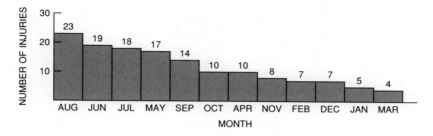

(b) Pareto Diagram (quarter)

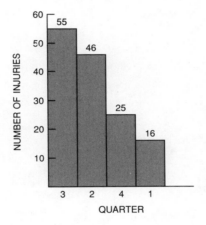

Exercise 4-3.

Complaints by Type; Pareto Diagram

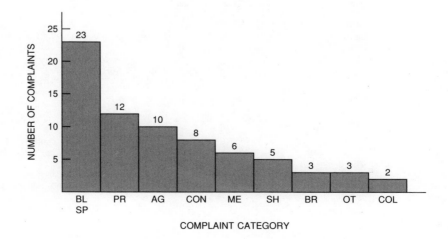

Exercise 4-4.

No Light; Cause-and-Effect Diagram

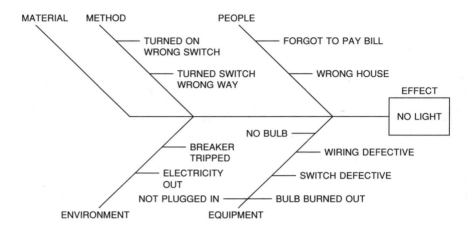

Exercise 4-5.

Flat Tires; Cause-and-Effect Diagram

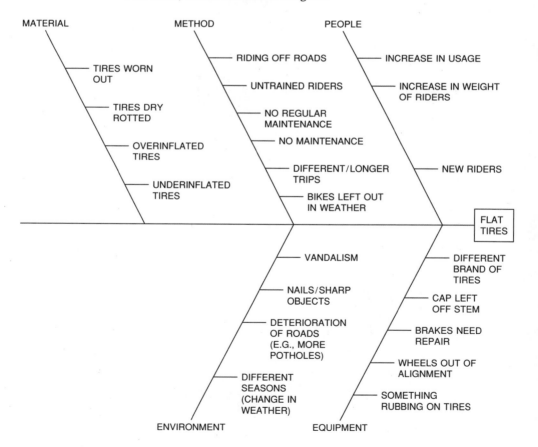

Exercise 4-6, 4-7.

Location specific

Exercise 4-8.

Travel Advance Signatures; Flowchart

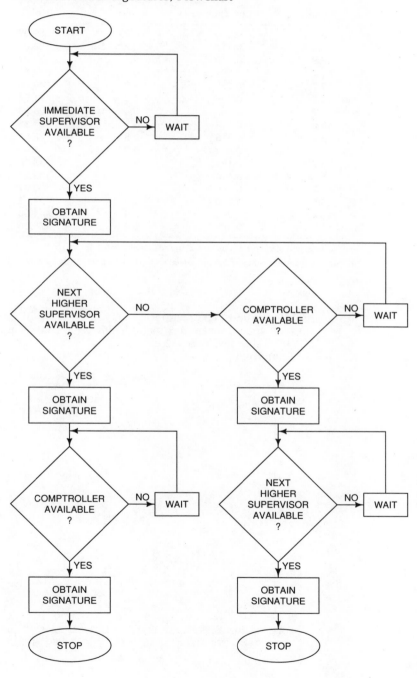

## Unit 5

Exercise 5-1.
   (a) Sulfur Trioxide Measurements

| Mean | Std. Dev. | Range | Signal-to-Noise | Coeff. of Variation |
|------|-----------|-------|-----------------|---------------------|
| 15.9 | 0.270 | 0.7 | 59.07 | 0.39 |
| 15.7 | 0.114 | 0.3 | 138.05 | 0.38 |
| 15.8 | 0.216 | 0.5 | 72.97 | 0.43 |
| 15.7 | 0.054 | 0.1 | 287.37 | 0.55 |
| 15.7 | 0.339 | 0.8 | 46.30 | 0.42 |
| 15.6 | 0.746 | 1.9 | 21.01 | 0.39 |
| 15.7 | 0.148 | 0.4 | 106.39 | 0.37 |
| 15.6 | 0.114 | 0.3 | 137.35 | 0.38 |
| 15.9 | 0.219 | 0.6 | 72.85 | 0.37 |
| 15.7 | 0.371 | 0.9 | 42.42 | 0.41 |
| 15.7 | 0.181 | 0.5 | 86.76 | 0.36 |
| 15.7 | 0.114 | 0.3 | 138.22 | 0.38 |
| 15.7 | 0.396 | 0.9 | 39.67 | 0.44 |
| 15.5 | 0.620 | 1.5 | 24.98 | 0.41 |
| 15.6 | 0.350 | 0.9 | 44.59 | 0.39 |
| 15.6 | 0.089 | 0.2 | 175.08 | 0.45 |

(b) Average standard deviation = Σ std. dev./lb = 0.27, $\bar{R}$ = 0.67

(c) Estimate of average standard deviation = $\bar{R}/d_2$ = 0.67/2.326 = 0.28

Exercise 5-2.

Melt Index and Temperature
(a) Melt Index: mean = 1.08, std. dev. = 0.054; Temperature: mean = 221.095, std. dev. = 0.532.
(b) Scatterplot

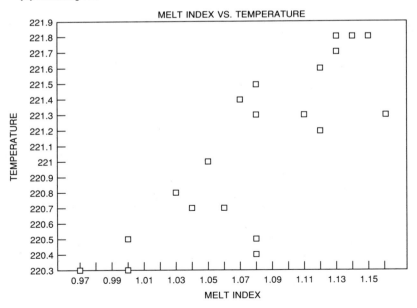

(c) Correlation coefficient = 0.816
(d) Linear relationship (not exact) exists between melt index and temperature.

Exercise 5-3.

| Population | Distribution's Shape |
|-----------|---------------------|
| 1 | skewed right |
| 2 | skewed left |
| 3 | symmetric |
| 4 | skewed left |

Exercise 5-4.

| | Seal Failure Times | |
|---|---|---|
| (a) | Company A | Company B |
| Mean | 1807.78 | 1507.25 |
| Median | 2012.00 | 1506.50 |
| Mode | 0.00 | 0.00 |
| (b) | | |
| Range | 1533.00 | 777.00 |
| Std. Dev. | 491.53 | 343.70 |
| Variance | 241600.94 | 118129.27 |
| (c) | | |
| Coeff. Variation | 0.27 | 0.23 |
| Signal-Noise | 3.68 | 4.39 |

(d) Company A seals are longer lasting (greater mean), but are less consistent (greater standard deviation).

Exercise 5-5.

Part Shrinkage
(a) Descriptive Statistics

| Mean | Range | Std. Dev. | | |
|------|-------|-----------|---|---|
| 9.96 | 2.10 | 0.93 | | |
| 10.44 | 3.30 | 1.26 | | |
| 9.90 | 2.40 | 1.06 | | |
| 10.08 | 2.40 | 1.07 | | |
| 10.80 | 2.10 | 0.87 | | |
| Average | 2.46 | 1.04 | | |
| | $\bar{R} =$ | 2.46 | | |
| | $\hat{\sigma} =$ | $\bar{R}/d_2 =$ | 2.46/2.326 = | 1.06 |

Exercise 5-6.

Iodine Content
(a) Run Chart

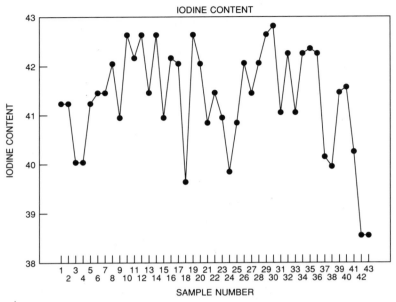

(b) Scatterplot (lag = 1)

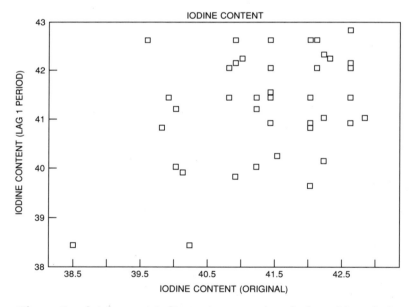

The scatterplot does not indicate strong autocorrelation, although there is some autocorrelation present.

|  | Lag | Autocorrelation Coefficients |
|---|---|---|
| (c) | 1 | 0.336 |
|  | 2 | 0.117 |
|  | 3 | 0.094 |

(d) $\pm 2/\sqrt{n} = \pm 2/\sqrt{43} = \pm 2/6.557 = 0.305$

Using the rule of thumb, the autocorrelation with lag = 1 is mildly significant. The other two are not.

Exercise 5-7.

$$s = 0.07$$
$$s^2 = 0.0049$$
$$S_{total} = \sqrt{s^2 + s^2 + s^2}$$
$$= \sqrt{3(0.0049)}$$
$$= 0.12 \text{ ounces}$$

Exercise 5-8.

| Component | Mean | Standard Deviation |
|-----------|------|--------------------|
| A | 40.00 | 0.4 |
| B | 40.57 | 0.4 |

(a)  $S_{diff} = \sqrt{s_A^2 + s_B^2}$
$$= \sqrt{(0.4)^2 + (0.4)^2}$$
$$= 0.57 \text{ mm}$$

(b) $\bar{x}_{diff} = \bar{x}_B - \bar{x}_A = 40.57 - 40.00 = 0.57$ mm; problem expected in about 32% of cases (i.e., difference more than 1 standard deviation).

Exercise 5-9.

$$\mu = 266,000 \text{ lbs}$$
$$\sigma = 100 \text{ lbs}$$
$$\mu_{10} = 10 \times 266,000 = 2,660,000 \text{ lbs}$$
$$\sigma_{10} = \sqrt{(100)^2 + (100)^2 + \ldots + (100)^2}$$
$$= \sqrt{10(100)^2}$$
$$= \sqrt{100,000}$$
$$= 316 \text{ lbs}$$

Exercise 5-10.

Residual Metal
(a) Run Chart

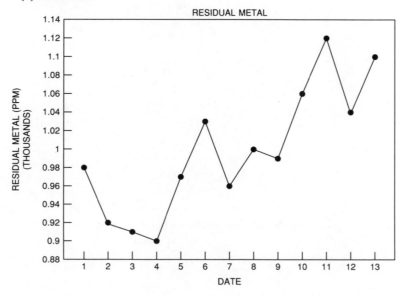

(b) Autocorrelation coefficient (lag = 1) = 0.33

| Date | x(t) Residual Metal | x − x̄ a | x(t + 1) Residual Metal | x − x̄ b | a × b |
|---|---|---|---|---|---|
| 1 | 981 | −13.38 | 918 | −76.38 | 1022.38 |
| 2 | 918 | −76.38 | 907 | −87.38 | 6674.84 |
| 3 | 907 | −87.38 | 896 | −98.38 | 8597.30 |
| 4 | 896 | −98.38 | 967 | −27.38 | 2694.22 |
| 5 | 967 | −27.38 | 1026 | 31.62 | −865.78 |
| 6 | 1026 | 31.62 | 954 | −40.38 | −1276.78 |
| 7 | 954 | −40.38 | 995 | 0.62 | −24.85 |
| 8 | 995 | 0.62 | 984 | −10.38 | −6.39 |
| 9 | 984 | −10.38 | 1055 | 60.62 | −629.47 |
| 10 | 1055 | 60.62 | 1118 | 123.62 | 7492.99 |
| 11 | 1118 | 123.62 | 1032 | 37.62 | 4649.84 |
| 12 | 1032 | 37.62 | 1094 | 99.62 | 3747.07 |
| 13 | 1094 | 99.62 | | | |

Mean = 994.38          Corr. Coeff. =          0.33
S.D. = 68.99
Var. = 4759.26

Exercise 5-11.

Melt Index Measurements
(a) Run Chart

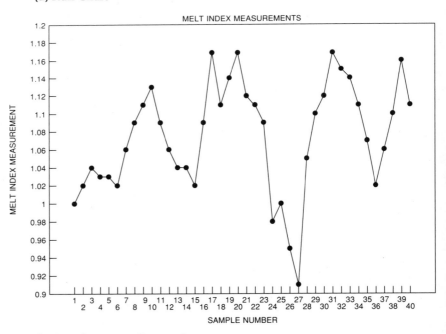

(b) Correlation coefficient (lag = 1) = 0.69

## Unit 6

### Exercise 6-1.

$n = 100$, $\mu = 9.5$, $\sigma = 0.8$;
$\Pr(X > 11) = \Pr(Z > (X - \mu)/\sigma) = \Pr(Z > (11 - 9.5)/0.8) = 0.0304 = 3\%$; $\Pr(X < 9) = \Pr(Z < (X - \mu)/\sigma) = \Pr(Z < (9 - 9.5)/0.8) = 0.266 = 26.6\%$

### Exercise 6-2.

Target $= 32 \pm 0.1$; A: $\mu = 32.02$, $\sigma = 0.05$; B: $\mu = 32.00$, $\sigma = 0.06$;
A: $\Pr(31.9 < X < 32.1) = \Pr(X < 32.1) - \Pr(X < 31.9) = \Pr(Z < (32.1 - 32.02)/0.05) - \Pr(Z < (31.9 - 32.02)/0.05) = 0.9452 - 0.0082 = 0.937$
B: $\Pr(31.9 < X < 32.1) = \Pr(X < 32.1) - \Pr(X < 31.9) = \Pr(Z < (32.1 - 32.0)/0.06) - \Pr(Z < (31.9 - 32.0)/0.06) = 0.95254 - 0.04746 = 0.90508$
$\Rightarrow$ Company A has smaller variation; probably better overall quality.

### Exercise 6-3.

$x_A = 32.13$, $\mu_A = 32.02$, $\sigma_A = 0.05$;
$\Pr(X \geq 32.13) = \Pr(Z \geq (X - \mu)/\sigma) = \Pr(Z \geq (32.13 - 32.02)/0.05) = 0.0139$
$\Rightarrow$ If the true process mean is 32.02 and the true process standard deviation is 0.05, there is only about a 1.4% chance of getting a value as large as 32.13. The process mean may have shifted upward.

### Exercise 6-4.

Normal Probability Plot

| Rank | 1 | 2 | 3 | 4 | 5 | 6 | 7 | 8 | 9 | 10 | 11 | 12 |
|------|------|------|------|------|------|------|------|------|------|------|------|------|
| $x_i$ | .87 | .90 | .91 | .91 | .92 | .93 | .94 | .96 | .97 | .97 | .98 | 1.05 |
| $F_i$ | 5.1 | 13.3 | 21.4 | 29.6 | 37.8 | 45.9 | 54.1 | 62.2 | 70.4 | 78.6 | 86.7 | 94.9 |

Data does not closely follow a normally distributed pattern.

(b) Mean $= 0.94$, Standard Deviation $= 0.055$

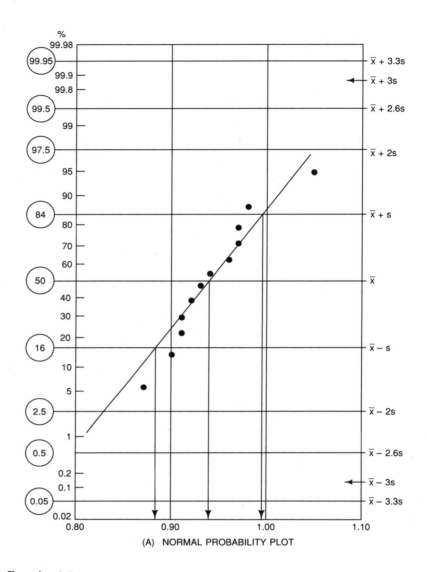

(A)  NORMAL PROBABILITY PLOT

Exercise 6-5.

Normal Probability Plots

| Rank | 1 | 2 | 3 | 4 | 5 | 6 | 7 | 8 | 9 | 10 | 11 | 12 |
|---|---|---|---|---|---|---|---|---|---|---|---|---|
| $F_i$ | 5.1 | 13.3 | 21.4 | 29.6 | 37.8 | 45.9 | 54.1 | 62.2 | 70.4 | 78.6 | 86.7 | 94.9 |
| Process A: | | | | | | | | | | | | |
| $x_i$ | .96 | .98 | .99 | 1.00 | 1.02 | 1.02 | 1.03 | 1.05 | 1.06 | 1.07 | 1.09 | 1.12 |
| Process B: | | | | | | | | | | | | |
| $x_i$ | 1.01 | 1.03 | 1.03 | 1.03 | 1.04 | 1.04 | 1.04 | 1.05 | 1.06 | 1.06 | 1.07 | 1.08 |

Both processes closely follow a normally distributed pattern. Process B has a higher mean (1.045 to 1.035) and a lower standard deviation (0.02 to 0.045).

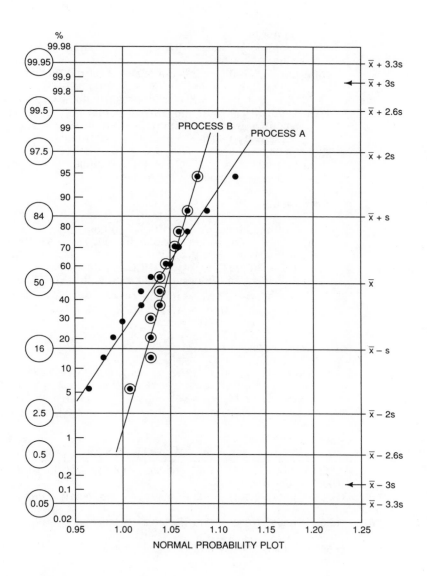

NORMAL PROBABILITY PLOT

Exercise 6-6.

$\mu = 1550$, $\sigma = 50$, $n = 100$;
(a) $\Pr(X < 1550) = 50\% \Rightarrow 50$
(b) $\Pr(X > 1650) = \Pr(Z > (1650 - 1500)/50) \Rightarrow 2$
(c) $\Pr(1525 < X < 1575) = \Pr(Z < (1575 - 1550)/50) - \Pr(Z < (1525 - 1550)/50) \Rightarrow 38$
(d) $\Pr(X > 1470) = \Pr(Z > (1470 - 1550)/50) \Rightarrow 94$

Exercise 6-7.

$\mu = 101.7$, $\sigma = 11.5$, $n = 4$;
$\Pr(\bar{x} > 113) = \Pr(Z > (\bar{x} - \mu)/(\sigma/\sqrt{n})) = \Pr(Z > (113 - 101.7)/(11.5/\sqrt{4})) = 2.4\%$

Exercise 6-8.

$X \sim n(2, 0.003)$;
(a) LSL = ?, but only 3% out of specification; $Pr(X < LSL) = 0.03 = Pr(Z < (X - \mu)/\sigma) = Pr(Z < (X - 2)/0.003)$; $\Rightarrow z_{.03} = -1.88$; $\Rightarrow -1.88 = (X - 2)/0.003$; $\Rightarrow X = 2 + (-1.88)(0.003) = 1.99436$; $\Rightarrow$ LSL = 1.994
(b) Symmetrical USL and LSL such that only 10% out of specification bushings are produced; $Pr(X < LSL) = 0.05$; $\Rightarrow z_{.05} = -2.57$; $\Rightarrow -2.57 = (X - 2)/0.003$; $\Rightarrow X = 2 + (-2.57)(0.003)$; $\Rightarrow$ LSL = 1.992, USL = 2.008
(c) $Pr(1.994 < X < 2.006) = Pr(X < 2.006) - Pr(X < 1.994) = Pr(Z < (1.994 - 2)/0.003) \times 2 = 0.0455$

Exercise 6-9.

n = 4 from 5 batches, $\bar{\bar{x}} = 1.5$, $\bar{R} = 0.006$;
(a) $\Rightarrow \hat{\sigma}_{\bar{x}} = \bar{R}/d_2 = 0.006/2.059 = 0.002914$; $\pm 3\sigma_{\bar{x}}$ limits $\Rightarrow Pr(\bar{x} < LCL) = 0.001350$; $\Rightarrow z_{.001350} = -3$; $\Rightarrow -3 = (LCL - 1.5)/0.003$; $\Rightarrow$ LCL = 1.5 - 3(0.003) = 1.41, $\Rightarrow$ UCL = 1.59
(b) Specification limits such that 95% within specification limits; $\mu_{\bar{x}} = \mu_x = 1.5$; $\sigma_{\bar{x}} = \sigma/\sqrt{n}$; $\Rightarrow 0.0029(2) = \sigma_x$; $\Rightarrow \sigma_x = 0.0058$; $\Rightarrow z_{.025} = -1.96$; $\Rightarrow -1.96 = (LSL - 1.5)/0.0058$; $\Rightarrow$ LSL = 1.5 - 0.011 = 1.489, $\Rightarrow$ USL = 1.5 + 0.011 = 1.511

Exercise 6-10.

Pr(outside specs) = $Pr(X > 800) + Pr(X < 700) = Pr(Z > (800 - 758)/19.4) + Pr(Z < (700 - 758)/19.4) = Pr(Z > 2.16) + Pr(Z < -2.99) = Pr(Z < -2.16) + Pr(Z < -2.99) = 0.01539 + 0.00139 = 0.017 = 1.7\%$

Exercise 6-11.

| Process | Calculations |
|---|---|
| 1 | $Pr(X > 1.505) + Pr(X < 1.495) = Pr(Z > (1.505 - 1.495)/0.0007) + Pr(Z < (1.495 - 1.495)/0.0007) = 0 + 0.50 = 50\%$ |
| 2 | $Pr(Z > (1.505 - 1.502)/0.001) + Pr(Z < (1.495 - 1.502)/0.001) = Pr(Z > 3) + Pr(Z < -7) = 0.13\%$ |
| 3 | $Pr(Z > (1.505 - 1.500)/0.002) + Pr(Z < (1.495 - 1.500)/0.002) = Pr(Z < 2.5) + Pr(Z < -2.5) = 1.24\%$ |
| 4 | $Pr(Z > (1.505 - 1.498)/0.002) + Pr(Z < (1.495 - 1.498)/0.002) = Pr(Z > 3.5) + Pr(Z < -1.5) = 6.7\%$ |

## Unit 7
Exercise 7-1.

(a) Activity: yard mowing; variable: time required to complete activity; common cause variation (random variation): personal fatigue, engine setting, time of day, dull mower blade; special cause variation (non-random variation): broken engine, rain, broken mower blade.
(b) Performance characteristics from processes having only common cause variation tend to exhibit stable patterns of variation; they are typically normally distributed.
(c) Control charts indicate when special cause variation is present.
(d) Centerlines are developed from (1) process data or (2) target values.
(e) Control limits are commonly set at $\pm 3\sigma$ because of (1) the characteristics of the normal distribution and (2) simplicity.
(f) Sample size: (1) The difficulty involved in collecting and analyzing

sample data from the process, (2) how meaningful multiple observations taken from a single sample actually are, and (3) sampling cost.
(g) Sampling frequency: (1) process and (2) cost dependent.
(h) Rational subgroups: samples that are as homogeneous as the process
will permit.

Exercise 7-2.

(a) In statistical control: when only common cause variation is present.
(Performance measures from in-control processes tend to be normally
distributed.)
(b) No. Since specification limits are externally imposed on a process, an
in-control process may or may not be producing within specification
limits.
(c) False signal: an out-of-control indication when process is in control.
(d) Lack of signal: when process actually goes out of control and no out-
of-control signal is given.

Exercise 7-3.

(a) Common cause variation: stable, consistent process; random variation
only; process noise.
(b) Special cause variation: unstable, inconsistent process; variation is not
just random (e.g., spike, trend, run).
(c) In general, common cause variation can only be reduced by management intervention.
(d) In general, special cause variation can be reduced by those directly
involved in the process.

Exercise 7-4.

(a) In general, when all points on a control chart are within control limits,
only common cause variation is present (i.e., data is scattered randomly around the chart's centerline).
(b) Leave the process alone.
(c) Report the out-of-specification product (in order to obtain management
intervention), but do not tamper with process. Tampering with an in-
control process will result in increased process variation.
(d) Probability of point outside $\pm 3\sigma$ limits: 0.27%; probability of point
outside $\pm 2\sigma$ limits: approximately 4.55%.
(e) Event log: a time-sequenced recap of events somehow logically aligned
with control chart (i.e., to help determine special causes of variation).

## Unit 8
Exercise 8-1.

$\bar{x} = 54.78$, $\bar{R}_m = 12.5$; $UCL_x = 88.03$, $LCL_x = 21.53$; $UCL_{MR} = 40.85$,
$LCL_{MR} = 0.00$.

Exercise 8-2.

$$\bar{x} \pm 3\sigma_x = \bar{x} \pm 3\bar{R}_m/d_2 \Rightarrow \text{spread} = 6\bar{R}_m/d_2$$

Exercise 8-3.

Factor $d_2$ converts average range values to esimates of $\sigma_x$ (i.e., $\sigma_x = \bar{R}_m/d_2$);
factor $E_2$ equals the constant 3 divided by $d_2$ (i.e., $CL_x = \bar{x} \pm E_2\bar{R}_m$, so $E_2$
$= 3/d_2$); factor $D_4$ is used to compute the upper control limit on a $R_m$ chart

(i.e., $UCL_{MR} = D_4\overline{R}_m$); factor $D_3$ is used to compute the lower control limit on a $R_m$ chart (i.e., $LCL_{MR} = D_3\overline{R}_m$).

Exercise 8-4.

Moving range chart: $UCL_{MR} = 93.87$, $LCL_{MR} = 0.00$, Centerline $= 28.72$; Individuals chart: $UCL_x = 1020.77$, $LCL_x = 867.96$, Centerline $= 944.37$; All points on both charts within control limits.

Exercise 8-5.

Moving range chart: $UCL_{MR} = 0.23$, $LCL_{MR} = 0.00$, Centerline $= 0.07$, $\Rightarrow$ All points within control limits; Individuals chart: $UCL_x = 1.16$, $LCL_x = 0.79$, Centerline $= 0.98$, $\Rightarrow$ All individual measurements within control limits.

Exercise 8-6.

Moving range chart 1: $UCL_{MR} = 34.1$, $LCL = 0.00$, Centerline $= 10.4$; Two points out of control (#9, #10); Point #9 (129) removed and $R_m$ chart control limits recomputed based on 29 values (i.e., 28 moving ranges).

Moving range chart 2: $UCL_{MR} = 26.5$, $LCL = 0.00$, Centerline $= 8.1$; One point out of control (#21); Point #21 (30) removed and $R_m$ chart control limits recomputed based on 28 values (i.e., 27 moving ranges).

Moving range chart 3: $UCL_{MR} = 20.9$, $LCL = 0.00$, Centerline $= 6.4$; All points within control limits, so x chart can be set up. Individuals (x) chart 1 (based on 28 values): $UCL_x = 115.1$, $LCL_x = 81.1$, Centerline $= 98.1$; All points within control limits. $\Rightarrow$ Both x chart and $R_m$ chart may be used to monitor process.

Exercise 8-7.

Moving range chart 1: $UCL_{MR} = 1.7$, $LCL_{MR} = 0.00$, Centerline $= 0.5$; Two points (#11, #37) above the $UCL_{MR}$; Point #10 (34.5) and point #39 (34.8) removed.

Moving range chart 2 (based on 43 values): $UCL_{MR} = 1.3$, $LCL_{MR} = 0.00$, Centerline $= 0.4$; All points within control limits, so individuals chart can be set up.

Individuals chart 1 (based on 43 values): $UCL_x = 37.9$, $LCL_x = 35.1$, Centerline $= 36.5$ (target, not sample mean); One point (#44) below $LCL_x$ and three additional points are right on $LCL_x$ indicating an out-of-control process. Note that if the process average (36.2) rather than the process target (36.5) had been used to establish the chart's centerline, all points would have been within control limits. Indicates that process mean must be shifted upward to establish an in-control and acceptable process.

Exercise 8-8.

(a) Lab 1 Data: Moving range chart: $UCL_{MR} = 1.29$, $LCL_{MR} = 0.00$, Centerline $= 0.39$; Point #23 above $UCL_{MR}$ implying an out-of-control process.

Lab 2 Data: Moving range chart: $UCL_{MR} = 1.38$, $LCL_{MR} = 0.00$, Centerline $= 0.42$; Point #14 above $UCL_{MR}$ implying an out-of-control process.

$\Rightarrow$ Both labs indicate that production process is out of control.

(b) Differences between Lab 1 and Lab 2 readings:

Moving range chart 1: $UCL_{MR} = 0.51$, $LCL_{MR} = 0.00$, Centerline $= 0.16$; Point #14 above $UCL_{MR}$ implying that labs differed significantly on at least one specimen; Largest difference on specimen #13; That difference deleted and moving range values recomputed.

Moving range chart 2: $UCL_{MR} = 0.39$, $LCL_{MR} = 0.00$, Centerline $= 0.12$; Point #21 above $UCL_{MR}$ indicating a significant difference between labs' results; Inspection of process data led to deletion of difference #20.

Moving range chart 3: $UCL_{MR} = 0.34$, $LCL_{MR} = 0.00$, Centerline $= 0.10$; No points outside control limits, so individuals chart may be developed.

Individuals chart 1: $UCL_x = 0.27$, $LCL_x = -0.28$, Centerline $= 0.00$; No points outside control limits.

$\Rightarrow$ Final $R_m$ and x charts may be used to monitor differences between labs' results.

## Unit 9

Exercise 9-1.

In-control process; $n = 5$, $\bar{\bar{x}} = 1.432$, $\bar{R} = 0.004$; $UCL_{\bar{x}} = \bar{\bar{x}} + A_2\bar{R} = 1.432 + (0.577)(0.004) = 1.434$, $LCL_{\bar{x}} = \bar{\bar{x}} - A_2\bar{R} = 1.432 - (0.577)(0.004) = 1.430$; $\Rightarrow$ All 40 sample averages within control limits.

Exercise 9-2.

In-control process; $n = 6$, $\bar{\bar{x}} = 50$, $\bar{R} = 4.0$; $UCL_R = D_4\bar{R} = (2.004)(4.0) = 8.016$, $LCL_R = D_3\bar{R} = 0.000$; $UCL_{\bar{x}} = \bar{\bar{x}} + A_2\bar{R} = 50 + (0.483)(4.0) = 51.932$, $LCL_{\bar{x}} = \bar{\bar{x}} - A_2\bar{R} = 50 - (0.483)(4.0) = 48.068$.

Exercise 9-3.

In-control process; $n = 5$, $\bar{\bar{x}} = 33.6$, $\bar{R} = 6.20$; $UCL_R = D_4\bar{R} = (2.115)(6.20) = 13.11$, $LCL_R = D_3\bar{R} = 0.000$; $UCL_{\bar{x}} = \bar{\bar{x}} + A_2\bar{R} = 33.6 + (0.577)(6.20) = 37.18$, $LCL_{\bar{x}} = \bar{\bar{x}} - A_2\bar{R} = 33.6 - (0.577)(6.20) = 30.02$; New sample: $\bar{x} = 37.8$, $R = 43 - 35 = 8$; $\Rightarrow$ Process mean seems to have shifted upward.

Exercise 9-4.

$n = 6$, $\bar{\bar{x}} = 1.001$, $\bar{R} = 0.002$; $UCL_R = D_4\bar{R} = (2.004)(0.002) = 0.004$, $LCL_R = D_3\bar{R} = (0)(0.002) = 0.000$; $UCL_{\bar{x}} = \bar{\bar{x}} + A_2\bar{R} = 1.001 + (0.483)(0.002) = 1.002$, $LCL_{\bar{x}} = \bar{\bar{x}} - A_2\bar{R} = 1.001 - (0.483)(0.002) = 1.000$.

Exercise 9-5.

(c) Indicate when nonrandom causes of variation exist in the process.

Exercise 9-6.

(d) The process dispersion is out of control. (Note: The two unanalyzed units could only increase the range. They could not decrease it.)

Exercise 9-7.

(d) The analyst is not using the chart correctly. (Individual values should not be plotted on $\bar{x}$ charts.)

Exercise 9-8.

(d) Probability that a point will fall inside the three-sigma limits for an $\bar{x}$ chart, if the process is in statistical control.

Exercise 9-9.

(a)

| Sample | 1 | 2 | 3 | 4 | 5 | 6 | 7 | 8 |
|---|---|---|---|---|---|---|---|---|
| $\bar{x}$ | 1.00 | 1.02 | 0.98 | 1.00 | 1.02 | 1.01 | 0.97 | 0.99 |
| R | 0.07 | 0.03 | 0.07 | 0.09 | 0.05 | 0.04 | 0.05 | 0.07 |

(b) $\bar{\bar{x}} = 0.998$, $\bar{R} = 0.059$
(c) $UCL_R = 0.13$, $LCL_R = 0.00$, $UCL_{\bar{x}} = 1.04$, $LCL_{\bar{x}} = 0.96$.

Exercise 9-10.

(a) $UCL_R = D_4\bar{R} = (2.282)(0.018) = 0.042$, $LCL_R = D_3\bar{R} = (0)(0.018) = 0.000$; $\Rightarrow$ All sample ranges within control limits.
(b) $UCL_{\bar{x}} = \bar{\bar{x}} + A_2\bar{R} = 0.651 + (0.729)(0.018) = 0.664$, $LCL_{\bar{x}} = \bar{\bar{x}} - A_2\bar{R} = 0.651 - (0.729)(0.018) = 0.637$; $\Rightarrow$ All points on $\bar{x}$ chart within control limits.

Exercise 9-11.

$UCL_R = D_4\bar{R} = (2.574)(5.7) = 14.6$, $LCL_R = D_3\bar{R} = (0.0)(5.7) = 0.000$; $\Rightarrow$ All sample ranges within control limits (i.e., the lab techs consistent with their own measurements); $UCL_{\bar{x}} = \bar{\bar{x}} + A_2\bar{R} = 180.2 + (1.023)(5.7) = 186.0$, $LCL_{\bar{x}} = \bar{\bar{x}} - A_2\bar{R} = 180.2 - (1.023)(5.7) = 174.4$; $\Rightarrow$ Four points outside control limits (2 each from Lab Tech 2 and Lab Tech 3); Significant difference between lab technicians.

Exercise 9-12.

(a) $UCL_R = D_4\bar{R} = (2.282)(1.34) = 3.06$, $LCL_R = D_3\bar{R} = (0.0)(1.34) = 0.000$; $\Rightarrow$ All sample ranges within control limits.
(b) $UCL_{\bar{x}} = \bar{\bar{x}} + A_2\bar{R} = 40.00 + (0.729)(1.34) = 40.98$, $LCL_{\bar{x}} = \bar{\bar{x}} - A_2\bar{R} = 40.00 - (0.729)(1.34) = 39.03$; $\Rightarrow$ All sample means within control limits.

## Unit 10
Exercise 10-1.
Overcontrol: often called tampering; increases process variation if process is in control.

Exercise 10-2.

Undercontrol: often called lack of signal; results in allowing an out-of-control process to continue to run out of control.

Exercise 10-3.

(a) Pr(detecting a process mean shift of one standard deviation in 2 samples) = Pr(detecting a $1\sigma$ process mean shift in either sample 1 or sample 2) = 1 − Pr(detecting a $1\sigma$ process mean shift in neither sample) = 1 − [(0.9772)(0.9772)] = 1 − 0.955 = 0.045

(b) Pr(detecting a $1\sigma$ process shift within 5 samples) = Pr(detecting $1\sigma$ process mean shift on sample 1 or 2 or 3 or 4 or 5) = 1 − Pr(not detecting shift on any of 5 samples) = 1 − $(0.9772)^5$ = 1 − 0.891 = 0.109

(c) Pr(detecting a $1\sigma$ process mean shift within 10 samples) = 1 − $(0.9772)^{10}$ = 1 − 0.794 = 0.206

(d) Pr(detecting a $1\sigma$ process mean shift within 25 samples) = 1 − $(0.9772)^{25}$ = 1 − 0.562 = 0.438

Exercise 10-4.

(a) Assume $\sigma$ = 0.03, original $\mu$ = 1.00, UCL = 1.09, LCL = 0.91; Pr(undercontrol when process mean shifts by $1.5\sigma$) = 1 − [Pr($X_i \geq$ UCL) + Pr($X_i \leq$ LCL)] = Pr($X_i \leq$ UCL) − Pr($X_i \leq$ LCL) = Pr(Z ≤ (UCL − $\mu$)/$\sigma$) − Pr(Z ≤ (LCL − $\mu$)/$\sigma$) = Pr(Z ≤ (1.09 − 1.045)/0.03) − Pr(Z ≤ (0.91 − 1.045)/0.03) = Pr(Z ≤ 1.5) − Pr(Z ≤ −4.5) = 0.93319 − 0 = 0.9332

(b) Pr(undercontrol when process mean shifts by $2.5\sigma$) = Pr(Z ≤ (1.09 − 1.075)/0.03) − Pr(Z ≤ (0.91 − 1.075)/0.03) = Pr(Z ≤ 0.5) − 0 = 0.6915

(c) Pr(undercontrol when process mean shifts by $3.5\sigma$) = Pr(Z ≤ − 0.5) − 0 = 0.3086

(d) Pr(undercontrol when process mean shifts by $4.5\sigma$) = Pr(Z ≤ − 1.5) − 0 = 0.0668

Exercise 10-5.
(a) 0.0027
(b) 0.00135
(c) Zone A begins $2\sigma$ from process mean; 0.9545 of area within $\pm2\sigma$; ⇒ zone A contains 0.9973 − 0.9545 = 0.0428; ⇒ Pr(two consecutive points in zone A when process is in control) = $(0.0428)^2$ = 0.0018.
(d) Pr(2 out of 3 will fall in upper A zone when process in control) = $(0.0214)^2(1 − 0.0214)$ = 0.00045
(e) Pr(both A zones) = Pr(between 2 and $3\sigma$) = 0.9973 − 0.9545 = 0.0428; Pr(both B zones) = 0.9545 − 0.6827 = 0.2718; ⇒ Pr(lower A or B) = 0.0428/2 + 0.2718/2 = 0.0214 + 0.1359 = 0.1573; ⇒ Pr(4 out of 5 will fall in lower A or B zones when process in control) = $(0.1573)^4(1 − 0.1573)$ = (0.000614)(0.8427) = 0.000516
(f) Pr(7 consecutive points in upper zones A, B, or C when process in control) = $(0.9973/2)^7$ = 0.00767

Exercise 10-6.

Yes. Zone rules, run rules, and control limits intended to help control chart users recognize nonrandom patterns. They may not do so successfully in all cases—even when the process is out of control.

Exercise 10-7.

Example of overcontrol. Control charts should be used to monitor process. Operators should be instructed to leave process alone unless an out-of-control condition is recognized.

Exercise 10-8.

(a) Half hour later.
(b) Assuming that first sample in sequence is taken immediately and that fourth sample measurement falls in zone A, 10.5 hours will have passed when sample 13 is taken. According to zone rules, no out-of-control problem is apparent, but close process scrutiny may be warranted because of pattern's regularity.

## Unit 11

Exercise 11-1.

In the process industries, processes are often multi-staged, feedforward or feedback controlled, highly complex input-output systems. In addition, process output are often homogeneous (e.g., gasoline) and stored together (e.g., common storage tanks). Several components of variation are usually present. Result is often that performance measures are neither independent nor normally distributed.

Exercise 11-2.

What to measure: (1) Characteristic listed in product specifications (i.e., connected to product success); (2) Characteristic closely correlated with some important specification or characteristic.

Exercise 11-3.

When and where to measure: Meaningful characteristic that is measurable early enough in process to allow corrective action (if necessary).

Exercise 11-4.

Gasoline is homogeneous. Therefore, five beakers of gasoline do not represent five independent measurements, which can be misleading. In this case, $\bar{x}$ and R charts are inappropriate.

Exercise 11-5.

Pump is one system. Taking vibration measurements on pump's base is actually obtaining four measurements of a single occurrence (with slight variation due to instrumentation and alignment of pump). In this case, $\bar{x}$ and R charts are inappropriate.

Exercise 11-6.

(a) $UCL_R = 15.52$, $LCL_R = 0.00$, Centerline $= 6.80$; $UCL_{\bar{x}} = 79.87$, $LCL_{\bar{x}} = 69.96$, Centerline $= 74.92$; All points are within range chart's control limits (i.e., variation within processes appears to be in control), but points are outside both control limits on $\bar{x}$ chart, indicating lack of process control.
(b) Unit 1 (samples 1, 4, 7, 10, 13): $UCL_R = 14.15$, $LCL_R = 0.00$, Centerline $= 6.20$; $UCL_{\bar{x}} = 78.82$, $LCL_{\bar{x}} = 69.78$, Centerline $= 74.3$; $\Rightarrow$ All points on both charts within control limits. Unit 2 (samples 2, 5, 8, 11, 14): $UCL_R = 15.06$, $LCL_R = 0.00$, Centerline $= 6.6$; $UCL_{\bar{x}} = 87.21$, $LCL_{\bar{x}} = 77.59$, Centerline $= 82.4$; $\Rightarrow$ All points on both charts within control limits. Unit 3 (samples 3, 6, 9, 12, 15): $UCL_R = 17.34$, $LCL_R = 0.00$, Centerline $= 7.6$; $UCL_{\bar{x}} = 73.59$, $LCL_{\bar{x}} = 62.51$, Centerline $= 68.05$; $\Rightarrow$ All points on both charts within control limits.

(c) There are three separate processes in operation. They cannot be monitored effectively with a single control chart. In this case, having 3 separate x and $R_m$ chart pairs (one for each process) is a better choice.

Exercise 11-7.

(a) $UCL_R = 0.14$, $LCL_R = 0.00$, Centerline = 0.05; $UCL_{\bar{x}} = 0.84$, $LCL_{\bar{x}} = 0.74$, Centerline = 0.79; ⇒ All points on R chart within control limits, but points fall both above and below $\bar{x}$ chart control limits indicating an out-of-control condition.

(b) $UCL_{MR} = 0.18$, $LCL_{MR} = 0.00$, Centerline = 0.06; $UCL_x = 0.94$, $LCL_x = 0.64$, Centerline = 0.79; ⇒ All points on both charts are within control limits.

(c) If pellets are loaded into the three railcar sections randomly (i.e., not from three separate production runs), pellets are mixed and represent output from a homogeneous process. Therefore, the three individual measurements in each sample are duplicates (i.e., same quality three times) and an x and $R_m$ control chart combination (i.e., average three measurements and treat them as a single value) is the better choice.

Exercise 11-8.

(a) All points within x chart's control limits, but clear zig-zag pattern exists).

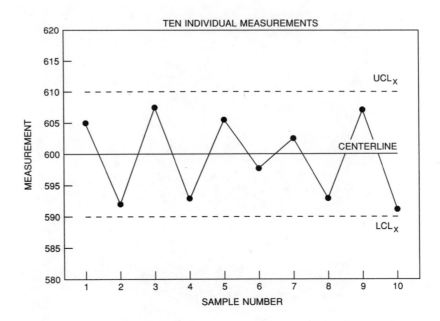

(b) $\sigma_x = 3\sigma_x/3 = 10/3 = 3.33$

(c) $\bar{R}_m = 12.67$, $\hat{\sigma}_x = \bar{R}_m/d_2 = 12.67/1.128 = 11.23$

(d) It appears that control chart was developed using data from several different processes, but that each separate data group shown in Table 11-C comes from several individual processes. Situation referred to as mixing.

Exercise 11-9.

(a) Two-Period Moving Range Based Control Limits: $UCL_x = \bar{\bar{x}} + A_2\bar{R}_m = 216.0 + 2.66(5.91) = 231.7$, $LCL_x = \bar{\bar{x}} - A_2\bar{R}_m = 216.0 - 2.66(5.91) = 200.3$

(b) Standard Deviation Based Control Limits: $UCL_x = \bar{\bar{x}} + 3\hat{\sigma}_x = 216.0 + 3(8.70) = 242.1$, $LCL_x = \bar{\bar{x}} - 3\hat{\sigma}_x = 216.0 - 3(8.70) = 189.9$

(c) Figure below indicates that autocorrelation is present in process (i.e., cycling). Therefore, standard deviation based control limits (b) are more appropriate.

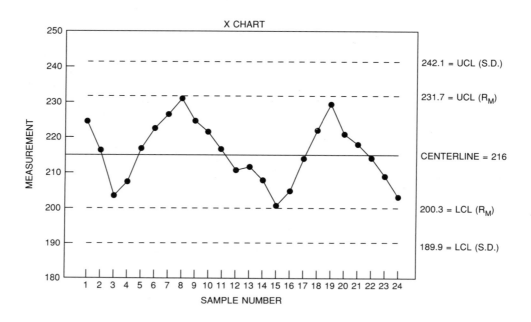

## Unit 12
### Exercise 12-1.

(a) $C_p$ = specs/spread = $200/(6 \times 30) = 1.11$
(b) $C_p = 200/(6 \times 40) = 0.83$
(c) $C_p = 200/(6 \times 70) = 0.48$
(d) $C_p = 200/(6 \times 20) = 1.67$

### Exercise 12-2.

(a) $C_{pk} = (\mu - LSL)/3\sigma = (650 - 600)/(3 \times 30) = 0.56$
(b) $C_{pk} = (680 - 600)/(3 \times 30) = 0.89$
(c) $C_{pk} = (650 - 600)/(3 \times 70) = 0.24$
(d) $C_{pk} = (650 - 600)/(3 \times 20) = 0.83$
(e) $C_{pk} = (800 - 720)/(3 \times 25) = 1.07$
(f) $C_{pk} = (800 - 720)/(3 \times 40) = 0.67$

### Exercise 12-3.

$n = 5, \bar{\bar{x}} = 1.432, \bar{R} = 0.004, \Rightarrow \sigma_x = \bar{R}/d_2 = 0.004/2.326 = 0.0017$
(a) Specification limits: 1.420, 1.440; $C_{pk} = (1.440 - 1.432)/(3 \times 0.0017) = 1.57$

(b) Specification limits: 1.415, 1.445; $C_{pk} = (1.445 - 1.432)/(0.0051) = 2.55$

(c) $Pr(Z \leq (X - 1.430)/0.005) = 0.025;$ ⇒ $-z_{.025} = (X - 1.430)/0.005;$ ⇒ $(-1.96)(0.005) + 1.43 = X;$ ⇒ $X = 1.43 - 0.01 = 1.42;$ ⇒ Specification limits $= 1.43 \pm 0.01$

(d) $C_p = $ specs/spread; ⇒ $1.5 = $ specs/$(6 \times 0.005);$ ⇒ specs $= (1.5)(0.03) = 0.045;$ ⇒ specification limits $= 1.43 \pm 0.0225$

(e) $C_p = $ specs/spread; ⇒ $2.0 = (2 \times 0.012)/(6 \times \sigma);$ ⇒ $\sigma = (2 \times 0.012)/(6 \times 2);$ ⇒ $\sigma = 0.002$

### Exercise 12-4.

$\mu = 758, \sigma = 19.4;$

(a) $Pr(\text{outside specs}) = Pr(X > 800) = Pr(Z > (800 - 758)/19.4) = Pr(Z > 2.16) = Pr(Z < -2.16) = 0.0154 = 1.5\%$

(b) $C_{pk} = (800 - 758)/(3 \times 19.4) = 0.72$

(c) $C_p = $ specs/$(6 \times \sigma);$ ⇒ $1.6 = $ specs/$(6 \times 19.4);$ ⇒ specs $= 186.24;$ ⇒ Specification limits $= 750 \pm 93.12$

### Exercise 12-5.

$\mu = 100, \sigma = 5.0;$

(a) 0.50

(b) $C_{pk} = (USL - \text{Mean})/3\sigma = (100 - 100)/(3 \times 5.0) = 0$

(c) In order to meaningfully calculate $C_p$, the process must be centered. Therefore, if the specs are $95 \pm 5$ and the process mean is 100, the situation is untenable. Either the process mean or the customer specification limits (or both) must be shifted.

### Exercise 12-6.

(a)

| Process | Average ($\bar{x}$) | $6\sigma$ | $C_{pk}$ |
|---------|---------------------|-----------|----------|
| 1 | 1.495 | 0.004 | 0 |
| 2 | 1.502 | 0.006 | 1 |
| 3 | 1.500 | 0.012 | 0.83 |
| 4 | 1.498 | 0.002 | 3 |

(b) Process 4

### Exercise 12-7.

(a) $C_p = 0.90;$ ⇒ $C_p = 0.90 = (USL - LSL)/6\sigma;$ Let $\sigma = 1$, then USL $-$ LSL $= 6(0.90) = 5.4;$ ⇒ USL $- \mu = 5.4/2 = 2.7;$ ⇒ $Pr(X > 2.7) = Pr(Z > 2.7/1) = Pr(Z > 2.7) = Pr(Z \leq -2.7) = 0.0035;$ ⇒ $Pr(\text{out-of-spec}) = 2 \times 0.0035 = 0.0070 = 0.7\%$

(b) $C_p = 0.75 = (USL - LSL)/6\sigma;$ Let $\sigma = 1$, then USL $-$ LSL $= 6(0.75) = 4.5;$ ⇒ USL $- \mu = 4.5/2 = 2.25;$ ⇒ $Pr(X > 2.25) = Pr(Z > 2.25/1) = Pr(Z > 2.25) = Pr(Z \leq -2.25) = 0.0122;$ ⇒ $Pr(\text{out-of-spec}) = 2 \times 0.0122 = 0.0244 = 2.44\%$

(c) $C_p = 1.00$ means specs equals spread. Therefore, only the area outside $\pm 3$ standard deviations will be out of specification (i.e., $0.0027 = 0.27\%$).

## Unit 13
Exercise 13-1.

(a) Two-Period Moving Range Chart: $\overline{R}_m = 0.010$; $UCL_{MR} = 0.031$, $LCL_{MR} = 0.000$, Centerline $= 0.010$; $\Rightarrow$ All points within control limits on moving range chart.

CUSUM Decision Interval Chart: $UCL_{CUSUM} = 3\overline{R}_m/d_2 = 3(0.010)/1.128 = 0.0255$, $LCL_{CUSUM} = -3\overline{R}_m/d_2 = -3(0.010)/1.128 = -0.0255$, Centerline $= 0.000$.

$\overline{x} = 0.785$, $\sigma_x = \overline{R}_m/d_2 = 0.010/1.128 = 0.0085$, $q = 1$, $D^+ = \overline{x} + q\sigma_x/2 = 0.785 + (1)(0.0085)/2 = 0.790$; $D^- = \overline{x} - q\sigma_x/2 = 0.785 - (1)(0.0085)/2 = 0.781$.

Sample Calculations:

$CUSUM_1^+ = 0.000 + (0.788 - 0.790) = 0.000$ (since $CUSUM^+ < 0$)
$CUSUM_1^- = 0.000 + (0.788 - 0.781) = 0.000$ (since $CUSUM^- > 0$)
$CUSUM_2^+ = 0.000 + (0.793 - 0.790) = 0.003$
$CUSUM_2^- = 0.000 + (0.793 - 0.781) = 0.000$ (since $CUSUM^- > 0$)
$CUSUM_3^+ = 0.003 + (0.770 - 0.790) = 0.000$ (since $CUSUM^+ < 0$)
$CUSUM_3^- = 0.000 + (0.770 - 0.781) = -0.011$

$\Rightarrow$ All points within CUSUM chart control limits.

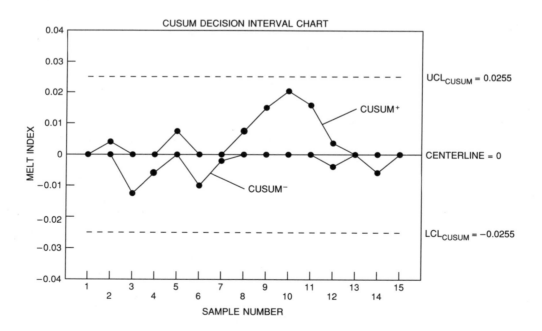

(b) 10 Additional Melt Index Values; All points within control limits on moving range chart. $CUSUM_{21}^-$ goes below $LCL_{CUSUM}$ indicating an out-of-control condition.

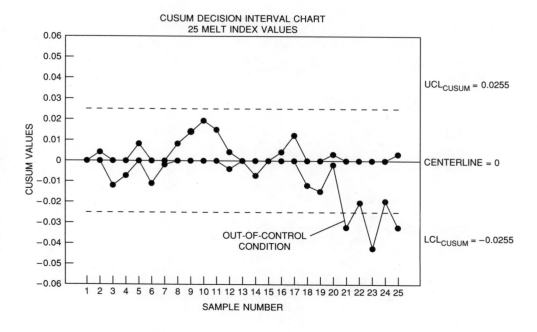

CUSUM DECISION INTERVAL CHART
25 MELT INDEX VALUES

Exercise 13-2.

(a) Data from Ex. 13-1; $UCL_{MR} = 0.031$, $LCL_{MR} = 0.000$, Centerline $= 0.010$; $\Rightarrow$ All points within control limits on moving range chart; $UCL_x = \bar{x} + 2.66\bar{R}_m = 0.785 + 2.66(0.010) = 0.811$, $LCL_x = \bar{x} - 2.66\bar{R}_m = 0.785 - 2.66(0.010) = 0.760$; $\Rightarrow$ All points within control limits on x chart.

(b) No points fall outside control limits on either $R_m$ chart or x chart.

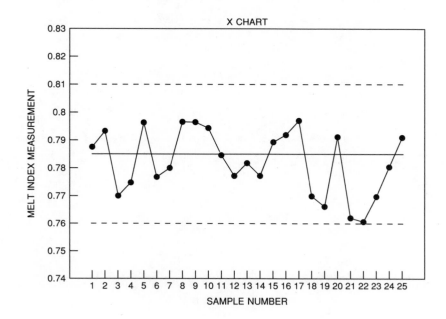

X CHART

Exercise 13-3.

Two-Period Moving Range Chart: $\bar{R}_m = 28.72$, $UCL_{MR} = D_4\bar{R}_m = 3.268(28.72) = 93.87$, $LCL_{MR} = D_3\bar{R}_m = 0.00$; $\Rightarrow$ No points outside control limits on moving range chart.

CUSUM Decision Interval Chart:

$UCL_{CUSUM} = 3\bar{R}_m/d_2 = 3(28.72)/1.128 = 76.39$, $LCL_{CUSUM} = -3\bar{R}_m/d_2 = -3(28.72)/1.128 = -76.39$, Centerline = 0.

$\bar{x} = 944.39$, $\hat{\sigma}_x = \bar{R}_m/d_2 = 28.72/1.128 = 25.46$, $q = 2$, $D^+ = \bar{x} + q\hat{\sigma}_x/2 = 944.39 + (2)(25.46)/2 = 969.83$, $D^- = \bar{x} - q\hat{\sigma}_x/2 = 944.39 - (2)(25.46)/2 = 918.90$

Sample Calculations:

$CUSUM_1^+ = 0.00 + (950 - 969.83) = 0.00$ (since $CUSUM^+ < 0$)
$CUSUM_1^- = 0.00 + (950 - 918.90) = 0.00$ (since $CUSUM^- > 0$)
$CUSUM_2^+ = 0.00 + (947 - 969.83) = 0.00$ (since $CUSUM^+ < 0$)
$CUSUM_2^- = 0.00 + (947 - 918.90) = 0.00$ (since $CUSUM^- > 0$)
$CUSUM_3^+ = 0.00 + (949 - 969.83) = 0.00$ (since $CUSUM^+ < 0$)
$CUSUM_3^- = 0.00 + (949 - 918.90) = 0.00$ (since $CUSUM^- > 0$)
$CUSUM_4^+ = 0.00 + (878 - 969.83) = 0.00$ (since $CUSUM^+ < 0$)
$CUSUM_4^- = 0.00 + (878 - 918.90) = -40.90$

$\Rightarrow$ All points within CUSUM chart control limits.

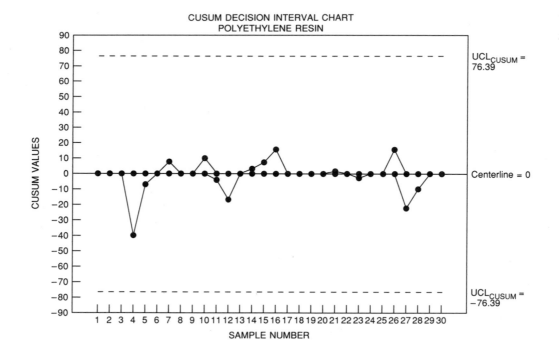

Exercise 13-4.

Two-Period Moving Range Chart: In order to bring moving range into control, two chlorine measurements were removed (#10, #37). No points fell outside the resulting control limits; $UCL_{MR} = 1.3$, $LCL_{MR} = 0.0$, Centerline $= 0.388 = \overline{R}_m$

CUSUM Decision Interval Chart:

$UCL_{CUSUM} = 3\overline{R}_m/d_2 = 3(0.388)/1.128 = 1.032$, $LCL_{CUSUM} = -3\overline{R}_m/d_2 = -3(0.388)/1.128 = -1.032$, Centerline $= 0.000$.

$\overline{x} = 36.24$, $x_T = 36.5$ (target), $\hat{\sigma}_x = \overline{R}_m/d_2 = 0.388/1.128 = 0.344$, $q = 1$, $D^+ = x_T + q\hat{\sigma}_x/2 = 36.5 + (1)(0.344)/2 = 36.67$, $D^- = x_T - q\hat{\sigma}_x/2 = 36.5 - (1)(0.344)/2 = 36.33$.

Sample Calculations:
$CUSUM_1^+ = 0.00 + (36.4 - 36.67) = 0.00$ (since $CUSUM^+ < 0$)
$CUSUM_1^- = 0.00 + (36.4 - 36.33) = 0.00$ (since $CUSUM^- > 0$)
$CUSUM_2^+ = 0.00 + (36.6 - 36.67) = 0.00$ (since $CUSUM^+ < 0$)
$CUSUM_2^- = 0.00 + (36.6 - 36.33) = 0.00$ (since $CUSUM^- > 0$)
$CUSUM_3^+ = 0.00 + (36.3 - 36.67) = 0.00$ (since $CUSUM^+ < 0$)
$CUSUM_3^- = 0.00 + (36.3 - 36.33) = -0.03$

First out-of-control point occurs at point #5 ($-1.98$). When that point is replaced by a zero (0.0) and the process restarted, point #6 is found to be below the $LCL_{CUSUM}$. The process seems to have significant problems. A run chart of the x values (below) shows a strong downward trend followed by a strong upward trend and a strong downward trend. Process appears to have considerable autocorrelation present.

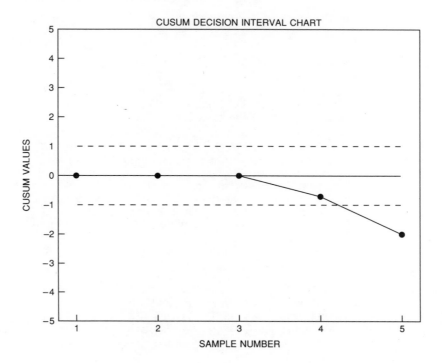

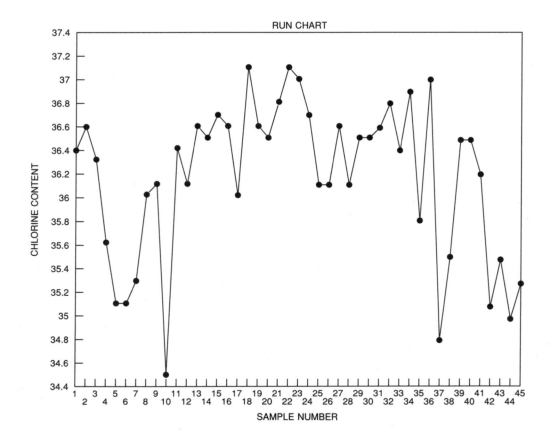

## Unit 14

### Exercise 14-1.

(a) $UCL_{MR} = 95.2$, $LCL_{MR} = 0.0$, Centerline $= 29.1$; $\Rightarrow$ All points within moving range chart control limits.

(b) $UCL_{MA} = \bar{x} + 3\bar{R}_m/(d_2\sqrt{n}) = 945.4 + 3(29.1)/(1.128\sqrt{3}) = 990.1$, $LCL_{MA} = \bar{x} - 3\bar{R}_m/(d_2\sqrt{n}) = 945.4 - 3(29.1)/(1.128\sqrt{3}) = 900.6$; $\Rightarrow$ All points within MA chart control limits (max MA $= 975.0$, min MA $= 922.3$).

(c) $\lambda = 0.5$ (from Table 14-9); $UCL_{EWMA} = \bar{x} + A_3\bar{R}_m = 945.4 + (1.536)(29.1) = 990.1$, $LCL_{EWMA} = \bar{x} - A_3\bar{R}_m = 945.4 - (1.536)(29.1) = 900.6$; Use $x_1 = 950$ as the first $x_t$ value; $\Rightarrow$ All points within EWMA chart control limits (max EWMA $= 973.0$, min EWMA $= 913.4$).

### Exercise 14-2.

(a) $UCL_{MR} = 0.229$, $LCL_{MR} = 0.000$, Centerline $= 0.070$; $\Rightarrow$ All points within $R_m$ chart control limits.

(b) $UCL_{MA} = \bar{x} + 3\bar{R}_m/(d_2\sqrt{n}) = 0.979 + 3(0.070)/(1.128\sqrt{4}) = 1.072$, $LCL_{MA} = \bar{x} - 3\bar{R}_m/(d_2\sqrt{n}) = 0.886$; $\Rightarrow$ All points within MA chart control limits (max MA $= 1.04$, min MA $= 0.92$).

(c) $\lambda = 0.40$ (from Table 14-9); $UCL_{EWMA} = \bar{x} + A_3\bar{R}_m = 0.979 +$ (1.330)(0.070) = 1.072, $LCL_{EWMA} = \bar{x} - A_3\bar{R}_m = 0.979 - (1.330)(0.070)$ = 0.886; Use $x_1 = 0.98$ as the first $x_t$ value; $\Rightarrow$ All points within EWMA chart control limits (max EWMA = 1.04, min EWMA = 0.91).

Exercise 14-3.

(a) $UCL_{MR} = 38.5$, $LCL_{MR} = 0.0$, Centerline = 11.8; $\Rightarrow$ All points within moving range chart control limits (max $R_m = 21$, min $R_m = 4$).
(b) $UCL_{MA} = 625.2$, $LCL_{MA} = 580.9$, Centerline = 603.1; $\Rightarrow$ All points within MA chart control limits (max MA = 608.5, min MA = 598.5).
(c) $\lambda = 0.8$; $UCL_{EWMA} = 603.1 + (2.172)(11.8) = 628.7$, $LCL_{EWMA} = 577.4$; $\Rightarrow$ All points within EWMA chart control limits (max EWMA = 610.8, min EWMA = 593.7).

Exercise 14-4.

(a) $UCL_{MR} = 19.3$, $LCL_{MR} = 0.00$, Centerline = 5.9; $\Rightarrow$ All points within $R_m$ chart control limits (max $R_m = 13$, min $R_m = 1$).
(b) $UCL_{MA} = 225.1$, $LCL_{MA} = 206.9$; Points both above $UCL_{MA}$ (#8, #9, #10) and below $LCL_{MA}$ (#16).
(c) $UCL_{EWMA} = 225.1$, $LCL_{EWMA} = 206.9$; Points both above $UCL_{EWMA}$ (#8, #9) and below $LCL_{EWMA}$ (#15, #16); $\Rightarrow$ Similar but not identical results on MA and EWMA control charts.

# Unit 15

Exercise 15-1.

(a) c chart, u chart
(b) np chart
(c) p chart
(d) binomial distribution
(e) Poisson distribution

Exercise 15-2.

(a) p chart: $n = 100$; Centerline = $\bar{p} = 0.10$, $UCL_p = \bar{p} + 3\sqrt{\bar{p}(1 - \bar{p})/n}$ = 0.10 + 0.09 = 0.19, $LCL_p = \bar{p} - 3\sqrt{(\bar{p}(1 - \bar{p})/n)} = 0.10 - 0.09 = 0.01$
(b) np chart: Centerline = $n\bar{p} = (100)(0.10) = 10$, $UCL_{np} = n\bar{p} + 3\sqrt{n\bar{p}(1 - \bar{p})} = 10 + 3\sqrt{10(0.90)} = 10 + 9 = 19$, $LCL_{np} = n\bar{p} - 3\sqrt{n\bar{p}(1 - \bar{p})} = 10 - 3\sqrt{10(0.90)} = 10 - 9 = 1$

Exercise 15-3.

(a) c chart: Centerline = $\bar{c} = 4$, $UCL_c = \bar{c} + 3\sqrt{\bar{c}} = 4 + 3\sqrt{4} = 10$, $LCL_c = \bar{c} - 3\sqrt{\bar{c}} = 4 - 3\sqrt{4} = 0$ (since negative blemishes are not possible)
(b) u chart: Centerline = $\bar{u} = 4$; For $k = 10$ (i.e., 10,000 square ft. roll): $UCL_u = \bar{u} + 3\sqrt{(\bar{u}/k)} = 4 + 3\sqrt{(4/10)} = 5.9$, $LCL_u = \bar{u} - 3\sqrt{(\bar{u}/k)} = 4 - 3\sqrt{(4/10)} = 2.1$; For $k = 5$ (i.e., 5,000 square foot roll): $UCL_u = 4 + 3\sqrt{(4/5)} = 6.7$, $LCL_u = 4 - 3\sqrt{(4/5)} = 1.3$

Exercise 15-4.

Total defects = 1393; Average number of defects (per assembly) = 55.72;
(a) Centerline = $\bar{c} = 55.72$, $UCL_c = \bar{c} + 3\sqrt{\bar{c}} = 55.72 + 3\sqrt{55.72} = 78.11$, $LCL_c = \bar{c} - 3\sqrt{\bar{c}} = 55.72 - 3\sqrt{55.72} = 33.33$

(b) Omit 22, 92, 22, 89, 93, 87, 33, 25, 20; Total defects = 910; Average number of defects (per assembly) = 56.88; Centerline = $\bar{c}$ = 56.88, $UCL_c$ = 56.88 + $3\sqrt{56.88}$ = 79.50, $LCL_c$ = 56.88 − $3\sqrt{56.88}$ = 34.26

Exercise 15-5.

$\bar{p}$ = 0.05, n = 50; Centerline = 0.05, $UCL_p$ = $\bar{p}$ + $3\sqrt{\bar{p}(1 - \bar{p})/n}$ = 0.05 + $3\sqrt{(0.05)(0.95)/50}$ = 0.142, $LCL_p$ = $\bar{p}$ − $3\sqrt{\bar{p}(1 - \bar{p})/n}$ = 0.05 − $3\sqrt{(0.05)(0.95)/50}$ = 0.000; ⇒ Four points are above p chart upper control limit (0.20, 0.16, 0.18, 0.16), so process is no longer in control.

Exercise 15-6.

Total "defects" = 554, Average "defects" (per shipment) = 13.85;
(a) Centerline = $\bar{c}$ = 13.85, $UCL_c$ = 13.85 + $3\sqrt{13.85}$ = 13.85 + 11.16 = 25.01, $LCL_c$ = 13.85 − $3\sqrt{13.85}$ = 13.85 − 11.16 = 2.69
(b) A u chart would be the same.

Exercise 15-7.

(a) Assuming that each month represents the same period of time (which is almost true), a c chart can be used.
(b) Total repairs = 184; Average repairs (during month) = 15.33; Centerline = $\bar{c}$ = 15.33, $UCL_c$ = 15.33 + $3\sqrt{15.33}$ = 27.08, $LCL_c$ = 15.33 − $3\sqrt{15.33}$ = 3.58

Exercise 15-8.

Total number of bolts produced = 471, Total number of imperfections = 490, $\bar{u}$ = 490/471 = 1.04. For $k_i$ = 27: $UCL_u$ = 1.04 + $3\sqrt{(1.04/27)}$ = 1.63, $LCL_u$ = 1.04 − $3\sqrt{(1.04/27)}$ = 0.45; For $k_i$ = 20: $UCL_u$ = 1.04 + $3\sqrt{(1.04/20)}$ = 1.72, $LCL_u$ = 1.04 − $3\sqrt{(1.04/20)}$ = 0.36

Exercise 15-9.

Centerline = $\bar{p}$ = 0.05; Maximum number inspected (n = 1485): $UCL_p$ = $\bar{p}$ + $3\sqrt{\bar{p}(1 - \bar{p})/n}$ = 0.05 + $3\sqrt{(0.05)(0.95)/1485}$ = 0.067, $LCL_p$ = $\bar{p}$ − $3\sqrt{\bar{p}(1 - \bar{p})/n}$ = 0.05 − $3\sqrt{(0.05)(0.95)/1485}$ = 0.033;
Minimum number inspected (n = 1003): $UCL_p$ = 0.05 + $3\sqrt{(0.05)(0.95)/1003}$ = 0.05 + 0.0206 = 0.0706, $LCL_p$ = 0.05 − $3\sqrt{(0.05)(0.95)/1003}$ = 0.05 − 0.0206 = 0.0294;

| Day | p | Individual $UCL_p$ |
| --- | --- | --- |
| 21 | 0.0697 | 0.0694 |
| 22 | 0.0699 | 0.0672 |
| 23 | 0.0697 | 0.0673 |
| 24 | 0.0697 | 0.0681 |
| 25 | 0.0697 | 0.0687 |
| 26 | 0.0697 | 0.0674 |
| 27 | 0.0697 | 0.0673 |
| 28 | 0.0694 | 0.0699 |
| 29 | 0.0698 | 0.0706 |
| 30 | 0.0698 | 0.0687 |

Individual control limits must be calculated on days 21–30. Eight are above their $UCL_p$ and the other two are nearly above their $UCL_p$. From day 21 on, the process is out of control.

Exercise 15-10.

(a) $n = 25$, Centerline $= n\bar{p} = 2$, $\bar{p} = n\bar{p}/n = 2/25 = 0.08$, $UCL_{np} = n\bar{p}$
$+ \; 3\sqrt{n\bar{p}(1 - \bar{p})} \; = \; 2 \; + \; 3\sqrt{2(0.92)} \; = \; 6.07$, $LCL_{np} \; = \; n\bar{p} \; - $
$3\sqrt{n\bar{p}(1 - \bar{p})} = 2 - 3\sqrt{2(0.92)} = 0.00$

(b) Yes. Both days exhibit points well above $UCL_{np}$.

Exercise 15-11.

(a) c chart (if welds are all for same joint); u chart (if welds are for different joint sizes).

(b) u chart (with k based on some measure of design complexity).

(c) c chart (if material shipment size is constant); u chart (if material shipment size varies).

(d) np chart (if number of material batches is constant); p chart (if number of material batches varies).

(e) c chart (if finished products are the same shape and size, etc); u chart (if finished products are different shapes or different sizes, etc.).

(f) c chart (if areas painted are all the same); u chart (if areas painted vary).

(g) c chart (assuming all shipping documents require same information).

Exercise 15-12.

(a) p chart (within some time period, such as a week).

(b) p chart (within some time period, such as a month).

(c) p chart (since number of patients vary).

(d) p chart (since number of patients vary).

(e) x chart.

(f) p chart (since number of patients vary).

(g) p chart (since number in regular care varies).

Exercise 15-13.

If the amount of off-spec paper produced daily follows an approximately normally distributed pattern and can be monitored by weight, an x chart/$R_m$ chart combination is an appropriate choice. If off-spec paper is relatively rare, however, such as one roll per day (on the average), and roll sizes are the same nominal size (e.g., 0.25 tons each), a p chart is an appropriate choice. A u chart is appropriate for monitoring the number of rolls of off-spec paper produced daily if the number is relatively small and the number of rolls produced daily varies.

# INDEX